# Reading
# in
# Education

## A Broader View

*The Charles E. Merrill*

**COMPREHENSIVE READING PROGRAM**

**Arthur W. Heilman**

**Consulting Editor**

# Reading in Education

## A Broader View

*Edited by*

Malcolm P. Douglass
*Claremont Graduate School*

CHARLES E. MERRILL PUBLISHING COMPANY

*A Bell & Howell Company*          Columbus, Ohio

Published by
Charles E. Merrill Publishing Company
A Bell & Howell Company
Columbus, Ohio 43216

Library of Congress Catalog Card Number: 72-96580

International Standard Book Number: 0-675-09006-7

PRINTED IN THE UNITED STATES OF AMERICA

# Foreword

Today, as we assert the need for relevance, for emphasis on process rather than product, for interdisciplinary approaches, for a broader view of reading, we can but review the *Proceedings* of the Claremont Reading Conference from 1936 onward to find all of these views being championed. At the very first conference in 1932, its creator and organizer, Peter L. Spencer, defined reading as the process of making discriminative reactions. He equated "reading" with what many of us consider *communication,* and some of us might broaden to meaning the process of *learning* itself—at the cognitive level and the affective, at the verbal and the nonverbal, involving the visual as well as other senses. Indeed, from the outset, the Claremont Reading Conference could have been called the Claremont Communication Conference or the Claremont Conference on Learning.

In this most interesting volume of readings selected from the conference proceedings of 1963–1971 (with the exception of one paper by Peter L. Spencer), a broad view of reading or communication is indeed brought into focus. Many of the papers are psycholinguistic or sociolinguistic in nature and/or scope, centering on the language user, his society, and the nature of the reading materials. A number of the readings reach far beyond the immediacy of teaching or learning reading. For example, Kenneth Johnson proposes that ". . . the school should strike at the very roots of the Black students' negative self-concept: social injustice." He emphasizes the need for the school and its reading program to actively help win the civil rights struggle! His viewpoint of direct involvement in society is cemented and augmented by a variety of papers contributed by sociologists, anthropologists, linguists, philosophers, medical specialists, authors of literature for children, and educationists. Such a position became even more significant when placed in juxtaposition with Sol Tax's hypothesis ". . . that at least some important values of a society are passed not from parents to children, or from teachers to pupils, but within peer groups."

A number of the papers are concerned with relevancy to the needs of learners. Jack Kittell points out that relevancy in reading *does not mean* transmitting and having learners store up as much information as possible, but instead, *should mean* guiding students to ways of making use of such information. Malcolm Douglass and H. Alan Robinson stress the fact that reading is not a subject but a process and hence is an integral part of the total school curriculum.

Several papers state and explore the concept that there is no one correct way of speaking English and the teacher's largest contribution to the reading program might be a sensitivity to, an acceptance of, and a real understanding of, the learners' dialects. Ronald Macaulay and Kenneth Goodman suggest that "mistakes" must be carefully considered in light of the student's dialect. As Macaulay points out ". . . when a teacher corrects a child who says *he don't,* she is not merely asking him to correct a slip or even to replace one word by another word, she is asking him to reorganize the set of rules by which this form was produced." Or, as potently pictured by Edward Moreno in his paper, "The View from the Margin," a teacher can "put down" a youngster by imposing ". . . his orthodoxy upon children of another cultural orientation. . . ."

Margarita, a child of Mexican American extraction during her first day in second grade is asked to introduce herself to the class. Already under undue anxiety, for, in her culture, modesty is a prime virtue, she blurts: 'I am Margarita.'

Then, the cold lash of reality across the face. In precise, and perfectly rounded syllables, the teacher retorts,

'Yes, but you know now that we are in an A-mér-i-can school. So your name is REALLY Margaret. Right, children?'

Much attention is placed upon individualization of instruction by R. Van Allen and others with careful attention paid to the difference between *teaching reading* and *learning to read.* Malcolm Douglass demonstrates the impossibility of teaching "all" of the reading skills—either time-wise on the part of the teacher or memory-wise on the part of the learners—and suggests that we ". . . think about how we can facilitate a behavior that is already present, even in the youngest child."

Obviously this book contains much of significance and relevance for the educator. Aside from its broadness of concept, it is broad in scope. It includes pertinent papers in relation to many facets of reading—the reading process, the social milieu, early language learning, methods and materials, sociolinguistics and psycholinguistics, reading disorders, literature for children.

The book, of course, contains varied views. It will reinforce many ideas for the reader; it may attack many convictions. In any case, it is bound to suggest a few new ideas to the most experienced reader. Above all, some of the papers cannot be prevented from stimulating thought and, perhaps, action.

Although it may be "stealing his thunder," this introduction closes with the conclusion to Norman Goble's paper which you will undoubtedly want to read *in context* in Part VI.

I propose that we concede that reading, at all ages, is a necessary and powerful educative instrument; that we set ourselves the objective of developing criteria of selection to shape the instrument more closely to the defined purposes of the general system—purposes derived from our concept of the goals of self and society; and that experience in the development and application of such criteria is a necessary part of the education of the teacher.

*H. Alan Robinson*

# Preface

Anyone who has given the subject serious thought will concur that the complexities of reading are endless. E. B. Huey put the problem succinctly when he wrote in 1908, in his recently republished book, *The Psychology and Pedagogy of Reading,* "Problem enough, this, for a life's work, to learn how we read!" And certainly the vast literature on the subject published since that time stands as testimony to our continuing efforts to grasp those complexities and to turn them into educational practices that will prove more successful in eliciting reading behavior in children and youth.

To add to that literature would seem foolhardy unless some specific contribution ensues. This is particularly so when one republishes articles and essays in a book of readings. What, then, will the reader find in this particular volume that is distinctive?

Aside from the quality of the writing itself, which the editor believes is a particular strength of this collection, this volume brings discussions on the subject of reading which expose various facets of this behavior not commonly treated elsewhere. And, on subjects familiar, the reader will find treatments that are novel, critical, or both. The purpose, then, is to present a collection of essays that treat reading as the complex process that it is, well-written essays that plumb many important aspects of this behavior in some depth. At the same time, it is to be realized that no one volume can provide a complete guide to the reading process.

The source of these articles differs from other books of its kind. With but one exception, each was drawn from a single source: Claremont Reading Conference Yearbooks from the past decade. The time span has some importance, but the source itself is more relevant if the reader is to understand how the present essays came into existence.

The Claremont Reading Conference is the oldest series of annual meetings considering aspects of reading behavior and their relevance for educational practice. The first conference was held in 1932, and the first yearbook was published in 1936. The conference series was inaugurated by Peter L. Spencer, now professor emeritus at the Claremont Graduate School, still the sponsoring institution. Profoundly influenced by holistic psychological theories, Spencer's initial purpose in calling the conference was to provide a forum in which an unorthodox, very broad view of reading, which he had conceptualized, might be subject to scholarly and practical inquiry. As H. Alan Robinson has pointed out in his Foreword, Spencer equated reading with communication. He saw the process of reading printed words as one aspect of a much more complex behavior, one which might be described as the process of creating meaning for *all* sensed stimuli. There were, in this view, specific skills and abilities associated with learning to read printed words, but there were many more elements having commonality with interpreting, or reading, other things—from other symbol systems to natural events or conditions observable in nature.

Whether or not one is inclined to agree with such a broad conception, the result in terms of the conference series itself was that it became commonplace for the widest variety of scholarly and professional people to contribute to it each year. Artists, geographers, physicians, philosophers, people from all walks of academic and professional life, joined in the dialogue. This tradition has continued with, however, a shift in emphasis. While Spencer sought to bring to the conference, and present through the yearbooks, an all-encompassing frame of reference for reading behavior, taking as his objective the problem of developing a rationale for all forms or aspects of reading, that objective has modified under the present conference leadership. That more modest goal has been to examine primarily the process of printed word reading, but still within a holistic frame. Thus the relevance of the work of individuals from different disciplines remains, although the focus of primary concern, while still very broad in terms of determining what has relevance, has to a degree been narrowed.

It is primarily for this reason and also because some practical limitations had to be drawn in delimiting the range from which essays were to be chosen, that the present collection is limited to items published during the present editor's stewardship. Many excellent earlier articles are available and serve as a reminder that time does not necessarily despoil educational literature. There are many wise as well as informative essays available in these publications, just as there are in Huey's book.

In the present collection, the attempt has been made to present essays focusing more or less directly upon the problem of literacy as it relates to the understanding of printed word reading processes. To view such reading in a broad context as has been the Claremont tradition immediately illuminates the relevance of anthropological, linguistic, medical, literary, and other such concerns along with the psychological and educational. And so the contributors to this collection come from disciplines, or represent interests or experiences, not commonly associated with "the problem of reading." At the same time, many old friends make their appearance here, but often, they, too, are found to be discussing aspects of reading or criticizing present practice in novel ways.

In the very breadth of reading lies a problem for the reader. A host of subjects are broached by the contributors, each one of which could have been expanded upon. At the same time, many important ideas are not considered, or they are only alluded to. Hence, there is the problem of balance, ameliorated only by the continuing realization that the basic concern, reading, is too immense in scope to allow a proper balance to be achieved. It is the editor's hope, however, that the very range of the discussions will encourage the reader to look elsewhere, not least among the volumes from which these articles were selected and from those published before.

In this volume, the reader will come across topics stated quite theoretically (meaning that he is called upon to turn theory into practice on his own). Others are more in the "how to do it" category. Still others attempt directly the wedding of theory to practice. The fifty-one articles or essays are grouped under six major topics. The first group approaches the question of the nature of the reading process and of reading behavior directly. And it is in this group that appears the only article not originally appearing in one of the yearbooks. It is the one by Spencer, having been extracted from *Reading Reading,* published in 1970. This collection, then, establishes a base for the variety of articles which follow.

The second group of readings presents a discussion of some of the elements which must be considered if the context for learning to read is to be broadly conceived. Like each of the other sections, the present readings do not purport to be complete or entirely rounded. The object is to introduce the idea that there is a complex constellation of ideas worthy of further exploration. Portions of some articles appearing in later sections bear on this idea as well.

Following is a selection of essays remarking on some of the elements to be considered in early development. Discussions of the significance of concepts of self, of the development of intellectual processes, and of language differences are followed by examples of instructional programs asserted by some to be more harmonious with the concepts presented earlier than standard or conventional programs for children.

The fourth group of articles is devoted to issues in vision and listening, with some commentary on their more mechanical counterparts of seeing and hearing. The next set of eleven essays includes a variety of discussions centering on the problem of selecting methods and materials for teaching and learning. The reader will find here numerous criticisms, and even indictments, of current, "modern" practice.

The final four sections are devoted to questions surrounding the relationship of literature to reading and to the causes of reading deficiency. In the latter concern, one group of articles is directed toward the special problems of minority groups. In a following set, individual differences are considered primarily from a physiological point of view. While the sources of reading disability may be many, the thrust of these discussions relates to that relatively small group of children who, given optimum conditions in other dimensions, would still experience great difficulty in learning in general, including the process of learning to read printed words.

The remaining two groups of articles focus upon the relationships of literature to reading behavior. The first presents discussions of the importance of literature to reading. The following set consists of articles by writer's of books for children. Here the reader will gain insight into the motives which possess the artists who devote their professional lives to creating a literature for children. Surely there is much wisdom here, in understanding children, in knowing what in literature appeals to the child's mind, and in appreciating how important intuitive behavior is in encouraging growth toward maturity in reading behavior.

*Malcolm P. Douglass*

# Acknowledgments

Many acknowledgments are in order whenever any book becomes a reality. First, I would wish to express my indebtedness to Peter L. Spencer not only for his fruitful efforts to expand our understanding of the complexities of the reading process, but as well for the many years of personal and professional association it has been my pleasure to have had.

I wish to express my appreciation to the many distinguished persons whose articles appear in this volume. Several have spent considerable effort up-dating or revising their text to account for changes in their own thinking or in the information upon which their article was first based. That so many scholars from such a wide variety of fields and interests would devote the time and effort to prepare these articles should give us all much heart. It is especially pleasing to be able to present their important contribution to a wider audience than is possible through the yearbooks alone.

Thanks are due, also, to many who assisted in planning the Claremont Reading Conference and its yearbooks, since these obviously form the basis from which the present effort was built. It is of course not possible to name them all, but special thanks go to the members of Alpha Iota Chapter of Pi Lambda Theta for their continuing interest and contributions. My colleagues at the Claremont Graduate School also have, continuously, contributed to the development of the conference and its yearbook. In this regard I should especially like to express my thanks to Donald McNassor, John O. Regan, and William R. Fielder.

Individuals who helped in so many different ways include Jean Phelps, executive secretary for the conference and yearbook; Marny and Russell Hubbard and Richard Marquard, her predecessors; Priscilla Holton Fenn, former director of the George G. Stone Center for Children's Books; Winifred Ragsdale, her successor. To Enid, Susan, John, and Paul Douglass, each in his own way, go my special thanks for the support and help one must have in seeing a task such as this to its completion.

*MPD*

# Contents

## On the Nature of the Reading Process

Hitching Posts for Reading Instruction in the Space Age,
   *R. V. Allen,* 3
Tradition Unmasked, *Peter L. Spencer,* 10
Reading as a Moral Process, *Clyde E. Curran,* 19
The Many Facets of Reading, *Malcolm P. Douglass,* 25


## The Context for Learning to Read

Self and Society, *Sol Tax,* 41
The Middle Ages Revisited: Reading in the Electronic Age, *Albert
   B. Friedman,* 59
Cultural Anthropology, Linguistics and Literacy,
   *Henry Lee Smith, Jr.,* 67
Reading and Relevancy, *Jack E. Kittell,* 77
Personality Traits as Factors in Reading Comprehension, *William
   Eller,* 85


## The Early Years

The Self-Concept of the Young Child as He Learns to Read, *Jean
   T. Kunz,* 93
Teaching Reading to the Under-Six Age: A Child Development
   Point of View, *James L. Hymes, Jr.,* 101
Piaget, Language, and Reading, *Margaret E. Smart,* 111
The Implications of Research on Children's Thinking for the Early
   Stages of Learning to Read, *John Downing,* 116
The British Infant School: A Model for Early Childhood
   Education, *Lois Fair Wilson,* 123
Bring Your Own: An Invitation to All Children to Bring Their
   Personal Language to School, *R. Van Allen,* 132

## Vision and Listening: Seeing and Hearing

Reading, the Visual Process, *Peter L. Spencer,* 141

Listening and the Discriminative Response, *Andrew Wilkinson,* 148

Problems in Aural Reading, *Helen Kennedy,* 161

## On Methods and Materials

What Price Standards? *Hubert C. Armstrong,* 177

Reading and Realism, *H. Alan Robinson,* 186

The Ideal and the Real World of Teaching Reading, *Harry F. Wolcott,* 196

Does Nongrading Improve Reading Behavior, *Malcolm P. Douglass,* 210

Sign and Significance: The Jabberwock Rides Again, *Jeannette Veatch,* 221

Culture and the Single Textbook, *Patrick Groff,* 232

Beyond Literacy: Pinfeathers or Wings in Children's Books, *Augusta Baker,* 245

Comprehension-Centered Reading, *Kenneth S. Goodman,* 251

Reality, Morality and Individualized Reading, *Helen Fisher Darrow,* 261

The Language-Experience Approach to Reading, *R. Van Allen,* 268

Twenty Language Experiences Which Form the Framework of the Experience Approach to Language Arts, *Wilhelmine Nielsen,* 275

## On the Teaching of Literature

Time Machines, Space Ships and Frog Ponds, *Frank G. Jennings,* 283

The Day the Anarchists Were Hanged—Some Thoughts on Literature as an Educative Instrument, *Norman M. Goble,* 298

Sign and Significance, *Northrop Frye,* 304

Drug Outcomes and Language Programs: A Problem of Communication, *John Owen Regan,* 311

## Views From the Margin

Fun Among the Phonemes, *John Farrell,* 319

The View from the Margin, *Edward Moreno,* 328

Schizophrenia in the Southwest, *Y. Arturo Cabrera,* 339

Raising the Self-Concept of Black Students, *Kenneth R. Johnson,* 349

# About Reading Disorders

Reading Deficit and its Relation to Social Maturity, *Alice C. Thompson,* 359

Developmental Dyslexia: A Diagnostic Screening Procedure Based on Three Characteristic Patterns of Reading and Spelling, *Elena Boder,* 365

Neurophysiological Aspects of Learning, *Robert E. Carrel,* 379

Some Neuropsychological Findings in Children With Reading Problems, *John B. Isom,* 384

Neuro-Physiological Studies of Learning Disorders, *C. Keith Conners,* 394

Perceptual Motor Training as an Aid to Development of Reading Abilities, *Clara Lee Edgar,* 403

Physical Concomitants of Reading, *Leon Oettinger, Jr.,* 411

# Authors Look at Reading

On the Importance of Imagination, *Maurice Sendak,* 423

The Significance of Satire: A Satirist Looks at Books, *Richard Armour,* 428

Children's Books, According to an Ex-Child Who Not Only Remembers But Writes Them, *Mary Stolz,* 435

Language: The Perimeter of the Suburbs, *Elaine L. Konigsburg,* 441

History for Those Who Couldn't Care Less, *Leonard Wibberley,* 451

An Afterword: On Sharing Poetry with Children at the Claremont Reading Conference, *Myra Cohn Livingston,* 457

# On
# the
# Nature
# of
# the
# Reading
# Process

R. V. Allen

# Hitching Posts for Reading Instruction in the Space Age

As a child I remember very vividly the visits of my Grandfather Allen. He lived in New Mexico where there was "elbow room" for a pioneering spirit, and we lived in the Texas Panhandle in a "crowded" farming village of nearly a thousand people. When grandfather came to visit us, he always got there three or four days after grandmother had arrived on the bus. He came in his buggy, drawn by a faithful horse that he loved as one of his own family. We had room for the horse as well as for grandfather, because my father had some of the same basic need for space that his father had, and we lived at the edge of town where we could have a garden, a cow, and chickens. We had a hitching post for the horse, even though the automobile had replaced the horse and buggy for ninety-nine out of a hundred persons.

When grandfather was not able to care for himself, he came to live with us and had to leave his horse in New Mexico. Just before he died, he begged to go back to New Mexico to die and we agreed that he could go. I was a high school boy at the time and will never forget my father carrying him to the car as he wept bitterly because we would not let him go back in his horse and buggy.

We are being ushered into the Space Age and as educators we have to decide what to take with us and what to leave behind. Times are changing rapidly and decisions must be made hurriedly in many instances. For that reason, we all need to have some hitching posts to which we can anchor our plans and our procedures. Some people will always try to find hitching posts to which they can tie their old, comfortable methods and materials—just like grandfather who never, never gave up the idea that there was a place for the horse and buggy in modern transportation. These people in education feel as strongly about the place of basic textbooks, ability grouping, self-contained classrooms, sequence of skills development, remedial classes,

3

standardized tests, workbooks, class size, and other vehicles which aid instruction as grandfather did about his faithful horse. But these people will not find hitching posts for their faithful friends in the Space Age. They are too slow, laborious, and inefficient. As hitching posts, they change too frequently to be of real value as basic guides. We must look for more realistic hitching posts for education in general, and for reading instruction specifically.

The Claremont Reading Conference is a good place to search out some of the possibilities, because it has always focused on the perceptive, creative processes rather than peripheral matters which are characteristic of many reading conferences. I find in the Yearbooks of the Conference many clues to the development of hitching posts for reading in the Space Age. Personally, I feel that one person has recorded more of the clues for reading in the Space Age than anyone else. I am struck with the vision and insight that Dr. Peter Spencer brought to us over the past many years, for he has been at the edge of the Space Age in reading for a long time. Let me quote just a few of the clues which he has given me:*

> We must change the classroom procedure in our schools from that of recitation hearing to a procedure of laboratories for learning.
>
> Memory is important, but one cannot remember that which one never experienced.
>
> Words are symbols of ideas. Words are not ideas.
>
> It is easy to restrict the occurrence and recurrence of words in a passage to be read, but it is less easy to determine how the passage will affect the reader or what he will make of it.
>
> "*Perceiving is creative. Re*ceiving may, on the other hand, be predominantly mechanical."
>
> We create our perceptions. Consequently, we create our ideas, our ideals, our aspirations, our goals, and even our dilemmas. None of these can be transmitted ready made from one person to another. Ideas and ideals are personal things. They are possessed only by their creator.
>
> We err when we think that perceptions are commodities which can be transplanted from one who created them to others who possess them not. Ideas are not found in books. . . . We cannot consume the products of thought as we can consume the products of industrial processes. We must do our own thinking, our own perceiving, and we must do our own concluding. Creativity is essential for our survival and our progress.

I could continue to quote the clues which Peter Spencer has given for describing some hitching posts for reading instruction in the Space Age. But

---

*Spencer, Peter L., "Reading in Creative Living," Twenty-second Yearbook, 1957, Claremont College Reading Conference, pp. 11-21. Peter L. Spencer founded the Claremont Reading Conference in 1932 and edited its proceedings from 1936 to 1958.

I believe that you can see that the hitching posts must be in the *minds and hearts of men* rather than in the ever-changing gadgetry which is produced by assembly-line methods. With the broad definition of reading which has been the continuing theme of the Claremont Reading Conference, we have "space" for looking at reading in the Space Age. The definition, "Reading is the process of making discriminative responses," continues to be today as useful as it was when it was first propounded by Spencer over 30 years ago. May I suggest that this definition become the first hitching post for reading in the Space Age?

From all the other possible points around which I might describe other hitching posts, three have been selected for our consideration. These are what Dr. William Van Til* has called the three great explosions of our time —

- the space explosion
- the population explosion
- the freedom explosion

The *space explosion* dramatizes the futility of any reading program goals which propose to teach children *enough*—enough word-calling skills, enough literature, enough speed, enough facts. Such folly in education has never been so real as it is today. Our hitching posts for reading instruction must be centered in more abiding values.

1.  *Each child must recognize that his future as a "reader" is determined to a much greater extent by the oral language which he produces and understands than by his skills in attacking new words.* May I suggest to you that this goal will never be attained through the teaching of someone else's language to the exclusion of the personal language of each learner? May I also emphasize the idea that the concocted language of today's reading materials has built-in regression for the language development of most students—both bright and dull? The hitching post of "highly controlled vocabulary" will become as out-of-date in the Space Age as the hitching posts for horses might be in downtown Los Angeles today.

2.  Each teacher must come to grips with the idea *that teaching is the art of raising the level of sensitivity* of each child to his environment, both within the classroom and outside. Can a child see more, feel more, say more, imagine, extend, extrapolate, synthesize, analyze, and generalize? Can he do these things with increasing depth of perception which can be communicated in ever maturing and more effective language?

*Van Til, William, "What Are the Real Basics in Education?" *Childhood Education,* Vol. 39, No. 3, November, 1962, p. 108.

Our public can ill afford any longer the luxury of maintaining classrooms where inefficient and ineffective teaching focuses on low-level learning experiences such as uniform work sheets, patterned materials, reading circles, and other materials and procedures that have short-range value to a few students and no real value for many.

If you are living in a community today where the public is reluctant to give adequate financial support, look at your schools before you blame the public.

Are you asking for money to build barns to store hay or for money to build launching pads?

As far as reading instruction is concerned, there is developing in our society a phantom curriculum which in a few years will do for most children automatically more than we now propose to teach in our first grades. Within ten years the "after 3 p.m." world of mass-communication, picture magazines, television, films, dime store do-it-yourself reading kits, and determined parents will provide for our schools a group of wonderful children who will defy our present practices of grouping and instruction. They will require a *personalized* (not individualized) curriculum. This, our public can, and will afford if we give them a chance.

Remember, the hitching post for teachers who are in harmony with the space explosion is the concept that *teaching is the art of raising the level of sensitivity of each child to his environment.*

The *population explosion* dramatizes the need for us to think of school organization in a framework different from our present "cage for every age" concept. Many visionary educators and business associates are working on this problem. Among other things, they are agonizing over what they see —thousands of vacant rooms in lovely homes in communities where 40 children are being crowded into elementary and secondary classrooms for what we call "education."

Our task today is to suggest some hitching posts to guide us in one curriculum area—reading instruction:

1. In the Space Age, children must have opportunity to acquire confidence in themselves as independent workers. There should be an expectancy that each child can search in his own storehouse of experiences and use his skills and information to solve problems which are meaningful and functional to him.

   I am not convinced that these expectancies can ever be developed in over-crowded schools where *all* children are required to attend school every day. Compulsory attendance every day is not functional now and cannot be accommodated with our population explosion. Its origin is in the horse and buggy days. It served its purpose, but it is not as basic a value as one of building confidence in children as independent workers.

2. The population explosion in the Space Age demands that teachers use a variety of methods and a great array of materials to meet the personal requirements of children as they mature in reading competency. The teacher, administrator, school board member, or parent who is out of step with the Space Age is one who is trying to find or to impose *one best* method or set of materials on all children in a classroom or a school district. Such an attitude about teaching a complex way of thinking to millions of people has never worked and it never will.

In the book of Deuteronomy in the Bible, I find God's answer to such a situation. Moses had just received the Ten Commandments and was commanded to teach them to the people. He must have been stunned by such an order. There were more than two million ex-slaves living in tents in a desert area. There were no basic texts, no classrooms, no counselors, no teachers! But God gave Moses a formula that is as useful today as it was at that time. He told Moses to tell the people that they should teach the Commandments diligently to their children

> when they were sitting in their house
>
> when they were walking by the way
>
> when they were lying down
>
> when they were getting up.

They were to be as a sign on their hands and as frontlets between their eyes.

They were to be written on their door posts and on their gates. God was saying that such vital and necessary instruction was to permeate the environment and that multiple approaches would have to be used to make the learning effective—in their hearts.

It was when the Commandments began to be taught by rote memory —as a system—that they lost their meaning.

Today, the reading program that is a system, a rote-learning process, is the one which lacks meaning to the learners.

The hitching post for teachers who are to teach children to make discriminating reactions to their environment must seek multiple approaches.

The *freedom explosion* dramatizes the need for us to treat children in our schools as human beings. The Space Age is bringing us in closer and closer contact with people who live in controlled-thought, authoritarian societies. As our children understand more and more the characteristics of such a society and its methods of indoctrination, we will find ourselves in an untenable position if we try to use authoritarian methods to teach children to live effectively in a free society.

What are the hitching posts?

1.  *Every child must gain the feeling that his own ideas are worthy of expression and his own language is a vehicle for communication.* The child in our elementary and secondary schools who is walled in by other people's ideas and language becomes dependent on outside sources for reinforcement in every aspect of living. Yet I have observed in many classrooms, beginning in kindergarten and extending through college, instructional procedures which always place the highest value on what someone else has said and written. Children are engaged in an endless succession of activities which train them to give someone else's answers to someone else's questions.

    What could be better training for successful living in an authoritarian society?

    Reading programs are prepared in detail before the children who are to use them are born. The stories are selected; the questions are formulated in workbooks or teachers' manuals; the answers are recorded on answer sheets for the teacher. In some programs of instruction which bear the name of "reading," there is an attempt to control the order in which children establish relationships between alphabet symbols and sounds.

    My hitching post has no place for such authoritarian-oriented procedures. I choose the one which is centered first of all in the language of each child. From there I would try to be sensitive to the many opportunities to help him mature toward an effective citizen, able to communicate his own ideas in a free society at the same time that he is using other people's ideas and is being influenced by their language.

2.  Freedom implies a freedom to learn, and with this goes the responsibility on the part of the learner to persist in the face of obstacles and to avoid distractions which lead away from the fulfillment of his plans.

    The hitching post in relation to this aspect of freedom is that *learning situations must be designed so that each child, as a person, must face up to inadequacies in skills and knowledge which are necessary to complete a task.* His ability to discipline himself in any learning experience is a mark of his growth toward self-direction and hence to worthiness to live in a free society.

May I ask you one simple question? How would you feel if someone reminded you every day that you belonged to an unworthy group or class? What would such a program do to you, personally, in helping you build confidence, to build toward self-direction, and to feel that you live in a free society?

Yet this is exactly what is happening in the vast majority of our classrooms in the reading program. With unscientific and unreliable data, teachers are placing children in groups which highlight unworthiness. The practice of destroying self-image through ability grouping is reinforced by an ageless procession of remedial reading teachers who tell the child again in a different way that he is no good!

As freedom explodes in every part of the world and in every aspect of life, we must be willing to and able to work with children in reading programs that help each child, as a person, to face up to his needs. It is only when we can do this that more of our children can grow up to be effective contributors to freedom as contrasted to the passive consumers which we tend to produce with some of our present practices.

There are certainly other hitching posts for reading instruction in the Space Age, but here we have reviewed enough to identify the effective, efficient reading program of the future as one which:

—is based upon the learner's language and experience

—reflects goals of a society which values creativity and divergent thinking

—includes learning experiences which generate productive thinking, allow freedom of expression, stimulate individuality, value ingenuity, and satisfy curiosity

—promotes personal satisfaction to the extent that learning to read and reading is a lifelong experience which requires ever maturing and more complex skills and knowledge.

**Peter L. Spencer**

# *Tradition Unmasked\**

> He's 17. Scared. Broke. No job. No hope. Why did he quit school? His biggest problem was reading. The average school dropout is at least 2 yrs. behind in reading when he quits . . . Reading problems are the main reason a million kids a year quit school (1).

This message accompanied a picture of an unhappy frustrated adolescent. It is typical of a large school population who have experienced difficulty with the visual reading of printed words. It constitutes a challenge to educational theories and practices since they may have been a contributing factor in that situation.

Educators are well aware that undesirable attitudes and deviant behavior may arise or be aggravated by failure to fit into the school environment. Students of child development have observed that these characteristics begin to show in the early grades as children find that their academic fate depends heavily upon the visual reading of printed words.

There appears to be general agreement that changes in the educational treatment of reading are needed, but there is little agreement as to the nature of the desired changes. Traditionally concern has centered mainly upon the visual sensing and interpreting of printed words. This has been regarded as distinctive type of behavior. Its relationship to other aspects of responsive behavior has received little consideration. Reading-behavior is identified by a specific type of stimulus rather than by the intrinsic psychological nature of the reading process itself.

This concept is clearly indicated by the definitions of reading presented in current textbooks. For example:

*\*Peter L. Spencer, *Reading Reading* (Claremont, Calif.: Alpha Iota Chapter of Pi Lambda Theta, 1971), Chapter One.

**10**

In this book we shall think of reading as an activity which involves the comparison and interpretation of ideas symbolized by written or printed language (2).

Authors may indicate that they are aware of broader ideas concerning the nature and functions of reading-behavior, but they still restrict their treatment to behavior activated by printed words:

Since the field of reading is already rather complex, and since most schools conceive of reading as work with printed materials, that point of view is taken in this book (3).

In 1940 the American Council on Education identified three concepts of reading-behavior: 1) the interpretation of written and printed symbols, 2) the interpretation of all symbol signs which denote, represent or stand for something else, and 3) the process of making intelligent adjustment to stimulation from various sources, including natural signs as well as conventional symbols. However, in the preparation of its report the committee centered its attention primarily upon the interpretation of written and printed symbols (4).

Nearly a quarter of a century later (according to the Harvard Report on Reading in the Elementary Schools) a conference of some twenty-eight experts prominent in the field of reading instruction agreed upon the "common-sense proposition that there are two major acts to be performed in the process of reading: 1) recognizing the printed word on the page, and 2) understanding and dealing with the meaning intended by the passage"(5).

It is disturbing to note that substantially the same idea of reading-behavior formed the basis for "Ye Auld Deluder, Satan, Act" enacted by the Massachusetts Colony more than three hundred years earlier. That act specified that every community of fifty or more householders must provide instruction for its children in the visual reading of printed words. The result was commonly termed "reading schools."

As other aspects of educational development were identified, "spelling school," "singing schools," "writing schools," "reckoning schools" etc. were comparably provided. Each area of educational concern was specifically identified and these areas have continued to exist, even in the composite curriculums of the modern schools. Hence, the American Public School has developed from what was properly termed a "Reading School" into an institution which treats of "reading" as merely one of many diverse areas for instruction. Possibly this is one factor which partially explains the difficulties experienced with reading.

Printed words are an important tool for communication in our society. In order that they may serve that function effectively it is obvious that they must be sensed and interpreted, that is, *read*. However, these same requisites apply to spoken words as well as to numerous other symbolic and even non-symbolic stimuli. Hence, the traditional "common sense" proposition which restricts the identification of reading-behavior exclusively to printed words is certainly open to question.

Tradition serves to provide stability in human behavior, but it may also serve as an impediment to creative growth. From time to time both individuals and their societies need to examine critically the role which tradition plays in their behavior. When Einstein was asked how he accounted for his making such unique contributions to the fields of mathematics and science, he replied, *"I challenged an axiom."* Since the field of education is so replete with "common sense," axiomatic ideas, it would be advantageous to apply an Einsteinian treatment to some of them. By so doing schools might be freed from untenable ideas and practices.

For example, outside the province of formal education reading-behavior is not restrictively associated with any specific type of stimulation. It is identified as a generalized behavioral response with reference to all sorts of stimulus situations.

> Throughout his history man has read many things: the flight of birds, the guts of sheep, sun spots, liver spots and the life lines on a hand. He has read the lore of the jungle, the spoor of the beasts and portents of a dish of tea. But whatever he has read, however he has read it, it has always been for "reasons." It was only when man invented symbols for the words in his mouth and for the ideas in his teeming brain, that other kinds of reading became useful, possible, or even desirable (6).

Some thirty years ago Anne Bryan McCall pointed out the need for a kind of reading which probably has great bearing upon the problem of school dropouts as well as on many other phases of humane living. She said:

> If parents could read their children's human behavior and tendencies; if older people could read youth, and young people were better readers of older people; if teachers and pupils, husbands and wives, brothers and sisters, friends and enemies, in short if all of us read one another better! if we were better readers of ourselves, if we could read at a glance our own abilities, our rich human endowments well enough to mend our mistakes and correct our misunderstandings, how many would live richer more efficient lives! (7)

Caution concerning extreme emphasis on the reading of printed words to the exclusion of other applications of reading-behavior is frequently given. For example, St. Augustine pointed out:

The world is a great book,
of which they that never stir from home
read only a page.

And Joaquin Miller warned:

The soul that feeds on books alone
I count that soul exceeding small
That lives alone by book and creed,
A soul that has not learned to read.

"Do you read me?" is frequently heard in air-to-earth conversations and other person-to-person communications.

These illustrations of references to reading-behavior outside the field of formal education are in sharp contrast with the restrictive "common sense" identification so characteristically found in educational theories and practices. Writers of general literature treat reading-behavior as an intellectual process which has wide general application.

This thought suggests the possibility that competence developed for one type of reading situation may be generalized and made available for use in other types as well—an idea which presents a potent challenge to those engaged in reading instruction. Finding ways to identify competence with applications of reading-behavior and determining ways to initiate and to expedite its spread to other reading situations constitute important aspects of educational development. It may well be that initially "all learning is specific," but there is no apparent reason why it need remain so. As a matter of fact, releasing ideas from the specific experiences from which they were originally derived is an important characteristic of educational growth.

The individual is continuously sensing and interpreting aspects of his environment. Ideas-about-things are conceived in the course of that process. These ideas are retained and, subject to their recall and association, are made available to supplement and enrich subsequent experiencing. John Barrett Kerfoot has remarked that learning to read in the real sense means enlarging our equipment and learning to use it creatively.

We read, then, quite literally, with our own experience. We read with what we have seen and heard and smelled and tasted and felt. We read with the emotions we have had—with the love we have loved, the fear we have feared, the hate we have hated. We read with the observations we have made and the deductions we have drawn from them; with the ideas we have evolved and the ideals we have built into them; with the sympathies we have developed and the prejudices we have failed to rid ourselves of (8).

The apparent differences between the conceptions of what constitutes reading-behavior as characteristically expressed in the educational literature and in general literary writings indicate a need for a more thorough study of the true nature of the reading process and how it functions in human behavior, that is, to *read reading* without being handicapped by restrictive specialized applications of the process.

The reading of language is important, but it is not a primary form of reading-behavior. Language elements are merely symbolic representations of ideas-about-things. The traditional "common sense" conception of reading-behavior is in difficulty in this respect. For example, the assertion is made: "Reading is developing meaning from patterns of symbols which one recognizes and endows with meaning. *Reading arouses or calls up meanings. It does not provide them*" (9). The providing of meanings which can be "aroused" or "called up" by means of symbolic stimuli must be essential to the process described. Why, then, is this not incorporated within the definition? Its omission seems to imply that the development of meaning is *prerequisite to,* but *not an integral part of,* the reading process. It completely disregards the organismic nature of the perceptual process.

Ideas-about-things are most effectively derived from direct experience with things in their own right. Therefore, reading-behavior includes the *reading of things directly* as well as the *vicarious reading about things* by means of symbolic representations.

Every activity of reading-behavior has aspects which to some extent are peculiar to it. However, the characteristics of sensing and interpreting what is sensed are common throughout. There are many sensory processes feeding data into a common conceptual hopper. Hence, all forms of experiencing are intrinsically related.

If we release the consideration of reading-behavior from association with any one particular stimulus type and if we then recognize that reading-behavior includes all adaptive behavior, educational theory and practices will be significantly benefitted. An holistic approach in the development of reading abilities is made feasible. Disparateness among reading acts will be minimized and characteristics which are common to all forms of adaptive behavior will be more readily recognized and stressed. This has important implications for persons who experience frustration with some particular form of reading-behavior.

Competence with reading-behavior is best thought of as an emergent phenomenon. Initially it is largely intuitive, but it develops through the acquisition of skills and the formation of concepts into a highly disciplined intellectually controlled behavior. While the development of skills with the processes of sensory reception and of behavioral response are important, the development of perceptual abilities constitutes the major problem in the creation of effective readers.

The traditional restrictive identification of reading-behavior which has dominated educational theories and practices concerned with reading-behavior must be unmasked and corrected. Reading-behavior consists of the *process of making discriminative responses with regard for any and all types of stimulation.* The narrow and restrictive association of reading-behavior with a single type of stimulus situation creates artificial problems which seriously interfere with the development of efficiency with the reading process. Many who experience frustration and damaging self-concepts due to difficulties experienced with the visual reading of printed words read other aspects of their environment effectively. Such terms as non-reader, retarded reader, slow reader, etc., are misleading unless the particular type of reading situation is also identified. For example, a non-reader of printed words may be a proficient reader of spoken words.

Progress in educational development is too important both for the individual and for our society to permit its being obstructed by faulty ideas or by inefficient communication. There is a crucial need to READ READING and to modify educational theories and practices so they more aptly fit with the findings.

Every reading activity has four sequentially intrarelated stages: 1) an activating stimulus situation, 2) a sensory reception stage, 3) a perceptual stage, and 4) a stage in which the adaptive response is consummated. Each of these stages has important educational aspects.

## The Nature of Reading-Behavior*

Reading is a behavioral pattern which functions in varying degrees of complexity and effectiveness throughout the life span of every individual. It is not a special type of behavior which is applicable for only certain kinds of situations. Educational development depends essentially upon the ability to determine what one needs to read and then upon achieving the skills needed in order to accomplish the tasks efficiently.

That one will read is determined by nature; but what he will read and how efficiently the reading will be accomplished depends upon how the native behavior process is developed. The growth of aptness in one's behavior can be facilitated by understanding the process by which it may be attained. Hence, in a very real sense, in order to devise effective developmental reading programs the nature and functionings of the reading process should be understood.

Since we have identified reading as the *process of making discriminative responses with regard for any and all types of stimulus situations,* we may proceed to analyze what such behavior entails. Evidently there must

*Spencer, *Reading Reading,* opening of Chapter Two.

be an activating stimulus, which affects the reader and causes him to devise and then to perform an adaptive response. Hence, it seems reasonable that the reading process may properly be structured into four sequential but intrarelated segments: 1) stimulus, 2) reception, 3) perception, and 4) response.

It is important to recognize that reading-behavior is a continuum just as all the other vital processes are. The human organism is continuously making adaptive responses which are intrinsically intrarelated both as regards the time sequence and the development of meanings and significance. This explains the function of the arrows in the following chart depicting the sequential stages of a reading act.

*Diagrammatic Chart of Sequential Stages in an Act of Reading*

| → Stage 1 → | Stage 2 → | Stage 3 → | Stage 4 → |
|---|---|---|---|
| Stimulus | Stimulation | Perception | Responding |
| Activators | (sensory | (conceiving) | (behavioral |
| | activation) | | performance) |

*Stage 1* – Anything which activates any sense receptor.

*Stage 2* – The activation of sense receptors. Transforming non-neural impulses to neural impulses

*Stage 3* – Cognition, recognition, association, creating meaning, giving significance, formulating plan of action, activating and directing response mechanism.

*Stage 4* – Performing the adaptive responses as directed, e.g., orally expressing the words and word patterns as perceived under visual stimulation.

The arrows in the diagram are designed to point out the ongoing emergent nature of reading-behavior. Each stage of the sequence exerts a direct dynamic influence upon the subsequent stage. They constitute an organismic unit. Whatever affects one of them affects all of them. The reading process consists in sensing, interpreting, and responding adaptively within stimulus situations.

While environment is an organismic whole, our sensory contacts with it are disparate in their nature and limited in their coverage. For example, the sense of sight is activated by a narrow band of energy waves known as *light.* In like manner the sense of hearing is activated by a different band of waves known as sound. Chemical stimuli affect the senses of taste and smell. Each of the other sensory processes is likewise limited to a certain type of stimulation. There are aspects of our environment which dynamically affect us but for which we have no direct sensory contacts, for example, ultraviolet and ultrasonic waves.

The fact that our sensory receptors are disparate in their functionings suggests that reading-behavior may properly be structured to correspond with a dominant sensory input. For example, we perform visual reading, aural reading, thermal reading, kinesthetic reading, etc. The recent maneuverings of space craft in outer space have focused attention upon gravitational reading.

There are important educational considerations regarding each of the sequential stages of a reading act as well as with each of the discernible applications of the process. Restricting a developmental reading program exclusively to a single aspect of reading-behavior is psychologically untenable and educationally inadequate.

Young people who are not adept with reading printed words often feel frustrated and confused with their school work. When such people come to recognize that reading is not some new thing which school teachers have devised to embarrass pupils, they commonly change their attitudes concerning it. When the instructor comparably recognizes that reading occurs in all behavior, he frequently finds instances wherein the pupil is a very good reader. Then, by playing up such instances, the pupil's confidence in his own abilities may be restored. Similarly, by pointing out and studying the instances of good reading, very often, the pupil achieves insight into what has impeded development in other applications of his reading-behavior. For example, one who reads people well may become a leader among his associates. He may find security and status with his friends. Inability to read printed words may under such circumstances become a challenge more than a mark of failure. Comparably, one who reads printed words with ease, but who finds extreme difficulty in reading his human associates, may be led to sense the likeness between the people represented in the books and those who are met in more primary reading relationships. One who reads readily spoken words but who finds difficulty in reading written or printed words, may be led to sense the essential similarity of the two applications of the reading process. Again, one who finds "sermons in stones, books in running brooks, and good in everything," may be led to develop that reading ability with confidence and respect. Premiums will be placed upon the aptness of behavior rather than restricted to accomplishment with a narrow range of situations.

## References

1. Advertisement, reprint courtesy of International Paper Co.
2. John J. Deboer and Martha Dallman, *The Teaching of Reading* (New York: Holt-Dryden, 1960), 3.
3. David H. Russell, *Children Learn to Read* (New York: Ginn and Co., 1961), 116.
4. W. S. Gary, ch., "Reading in General Education; an Exploratory Study" (Washington, D.C.: American Council on Education, 1940), vii.

5. James B. Conant, *Learning to Read; a Report of a Conference of Reading Experts* (with foreword by James B. Conant) (Princeton, N.J.: Educational Testing Service, 1961), 4.

6. Frank G. Jennings, "Aspects of Reading," *Claremont College Reading Conference Yearbook,* No. 21 (1956), 113–114.

7. Anne Bryan McCall, "How Well Can You Read?" *Claremont College Reading Conference Yearbook,* No. 11 (1946). Reprinted by permission from *The Woman's Home Companion* (July 1936).

8. John Barrett Kerfoot, *How to Read* (Boston: Houghton-Mifflin Company, 1916), 10.

9. Dorris M. Lee and R. V. Allen, *Learning to Read Through Experience,* Second Edition (New York: Appleton-Century-Crofts 1963), vi.

# Clyde E. Curran

# *Reading as a Moral Process*

Reading and morality are so connected, it can be said that reading, as it is taught in the schools today, is a moral process. To make sense out of this assertion, it is necessary to define reading and morality. I will use the word reading to mean the development of meanings from various stimuli, but in this instance particular reference is made to printed word symbolization. Morality, as I am defining the term, refers to those social forces that induce people to behave as they do. This is the way Sumner uses the word when refering to customs and mores.

There are at least three ways in which reading is moral in that it is connected with customs and mores: 1) The teaching of conventional meaning or common usage is moral. Children need to know language usage not only to communicate, but to become proper members of society. 2) The structure of language tends to determine the range and character of thinking. When we teach reading, including such things as those which appear on the pages of a book and the structure of language upon which they are based, we teach the dimensions within which students think. 3) Moral judgments are exercised in the selection of books. Even prize-winning books have moral sanction. These are the books that *must* be read.

How reading as taught in the schools ties into customs and mores was presented at the opening of this talk to help bring into focus what seems to me to be the most important yet most neglected dilemma in education today. In my mind, the problem takes the form of a nightmare. A scene from Fellini's film *8½* contains the same nightmarish quality that my dream version of the teaching of reading has.

In *8½* (this is an autobiography), Fellini is told by his staff of physicians he must get away from the enormous pressures motion-picture making entails. They prescribe residence in a health resort in which hundreds of people suffer from Fellini's illness—world weariness. Each morning the patients form in long lines to get a cup of mineral water. These lines move across the screeen in various directions. The setting for this scene is an old Roman garden. What Fellini is driving at is not apparent until these rows of sick people become frozen into rigid lines. When the rigidity sets in, what was an uninteresting series of loosely connected events becomes a nightmare. The beauty of the rural atmosphere in which it occurs only adds to its sense of awfulness.

My dream about the teaching of reading takes a visual form similar to the lines of sick people in Fellini's film. The Roman garden is replaced by beautifully designed and equipped classrooms and libraries. The lines of sick people are supplanted by long rows of handsome teachers matched by longer rows of delightful-appearing pupils. The teachers have mastered every technique of teaching reading, they use nothing but the best books, and the pupils learn to read. The older pupils have all read the Hundred Great Books. Only at the end of the dream does the nightmare quality enter, then the meaning of the total dream becomes apparent. Despite all the good conventional things that are happening in the classroom, when teachers and pupils leave school, *they do not read.* Teachers who are not readers are successfully teaching reading to students who do not read. This enterprise is being applauded by a gallery composed of some parents, but mostly of liberal arts professors. Needless to say, the members of the gallery are not "readers" either.

My nightmare contains a lucid explanation why teachers and pupils are not readers. The entire teaching enterprise is geared toward reading the Hundred Great Books. Those who have partaken of the Hundred Great Books find lesser material intolerable. But who can possibly stand to reread the Hundred Great Books? And so they stop reading.

This is a dream. What about the reality? It is not difficult to describe. Teachers are teaching reading and teaching it well to youngsters who are learning it, but there are very few "readers" among teachers and even fewer among students.

Who is a reader? What are the characteristics of a reader? Before going into this in detail, I would like to underscore the following sentence: *The reader's approach to reading is amoral.* It has nothing to do with acquiring an education. This needs to be repeated. Reading done from the perspective of a reader has nothing to do with getting an education.

I know of no better way to reveal the telling quality of a reader than the following anecdotes about two readers. One was a girl who was quite young when I first met her. The other was a young man with whom I became acquainted at Stanford. Dorothy was the twelve-year-old granddaughter of a neighbor. The grandmother would complain, "All she does is read. She never wants to do anything else." Dorothy was married at nineteen, divorced at twenty. I saw her about two weeks after her divorce. When I said I had heard the news about her broken marriage, I could see she wanted to give some explanation. In one sentence she gave the perfect reason for her divorce. "My husband didn't like to read."

Randy McCallister entered higher education rather late. He was twenty-four and a sophomore at Stanford when I, working as a dormitory counsellor, met him. During one of our frequent conversations, he spoke about students who get all "A's." In his opinion they have low standards. I asked him what he meant by this. He reasoned in the following way. If a student studies hard enough to get an "A" in a course like Economics I, etc., he must neglect important things. After hearing Randy's opinion on academic excellence, I wanted to know what he thought of his two years of study at Stanford. I asked him what he thought of his Stanford education up to that point. After thinking a minute, without a hint of facetiousness he said, "It has been all right, but it has interfered with my reading."

What are some of the qualities of a reader?

Readers do not read for self-improvement. There is a quotation from Dryden—"Love is love's reward." Reading is its own reward. Readers are not bookworms. They don't read compulsively. A bookworm has to finish every book he starts. Readers start many books they don't finish. Readers subscribe to this law: If a book is not worth reading, why finish it? Think of the large mass of printed stuff that would go into the garbage can if this law was widely adopted.

One way to spot a reader is to find a person who has not only read and reread everything his favorite authors have written, but nearly everything that has been written about them and their writing. It's a humbling experience to hear a reader talk about his favorite author as he, with unchecked enthusiasm, completely disregarding the simplest tenets of criticism, tells about the ways this author has made him feel alive. A listener who is alive himself will wonder if readers have not come upon one of the mysteries of life. Readers love books but they are not collectors. Paperbacks are the books meant for readers.

It is a pleasure to watch readers in a library. They wander through a library in a purposeless-meaningful way that suggests they're propelled by the kind of affection found in courtship. In contrast, a researcher with calm efficiency goes directly to the business at hand. A researcher is like a cook who has baked a cake many times and knows exactly what to do and how it will turn out. In their meandering amazed manner, readers seem to be saying by their seeming show of wonder that they find the existence of libraries a miracle.

The list of attributes of readers could be extended, but I think enough has been said to underscore the idea that a reader is not automatically developed through teaching reading. But before leaving the characteristics of a reader, I would like to say a word about two misconceptions. It is often said that readers do nothing but read. This is not true. They eat and sleep like everyone else. Another misconception concerns isolation. Readers are not isolates. They must read their favorite passages to someone. When they burst with enthusiasm upon finding something that needs to be read aloud, they seek an audience.

How are readers developed? This question sets the slogan impulse going. Smile! Be diligent! Become a reader! Think!

Have you ever thought about the "Think" signs in IBM offices? And as you think about thinking, you wonder if the thinking you're doing about thinking is what the sign implies when it says, "Think." When you reach this point, you realize you're not thinking about thinking at all. You're thinking about thinking about thinking. At this juncture you long for another sign: "Don't Think."

Reading as done by readers is philosophical when philosophy has a special meaning. As it developed in the west, philosophy is predominantly rationalistic, when the word "calculating" could be used as a synonym for "rationalistic." Early in its history (by Plato's time) philosophy became abstract in the sense that general semanticists use the term; that is, at the third level of abstraction—the first level being direct perception; the second, applying words to sense perceptions; the third, the relationship between symbols. Mathematics might be defined as third-level abstraction, or relationships between symbols. Philosophy in the west is largely abstract in this sense. The data of philosophy are derived from relationships between conceptual schemes and concepts. One of the honorable achievements of western scholarship, for that matter of all western culture and art, is abstract philosophy. This achievement has been so monumental it obscures the fact that throughout western history a non-abstract form of philosophy has existed: It is sometimes spoken of as wisdom. When I said reading is philosophical, I had this kind of philosophy in mind. At one time philosophers and poets walked the same path. As abstract philosophy developed, the professional thinker and the poet moved in different directions, the poet toward the more obscure depths of human experience, the philosopher toward the relationship between symbol systems. Yet wisdom, as philosophy, growing outside the boundaries that are spoken of as western philosophy, has remained in the poet's camp. The difference between the philosopher (as he is concerned with wisdom) and the poet is the poet sings about his experience while the philosopher discourses upon his experiences. What is significant is that both draw their working material predominantly from their own experiences and not abstract conceptual schemes.

Philosophy as wisdom can properly be called meditative in contrast to calculative. Examples of meditative philosophers are Emerson and Marcus Aurelius. An example of a philosopher who possessed little or none of the meditative but who was a brilliant rationalist is Kant. Both meditative and rationalistic are found in Santayana. Recently because of the rise of modern existentialism, a meditative philosophy which employs rationalistic analysis, there is a new interest by abstract philosophers in the kinds of human problems that have been traditionally handled by poets, dramatists, novelists, and meditative philosophers. Reading when done by readers is one form of meditative thought.

I said reading is one form of meditative thought because what I have called the meditative can be broken down into three forms: moral, spiritual, and esthetic. The principal problem of moral meditative philosophy is identity or how a person instates himself as a human being. Despite the great variety and the tortuous technicalities in modern existentialism, identity is the problem it deals with.

The reader belongs to the spiritual form of meditative thought. Spiritual does not mean an essence hovering above or lying within a thing or person, but means the concrete nature of the thing or person. The spirit of a waterfall is the water falling. Its spirit is experienced by looking at it or better still by standing within it and getting wet. The spirit of a man is what he does, what he thinks, how he influences other people, the concrete manifestations of himself as a person, etc.

The spiritual form can be divided into the subjective and objective. When the reader is so caught up into what he is reading that he loses himself, he is in the objective spiritual meditative realm. Almost any form of literature at times can affect a reader in this way. The most common example of readers forgetting themselves because they are carried away by the magic of what they read is the adventure story or drama. Technical material in science and philosophy, however, can also accomplish this.

The subjective spiritual form of meditation overcomes a reader when, without conscious intent on his part, the material he is reading makes him see himself in a way he had not done before. As he reads, a word or a phrase jumps up before him and serves as a mirror. The person who reads the Bible many times and suddenly is struck by a truth that he never realized before, a truth that gives him a much more penetrating understanding of himself than he had before, serves as an example of the subjective spiritual form of meditative thought. Self-knowledge, when it comes, is never easy. Reading as done by a reader can provide such knowledge. One of the other most common ways to acquire such knowledge is through suffering or shock.

The esthetic differs from the spiritual in that it is dominated by a prevailing quality of loneliness. Again the question arises, "How is a reader taught to be *a reader?*"

This is like asking how the mystery of love is solved. Where is it to be found? Where does wonder abide? The reader knows this place. It is a simple place. How to get to this place is a mystery. What makes a mystery a mystery is that it cannot be explained. Despite how hard an individual tries to explain it, it cannot be explained. This doesn't mean that a mystery can't be experienced. Mysteries can be experienced but not explained. Reading as the reader does it is a mystery.

I know a story that contains the key to this mystery. This is a story about a teacher, Mr. Jones, and a pupil, Johnny. Mr. Jones knew there is something more to teaching, especially the teaching of reading, than the usual lessons and recitations. To get at this "something more," he designed a lesson on how to reach out and touch a star. What he was interested in teaching was lyricism. He defined lyricism this way: A creature is lyric when it so completely obeys its inner laws that to watch it makes you feel like singing or dancing. A cat jumping at its shadow is lyric. A child doing anything that is completely childlike, even if it's not very proper, is lyric. An old person sitting in the sun, not just vegetating but who is actually aware of the warmth of the sun and the multiple sights and sounds that surround him, is lyric. Professor Watinobi, when, upon finishing an elaborate mathematical explanation, turns from his figure-filled board to his class and says, "So," is lyric. Reading when done by a reader is lyric.

As Mr. Jones began his lesson on how to reach out and touch a star, he could see that Johnny wanted to be heard from. Ordinarily he wouldn't pay attention to a student raising his hand at such a crucial stage in a difficult presentation. But Johnny was so urgent that he called on him.

He said, "What is it, Johnny?" He was just a little exasperated.

Johnny answered, "But Mr. Jones, last night I did reach out and touch a star."

Now many teachers would say, "What does he mean by that? Why did he say that? Is he telling the truth?" But not Mr. Jones. He knew Johnny was telling the truth. Furthermore, he knew what Johnny meant, because last night Mr. Jones reached out and touched a star.

Malcolm P. Douglass

# The Many Facets of Reading

There is probably no educational topic more likely to attract one's attention than a discussion of what we in the United States have come to call "the reading problem." This widespread interest is, it may at first seem strange to note, largely an American phenomenon. And it has led us to invent a number of institutions that are equally unique to this country. Among them is something called a Reading Conference. Each year scores of meetings are held throughout the land devoted to the subject of reading. Rarely, if ever, do people in those other countries of the world aspiring to universal literacy hold such conferences. Similarly, we may note that the "reading specialist" is also an American phenomenon. Only in the United States can one possibly find a person formally trained and licensed as a "remedial reading teacher," or for that matter, one claiming the title: Professor of Reading. Binding the various professionals interested in "reading" together are national, state, and local organizations consisting of tens of thousands of individuals, together representing one of the largest groups to be found concerned with a particular interest in education. While our monopoly over such things may be broken some time in the future, the widespread extent of their occurrence in the United States contrasted with that of other countries shows that we have established an enormous lead over any would-be competitors.

Why this great interest in the United States in reading behavior when people in other countries do not seem to care? The obvious answer is, of course, that we perceive ourselves as experiencing great difficulty in causing people to become readers. And indeed we do have a serious "reading problem." Official estimates show that at least 25 percent of our school-age population is experiencing sufficiently severe difficulties that their access to "the good life" is being blocked in a significant fashion (1). Additionally,

25

we know that in our major racial and ethnic minority groups, that figure frequently exceeds 90 percent where such people are living under ghetto conditions.

A glance at those foreign countries having as a national goal universal literacy indicates a much lower level of difficulty than we commonly encounter. In the Scandinavian countries initial reading difficulties amount to four or five percent. That figure is halved in the ensuing three or four years by giving additional individual attention. So for them, there is no reading problem. Consequently, they do not join organizations nor do they plan or attend conferences devoted to that subject; as well, they do not find the need for highly specialized professionals in reading behavior.

In my analyses of the incidence of initial reading disabilities at the international level, I find that the Scandinavian experience of about five percent appears for the most part to hold from one country to another, with the exception of Great Britain where the rate of initial reading disability apparently amounts in the overall to about half of that experienced in the United States. It is still not high enough to cause the great alarm in the population that is the case here, perhaps partly because they do not experience such mass deficiencies within certain sub-groups in their society. While my survey is not complete, I believe I have at hand enough data on the incidence of reading disability from enough sources that I will not find these figures to vary significantly in the future.

Of course, the question arises immediately, "Why are we so different?" Why do we have so many reading problems? And, of course, what can we do about it?

I suspect we could very well in the not so distant future reduce the number of reading disability cases in this country to at least a ten percent level of initial incidence, furthering that reduction to perhaps five percent. However, to achieve this, I believe it is going to require some major shifts in our thinking about the nature of reading behavior, *and* where our instructional emphases ought to lie with respect to stimulating the processes of reading.

### The Case for Phonological Irregularity as a Major Cause of Reading Disability

It has been popular to account for the higher incidence of reading disorders in this country by claiming that the English language has a special character of its own that makes it harder to learn—at least, harder to learn to read and write, if not to speak. It is generally believed that written or printed English is so irregular in its representation of the phonological system that it is therefore simply foreordained that more people are going to have more problems in mastering the language. While there is no doubt that most of the other languages in the world which utilize a phonetic symbol system appear to be more regular than is English, those differences are probably more apparent than real. As well, if we continue to place undue faith in this reasoning, there is the real danger we will fail to give proper emphasis in our instruction to matters of far greater consequence in the learning to read process.

There are at least three reasons why the "case of phonological irregularity as a major cause of reading disability" is open to question. First, we note that within our population generally, the problem of reading disability is expressed selectively. That is, how can we explain the very high incidence in certain segments of our population—particularly the Negro, the Mexican-American, and American Indian people—while at the same time noting that even within these groups, those who have achieved in terms of socioeconomic levels perform as well or better than their White counterparts? Perhaps differences are more directly related to conflict between values and the school or the standard of living. Certainly, one of the notable characteristics of those other countries with which I have knowledge is the homogeneity of those particular cultures—and the agreement on the value of schooling that they enjoy.

A second incongruity that calls into question the notion that our language is accursed, at least in its printed form, derives from recent linguistic research. Linguists during the past five or so years particularly are coming up with the notion that indeed the orthographic system for representing the oral language is finely tuned to that language. While surface analysis suggests oddities, sometimes in the extreme, depth analysis (which has only been available to us since the invention of the electronic computer) yields different information. That very distinguished linguist, Noam Chomsky, for example, has recently written on this point:

> It seems to me that the most direct contribution that contemporary linguistics can make to the study of literacy is in clarifying the relation of the conventional orthography to the structure of the spoken language. This relation is, I believe, much closer than is ordinarily supposed. So much so, in fact, that conventional English orthography in its essentials appears to be a near-optimal system for representing the spoken language; it is to a large extent merely a direct point-by-point transcription of a system that the speaker of English has internalized and uses freely. . . . Correspondingly, conventional orthography is highly appropriate, with little modification, for a wide range of dialects. To the extent that this point of view can be substantiated, it would follow that the teacher of reading is not introducing the child to some new and obscure system that is only distantly related to the spoken language he has, to a substantial degree, already mastered. Rather, the teacher is engaged in bringing to consciousness a system that plays a basic role in the spoken language itself (2).

Chomsky is a linguist to be reckoned with, and I find support for the argument in other research as well. But I am also attracted to the very important role Chomsky gives to intuitive behavior in learning. He argues that in teaching children to read printed words "the rules of sound-letter correspondence need hardly be taught." (3) He suggests that the teacher's role is primarily "to enrich the child's vocabulary so that he constructs for himself the deeper representations of sound that correspond so closely to the orthographic forms." (4) Chomsky is also asserting the paramount importance of experiencing and the opportunity to talk about or otherwise share those experiences in the learning to read process.

Finally, in my suggestion that the particular character of our language cannot be held responsible for our difficulties, consider the fact that the modal age for beginning formal instruction in reading printed words is significantly higher elsewhere than in the United States. In the past, formal instruction here has begun around the age of six, upon entry into first grade. Increasingly, formal instruction is taking place at earlier ages—in the kindergarten year and even before. While the applications to school situations of Piaget's discoveries about cognitive development are in their infancy, it is nonetheless logical to hypothesize that formal instruction is much more compatible with Piaget's "formal operations" stage of development which begins about age seven. The congruence between cognitive mode and instructional technique is perhaps a more critical factor in learning through formal instruction. One apparent remedy would then be to postpone instruction to that age when formal teaching is more likely to be effective— at seven, *or older* for many normal children—rather than is presently the case where the pressure is certainly in the opposite direction. Or, we might find procedures for teaching more compatible with the younger child's way of reasoning.

## The Complex Nature of the Reading Process

I am suggesting, then, that there are other factors at work—complex ones about which we so far know very little. Given the extent of "the reading problem" in the United States, however, it at first seems odd that we are so ignorant of that process we so eagerly seek to instill in the young. In fact, it has only been in the recent past that there has been any widespread interest in analyzing reading behavior, let alone how that behavior might be encouraged through modifying those classroom procedures that presently provide such unsatisfactory results. Within that mountain of published material related to "reading," only the smallest fraction of it is devoted to any concern for describing the process itself. It has by and large been assumed that there is a common understanding of its nature. However, there is a trend, which began only within the past few years, toward specific descriptions of the reading process. However long overdue, it must be welcomed.*  Nonetheless, it is unfortunate in my view at least, that most of these attempts to describe reading remain so narrowly based. By restricting their concern to behavior associated with responding to printed words, I submit, the true complexity of reading behavior escapes our notice. The consequence is very much like that resulting from the argument over the impact of phonological irregularity upon reading disability; it prevents us from seeing the forest for the trees.

I would argue, then, that reading is a complex process whose dimensions are infinitely broader than we have generally assumed them to be. Parenthetically, I would also say that while we have underestimated the complexity of the process itself, we have over-complicated the teaching of reading unmercifully.

## A Broad View of Reading Versus the "School View"

Our continuing insistence upon thinking of reading as a behavior exclusively associated with printed words is perhaps understandable if not logical. We have a peculiar "school view" of reading which derives, at least in part, from our anxiety over teaching that behavior more successfully. That concern has been endemic in our society for at least two hundred years but the result appears to be such that it might well pay us to shake loose from such narrow thinking. In our lives outside of school, of course, we use the term "reading" to connote an interactive process with a much broader range of stimuli than printed words. Since there is a great deal of wisdom buried in language, it might be worth our while to discover *why* it makes sense to think of reading in *that* context, which is simply the process of creating meaning for *any* stimulus for which the human organism can develop a meaningful awareness, rather than as a subject in the curriculum isolated and remarkably unrelated to the rest of school activities. Out of school, meanwhile, we "read" anything: faces, gestures, tracks, numbers, pictures—the list is endless, and it *includes* printed words.

Almost forty years ago, Peter L. Spencer employed the generic sense of that term in developing a theory of reading. The basic concepts he developed I believe to have continuing validity. His basic point of view is contained in this statement:

> It is obvious that in order for printed words to perform their intended function, they must be read; that is, they must be sensed and interpreted.

*The Claremont Reading Conferences provide the notable exception of this case, having been founded in 1932 for the express purpose of developing a theory of the reading process.

But, that is likewise true of spoken words and of everything else which we experience . . . Certainly, sensing and interpreting the printed words on a page constitutes an act of reading; but, the assumption that it constitutes the whole of reading behavior is open to serious question (5).

Spencer thus opens up the whole educational question of the necessity for drawing boundaries between one kind of reading and another. At the same time he broadens the problem of understanding the reading process by suggesting that there are some aspects of reading behavior common to all types of reading, while other aspects obviously are distinctive. The educational problem, then, is to discover the nature and extent of those similarities and differences and, at the same time, to determine some order of importance for each in devising instructional strategies. In this way, criteria can be built for developing a balanced curriculum.

### Elements in the Reading Process

Let me turn now to the next steps in the application of this theory of the reading process. In this view, there are four major elements interacting as any reading proceeds. These are continuously engaged since reading is an on-going process which requires *time* if meaningful behavior is to result. The first of these elements resides entirely outside of the reader and has its own special character. That obviously is the environment of the reader, consisting as it does of a wide range of sources for stimulation, *among* them printed words.

The remaining three elements interacting in reading behavior are to be found within the reader and are consequently very largely removed from direct observation and study as to their unique character. Additionally, they share common ground with all forms of reading behavior.

The second element in reading, then, is that process by which the human organism changes visual, auditory, and other forms of stimulation into neural responses. Patterns of light and sound, of texture and motion, etc., are converted by the sensory apparatus for transmission within the human body. While much about these processes of conversion and transmission of stimuli from the environment is known, it remains an extremely complex behavior, not simply because, for example, the eye is an extraordinarily complex organ by itself, but because visual processes do not occur without involving in various degrees the other sensory modalities. This condition of interaction is the case for all sensory stimulation. In the reading of printed words, for instance, we observe that, although visual perception is essential, the actual reading depends even more greatly upon auditory imagery built up through past experiences, activated in some fashion through visual perceptual experiencing. This critical importance of hearing in visual reading is not as widely recognized as it should be; *in fact,* the aural mode is primary in reading printed words since the ability to speak in large measure appears to carry with it the capacity for building that imagery necessary if reading of printed words is to occur. For example, it is the lack of ability to *hear* that creates the serious visual reading problems encountered by the profoundly deaf. Especially is this so when printed word reading is taught to deaf people, as is so often the case, by way of some version of the oral method. It is reasonable to assume that the imagery necessary to the reading of printed words might be built through motoric experiencing (rather than auditory experiencing) as is available through finger spelling. However, if the reading of printed words is dependent upon auditory abilities, then the literacy problems of the profoundly deaf undoubtedly will continue. But I mention this here primarily to illustrate the importance of hearing in printed word reading as well as the interactive nature of the sensory processes.

Two elements in the process remain; they are those of perception and of responding. The mystery of these behaviors remains locked in large measure deep within the human organism; yet we know that their processes involve every aspect of that organism: they consist of motor responses, intellectual or cognitive—or thinking—behavior, each colored by affective or emotional tones. Again, I need to stress the totality of these involvements; there is no separation possible here either.

## The Importance of Mind and Heart in Learning to Read

It can readily be surmised that of all the interacting elements, certainly the last two are at once the most complex and at the same time those that we know least about. While scientists no doubt will continue to unlock many more of the mysteries that surround the human mind, there hardly seems doubt that within this aspect of reading behavior we come across the most illusive and difficult of questions to resolve in our quest to understand the nature of the reading process. It is in order, then, that we realize there is a great deal of unexplainable behavior in reading as well as a great deal of feeling tone surrounding the whole process. Until science moves us much further along, we ought, therefore, to accept the idea that intuition is playing a very large part in the acquisition of reading competencies.

Even if science provides us with sufficient information soon so that we can explain those behaviors that heretofore have been "explained away" by way of the notion of *intuition,* there seems little doubt that our major emphasis in teaching any kind of reading, but particularly here reading printed words, should be upon stimulating thought and providing opportunities for communication of all kinds. While I have shared in the thought that the linguist probably has little of direct value to say to the teacher of reading, I must at least retract that idea for the moment to push Mr. Chomsky forward to center stage once again, for he concludes as I would, that

> there is little reasonable doubt that the dominant factor in successful teaching [of reading] is and always will remain the teacher's skill in nourishing, and sometimes even arousing, the child's curiosity and interest and in providing a rich and challenging environment in which the child can find his own unique way toward understanding, knowledge, and skill (6).

### Arranging the Environment to Stimulate the Development of Reading Behavior

As counterpoint to these views of the nature of reading behavior and the over-riding importance of mind and heart over orthography and the functioning of the sense modalities, I believe there are a few ideas that might profitably be kept in mind as we arrange that challenging environment Chomsky speaks about. These considerations I derive from the broad concept of reading and I hope the logic of those derivations remains reasonably clear as I proceed.

First, I believe we should be careful to separate the idea of teaching reading from how reading is learned. In many, if not most instances, we cannot explain how a child achieves the integration of all those competencies that come into play when reading occurs. Even if it were desirable to teach all of the seeming peculiarities of our orthographic system (which I do not in any case believe), it is clearly not feasible. There is simply not enough time in the school day, even if we went the last distance and threw out all of the subject matter curriculum *and* P.E.—a not impossible prospect in some schools, I fear. The evidence strongly suggests, in fact, that the teaching of rules, grapheme-morpheme correspondences, and all the various skills is, if not totally ineffective, certainly excessively inefficient. The fact that our own memories of how we learned to read printed words, and how we expanded our capacities to their present well developed stage, suggests a bit more humility on our part as to the effects of direct teaching. Rather, I think it encourages us to think about how we can facilitate a behavior that is already present, even in the youngest child. Consider, for example, that, in addition to the many pieces of intelligence acquired in the earliest years, all children entering school have, as well, some facility for reading words in their printed form.

A second idea relates to the fact that all reading is a silent act that cannot be directly observed. We see only the smallest part of the tip of the iceberg when we see eyes move, fidgeting behavior, or other apparently overt signs that reading is or is not taking place. We use various devices, among them a strange one called "oral reading," to give us evidences that reading has occurred. But workbooks, oral reading (or saying words already read out loud), even talk about the "author's meaning" only provide clues as to whether or not a child has been reading. There are other ways of inferring whether reading has occurred, if we need such. I suspect, however, that we are spending far too much time in these activities; it would be better to give children more time to read rather than asking them so often to prove that they have read something. In more simple words, reading is very private behavior and must necessarily and thankfully remain so.

A third idea has to do with the individualistic nature of the reading process. Reading is simply not a group activity. Why it should be taught that way escapes my imagination, except that I know the "three group" method was presumably designed to provide for individualized instruction. Actually, it is more reasonable to assume that total class instruction provides better opportunities for individual learning since the teacher cannot exercise as much control over the wide range of interests and capacities found in any classroom. I do not advocate returning to those old days, however, because it is obviously so easy to individualize learning opportunities—if we can reduce our urge to check upon progress a bit.

My fourth comment relates to the fact that any reading is a personal experience. The emotional aspects in all language performance provide the most critical of the elements in reading. Since language provides a window into the interior being of every person, criticism of the ability to use that language (in whatever form) constitutes a personal judgment of the worth of that individual. Consequently, negative criticism, expressed or implied, is destructive of human relationships if persisted in for any great length of time. I therefore think we should become very sensitive to those messages that in fact tell a child his language accomplishments are poor or otherwise unacceptable.

A fifth idea is that the quality of any reading is dependent upon experiencing. Any experience obviously must be unique to the individual; and it is upon those unique experiences that ideas develop. We ought to give much attention to the quality of experiences—to those first-hand encounters with the environment out of which ideas and feelings emerge. If the experiences children have are relevant to their own lives, they will also be meaningful; however, there must also be a place for those experiences in the school setting and opportunities to communicate the meanings such experiencing has for the child. If these conditions exist, it seems difficult to imagine any child not making good growth in his ability to read and to write.

Finally, verbal language is interrelated; development in one aspect strengthens the others just as it affects beneficially other modes of reading.

For historical reasons alone, as far as I can determine, we have assumed that a child learns to read the printed mode before learning to write it. However, it may be much more sensible to argue that, like learning to speak and listen, the capacity to read and write the language also develops concurrently. It can perhaps also be argued that as listening is intimately related to the development of oral speech, writing is similarly important in the development of the ability to read print. This follows, it seems to me, because writing requires the child to utilize auditory images first. Translating those images into an orthographic system follows in the sense that oral language is the result of practicing so as to obtain congruence between speech and auditory images for that speech gained through listening. Any child who can write phrases and sentences meaningful to him can read printed words. There are perhaps other reasons to explain this phenomenon, but in any case we might infer as a consequence that the initial school experience be in writing, followed by encounters with printed words in books, all of this of course, to be followed by continuous and extended experiencing of both.

## Can "Reading" Be Taught?

No matter the context in which it is viewed, reading is clearly a multi-faceted behavior of immensely complex dimensions. But if we subsume the "school view" of reading under the broader context suggested here, then that behavior is seen as an even more intricately involved process. So involved is it that one is immediately led to the question as to whether reading can actually be taught. I suspect it cannot, at least as directly as we try to teach it. That is, instruction in reading as we commonly perceive it, striking at such a narrow band of the total process, appears to by-pass many of the most important aspects of that behavior. Hence, it would appear that situations and opportunities are created, by plan or quite incidentally, that either encourage the development of reading behavior or snuff it out. More accurately, I should say that situations and opportunities apparently arise throughout the life of the child—part of which is spent in school—that determine what kinds of reading will occur and what the quality of that reading will be.

If reading for the most part is not taught directly, then how can we explain its emergence? I think there is little doubt that one factor alone is responsible: that is the apparent natural human propensity for language in all its forms. It is impossible for a person to grow up without the ability to speak and to interpret spoken language, as long as there is one other speaking person around. What, then, is so different about learning to read and write one's language that it requires such specialized teaching of skills and other techniques for analyzing words in their printed form? John Regan has pointed out that indeed children might not grow up speaking, or at least not achieve the remarkable development of that ability we observe in all normal behavior in the first four years of life, if they were taught to speak in the same general fashion as children are taught to read and write (7). In so saying, he was pointing to the fact that much of what we currently attempt in the way of instruction in reading and writing may well cause more interference than encouragement in the development of those abilities. In any event, our formal instruction clearly lacks virtually all of the elements in teaching and learning that a parent seems naturally to use in those early, productive years. Is it perhaps worthwhile to make at least a note of this fact and consider whether there are meanings for the classroom within it?

Just as people learn the oral tradition, might we then not expect the written or printed tradition also to emerge? Is there good reason to assume that writing and print are *that* different? In observing young children, we see the same natural proclivity that characterizes the behavior of older members of the species, i.e., the devising of various kinds of symbol systems to stand for ideas resulting from experience. For example, "pretend writing" is something every child will do if he just gets the idea somewhere. Before he knows the formal system—the approved version—he will write his own squiggles to stand for words in stories, squiggles that will be "read back" with a high degree of accuracy at a later time if we encourage it. It is true, also, that all children come to school with some knowledge of that formal system. These are mainly words that come from the breakfast table, the endless hours spent at the television, or from some other familiar activity. Today's *Cheerios* and *Sesame Street* have taken the place of yesterday's *Disneyland* and *Batman.* Still, children respond meaningfully to such symbols when they are in their experience. This suggests that the critical conditions for learning to read are found in the daily lives of people, in the quality of that life—in opportunities for developing ideas, and in finding various ways of sharing them. Teaching can have great effects if effort is bent in these directions.

## Reading and the Problems of the 70's

If reading "comes naturally" as the saying goes, then we must look especially at the problems of racial and ethnic minorities along with our overall concerns, for those problems are staggering to say the least. In my analysis of reading behavior I have emphasized above all else that it is an activity involving attitudes and ideas, feelings and experience. Many people in our society, however, feel alienated and believe they have been denied equal access to the affluent America of the 1970's. These feelings are real and have basis in fact. They also increasingly believe that it is necessary above all else to raise levels of literacy in order that they will have those tools they think are critical for survival in a world that seems to demand ever higher levels of competence. Reading as a consequence is viewed as the key to the affluent world of the middle-American. The "cure" is assumed to be more effective teaching of printed word reading. However, reading broadly viewed suggests the most important key that will turn open that door to reading and writing the printed language will be applied in the community itself. For there are important precursors to the successful stimulation of reading behavior, either broadly or narrowly construed. While the school can undertake important reforms, the nature of reading behavior and the manner in which I believe the reading process grows and matures are more dependent upon finding solutions to the social and economic ills that beset important segments of our society. The most important change the school can make—one of no mean consequence—is to *become a school for the people it directly serves* rather than a reflection of the middle-class culture at large. It is no accident that "middle-Americans" have in the overall the smallest number of reading problems: the schools in our society reflect that relatively homogeneous economic, social and cultural world of the "middle-class." As well, schools in the ghetto still by and large also reflect that world rather than that of the people they serve.

To change the school in those areas serving minority populations is nonetheless insufficient in achieving a solution to the very grave problems of which high levels of reading disability are symptomatic. I am urging, then, that ways be found to reduce the very wide range of differences that divide people from one another and from the mainstream of society. At the same time, however, we should not seek to reduce the range of those differences which lead to healthy diversity.

But time is running out. In the past, when a people have sensed the possibility that improvement was in fact possible, they have grown increasingly dissatisfied and have frequently rebelled. This is in the American tradition, as Alexis de Tocqueville, that perceptive chronicler of American life, pointed out almost 150 years ago. In his famous volume, *Democracy in America,* he wrote:

> The evil which was suffered patiently as inevitable seems unendurable as soon as the idea of escaping from it crosses men's minds. All the abuses then removed called attention to those that remain, and they now appear more galling. The evil, it is true, has become less, but sensibility to it has become more acute (8).

Perhaps we now have sufficient evidence to conclude that history is coming as close to repeating itself as is ever possible. Awareness is growing. Anger and dismay are being expressed, often in unfortunate ways. That there is an endemic reading problem and it does indeed "appear more galling" is ever more widely recognized among those who are most afflicted if not among society at large. As we become aware of the true dimensions of the problem, it becomes increasingly clear that it *is* at once both intolerable *and* unendurable.

So I end on a note of urgency, but also one of hope.

I believe it is imperative that as teachers and others thinking about school problems, we think more reflectively about the nature of the reading process and the priorities for teaching that emerge from our thoughtful considerations. I have emphasized a broader conception of the nature of reading in the belief that such a view does indeed contain within it important ideas for distinguishing the very important from that which is not as important in planning a curriculum for boys and girls. If the human animal distinguishes himself from all others by his propensity for, and ability to use language to express thoughts that in turn stand for remembered experience, as I believe is the case, then we can be humble in the presence of these developing abilities that will out if we will let them. At the same time, we will have good ideas how circumstance may be arranged to maximize their development.

## References

1. "The Right to Read—Target for the 70's," Address by James E. Allen, Jr., U.S. Commissioner of Education at the 1969 Annual Convention of the National Association of State Board of Education, Los Angeles, September, 1969.
2. Noam Chomsky, "Phonology and Reading," Chapter I in *Basic Studies in Reading,* Harry Levin and Joanna P. Williams, eds. (New York: Basic Books, Inc., 1970), 4.
3. *Ibid.,* 15.
4. *Ibid.,* 18.
5. "Reading Reading," unpublished manuscripts of an address given by Peter L. Spencer at the International Reading Association Conference held in Fresno, California, September, 1970.
6. Noam Chomsky, *op. cit.,* 3.
7. John O. Regan, "The Problems in Teaching the Mother Tongue: An Anthropological Standpoint," paper delivered at UNESCO Conference on the Mother Tongue, UNESCO Institute of Pedagogy, Hamburg, December 1969.
8. Quoted by Charles E. Silberman in *Crisis in the Classroom* (Random House, 1970) 20.

# The Context for Learning to Read

# Sol Tax

## Self and Society

My major point is that the process of learning or changing "motivation" is a *social*, not an individual, process. An individual does not behave alone but usually in response to people important to him. We can call these people his "reference group." The matter becomes complicated when there is more than one reference group and a single piece of behavior pleases one and displeases another. This happens in different degrees to everyone and in all societies. In such cases, the individual tends to behave like the proverbial mule who starves to death because he is half-way between two stacks of hay. When a child behaves this way, many of us define his behavior by saying that he "lacks motivation." Since it is human to behave, it could only be pathological—and individual and unusual—for someone to lack motivation; that is, to stop behaving. So, when a teacher says that Johnny "lacks motivation," she is only confessing that she does not understand why Johnny does not do what she thinks he ought to do.

The fault of the teacher is not that she does not understand Johnny's behavior (or lack of behavior) or that she has given up even trying; but that, in giving up she blames the child, stigmatizing him as pathological, saying he lacks motivation. Thus she adds insult to injury and further destroys the relationship between herself and the child, and between the child and other children not so stigmatized.

I want now to return to the original proposition, that learning or changing is not an individual but a social process. Let me clarify how the social is in turn imbedded in the cultural, the very existence of which it is difficult to accept or even recognize. We are all human, and therefore the same. But part of being human is that we are also different. Coming to know another person is coming to see the respects in which he and I are alike, and the respects in which we are different. Comparisons are usually made along three cross-cutting axes. First, there are individual personality differences whereby any two of us can appear to differ radically even if we are brought up in the same circumstances. Second, there are "situational" differences; two men who are hungry, or two who are members of different minority groups, may exhibit surprisingly common behavior. Third, there are the cultural differences whereby persons of one traditional culture live by a common set of values and behavior that may radically differ from those of another traditional culture.

All humans are products of one or another culture which sets them on a narrow pathway. As we grow up, we do not even know that this is only one of many pathways. We are raised with blinders on our eyes so that we see other people in terms of our own cultural ideas of proper behavior. When we first try to know a person who has grown up in another culture, we therefore misinterpret his behavior. We do recognize personality and situational differences—there are lazy and industrious people in all societies, and we recognize the difference between rich and poor—and we assume that's all there is to it. So we not only fall into an error of simple misinterpretation, we also make incorrect value judgments. We say that this stranger is lazy because anyone who behaves like that in our own culture is lazy. In fact, we are guilty of a bad analogy; it is as though we said that a lilac bush is defective because it has no thorns or red roses. When we assume that culture is not a factor, we interpret as bad or defective behavior that is legitimately different.

Many of us think of cultural differences as existing only in far off places, among Malinowski's Trobrian Islanders, or Margaret Mead's Samoans. But in fact they may exist between any two peoples who have come in contact but have not completely lost their identities. A difference in language or dialect is one sign of this. Two speech communities are likely to indicate two cultures as well, and if they are not very different, there is a greater danger that we will remain blind to the difference. In education the problems which arise from large cultural differences are not necessarily more difficult than those which arise from small cultural differences. When the differences are small, the effects are subtler and sometimes more, rather than less, critical.

Our forefathers came from Europe and took this continent from American Indians. They were disposed to change, and they assumed that everybody else also wanted to change in the direction of the dominant society and culture which they established. When the North American Indians did not fulfill this expectation, they received the blame. They were ignored and left in isolation without the means for making an economic adjustment of their own choosing. Though today they still value their own ways and refuse to change, they also want to eat. The dominant establishment of course considers that *they* are the problem.

While northern Europeans were appropriating the North American Continent, the Spaniards and Portuguese were taking the rest; here the dominant indigenous people happened to be peasants quite like those in Europe, and they adjusted rather differently. In California and our Southewest there were non-peasant Indians who remained isolated; but the mixture of European and Mexican peasant cultures which moved in upon them provided a new Spanish-speaking culture which satisfied the Spanish-speaking peasantry. In effect they were indigenous people when we moved in on them; they had their own culture which they saw no reason to change. Puerto Rico also had its settled culture; its people also had no desire to change their ways simply because we moved in on them. They migrated to our mainland only to seek a living.

To get labor, our forefathers who took over the continents also enslaved Africans. When slavery was legally ended, it continued in other forms, and the present need to end it once and for all constitutes the major domestic problem of our day. The myth that the Africans in this country lost their culture was part of the process of our dehumanizing them. Whites pretended that Negroes had no distinctive culture—were just like us except that they were inferior; and in the caste system the Negroes had to adjust to the white man's conception. It may turn out that many Blacks are more like American Indian tribes than like economically-oriented Japanese. If so, as in the case of American Indians, equality on white terms will not suffice. We shall only know when we have lived with equality for a while.

In the meantime, we face policy issues in education which result from these cultural differences. One can begin with the Coleman Report and the Civil Rights Commission demands. In 1965, the Coleman report on "The Equality of Educational Opportunity" stated that a student's classmates are the single most important influence on how much he is likely to learn. Coleman found that "Improving the school of a minority pupil may increase his achievement more than would improving the school of a white child increases his [achievement]." But more significantly, he found that the socio-economic and educational backgrounds as well as the aspirations of other students in the school were more important in predicting a student's achievement than the strength or weakness of school facilities, curriculum, teachers, or than the amount of money spent on each pupil, or any other special feature of the school itself.

The United States Commission on Civil Rights 1967 report, "Racial Isolation in the Public Schools," said that in addition to the social class factor, the racial composition of a classroom plays a secondary but still important role in school learning: "Racially isolated schools tend to lower Negro student's achievement and restrict their aspirations. By contrast, Negro students who attend predomiantly white schools more often score higher on achievement tests and develop higher aspirations." (Summary,

C.C.R. Clearinghouse Publication, No. 7, p. 4.) The Commission established that both Negroes and Whites do better when a classroom becomes predominantly White, while in contrast, special compensatory education programs in ghetto schools do not overcome the social class, peer factor. Thus, students in segregated ghetto schools with stepped-up education programs do not achieve better than students in equally segregated schools without special programs. The conclusion reached is that, whatever the other consequences of integration, in the long run it should have a positive effect on Negro achievement.

In November, 1967, a conference also sponsored by the U.S. Commission on Civil Rights reported the growing body of research on student achievement. Again the view was reinforced that compensatory education in Negro ghetto schools has been a dismal failure. Negro students learn more in normal, mostly white classrooms than in the most elaborately improved all-Negro schools with small classes, extra teachers, and special programs. Reviewing the research reports presented to the conference, Harvard Social Relations Professor Thomas Pettigrew concluded that it has been established beyond a reasonable doubt that the main resource that schools can offer a "disadvantaged" child (that's his term; I do not use it) is association with more advantaged children. Children of all backgrounds tend to do better in schools with a predominantly middle-class milieu. One explanation for the higher achievement levels in integrated schools seems clear: when the make-up of the classrooms is more than half White, the middle class atmosphere tends to prevail. As soon as a school becomes more than half non-white, the learning of both Negroes and Whites suffer, presumably because the middle-class atmosphere no longer prevails in the classroom. Compensatory programs apparently have not been as successful as simple integration in creating an achievement-oriented classroom environment.

This is insulting to Blacks in our society. An injustice is involved here because the only analysis of why white middle-class children are needed for the education of Negroes is that only they produce an atmosphere conducive to learning. But all arguments favoring "integration" of the schools in this country assume that the goal of the American educational system is to pass on the majority culture. It might be interesting to consider the differences between what most white educators consider the goal of education and what might be considered the goals of education by those Blacks who do not accept integration as a desirable outcome. Nobody has even asked Blacks or any other minority group to enter into a general discussion of what they see as the goals of education. In terms of their own educational goals, who knows that they cannot produce an equally effective atmosphere for learning?

Meanwhile, however, the conclusion of the Coleman report, of the Civil Rights Commission, and of others should hardly surprise us. Everything we know about how cultures diffuse from one social group to another is violated by the notion that members of Group B will absorb the culture of Group A when their only face-to-face contact is one person who represent that culture, the teacher. Students of acculturation know that it is impossible to impose the culture of one group on another by providing only a single, weak link.

In a ghetto school, ghetto behavior—but not an alien culture—is passed on "naturally." The least required if another culture is to be transmitted is contact with a *community* of people of the other culture, which may then diffuse its culture by a voluntary process of selection. Only voluntary selection makes possible the passing of useful information without threatening identity and values. Not everything that is proposed to pass on will pass through this subtle filter to be internalized by the recipients. This explanation removes the element of insult, but we must do more than that.

The crux of the matter with regard to education is the question of whose culture is to be transmitted. I raised this question in connection with the colonial situation in a paper some twenty years ago* when European pioneers still held colonies in Africa and elsewhere. Man would not have evolved—we would not be here today—if cultures could not be passed on from one generation to the next. What is wrong in our time is that people in power assume that their culture is what must be transmitted to the next generation, even of people of other cultures. People want to maintain their own values and ways. If these are sharply different, competition arises between the superordinate group which has one culture and the subordinate group which has another.

In the United States where "minority groups" are based on race, religion, national origin or some peculiarity of culture, ethnic sub-societies are not typically territorial. The situation also differs from other colonial situations in that most minority nationalities are anxious not to be nationalities. Rather they strive to be Americans and identify with American values and aspirations. Problems arise only when the dominant group refuses to accept them, and segregation is forced on them.

Among the exceptions to this are American Indians who want more than equality. They want recognition of their identity as a sub-national group and want that identity protected. Indians want to share the economic and social advantages of the larger society while maintaining their own values and their own communities.

---

*"The Education of Underprivileged Peoples in Dependent and Independent Territories," *The Journal of Negro Education,* Vol. XV, No. 3, Summer, 1946.

It was long clear to those of us who learned from American Indians that one of the striking differences between Negroes and Indians as minority groups in the U.S. was that Negroes were fighting for equality in our society and did not want to talk about cultural differences, at least not until they had achieved the legal equality they were fighting for. Indians, on the other hand, did not want to be part of our society. They wanted to share in its benefits to the degree that they wanted to participate but they wanted to be free not to participate and to maintain their own ways and culture.

As Negroes have begun to achieve their freedom, they find ways in which their own upbringing and their own traditional ways of behaving are more interesting to them and have values the white way does not have.

We in the United States must now ask whose culture is to be transmitted. Is the dominant white, middle-class culture to be transmitted to Indian tribes, or to people with Spanish surnames as they are now euphemistically defined? And particularly, whose culture is to be transmitted in ghetto schools? If it is to be our dominant white culture, some serious problems arise.

First, let me point out that nobody has seriously raised this question. Occasionally I have tried to do so in a conference and the response is, "Well, they have to get along in our society; what do you want to do, preserve some culture which forbids them a proper economic and social adjustment to the larger milieu?" My only answer can be that this is not necessarily the only alternative. Then I enter into a discourse on cultural pluralism and the possibilities in our society for some alternative solutions. However, these cannot be seriously considered until these minority groups achieve sufficient equality to make their own demands for individuality; that is, until they achieve enough "power" as they call it (an appropriate term) to be able to make their own wishes felt as to what they want to become.

The mass notion that culture is passed on in society from generation to generation gets in the way of constructive relations between parents/children, teachers/pupils, adults/teen-agers. It is time to shake some notions —so far taken for granted—about how culture passes from generation to generation.

The evils of paternalism and the habit of doing things to people against their will for their own good is not only a propensity of colonial governments insistent on civilizing the heathen, but also a habit of parents and teachers. Using the formula A over B, A can stand for a parent, B for his child; A for the teacher, B for the pupil; A for a European government, B for its colony; A for the Bureau of Indian Affairs, B for an Indian tribe on a reservation.

Let's say that, in all these cases, A is in the position of having authority over B or responsibility for B's welfare. In the case where this a completely benevolent authority, A sincerely feels the responsibility for B's welfare. A wants to help B. There is no conflict of interests—A and B both want what is best for B. As I once put it:*

> Now suppose that A and B disagree about what is good for B. Mother thinks Johnny shouldn't eat so much candy; it will injure his teeth. Or the pupils in a class decide to chew gum, and the teacher forbids it—regretfully—for the same good reason. Or the Indian tribe decides it wants to have its own school on the reservation but the Indian Service says they should go to public school so they can learn the ways of the white man, for their own good. In each case A and B are interested only in the good of B. But they disagree on what is good. This now is the problem—who should have the final word? Should the child eat the candy? Should the Indians keep their own school? This is the stripped-down model of the question I want to discuss, and only this. I am excluding all other problems, and deliberately over-simplifying. Especially remember that there is only one A and B. The model is quite different if we include Johnny's little sister, because then mother cannot worry simply about what is good for Johnny; maybe she thinks that what Johnny wants to do would be bad for sister May. To bring into our picture the rest of the family, or friends or neighbors, changes the model entirely, introducing conflicting interests . . .
>
> Now, simply stated the problem is this: who gets his way, A or B? Does Johnny eat the candy? We have all been in this position, and it is, of course, never so simple as the model. But the principles involved now come out rather easily, and the model permits us to compare the problem of the child with the problem of the community. Let us take the case of the parent and child first.
>
> Among the objectives that a good parent has is to protect the child from harm until he is able to protect himself. The younger the child, the greater the need for protection, but training for independence begins early and needs to increase rapidly. There is no single general rule to help a parent decide when and whether Johnny should have his way. The first rule is the quicker the better for any good influence on a child. There are two main limitations. One is safety; the parent cannot let the child do serious damage to himself. The other is more difficult. A child doubtless needs the feeling of protection that an authoritative parent may give him; but this is just the kind of protection he should lose as soon as possible. Aware of these two cautions, the parent ideally gives the child his head as early and as often as possible. Child psychology is not my field, but it is my understanding that no age is too tender—on principle—to begin.
>
> The second rule is almost equally obvious, difficult as it may be to apply in practice. The child should be permitted to have his way only as he is able to understand the consequences of alternative decisions. Theoretically, for example, Johnny may be allowed to decide whether or not to eat the candy only if he knows the feeling of a dentist's drill. When this

---

*The Freedom to Make Mistakes," in *The Documentary History of the Fox Project*, F. Gearing, et. al., eds. (Chicago: University of Chicago, 1960), pp. 246–48.

point is reached is difficult to know; and it is easy to be wrong in either direction. I suppose that the safe rule is that if there is no great absolute danger to the child of a wrong decision, then he ought to have his way even if the parent can't be sure he understands completely.

I have said nothing so far about whether it matters who is "right"—parent or child. It may seem strange, but this question appears to be beside the point. The parent and the child both believe they are right. If either of them thought he were *not* right, there would be no disagreement. So we expect the parent to believe in every case under discussion that he is right, and the child wrong. The problem still remains, therefore, of the circumstances in which the parent decides to let the child make the decision in spite of his certainty that the child is wrong.

The point is this. If the child in our model case is to be free to make a decision, it means he is being permitted in the parent's view to make a mistake. Therefore, freedom to make decisions must mean freedom to make mistakes.

If freedom means anything other than to think dark and bitter thoughts—and every slave everywhere has that poor freedom—it must mean freedom to act. That implies freedom to decide how to act. And any decision implies the possibility of error. It is, therefore, a grievous mistake to deny a child the right to make the decision about his own action only because the parent—or teacher now, if you will—believes the child is wrong.

This is not only a matter of logic, however. Think but of the common phrase that experience is the best teacher, or that one learns from his mistakes, and it becomes evident that to deny the child the right to make mistakes deprives him of his opportunity to learn, to grow, to become independent . . .

The salient rule, therefore, remains that *provided* that emotional factors and real and present danger are not pressing—and *provided* that the parent is reasonably satisfied that the child understands the consequences of the decision—then the child must have it his own way. The same rule, exactly, applies in the classroom or in a student organization with an adviser dedicated to guide its activity. In the last analysis, the children have to decide for themselves, and they must be permitted to decide in a way that their elders know is wrong.

. . . (Thus) if a parent wants to make the decision, he has the power to do so. But if he wants to perform properly the function of bringing up the child, he should never exercise the power except in the limits posed, and never simply because he is sure that he is right . . . I should think it proper for the parent to make the decision for the child because there is no time to understand the child's point of view, or no time for the child to understand all of the issues. These are human limitations. But it is wholly improper to make the decision on the grounds that mother—or teacher—knows best.

With this general principle in mind, we can address two interrelated issues: 1) the relation of one generation to the older generation which is in some degree of control over it; and 2) the "channels of cultural transmission," the paths through which information is passed in society; who learns what, how much, from whom, under different circumstances?*

Possibly because genetic transmission goes from parent to child, thus from the older generation to the younger, most of us assume that culture also passes primarily from parents to their children. But this is something to discover, not to assume. We must look at the question afresh, empirically, since unlike information that passes through the genes, non-biological information passes from person to person in many ways, not exclusively or necessarily from parent to child.

When we say "from generation to generation" we do not necessarily mean that there are finite generations. The age grades in society do not flow evenly, and any lines we draw are arbitrary. Nevertheless, as far as I know, nobody has followed through from this general common-sense understanding to some of its logical conclusions.

Any population consists of people of a variety of ages, a few of them very old, a few very young, and different distributions in between. It is possible to divide the entire population continuum into arbitrary groupings from infants, children, teens, young adults, the middle-aged, to the aged, or however; and we tend to speak of generations as though they were real. Thus we say that values are passed on "from generation to generation"; we speak of teen-agers as though they were a real and permanent group, and so on.

This is understandable because there are several social realities which suggest this picture of discrete generations. First, everybody is part of a nuclear family in which the generations are clearly marked.

Second, in our society we have many social institutions which cater to generations: the schools, for example: primary school, secondary or high school, and college. In each of these, and in every classroom, there is a group of children and characteristically a teacher who may be twenty years older than the children. And there are many other institutions which make something concrete of generations thought of in this way.

Third, we have laws and customs which make mass age distinctions. In many cases, twenty-one is the legal cutting edge, and we tend to talk of this as real. People under twenty-one are in one generation; people over twenty-one are in another generation. Sixty-five is another such cutting point and an important one. Thus, in these terms, society is roughly divided into three age grades: the youngsters under eighteen or twenty-one, the people who have no rights; people between twenty-one and sixty-five who have rights but they have to work for them; and people over sixty-five who have some rights for which they do not have to work. These are the three age grades through which we pass in our society. All societies have age

---

*The research on which this section is based was made possible by a grant from the Wenner-Gren Foundation for Anthropological Research.

gradings of one kind or another, sometimes more and sometimes less systematized, and often very different from our own. These things are cultural, and cultures differ, and you would find a great variety of examples around the world.

In our society we tend to emphasize these group generations as if they existed in reality. Furthermore, the distinctions made in terms of family, the educational system, and law and custom are enough alike to reinforce—rather than contradict—one another and thus give an apparent social reality to the common acceptance of generations. Nevertheless, these generations, reified in this manner, have limited reality. There is, in fact, a continuum of ages of people from which the "generations" are cultural abstractions.

What are the realities then? The realities are 1) the age continuum and 2) specific recognized institutions in each society, many of which have some age or generational characteristics. Although the classifications of the population by age are arbitrary, any age grade can be recognized as significant and related, accurately or not, to any institution. For example, we associate school with children, which is only a rough approximation because, of course, there are night schools for adults and the like. And characteristics are attributed to an age grade; for example, we say, teen-agers are rebellious, or old people are conservative. But we are going to put aside these usual practices to start afresh.

If we start with the age continuum, we can ask, "How does culture pass through time?" Let us consider only person-to-person passage of information, and pose two alternative models. Model A refers to a passage of culture from parents to their children, from teachers to pupils, from oldsters to youngsters. Model B refers to passage from slightly older to slightly younger people. A is the model which we think of as the generation to generation pattern which, I repeat, is popularly assumed when the phrase is used; I call it "long-jump percolation." B is a pattern I propose to establish as the short-age interval passage of culture which I call "short-jump percolation."

It has long been recognized that some culture passes through peer groups. For example, children learn games from other, sometimes older, children. Or we recognize teen-age culture. We tend to think of these as interesting but isolated phenomena, while assuming that the major adult knowledge and values come to an individual first from his parents, then his teachers, then social and political leaders, newspapers, books, television, etc. In contrast, I now seriously put forward the proposition that a chief way—not an incidental way, but a chief way—the traditional adult culture is transmitted in all or most societies is through the peer group. It is possible that it is most common for culture to be passed on through "short-jump percolation" and that it is an illusion of our culture and other cultures that parents, teachers, leaders and others teach anything to people 20 or 25 years their junior. There are several observations that lead to this somewhat extreme suggestion.

First, in some known cases, of which there are many in this country, a young child learns his language, not from his parents, but from members of a speech community which is alien to the parents. The speech community is the general community, the language of the neighborhood in which a person is living. In many cases the parents have moved from another country. They learn English as a foreign language, and their phonetics will never be the same as that of a native. Furthermore, they may exhibit many morphological, grammatical, and vocabulary patterns which differ from the speech language into which they have moved. If their children are born after they have arrived here, the children theoretically have a choice between learning the language from their parents or learning it from the wider speech community. The only way to test whether language is or is not learned from parents is to find situations in which the parents are not part of the speech community. Although this question has not been well-researched, it appears that even before these children go to school, they do not share the peculiar dialects of their parents.

Linguists with whom I have discussed this have told me that this observation may be faulty; the child may learn his parents' language first and then quickly forget it as soon as he comes into contact with people outside. Nevertheless, the observation remains that children of three to five years of age frequently speak the language of people around them rather than the language of their parents. Assuming only that we are not talking about an isolated family and possibly excepting the first-born who might not have contact with children outside the family for a year or two, we can see that language does not *necessarily* pass only from parent to child. It is not necessary to suppose that a year-old child learns directly from outside the family, only that he learns from an older sibling, who learns directly or indirectly from others than their parents. The whole community of all ages is in communication, not simply the child and his parents.

Further, there is a general body of theory, current in anthropological and linguistic circles, which suggests that language and thought are extremely closely related. In other words, we think in terms of a language. Thus, there is reason for supposing that if language is learned from slightly older people rather than from people twenty years older than oneself, many other aspects of the culture may also be passed from the general cultural community, rather than from the parents as we usually assume.

If this is the case, it raises the question of whether basic values do not also come from a value or culture community outside the family which corresponds to the speech community. It is possible that, with the exception of extreme cases of family isolation, language and culture are learned from the wider community. We do not usually recognize this because, in most cases the parents' and the community's language and culture are very similar. Furthermore, we have a predilection to believe that parents are important in culture transmission.

A second consideration which supports the contention that culture is largely passed on through "short-jump percolation" emerges from the fact that, as we all know, within the family there is hostility as well as love. Leaving sex aside, there is a complex of authority and dependence which makes for a syndrome of ambivalence. The anthropologist, Radcliffe-Brown, described this as a conflict between consecutive generations, with a hostile respect relationship of child to parent, especially of the same sex. In turn, the parent is hostile to his parent, the child's grandparent, while in contrast the grandchild-grandparent relationship is a benign one. Radcliffe-Brown described the generation principle at some length and compared societies in terms of this almost universal principle of hostility between consecutive generations and the benign relationship between alternate generations.

Not only is there hostility between one generation and the one immediately above it, but the latter has authority over the former. I would suggest that this is not a good climate in which to pass on knowledge, rules, and values which are very close to the heart of the hostility. The attempt to pass on rules and values from one generation to the generation below it tends to result in a vicious circle of misunderstanding in which the parent is frustrated in what seems to him his duty. Further, the child either pretends to accept and then acts otherwise, or he rebels outright, depending on the power and the reward-punishment situation that is involved.

This may explain why, in spite of the fact that very little cultural information passes from parents to children, the culture requires the pretense that it does. This is also a general problem for the administrator with power and the administered. Parents-child, teacher-pupil, imperial power-colony, all are members of the same class, and in different ways they find the same difficulties in communication. Comparisons can be made and a principle erected of the kinds of relationship that are established in authority situations and why we so frequently go wrong when there is disagreement between consecutive generations.

We can distinguish between two kinds of authority or power. I talked about A over B, where A has power and uses it only for the good of B; and when A and B disagree on what is good for B, A uses his power to enforce his opinion. I call this "Authority Type X;" B accepts, or pretends to accept, the decision because he has no alternative, no choice. But he is not convinced it is what he wants, and the pretense on both sides is clear to him, though it is not clear to A. I have already mentioned some of the consequences of this situation.

However, there are cases in which A and B are independent and coordinate, not A over B, but B becoming dependent on A for something he (B) wants; that is, B deliberately places himself under the power of A. He is not there by birth or some other force of circumstance, but by his own volition. A makes decisions which concern B and are claimed to be for the benefit of B. A has no real, legal authority. B can free himself, but he stays under the authority of A for whatever rewards there are for him. This I call "Authority Type Y," and it is the kind of authority found in peer groups, and in any other group with "natural leadership."

In the X situation, A feels juridical or traditional responsibility for B and he has "duties" which he feels he cannot give up. He feels he must "exercise his responsibility." In the Y case, A has no juridical, legal, institutional, or traditional responsibility or authority. He can use B or misuse him, as long as B lets him do so. He can also wash his hands of B. A young person finds himself in the B part of several X relations: son or daughter, pupil, and indeed a "B" to every adult who chooses to take responsibility and pre-empt the position of authority as though it were juridical. Grownups are all classified with parents and teachers as having something of the same propensities. The occasional adult who behaves differently, frequently an old man, fifty or sixty years older, is appreciated for the difference.

In contrast, children almost always find themselves in the Y type relationship with their age-mates. An older sibling sometimes gets into the A position of the X type of relationship when he becomes the surrogate parent. Similar is the school monitor who acts as a surrogate for the teacher. In such cases, B does not take the authority as real; but often the older sibling or the monitor may be the A in a Y relationship as well. These exceptions, however, do not change the general rule; the habit is to establish Y type positions within age intervals of up to about five years, and the X relationship generally where the age interval is over fifteen years.

The argument here is that the climate for acceptance of information, including value judgments, is much more favorable in Y than in X type relationships. I am suggesting that information is received from persons who are superordinate in either the X and Y positions, but the question is which is more easily accepted in a case of conflict; and here there may very well be a difference according to the kind of information involved. Clearly there is a significant difference between learning values or learning arithmetic for example. The latter might be more acceptable from somebody fifteen years older than is the case with values, questions of right and wrong.

The X relationship by definition sets up a misunderstanding, a pretense because B does not accept the information but has to pretend acceptance. He cannot get out of it; he has no alternative. In the Y type relationship, accepting the information is functional for him in a different way. If a child is told by his parents that he should behave in a way that contradicts what he needs to do to operate among his peers, he cannot accept the parents' judgment if he is to continue to operate. He learns how to simulate behavior that permits him to operate in X relationships and indeed he learns these tricks from, and they are approved of by his A's in Y relationships. Further, peer group relations persist through life, after the A's of the X relationship have lost their power. Thus again it is not surprising that Y type relationships are most often dominant over X type relationships. Otherwise the world would not go on; Y types are the social relationships that persist. Status in human society comes in some degree from parents, but essentially it is sought from and competed for among one's peers.

Culture is always changing, with greater or lesser speed, and in all of its parts, but of course unevenly. Parent-child or teacher-pupil, representing a twenty-five-year interval of change, must have different values. So the model here offered shows how changes occur, even in relatively homogeneous societies.

I will not go further into the complexities of the model which can be followed if one imagines time passing and people passing through time. This general way of thinking about what might pass from one generation to another, and the channels through which it passes, suggests that at least some important values of a society are passed not from parents to children, or from teachers to pupils, but within peer groups. Yet unstudied in any detail, or comparatively, is exactly who learns what from whom. Possibly one of the reasons this has not been studied is that it is an extraordinarily delicate point we would prefer to hide. In the same way that nobody really wanted to study the realities of Freudian sexual behavior, considerable resistance might be encountered if one were to inform teachers or parents that they are not passing on American culture. The facts of this proposition need still to be examined empirically, but its implications for action must be worked out by educators, not anthropologists.

\*    \*    \*

The theme "Self and Society" as it ties into problems of education, particularly education in literacy and verbal facility, is closely related to a five-year research program in cross-cultural education which some of my colleagues and I have carried out under a grant from the Carnegie Corporation.

In addition to carrying out field work with the Cherokee Indians in Eastern Oklahoma, we also established a national forum, a newsletter called *Indian Voices*. It is edited and written entirely by Indians, and in it American Indians across the nation exchange views with one another. Through *Indian Voices* we have tried to counteract the Indians' identification of literary with the white man. If Indians can find reading and writing functional in their own terms, clearly they would be, as you might say, "motivated" to read and write. When people who know that reading and writing exist, but do not themselves read or write, it is because they have not found reading and writing useful or functional in their own terms and in their own situation.

It is remarkable that there are many peoples who were more literate three or four hundred years ago than they are now. In Mindoro in the Philippines where people are poor, benighted, illiterate, etc., in European terms, there are literate people who write on bamboo in a language which was once widespread in all the islands of Southeast Asia. What happened?

Similarly missionaries long ago introduced writing in native languages to the natives of the small, scattered islands of Micronesia, who themselves carried it from island to island and are now generally literate in their own language. Since they live far apart, literacy is useful for sending messages across the waters; they find it functional. They see it as their own language and do not associate literacy with Europeans any more than American Indians associate the horse with the white man, who brought it to Mexico in the 16th Century. The point is that in order for people to be interested in reading and writing, literacy must be functional for the individual and his reference group and in accord with its cultural values and sense of identity.

People in general will accept any innovation and make any change provided, positively, that is functional in their own terms, and provided, negatively, that it does not violate the values by which they have learned to live or threaten their identity as individuals, which is tied to the identity of their tribes. Speaking of a people as conservative or as unwilling to learn or as unmotivated, etc. merely avoids the real questions.

A child raised in an American ghetto who is expected to become literate knows very well that literacy will not make him into a rich lawyer or doctor. He has too many examples around him of people who know quite a lot which does not get them anywhere. Thus the line, "you can be a success if you only do your homework" does not go very far. Schooling is not seen as truly functional by the child, or his reference group, or his society. Can we achieve equality fast enough to make education functional when education is required to achieve equality?

We must begin with the question of "How do you make education functional?" I am not referring to the long run but to the short run, or how to make education seem real and functional in the classroom. The sum of the short runs will result in the long run. How can a teacher avoid violating the child's values when in ignorance he assumes they are the same as ours, and every word used might be an insult? For example, it is widely accepted by the knowledgeable these days that standard English must be taught as a second language to children who do not come from a home in which standard English is spoken, since one must assume that they have a language at home. If the teacher says, "You don't speak English," children will rightly ask themselves, "What language do I speak then? What language do my parents speak? Don't we have a language in our family?" When English is taught as the first language, clearly there is a violation of values and a questioning of identity. This applies throughout. The books our teachers are likely to use threaten the identity and violate the values of all children for whom they were not written. Pictures of Dick and Jane's new-found, coffee-colored, middle-class friends are helpful to white suburban children, but doubtlessly add to the confusion of the ghetto.

We have still to learn to recognize that Blacks have a positive legitimate culture. I am sorry that like others of my age, I did not apply what I learned and get on picket lines early enough. On the other hand, it is probably just as well that youthful Negroes in the South began their own rebellion which then some others of us joined. But we cannot wait any longer to apply what we know.

The Cherokee in Georgia were in many ways more educated than the European immigrants with whom they came in contact. When Sequoya invented a syllabary system of 64 signs for the Cherokee language, 20,000 Cherokee became literate in their own language within three years. In 1820 they started to print a newspaper partly in English and partly in Cherokee syllabary. It carried news from Boston and other places which were of the same high civilization that the Cherokee had achieved.

During Andrew Jackson's presidency, the Cherokee were forcibly removed. They maintained their state in Eastern Oklahoma, and they maintained their printing presses. They built separate seminaries for boys and girls which were the first schools west of the Mississippi in which Greek and Latin were taught. They were managed entirely by the Cherokee Nation. These same Cherokee-speaking people in Eastern Oklahoma are among the poorest and least educated Indians in Oklahoma!

What happened is that in 1900, Oklahoma became a state, and treaties were again broken. The Indians were over-run by whites who squatted on their land before it became a state. Indian national independence was no longer recognized; the tribe was "terminated." The Nation became powerless and lost interest in its own development. Indians could no longer develop independently on their own terms and would not develop in the way the white man wanted them to do. It must be remembered that the Whites who surrounded them were poor, uneducated farmers. Indians were and still are obliged to go to country schools run by the white community, and the fact that they do not go to school and do not get educated is hardly surprising.

Our project tested the hypothesis I have presented here, and in only five years, reversed the situation. We brought back printing with a new type font. The Cherokee had not forgotten how to read and write, and now became again creative. They now have a Cherokee newspaper, a programmed primer so more people—especially the young—can learn to read and write on their own; a bi-weekly radio program in Cherokee which became so popular that it was soon extended from a half hour to an hour.

One of the notions to be tested was whether, if a people are literate in their own language, they will easily become literate in another. For these purposes, then, the project developed the first Cherokee typewriter in history, helped Cherokees to begin the Cherokee-language *Cherokee Nation Newsletter* and the bi-weekly radio program with national news and news of the Cherokee community, including advertising in the Cherokee language. The *Cherokee Primer,* from its first printing in April, 1965, until the end of the project two years later, was distributed to some 1500 Cherokee speakers.

The active literacy program included four literacy classes in three schools for Cherokee speaking children; three school programs in Cherokee literacy using the *Primer* but without the help of the project staff; adult and children's Cherokee literacy classes in Cherokee churches using the *Primer;* and adult Cherokee literacy programs in three schools using the *Primer.*

These and other aspects of our projects tended to revive the Cherokees' latent interest in their own language, and therefore their self-esteem. Furthermore, for the first time, the people around them began to see that these poor Indians who had been "swept under the rug" in the Ozarks were really quite some people after all. This was the effect both where they were feared and where they were at least slightly respected. This redefinition of Cherokees to Whites, and of Whites to Cherokees also involved Cherokee language courses for adult English speakers, and we developed a dictionary and texts so that white people could learn Cherokee. We also offered a high school course in the Cherokee language for a mixed group of Whites and Indian.

There is much more to say about this project, but to return to the original topic, "Self and Society." From the beginning of any child's consciousness, whether that is before or after birth, the human infant must be presumed to assume his own individuality. It is not a male or a female, which already classifes rather than individualizes; nor an infant, which equally classifies. It is rather the only significant being, demanding full attention to its unique self. In contrast, it may be presumed that this creature sees all others as a mass of non-self, the generalized "other." Becoming socialized then is to be forced out of the illusion of uniqueness, forced to accept that one is only a member of classes, and at the same time forced to break down the generalized mass of the other into classes and even into individuals.

In this basic sense, socialization is perhaps never successful. In our complex society, life is a never-ending struggle by the individual against his own homogenization; but, on the other hand, few of us learn to individualize others. Many of the other societies which anthropologists study provide solutions which could help us. This is most remarkably true of what are called tribal or kinship societies. They are usually small, and statuses are ascribed from birth. Every individual is classified in so many ways that he is in effect again individualized. He needs only to recognize his ascribed statuses which are his by birthright and need not be earned or even verified. These statuses are never brought into question. Since he learns precisely and positively who he is in relation to every other individual in his total life environment, he solves at once and without struggle the problems of his own individuality and those of others.

How could we return to this human condition when there are billions of people in a single system of mankind? I think it is possible that eventually our technology may help us. As one might expect, the first products of our new technology appear to be working against individualization; they depersonalize and dehumanize. However, in the large society, this new technology is necessary if individualization is to be possible. Only by electronics can the statuses, associations, interests, and desires of each of us be registered and used in social decision-making. Then again the individual can be taken into account as he was in the small society. It seems possible that the technology which is haunting us now may eventually help us resolve our problems. Thus I can end on a note of challenge and perhaps even optimism.

**Albert B. Friedman**

# The Middle Ages Revisited: Reading in the Electronic Age

In many ways the modern world seems to be entering an age, the electronic age, which is recreating the conditions of the Middle Ages. For the Middle Ages was an ear culture, an oral culture. With the introduction of printing, silence fell upon the world, and the eye became dominant in cultural affairs. We now are watching the waning of the age of typography. Electronic mass media, movies, television, radio, tape recorders, telephones, and phonographs are overwhelming the printed word as the really significant vehicle of information, persuasion and entertainment. What are the repercussions of our passing out of the age of print, out of the Gutenberg era? What threats does the cultural establishment face? Are we indeed returning to the Middle Ages? Or can it be that our anxieties are unfounded; that the new age will give us vastly more than it will deprive us of?

I have said the medieval world was a world of the ear. Only clerics and a few lay administrators could read or write or keep records. Even kings were illiterate; one of the early Henries was called Beauclerc—the great scholar—because he had managed to learn to sign his name. The kings, nobles and burghers were entertained by their household musicians or by minstrels and conteurs, who recited to them from trained and capacious memories. Many minstrels were capable of improvising ambitious poems of thousands of lines right on the spot, improvising out of their stores of stock formulas. The lesser laity richly entertained themselves with ballads, dance-songs and long recitals of adventure narratives. It was nothing unusual for an amateur village storyteller to have in his memory a repertoire of tales and verse that could keep him going for several days without repeating himself.

For pious and religious fare, the upperclasses had their chaplains to read to them; the lower classes had their parish sermons or travelled great distances to hear itinerant preachers, for the Billy Graham phenomenon is ultimately medieval. In many places, the really telling religious instruction was conveyed through wall paintings: François Villon, the vagabond poet of fifteenth-century Paris, tells us his mother's whole religion was gleaned from the murals in the nearby church—she saw the damned souls graphically suffering in hell and knew she didn't want that. In England and France, the creed, saints' lives, and the key Biblical stories were dramatized in cycles of playlets that were performed on wagon floats. Bleachers were set up at stops along a procession route; the wagon drew up; the play was put on; the wagon moved to the next stop, making way for the next wagon with the next play in the sequence.

The important point that I must incise is that very, very few medieval people read—read squiggles of black symbols on paper, that is. The art of the oral extemporizer demanded that he be illiterate. It was precisely because his verbal expressions, formulas and themes were not backstopped by written words that he had to trust to his memory, and he developed his memory to be worthy of the trust. Minstrels only very rarely used prompt books (or prompt manuscripts, I should say). The poets, it is true, did compose on paper, but not works to be read *by* their patrons—rather works to be read *to* their patrons. For poetry in the Middle Ages, as in Roman days, was not published by being amplified in numerous copies; it was published by being publicly recited, if necessary in installments, by the poet or a chosen performer. Only the chaplain, parson or monk had occasion to read print, and even these devoted souls, and even when they were alone, did not read silently to create an interior, a mental sound movie. *They read for their ears via their eyes—they read aloud.*

For silent reading, which any fourth grader among us has been trained to do, was something of a miracle in the Middle Ages. Everyone, whether doctors of the Church or lowly clerks, mumbled. St. Augustine writes with awestruck admiration of his mentor, St. Ambrose, who could read, and seemingly comprehend what he was reading, and without even moving his lips! Ambrose had taught himself this technique in self-protection. Eager young monks usually surrounded him in his cell and when he read aloud they kept breaking in to ask questions on the sentence he had just finished. The old man found these interruptions unendurable. With unsaintly cantankerousness, St. Ambrose learned to cover his tracks by reading silently.

St. Ambrose had few followers in silent reading. There was little purpose in it: reading was a social affair. People read works in small groups since manuscripts were rare and expensive and there were few literate people. In monasteries, which were of course the centers of learning, at mealtimes one monk read as the others munched. It happens that solitary reading was in fact encouraged among the monks, though it will surprise you to learn that the average monk read personally and solitarily only about one book a year. Thus, even though there was reading in the Middle Ages, it was actually an oral rather than a visual affair—it was a phenomenon of an ear culture.

Then came Gutenberg. Print amplified works of learning and literature by many powers. It has been calculated that fifteen to twenty million copies of thirty to thirty-five thousand titles were printed in the first fifty years of printing. There was now a point to more general literacy.

The revolutions caused or abetted by the invention of printing are too numerous and controversial and too well-known to need more than the briefest potting here. Printing is said to have clinched the Renaissance by making cheap editions of the classics available. The solitary reader entered upon the scene: individualism in thought was encouraged by his presence: modern man and the modern age were born. Individualism plus printed Bibles plus religious tracts and theological-works-for-everyman equal the Reformation. Printing consolidated and fixed the European vernaculars, and this trend, added to the centralism encouraged by the new literacy, hastened political nationalism. And not to forget economic man, easier communications stimulated ambitious networks of trade, leading to commercialism, leading eventually to the industrial revolution. Of course, there may be those here who think the Reformation, nationalism and commercialism not altogether good things. But now that the sun is setting on the age of Gutenberg, our nostalgia—not to mention our lively fear of what is in store for us—predisposes us to be charitable.

In this new age, we are coming more and more to be freed from the tyranny of print. Print has been tyrannical in two ways. First there has been the tendency exhibited by everyone from Shakespeare's Mopsa to Will Rogers and beyond, the tendency to regard whatever is seen in print as true. "Seeing is believing." Hearing is hearsay. The formal, official solidity of the typographical impression somehow canonizes what it is stating. In our context however, the tyranny of print refers rather to the feeling of admirers of the oral culture that print has unfairly eclipsed the oral and audial means of expression, a situation which the electronic media are redressing.

The truth of the matter is that civilized man's dependence on print has never been complete. Even the most cultured and bookish man gets only a small part of his information and entertainment from print. Our important knowledge, the knowledge which we use to structure reality, and deal with other people, and make ourselves effective in our jobs, comes through talk, comes through social experiences, and cultural dialogue, comes through what all our senses, not just the deciphering eye, have presented to us. We are really still three-quarters if not more in an ear culture. That said and admitted, our business is with this one-quarter dependence on and enjoyment of print. Is this being eroded away by the tendency to telephone rather than write a letter, to look through a picture magazine rather than read an unillustrated article, to view TV or go to a movie rather than read a book, or to listen to the radio rather than read a magazine? Will reading eventually become dispensable and be superseded by some combination of other media?

On this point it is hazardous to be positive, but one may safely predict that if things sift themselves out sanely, each medium will eventually take over the functions for which it is best fitted. In some sectors print and reading will have to retreat, and deservedly. Let's face it: print has been superseded in some areas much to the benefit of our general culture. Print, for example, was never able to do for music what the radio and the phonograph have. How could print preserve for us the vocal artistry of a Caruso or an Ivogun or the virtuosity of a Casals, a Cortot or a Toscanini?

The dissemination and appreciation of drawings, paintings, sculpture and architecture have been greatly encouraged by the press, but not by the printing press that turns out alphabetic symbols. The presses that have brightened our culture with reproductions of the graphic arts, with illustrations of the plastic arts, the presses that have gathered whole museums into books, have been presses of another kind. If a picture is worth a thousand words, who can deny the economy of photo-journalism of the sort that has been brought to its highest development in *Life Magazine?*—though it is sad of course that the brightness and excitement of the pictures tear the reader's attention away from the letterpress.

Similarly, TV and movies have peculiar and real advantage over the printed word in dealing with many genres and many types of content: in the great rivalry now going on, these successes will mark out for the various media their destined modes, levels, possibilities and audiences. The man of liberal culture will soon learn where to go for what, and the man who nurtures an unreasoning prejudice against one of the media does so to his own great disadvantage.

I suspect that at this point many of you are convicting me of having much too naive a tolerance for the newer media. Maybe so. But one snobbery I must combat, and that is the hard and fast division that some advocates of reading make when they lump TV and radio and films together as mass media and smugly exclude reading from that baleful category. Now I admit that there is some truth in this classification. Books and serious journals are the chief organs through which the informed, cultured elite express themselves and fuel themselves. Admittedly, too, TV, the movies and films can readily be charged with all the evils of mass communication: conventional piety; bland, unreasoning optimism; conformist values; a low common denominator of taste; blithe sentimentality; worst of all the tendency to regard the audience as a consumer and to slant the level of the performance toward what a condescending producer imagining his customer wants. The evils are quite real and lie in the first necessity of a mass product, which is, of course, to have mass appeal. A book can be a modest success if it sells 10,000 copies; a successful TV program requires millions of viewers, a successful film, millions of admissions.

But what we are forgetting here is that the book represents the first translation of a craft into a mass product; printing created the first modern production line. Our reading snob, however, will shrug off this favorite assertion of Marshall McLuhan's as a mere historical note of no significance in the modern context. He may also find ways to step around the four hundred million paperbacks that were printed last year. Nor will his snobbery be shaken when one points out to him how much hardcover book reading is the reading of such trash as that turned out by Frank Yerby, Thomas Costain, Frances Parkinson Keyes and the detective and spy story writers. Where we really have him of course is in the popular magazines and newspapers. The average consumption of books in this country is probably not more than three or four per capita; the reading matter of the vast reading public is made up of daily newspapers and of general magazines like the *Saturday Evening Post, Time, Newsweek* and the *Reader's Digest.* In these magazines, all the sins of style and the crass attitudes of the mass media are redundantly exemplified. Indeed the *Reader's Digest* has always been for our intelligentsia the most vicious example of superficiality, readability-at-all-costs, bogus intensity, shallow optimism, and shameless catering to the more genial mass prejudices. The article which was already painfully surface and glib and intellectually vapid in the magazine in which it originally appeared is further superficialized for its regurgitation in this frighteningly popular digest. But I needn't labor this point. Reading is itself a mass media; on that score we can't be snobs. Most persons we teach to read will spend their skill on material of no better quality than the average TV or radio program. The only reading worth making a case for is discriminating reading, the reading of material that is written with style and fully engages our minds and sensibilities.

And what is the case for serious reading? Why is this skill worth preserving? Will reading continue to be practiced or are we in fact entering the postliterate age of the gloomy prophets? In the tough, pragmatic future, no skill is going to be artificially maintained for long. What can reading do better than the electronic media?

The first thing that impresses us about type or print is its physical solidity and stability as a symbol. Voices evaporate to reverberate only briefly in memory; visual impressions go out of focus and fade altogether. But actually when you come to think about it, typography is no sounder or stabler than the means of preservation used by the new media. Tape and records preserve the voice; paper, celluloid and plastic preserve visual sequences. Print will unquestionably have lively competition as a preserver of information.

In the library of the future, we will not go to a card catalog but to a computer, into which we will punch a request for the information we want. When the computer has coughed out a few strings of code, we shall go to a dim, soundproofed, hearing-and-viewing-room, dial the code goups given us by the computer, and from one of the 12 or 15 national information centers there will be transmitted to our screen or to our amplifier the information we are after. Perhaps in some cases we shall merely be shown pages, slowly turned, of one of these old-fashioned twentieth-century things called books. For we shall still be reading. There are those books whose value is not in their information, books in which how the thing is being said is a part of what is being said, books also whose authors calculated part of their effect from the expectation that they would be read—and these books alone, if nothing else, will maintain reading. Science may choose to code information electronically but civilization will not let 2500 years of imaginative literature go down the drain, though in the future we may very well talk more about Gielgud's or Olivier's production of *Hamlet* rather than Kittredge's or Neilson's edition of *Hamlet.*

Even as a medium of information, print has its points. We not only read locally and linearly, but we take in the whole bloc of information, the paragraph or passage, in a sizing-up glance. Printed material, unlike other media, permits us to scan. We read the topic sentence, skip through the paragraph sampling as we go, reading carefully again only where the writer becomes emphatic. We know from its typographical position when a conclusion is coming, and attend more closely to that. We may pass over whole pages if our sampling indicates that what is being written is obvious to us or not what we want. And if the conclusion seems to be based on points we had neglected in a moment of inattention, we can easily turn back and recover the thread of the argument.

One important characteristic of reading which we do not much think about is that readers make up a non-contiguous society and reading is a non-simultaneous art. To take the matter of simultaneity first: a movie, a TV or radio program, even a staged play, exists for the individual only while it is being publicly performed. The individual shares the performance as a social act with a hundred, a thousand, perhaps fifty million other persons at the same time. In reading, the individual puts on a private performance for his own benefit and at a time of his own choice. A reader can follow up a personal interest actively by taking down or borrowing or buying the books he needs; the TV viewer is at the mercy of what the TV producers lay out for his passive absorption.

To explain the non-contiguity of readers involves my reintroducing a notion I touched on earlier. Print, unlike the other media, is destined to remain, I think, as it is now, not only the purveyor of reading material to a vast general public but also the organ for the expression and dissemination

of original, avantgarde, creative opinion. The media which depend of economic necessity on mass audiences cannot afford to offer a platform to the
intellectual and artistic elite. Thanks, however, to the more modest audience demands of book publication, the leaven so vital to cultural health and
progress can be made available in books to the limited number of readers
who value advanced thought and experiment. A book's audience or readership need not be contiguous, that is, it need not be assembled all in one hall,
like a theatrical audience. They may be scattered all over the globe. This
fact accommodates the intellectual elite who are few in any one community.

Also, as we observed, a book's readership is not simultaneous, that is,
not all readers of a given book will be reading it at the same time—in the
way that all viewers of a TV program are watching it simultaneously. This
non - simultaneity too serves the intellectual elite, for they are not obliged
to consider a book until they are prepared to understand it, or having read
it unprepared they can return to the book when better equipped, or hearing
of the book when they are not interested in that aspect of the subject, they
can securely postpone taking the book up until it comes into line with their
interests.

Perhaps I have made too much of reading as the vehicle par excellence
of elite, advantgarde opinion. But it is precisely because reading is the media
for advanced opinion *as well as* being a mass media that it provides a
channel of communication among various sectors of opinion and among
groups with differing standards and tastes. The influence of the elite exerts
itself by seeping down to lower levels. The elite of course are not really
exclusive; they *do* want to have influence. The beliefs and interests of the
mass mind and the middlebrow mind are the constant preoccupation of
intellectual leaders because they realize only too poignantly that their ideas
will have consequences in action only if they can be generalized on a broad
base and win a wide circle of partial or total adherents. In the scale of
readers, therefore, every kind of literary taste is represented, every species
of interest, every degree of intellectual intensity. And in addition to stimulating cultural variety, reading facilitates cultural mobility. The reader who
individuates to the point that he detaches himself from mass sensibilities,
has available to him on the next shelf at the library his avenue of escape.

Finally there are those obvious values in reading that only need to be
asserted to be conceded. On the psycholinguistic side, the act of reading
strikes every reflective analyst as almost miraculous. It baffles reason to
follow how the uttered or interior phonic stream which we generate from
type-symbols cues unfathomably complex acts of image-production and
thought. More than any other media, reading requires active participation
on the part of the receiver, the reader. The imagination is given greater
scope to operate in when one is reading than in any other form of communication. The thoughts, images, emotions and other responses that a given

passage of print stimulates in the mind are subtly conditioned by the individual reader's tastes, associations, experiences, intentions and sensuous predilections. Reading would be emphatically worth fostering if only for the mental exercises it involves.

But most of us read not to exercise the mind and not exclusively to gather information; we read for the sheer pleasure of indulging our imaginations. People may neglect duty, but pleasure motivates us irresistibly. It will take a radical reorganization of human nature for men to forego perhaps the greatest of innocent human delights, the fabrication of private sound movies in our heads out of intrinsically meaningless clusters of type.

# Henry Lee Smith, Jr.

# *Cultural Anthropology, Linguistics and Literacy*

I feel that one who is billed as an anthropologist and as a linguistic scientist needs at the very outset to make clear exactly what his approach or frame of reference is to a problem that is so multi-faceted as that of reading. In the first place, I believe we must start with the very, very beginning—the thing that makes reading and discriminative responses a possibility. All living things respond to their environment. But only man responds with considered responses or, if you will, discriminative responses, because only man can talk. It is the gift of human language that makes human life and human beings possible. Man is able to think about consequences, is able to ponder and to weigh choices because he thinks like a man. And thinking like a man means thinking through and by language.

When I went to school, language was defined as a means or a vehicle for communicating thoughts and ideas. I have often thought about this so-called definition and realized that it is really not a definition at all, because it does not tell us what communication is; it does not tell us what a thought or an idea is. But to the linguistic scientist and cultural anthropologist the greatest omission of all is that the definition tells us nothing about the structure of the vehicle which is supposed to communicate the undefined thoughts and ideas. The linguist, the cultural anthropologist concerned with linguistic systems, would start off a definition of language something like this: "Language is a system of arbitrary vocal symbols." The definition will be completed later, but I want here to stop and pause for a moment on the word "symbols."

It is necessary to realize, first and foremost, that language is vocal, that the symbols are vocal symbols, and that the vocal symbols of *spoken* language (a tautology) precede or are prior to the symbols of writing systems. Language is made up of noises—the noises we make with our faces

**67**

—it is not the scratches we make with our fists. All linguists and all cultural anthropologists will insist on the primacy of spoken language and point out that writing is secondary. This is in no way to denigrate writing. This is in no way to minimize the importance and the necessity and the value of the printed page. Quite the contrary, this is to realize that writing is probably the keystone of civilization. Literature is certainly the record of the best that has been thought and said in any cultural world. Writing is man's second greatest invention. But language is the first and greatest.

Language is a system of arbitrary vocal symbols. By virtue of the possession of these unique symbol systems that we call human languages, man is unique. To quote from Leslie White, former chairman of the Department of Anthropology at Michigan, "There is a fundamental difference between the mind of man and the minds or mindings of all other species. The difference is one of kind, not merely one of degree. Only man has the ability to originate and bestow meanings upon things and events and to comprehend such meanings bestowed by others. Holy water is a good example of this kind of behavior." He continues, "Holy water has a meaning that ordinary water does not have. This meaning has, of course, a value, an importance, to millions of people. Upon what does this meaning or value depend? Certainly not upon the physical structure or chemical composition of the fluid. It depends upon the unique ability of the human organism to originate and bestow meanings upon acts and upon objects external to itself." Mankind alone has the ability to bestow meanings upon things and events which are external to himself. We will return in just a moment to this peculiar ability to symbol.

But first let me say one more thing about the structure of the vehicle which we call human language. It is a system that shapes, as well as carries, thoughts and ideas. It is not so much that we think first and then talk; but rather, perhaps, that we think because we can talk. The structure of the language itself is one of the principal shapers of what we call thoughts and ideas. In languages of our family, the favorite sentence type has been described as actor-action-result or actor-action-goal—"I like cheese," "Boy meets girl," and so on. The result of the action is that which we see as important in the world. So important are the results of our actions that we in the western world generally consider it is sinful to remain contemplative. We must act. The American would rather do something and err than to sit at dead center. There is something in the nature of the favorite sentence type of our language which forces us to see events as caused by other events in the past. There is an obligatory structuring in languages of our type that makes us talk about actions in a time sequence.

To put it another way, all of the languages of our type have an obligatory tense system. We cannot conceive of an action except as taking place along a time line. To us it is very simple and understandable to say, "The man is dead." But this is a ludicrous statement to the speaker of Chinese. He looks at us and says, "How strange. You say the man is dead. He is stretched out lifeless before you. He has been dead for some time in the past. He is at present lifeless. And he will remain so for a considerable time in the future. And yet you say the man *is* dead. We say, 'man, dead.' " And as you see it, that's all that is really necessary. But we must place things in a time sequence, and we say, therefore, the man is, at the present time, dead, and don't realize how rather strange that may seem to speakers of other languages whose culture is shaped by other linguistic systems, who are, if you will, partners to an agreement to structure their experience along different linguistic lines. As a man talks, yea, verily, so does he think and feel.

By the use of culture we are brought to the questions, What is culture? And how are language and culture related?

One time when I was working in my study, my little daughter, who was then six or seven years old, was playing with some little friends outside. I heard her say, "Let's pretend this rock is a wolf." No other species could make that statement, because no other species can make any statement of that kind, because that particular kind of statement depends upon the behavior Leslie White calls "symboling." In order to understand that, we must understand the difference between a symbol and a sign, as White uses the terms, and understanding what White means by "symboling." "Symboling" is the uniquely human process of "bestowing" meaning on things and events in our environment. Meanings so bestowed cannot be perceived directly through the senses, and White describes symboling as "trafficking in nonsensory meanings." He put it very well when he says, "No animal other than man can have or be brought to any comprehension of holy water, or fetishes, or sin, or Sunday." (1) But, to White, a sign is an event that indicates something else. There are two kinds of signs—those whose meanings are inherent in themselves, like steam escaping from the radiator of an automobile, or geese flying south; the second kind of sign is one whose meaning is not inherent in its physical structure, but whose meaning is learned by conditioning. For example, you can condition a rat to respond to a green triangle as meaning, if you will, food behind the door, and a red circle meaning an electric shock. The rat very quickly learns which door to avoid. (We have found out in certain psychology classes that sophomores can also be so conditioned, and hence, sophomores can be made to behave just like rats, which shows the malleability of the human spirit.)

There is, however, something far more important in our life than conditioned responses, though conditioning is obviously of paramount importance in any learning—human, rat-like, or any other kind. But the sign is something comprehended through conditioning and directly through the senses; a symbol can never be comprehended directly through the senses, but can only be given its meaning, and be understood and communicated to others who are members of the same culture and speakers of the same language.

Now I have to pause and read something to you. (I make a collection of horror stories from newspapers.) As a scientist of linguistic behavior, I try to keep abreast of the kinds of things that are being said and written about language in the public press. I had noticed the great interest being expressed in that winsome creature, the dolphin, and how deeply we are concerned in training him. I have here an article from the *Buffalo Courier-Express.* It was contributed by the Science Service, Incorporated, so it is a syndicated type of thing. I don't wish to blame the *Buffalo Courier-Express* for it entirely. It is headlined

ARE DOLPHINS REALLY TALKING?
SCIENTISTS UNABLE TO AGREE

Now first I have to tell you that for many years anthropologists concerned with primate behavior and primate evolution have been watching gibbons and other primates, and have pretty well decided that the gibbons, very winsome little creatures themselves, have at least fourteen calls—signs, if you will, a system of signs, with *signs* being used in the way in which we have been limiting the term. The gibbon can emit a call which means food, and another call which means danger. But no gibbon yet has been able to say, or, shall I say, to *sign,* "There's a nice bunch of bananas here, but that leopard that's been bothering us is coming up on my right. I'm going to throw a stick over there and distract his attention, and while he goes over there, circle my left and get the bananas and I'll meet you behind the third tree and we'll have lunch." No gibbon can even put together the two signs food and danger in any context which would make his bearer able to make a discriminative response. He's either got to say "food" and hope the danger dissipates, or "danger" and hope that he can wait another hour for lunch.

There is a difference, in kind, not just in degree, between what the most intelligent, winsome animal and human beings do. Dolphins, believe me, will do anything for a fish. They have found out, being highly intelligent creatures, that mankind is an easy mark. "All you have to do is to jump out of the water and make noises and they'll give you anything you ask for." Dogs found this out 60,000 years ago. They came sneaking in and discovered that, if they lurked around human habitations and picked up the garbage (which at that time as an important matter, as it still is in many municipalities), mankind would throw them the bones. They domesticated themselves. And now I'm wondering if the dolphins are not doing the same thing all over again. Let me read from the article. Quite well along we find:

> Each of the 32 different whistles may represent a complete expression, in which case dolphins would be limited to voicing 32 needs or emotions. But if each represents a syllable or a word, they could be combined into innumerable expressions, into a language, provided the animals have the intelligence to use a language. A small minority of scientist-types are so impressed with a dolphin brain they think this mammal is as smart as people. A few will even go as far as saying dolphins may be more intelligent than humans. Dr. John Lilley, controversial director of the Communications Research Institute at Miami, thinks dolphins may be the first non-human species with which man will hold intelligent conversations. Efforts are being made to translate dolphinese into English by matching recordings of their sounds with movies of their actions and by employing a computer-like device that memorizes dolphin whistles and buzzes. But Lilley is going about it the other way. He is trying to teach dolphins to speak English. His prize pupil is Elvar, a frolicsome seven-foot, 350-pound male bottle-nose. By rewarding him with fish and sending pain- or pleasure-evoking jolts of electricity into his brain, Lilley and helpers have trained Elvar to vocalize in the air. The dolphin reportedly can match in number and duration a series of as many as twelve nonsense syllables shouted by a human. This is far more than parrots and mynah birds can handle. According to Lilley, Elvar can mimic such phrases as "More, Elvar," complete with southern or New England accent (1).

As a linguist and behavioral scientist, I find this shocking. In the light of what I have said previously, need I say more? Personally, I resent it.

But to resume. Leslie White says that "the things and events that are external to man and that are the result of symboling should be called symbolates." White defines human culture as "things and events in the real world dependent upon symboling—that is, *symbolates*—seen in an extra-somatic context" (2). To the cultural anthropologist, symbolates are equated with human behavior, and symbolates are looked at and studied *outside* of the individual human being, and seen as systems of norms. A linguistic system or language is an ideal example of such a cultural norm system, and we study language and describe and analyse it as though it were "pulled out" of the people who use it.

The linguistic scientist, then, is concerned with studying the linguistic system, not as it resides in an individual at one instant in time, but the way it resides in every person enculturated in that culture and therefore a speaker of that language. He is concerned with seeing the language as an all-encompassing, obligatory norm system which the individual must internalize or learn, although he may place upon it the stamp of his own individuality. But the psychologist, who may also be seen to be concerned with things and events in the real world dependent upon symboling, *is* concerned with the individual; he sees symbolates in an *intra*-somatic context. He is interested in the varying abilities of individual human beings in learning linguistic or other cultural systems of behavior, and in noting how skillfully each can manipulate these. He is seeing the locus of the symbolate in the individual's soma, but the *culturologist* is seeing the locus *outside* the soma. And the sociologist, the student of society, sees the symbolates in an *inter*-somatic context. Here the societal group is the smallest unit, and human beings are seen acting and interacting as members of these social groups. The sociologist takes it for granted, so to speak, that each of the individuals has been enculturated, or is being enculturated; that is, that he has internalized the cultural norms. So there are three approaches to the study of human behavior: one from the societal science vantage point, one from the vantage point of the culturologist, and one from the vantage point of the psychologist. All of these approaches are essential. Not one of these behavioral or social sciences should be called *the* science of human behavior; they are *all* sciences of human behavior. Each one is necessary if we are to understand the complexity of the human being as an individual, as well as the complexity of men interacting and acting as human beings alone can and must.

To finish our definition of language, then: "Language is a system of arbitrary vocal symbols through which human beings in the same culture interact—and hence *communicate* (here "communication" will be equivalated with "interaction") in terms of their common cultural experience, or their common cultural expectancies." Language is inextricably interwoven with the rest of culture. It is the *sine qua non* of culture. It is the alpha and the omega of culture. Only when man is in possession of this unique symbol system can he create symbolates. And the rest of culture, then, is simply an integrated projection of man as a symbol maker and symbol user. Culture is not just tools. It is not just the product of man's hands, it is also the product of his head and of his heart as well. It is the totality of the way of life of a society. It is the sum total of the values and of the attitudes and of the assumptions. It is man's unique adaptive mechanism; and without language culture is impossible. Culture can exist and be transmitted generation after generation only through the mediation of language. Language is not only, then, a system of culture, but the prime system of culture, because language alone, through itself, is able to relate itself to the other systems. Thus all of the systems of culture, including language itself, can be described and analyzed through language, but no other system can describe itself or relate itself to the other systems.

What of writing? Writing is one of the most important systems in the culture of every literate society, but it is a *secondary* or *derived* system in that it symbolizes language. Language can be seen as man's structuring or categorization of his experience—his symbolization of experience. Writing is a symbolization of language, hence a symbolization of a symbolization.

But how often we read or hear, "The English language has twenty-six letters." This is a flagrant confusion of the two symbol systems; what is meant is, "The form of the Latin alphabet used to *write* the English language has twenty-six letters, or literal symbols." The English language quite obviously does not have twenty-six letters, but consists of a complex system of sounds, which lead into shapes or forms—words, endings, and so on, and which, by virtue of their structuring in distributional patterns are then able to make sense and to carry *message.* We often think, then, of words (and generally words as they are written on the printed page) as being the be-all and the end-all. Again, I am not denigrating words written on the printed page. But once again let us put first things first.

The two great myths are, first, the confusion between language and writing, and, second, the belief that if you "have" a vocabulary of a certain number of words, you control the language. But it is not amount of vocabulary, but *control of structure* that counts. If you are in control of the structure of a human language, it is very simple to ask someone, "What do you call that?" When answered, you have another word in your vocabulary. Vocabulary is easy to come by. It normally increases in a regular ratio as the human being ages and as his experience of the world increases. And one of the best ways to increase our experience of the world, albeit vicariously, is through reading.

Part of the vocabulary myth is the belief that words *have* meaning. Words don't have meanings. Words are able to do their work for us because they reside in structural linguistic patterns of distribution. And this complex system, this structure, is, by and large, internalized or learned by the physiologically normal human being by the time he is three-and-a-half years old. From three-and-a-half to five-and-a-half, he is simply putting on the finishing touches.

I can well remember when my number two boy was three-and-a-half years old. It was his sister's second birthday, but we decided to give him a present because he wasn't invited to the party. I was about to give the present to him when the thought crossed my mind, "The kid's three-and-a-half. Thousands of times I've told audiences that the language learning process is practically complete by three-and-a-half. Let's see." (Anthropologists are constantly experimenting with their children.) His grubby little hand was outstretched, and as I gave him his little present, I said to him, "Many happy returns on your three-and-a-halfth birthday." And he said, "Thank you, Daddy." And I said, "Now, tell me, would you do Daddy a favor?" "Yes, Daddy," he said brightly, "what is it?" I said, "Go get Daddy the frammis." Now my number one boy is a very literal-minded lad and would have said, "What's a frammis?" But not my number two boy. He never yet has been caught without the answer. He said, "Where is the frammis, Daddy?" And I said, "It's on the fortecyte, where it always is."

So he went into the living room where his older brother was and said, "Daddy wants the frammis. He says it's on the fortecyte. Where's the fortecyte?" Well, his older brother straightened him out as only siblings can. But I was happy, and he was happy. I had proved my point, and he had his present. No, "frammis" and "fortecyte" are doubletalk, but because those items resided in a structural pattern, my son knew that "frammis" had to refer to something that a child of three-and-a-half could carry in his hands. He knew a fortecyte had to be something upon which a frammis could repose. A fortecyte couldn't be too high, because a kid of three-and-a-half would have to be able to look on the top of it to see if the frammis was there, so he could get it and bring it to his old man. All this he knew, because he knew his father wouldn't deceive him. In other words, he "knew" frammis and fortecyte were both *nouns,* although that was a term he did not come across until years later in school, and doesn't understand yet.

So it is the structuring of the system in which words reside that allow them to do their work for us. I do not have to remind you that there is a great deal of difference between a *light* pole and a light *Pole.* There is a radio announcer in Buffalo who constantly gets these patterns of stress mixed. I can remember when, during one of these long weekends with lots of accidents, he said, "A Mr. Ditchkovsky, in the town of Elma, lost control of his car and ran into a light *pole.*" By the same token, I do not have to remind you there is a great deal of difference in the sentence, "What are we having for dinner, Mother?" and "What are we having for dinner? Mother?" Here, just by raising the pitch one level, I have signaled to you that the word Mother is in an entirely different relationship with the rest of the sentence. Now the child has learned these stress patterns and these intonation patterns, along with everything else significant in the structure of his language, before he comes to school. It is a mammoth waste of time to try to teach him his *language* because he is not *literate.* He goes to school not to learn his language, but to learn how his culture and his society has decided to represent that language in writing.

Again, first things first. The problem is to determine the most efficient way of making a person literate, because if he can become literate, all of the magnificant vistas that reading opens can be his. But until he is literate, until he controls the reading process, he is bound in shallows and in miseries. Consequently, the cultural anthropologist as linguist is concerned with how he can define or help define the *nature of the problem* of teaching literacy. People who confuse language with words on the printed page have given me the impression at times that they not only think that words so seen *have* meanings, but that these words *are* meanings. This is dreadful. I can remember once when I was visiting a reading class when the story the children were reading was called "The Bridge." There was a picture of a suspension bridge at the top of the page. In the teacher's manual it said, "Teach the word *bridge."* You know what some of these manuals are like; they remind me of my wife when she says, "Don't give me a recipe unless its starts off 'Face the stove.' " Well, this was one of those teacher's manuals that says, "Teach the word bridge." And the literal-minded teacher, believing the mythology, thought that the children, because they couldn't read b-r-i-d-g-e, didn't know what "bridge" *meant.* She had begun laboriously to teach the *meaning* of the word bridge. I couldn't stand it any more, and neither could the kids. I asked this woman if she would mind asking Johnny and Billy and Mary in the front row what "bridge" meant. She said, "All right, but it's not in the manual." So she started off and she said, "Johnny, what's bridge?" And he said, "Bridge is what we call my grandmother's false teeth." And he looked at me and he smiled. The teacher looked a little abashed, and she said, "Susie, what's bridge?" She said, "Bridge is what my Mother plays and my Father gets mad because when he gets home, supper's not on the table." Well, she knew by that time she was licked. Not one of these kids, of course, was going to come out with the more usual association of arbitrary linguistic symbol and cultural artifact, because they were having too much fun.

If you can teach the child to go from the printed page back to the *oral counterpart,* the meaning will be released. You do not go directly from printed page to meaning; you go from printed page to oral counterpart, which releases the meaning already there. And yet, we have been teaching, many of us for years, as though the process were one where you go directly from printed page to meaning. Reading has been confused with *understanding.* It's vastly different. You may be able to read with unerring accuracy a sentence such as, "The morphophone is not only a 'holding company' for phonemes, but should also be seen as the basic unit of the morpheme," and not have the slightest idea what it means. That is, you couldn't come up with a paraphrase that would satisfy a linguistic scientist because you are not aware of the special vocabulary used in linguistics. But you can *read* the sentence. I'm concerned with reading in *that* sense, because until the reading *process* is in control, understanding can never come.

Perhaps another story about my number two boy will help illustrate this. Like all youngsters of this day and age, he sat glued in front of the television screen. He became very adept in singing commercials of all types. (He couldn't carry a tune, but how he loved the words.) There was one at that time which was on the screen constantly, the commercial for Tide, showing the big box with the letters coming on separately to a tune— "T-I-D-E, Tide." I'm sure you remember. So once, shortly after his three-and-a-halfth birthday, his mother and I were in a supermarket with him, and he pointed to a mammoth display of Tide boxes and said, "Look, Mommy, Tide." A woman who was standing near us said, "Isn't that amazing! That child can read!" I said, "Madam, he is simply reacting to that as a sign. He looks at television." She replied, "Well, isn't he reading?" I said, "No. You see, if that initial letter 'T' could have been changed to 'R' and he had said, 'Look, Mommy, *Ride;* don't they know it's *Tide?',* then he'd be reading." This is the discriminative response that must be able to be made before literacy can be achieved. And until literacy is achieved, there can be no reading, in *any* sense of the word.

Linguistics, because it is concerned with the relationship of the linguistic system as a cultural system to a second cultural system, the writing system, is able to furnish insights into the nature of the problem. Whereas people have been basing reading instruction on a false and misunderstood relationship between language and writing, words and meaning, the linguistic scientist says, "Let us look at first things first and understand the nature of the writing system, and then see how it relates to what it represents, language."

Now please don't say that I am saying that the linguist has *the* answer to the teaching of reading. This is absurd. No one discipline can come up with *the* answer to this complicated problem, the nature of which we are just beginning to understand. But I believe that linguistics and cultural anthropology can furnish important insights. (You know what the man said about insights. "Insights, well, it's like a flat tire. The insight doesn't fix it, but it helps to let you know why the car doesn't run so well.") Well, we certainly can tell some people why reading instruction has not been as efficient as we all would like. It has been based on a series of mistaken premises. If the linguist adds his insight to the training expertise and dedication of the great group of teachers of literacy, the world will find that Johnny will read far better.

Therefore, in conclusion, let me just say this. I do believe that linguistics and cultural anthropology can add dimensions to the understanding of the nature of this problem. To be literate, to be able to read, opens up the world of knowledge, gives us access to "the best that has been thought and said in the world." Even if it may sound old-fashioned to some, I'm still deeply convinced that the book is the best visual aid.

### References

1. William J. Cromie, "Are Dolphins Really Talking," World Book Encyclopaedia Services, Inc. Reprinted from the *Buffalo Courier-Express* (December 18, 1966).
2. Leslie White, "Symboling: A Kind of Behavior," *The Journal of Psychology* 53 (1962).

**Jack E. Kittell**

# Reading and Relevancy

One needn't be uncommonly perceptive to be aware of the increasing use of the term *relevant* or its noun forms, *relevance* and *relevancy*. So noticeable, in fact, is its expanding use that it must be classified as one of the "in" words of our times. Although it has certainly become a part of educationist jargon, its use has not been restricted to that profession but also seems to enjoy rather widespread deployment in other fields of endeavor. With such popularity it surely deserves at least a brief focus of our attention. Even without a criterion of grammatical meticulousness one becomes impressed with the ambiguity of such frequent uses of relevance as "Make schools relevant," "Is it relevant?" and "We need more relevance." Such statements seem incomplete unless, as Peter Wagschal has pointed out in a *Phi Delta Kappan* editorial, one adds "to (something)." Dictionaries too support the meaning of appropriate relatedness. Why, one wonders, do so many speakers and writers fail to complete the connection by not stating to what, education or programs or books are or are not relevant? One suspects that such ambiguous statements of relevancy are basically "cover-ups"—a method of appearing to be "in" by using the "in" word *relevant* but in reality skirting the basic issue of commitment to something, of coming to grips with reality.

"I FEEL
SO
BREAK
UP" (1).

DEAD
END
(3)
what
isn't?

To what, then, should school life be relevant and more particularly, to what should reading be relevant? The ambiguous ones when pressed with these questions usually reply, "Well, school life and reading should be relevant to modern American life." Having said this with appropriate piousness they consider the subject closed. But such an answer is but a beginning in satisfying the demand for relevancy. Does being relevant to modern American life mean accepting the

77

present condition and helping children and youth adjust to a life of mind-blowing, copping out, racism, technological enslavement and affluential pollution? Or does it mean being relevant to some arbitrarily contrived grand design into which the future ought to be pressed and molded? Supporters of both viewpoints are plentiful.

With the validity of both viewpoints open to question, to what might we turn as valid dimensions of relevance? I submit that the valid dimensions of relevance include 1) human potential, 2) human aspirations, 3) human dignity and 4) human interaction. These certainly are of our time as well as of all times. We can ill afford to ignore them and I suggest that it is in terms of these basic characteristics of humans that we must direct the relevancy of school life and reading.

## Making School Life and Reading Relevant to Human Potential

What might this mean for reading? It must mean that our provisions for learning to read be based on assumptions that all children possess potentialities that far exceed anything we have expected of them in the past. Particularly is this true of potentiality for making discriminative responses within the broad spectrum of total communication. Otto in a recent issue of *Saturday Review* presents a strong case for developing the relatively untapped potential of all of man's senses (4).

This must mean that the life of the school day join with the rest of each twenty-four hour day and become an integral part of real life—not as the corrupting influences make it seem but as the basic needs of human beings demand it be for survival. Can school life, can reading instruction at any level afford to ignore the electronic and graphic languages of color, rhythm, sound, form, space and texture? The improvement of the perceptiveness of all senses cannot help but make reading more meaningful.

To be relevant to human potential must also mean that reading instruction break open the dialect cages that prejudice so easily constructs and in which humans become so cruelly imprisoned. Not only must reading instruction free the dialectally enslaved but it must also guide the way to freedom of thought, expression and self-fulfillment.

"ONCE I HAD BRAINS
AND A HEART ALSO:
SO, HAVING TRIED THEM
BOTH, I SHOULD MUCH
RATHER HAVE A HEART ..."
                    The Tinwoodman (5)

Human potential includes the ability to be effectively self-directing and school life and reading to be relevant to such potential must provide options and the freedom of choice necessary to utilize those options. The wise and effective uses of freedom are not learned under constant and complete control no matter how well intentioned, but rather by experiencing appropriate consequences of using freedom.

## Making School Life and Reading Relevant to Human Aspirations

It is now believed by some that man's aspiration to know and his insatiable demand for information along with his propensities for technological development will of necessity soon result either in methods of transmission other than print or information will remain perpetually suspended (7).

"The National Library of Medicine in Bethesda indexed almost a quarter of a million technical articles, books and monographs last year; the nation's space program yearly adds more than a million pages of technical data to the pile. Scientists and engineers turn out more than a million reports, articles and publications annually.

These amounts are expected to double in only five years"(8).

"It's a Barnum and Binary World
Just as ideatic as it can be,
But it would only be make believe
If it wasn't for you and me (9).

What does this mean for the relevancy of school life and reading? Certainly it should mean that the purposes of education and reading should not be to transmit and have each child store up as much information as is humanly possible. It should mean that school life and reading should be devoted to enabling students to identify and develop values to guide them and skills in selecting, evaluating and using the wealth of information that modern technology makes available to them. It must mean that making discriminative responses to and through a variety of media in addition to print is relevant to a rapidly changing symbol-centered society.

Man's aspirations are not limited to the purely cognitive aspects of knowledge as important as those aspects may be, but he aspires also to knowing in the affective domain. To be relevant to those aspirations reading instruction must provide for connecting the dreams, the hopes, the fears, and the poetic of each student with

"IT TAKES ALL THE
RUNNING YOU CAN
DO TO KEEP IN
THE SAME PLACE."
Lewis Carroll (10)

those of his cultural heritage, immediate and past. It is relevant then to help students interpret the models from their heritage. One way of doing this is through literature, particularly poetry.

Nancy Larrick after five years of working with the Lehigh workshop in poetry for children has concluded that children are attracted to literature that has a sense of reality (11). To ignore the necessity of beginning with *their* sense of reality in order to bridge to more lasting masterpieces is to lose the learner. Human aspirations are rooted in the here and now. As a product of the individual's experience they are shaped and colored in individual, unique ways.

> **"HOW COME NOTHING'S LIKE IT WAS UNTIL IT'S gone" (12)?**

School life that does not include reading material such as *The Quarreling Book* by Charlotte Zolotow, *The Jazz Man* by Mary Hays Weik, *The Outsiders* by S. E. Hinton, *Durango Street* by Frank Bonham, *The Autobiography of Malcolm X* and *The Mad Sampler,* or does not include items such as the popular songs, "Sounds of Silence," "I Am a Rock," "A Most Peculiar Man" and John Lennon's "In His Own Write" is likely not to provide a base from which students can realistically bridge toward fulfilling their aspirations. In short there must be provisions for both media and messages which are meaningful to students.

## Making School Life and Reading Relevant to Human Dignity

Perhaps in no other period in history have the young of a society been more obviously alienated than at present. Perhaps at no other time have they been so aware of hypocrisy, of sham, of ugliness. Otto has described the situation in stark terms.

> **"THE MODERN SCHOOL IS REALLY GREAT, YOU LEARN TO READ AND WRITE AND HATE."**
> A student (14)

"Psychological and psychiatric jargon dealing with emotional dysfunction and mental illness has become the parlance of the man in the street. In addition, from early childhood in our educational system we learn largely by our mistakes—by having them pointed out to us repeatedly. This results in early "negative conditioning" and influences our attitude and perception of our selves and other people" (14).

> **HOLLOW PEOPLE EMPTY WORLD**

Almost from the very beginning the infant begins processing his environment by becoming involved with it. Through direct involvement with his physical and social environment he forms meaning and concepts about himself and about "others." In large part the language environment which is processed determines the normal dimensions of the child's view of reality and it forms the only readily accepted means for expressing those perceptions, meanings and feelings which are unique unto each individual. Language is a direct channel to all that is private—to the very essence of the being.

We have been recently made aware of the linear constraints of print by McLuhan (15), Mead (16), and others. It has become obvious that youth today have lost faith in verbal language—particularly that in print. Some reasons seem rather apparent. To be placed by compulsion in an unnatural setting and confronted incessantly with someone else's goals, someone else's language, someone else's standards and to be impressed just as incessantly with the deficits of one's own language which because of its pervasive character means one's own worth as a person and the worth of one's environment constitutes a situation which cannot be tolerated by the human ego without some scarring. The drop-out rates, suicides, drug cases, academic failures, the rebellion of youth all are eloquent testimony to the validity of Carl Roger's question as to whether anyone can really teach anyone else anything and whether what little might be taught isn't relatively worthless.

> **"EDUCATION IS SOME-THING WHICH TAKES UP SPACE IN MY LOCKER."**
> a student (17)

The basic need to feel of worth, to feel confident in oneself, to feel secure enough to inquire after life cannot be ignored by schools that are relevant to human needs. "In order to learn to read a child must have preserved enough courage for active curiosity" (18).

It would seem that if we learn nothing else from the present turmoil, we should be convinced that if school life in general and the instruction and uses of reading in particular do not support and enhance human dignity, schools as we have known them will cease to serve any vital function.

> **"DO IT RIGHT OR GO TO HELL!"**
> ghetto student (19)

## Making School Life and Reading Relevant to Human Interaction

> **PLASTIC PEOPLE WITH PLASTIC TEARS**

Increasingly as we experience environmental press we are aware that man is indeed a social animal. By interrelating with others of his species—those comprising his social environment—he becomes human. To some anthropologists, biologists and sociologists human interaction is communication (20). Almost all living organisms are involved in some system of communication—some system of interrelationships. Closely associated with that concept is another that conceives of communication as a multichannel system and still another that communication is continuous, that is, at least one channel is in operation at all times.

"DING DONG BELL DUMMIES GO TO HELL."

a student (21)

Certainly, verbal communication as one of the major channels has received the greatest attention historically, as well it should. Since the advent of the printing press however, written communication has received almost exclusive attention. This perhaps to the detriment of the overall effective interaction of human beings. There can be no doubt about the values of print. But print has had an all pervasive restricting influence on how we think, perceive and act. McLuhan (22), Sidwell (23), and others have declared print to be the mark of the middle class, the isolator, the passive medium.

Though print should not be discounted for those functions of communication and expression which it can serve best, evidence accumulates indicating that effective communication is too important to be left to words alone. In fact, a recent research study of the communication of feeling discovered that the effects of the non-

"PEOPLE SAY THAT LIFE IS THE THING BUT I PREFER READING."

Logal P. Smith (22)

verbal aspects of spoken language can outweigh, by far, the verbal factor (25). The non-verbal aspects of communication can no longer be considered as inconsequential and ignored. In fact, they carry some direct implications for making reading relevant to human interaction.

"AND WHAT IS THE USE OF A BOOK," THOUGHT ALICE, "WITHOUT PICTURES OR CONVERSATIONS?" (26)

Even when a particular environment places relatively strong emphasis on the verbal aspects of communication the child has a tremendous task of translating the varied and rich means of communicating by oral language and pitch, stress, juncture, volume, gesture, touch, distance, etc. into the rather restricted symbols of written language in either the process of writing or the reverse process of reading. For children whose predominate means of communication are non-verbal the translation task must seem virtually impossible.

What makes this problem of translation so important is that effective human interaction is so crucial to human survival. In large part, such interaction depends on how one person perceives and feels about others and how one perceives oneself as a member of a social environment. An obvious but little utilized fact is that most of human emotional responses are learned and continue to be expressed in non-verbal terms.

"I DON'T REALLY KNOW ME:
SURELY IT'S IMPORTANT
TO KNOW ONESELF.
SOMEDAY, WHEN I HAVE
TIME AWAY FROM SCHOOL
AND HOMEWORK ... I'LL
MEET ME ..."

a student (27)

One task of school life and reading must be to develop in each individual an awareness of his rich reservoir of communication competencies, both verbal and non-verbal. The school should help each child consciously utilize his competencies, particularly the non-verbal, and to verbalize about them, translate them into words and finally, to utilize them deliberately in written language both as a reader and a writer. Such an approach demands that the learner be an active participant, not a passive receiver. Such an approach will enable the student to integrate the dominance of the noun metaphor of the printed medium with the verb or process metaphors of the electric and electronic media. Such integration will enable the student to make reading a "happening," a "be-in," "to make the scene" and "cool it." Life is action. Print is static. Speech actively involves all of the senses as do the electronic media. Reading demands an isolated, extended visual sensitivity. The classroom as we know it is almost entirely the by-product of print (28). Reading that is relevant cannot ignore the dynamics of human interaction.

EVERY RADICAL ADJUSTMENT
IS A CRISIS OF SELF ESTEEM

To make school life relevant to human interaction then demands that teachers be able to communicate in the student's mode. Schools must provide for the necessary interrelationships that enable and encourage each student to bring his unique perceptions, his unique language, his unique aspirations and potential into interaction with the richest environment that can be provided in his school life.

In summary, school life and reading should be relevant to 1) human potential, 2) human aspirations, 3) human dignity and 4) human interaction. Throughout this discussion it has been recommended that school life and reading be student centered and action oriented, that all of the senses and the wealth of communication competencies with which each child begins school be exploited through increased awareness and active involvement in controlling his own learning. Human survival demands nothing less.

### References

1. John Rouse, "I Feel so Break Up," *Media and Methods* 5 (May, 1969): 31–35.
2. Peter H. Wagschal, "On the Irrelevance of Relevance" LI *Phi Delta Kappan* (October 1969): 61.

3. *The New Yorker* XLV (October 18, 1969): 154.

4. Herbert A. Otto, "New Light on the Human Potential" LII *Saturday Review* (December 1969): 14–17.

5. L. Frank Baum, *The Wizard of Oz.*

6. Quentin Fiore "The Futures of the Book," *Media and Methods* (Ultronic Systems Corporation) 5 (December 1968): 23.

7. Ibid., 20–26.

8. Ibid., 20.

9. Don Fabun, *The Dynamics of Change* (Englewood Cliffs, N.J.: Prentice-Hall, Inc. 1967), "Automation," 13.

10. Fiore, op. cit., 22—*Through the Looking Glass.*

11. Nancy Larrick, "Reading in the Age of Violence," *The Hues of English* (Champaign, Illinois: The National Council of Teachers of English, 1969).

12. Fiore, op. cit., 22.

13. Otto, op. cit., 16.

14. Bob Swartz, "Five Biased Poems," *Media and Methods* 5 (April 1969): 48.

15. Marshall McLuhan, *Understanding Media* (New York: McGraw-Hill Book Co., 1964).

16. Margaret Mead, "Youth Revolt: The Future is Now," LIII *Saturday Review* (January 10, 1970): 23–25, 113.

17. Mary Smyczek, in *Media and Methods* 5 (April 1969): 36.

18. E. Sylvester and M. Kunet, "Psycho-dynamic Aspects of the Reading Problem," *Journal of Orthopsychiatry* 13 (1963): 69–76.

19. New Dimensions in Education Advertisement in *Media and Method* 5 (April 1969): 21.

20. See: Ray L. Birdwhistle, "Communication as a Multi-Channel System," *International Encyclopedia of the Social Sciences* (New York: 1965).

21. Mary Sandok, "Where Do Dummies Go?" *Media and Methods* 5 (April 1969): 44.

22. "Afterthoughts," in *Media and Methods* 5 (December 1968): 20.

23. McLuhan, op. cit.

24. R. T. Sidwell, "Cooling Down the Classroom: Some Educational Implications of the McLuhan Thesis," *Educational Forum* 32 (March 1968): 351–8.

25. Albert Mehrabian, "Communication Without Words," *Psychology Today* 2 (September 1968): 53–55.

26. Fiore, op. cit., quoted on page 25.

27. Judy Endicott, "What Would You Learn Without Schools?" *Media and Methods* 5 (April 1969): 33.

28. Neil Postman and Charles Weingartner, *Teaching As A Subversive Activity* (New York: Dell Publishing Co., 1969).

**William Eller**

# Personality Traits as Factors in Reading Comprehension

A scrutiny of the professional literature dealing with reading comprehension reveals a tendency to treat comprehension almost entirely as a cognitive function; that is, hardly any consideration is given to affective influences upon understanding of the printed word. This tendency should not be viewed with much surprise, inasmuch as the details and pedagogies of reading comprehension have been developed predominately by elementary educators and language arts specialists, neither of whom are highly sophisticated regarding the affective aspects of learning. It might even be argued that these groups are not very knowledgeable about the cognitive aspects of learning either, but a teacher or editor usually finds it easier to deal with the cognitive functions even if he doesn't quite know what he is doing.

A serious student of the communications processes must sooner or later come to the realization that the affective life of a listener or a reader has an immense influence upon his assimilation of the spoken or printed word, especially when the higher order comprehension skills are called into use. There are at least two sources of justification—one informal and the other scientific—for the claim that personality and emotional factors are important in reading comprehension: 1) all of us have observed, at least in others, that even highly educated persons have blind spots in their rational vision, areas in which they do not "see" very clearly. Unfortunately, we often are not able to discern these blind spots as readily in ourselves as in others, although many of us who work in the semantic arts have developed some procedures with which we try to counterbalance or offset certain of our predispositions. 2) The constantly increasing volume of research of the social psychologists and communications theorists includes numerous studies which reveal the complexity of language comprehension and the impact of the recipient's personality in that complex.

Existing evidence seems to indicate that literal reading comprehension is not affected much by the emotional state of the reader, but that the higher level types of comprehension are distinctly responsive to personality factors. McKillop (1) explored the relationship between expressed attitudes and responses to different types of questions reaching from the very specific and structured to those requiring interpretation and evaluation. She found that the correlation between the reader's attitudes and his answers to the questions varied with the complexity of the questions. For fact and detail items the relationship was slight, whereas for judgment and prediction items the influence of the reader's attitudes was easily observed.

Piekarz (2) also found, in her doctoral study, that the affective characteristics of the reader do not have much influence on his responses to the questions involving literal comprehension, whereas his personality and predispositions seriously influence his answers to interpretation and evaluation questions.

> A strong negative parental attitude did not seem to interfere with accurate understanding at the literal comprehension level but it did prevent objective and rational understanding at the interpretation and evaluation levels. Those children with favorable attitudes towards their own parents appeared to grasp the author's intended neutral meaning easily and accurately and were able to answer all kinds of questions correctly. The children with strong negative feelings and attitudes towards their own parents answered literal comprehension questions dealing with the identification of clearly stated facts fairly successfully. Their answers to interpretative and evaluative questions, however, showed evidence of distortion and misunderstanding. It seems, therefore, that it is in those areas that distinguish critical from non critical readers that attitudes play their most effective, and oftentimes pernicious role (3).

In a relatively short article it is, of course, not possible to answer fully the question, "How does reader personality interact with reading comprehension?" For one thing the contributions of communications psychologists which are relevant to the issue would require several pages, even for a summary presentation; in fact, publication of the communications research of Hovland, Janis et al. (4) at Yale has required a series of hardbound books. Secondly, many of the relationships reported herein could be challenged or argued because they are based on certain theoretical frameworks. Experimenters starting from other theories seem to get different results, at least part of the time. Furthermore, the theoretical framework and ensuing research are often the work of psychologists who are not specifically interested in reading comprehension but in broader communications processes. Therefore, the results of many of the experiments of social psychologists have to be more or less specifically interpreted in terms of reading comprehension.

One personality factor which has been related to reading comprehension by research workers is self-esteem. Janis (5) found that persons with low self-esteem are quite susceptible to persuasion. From this evidence it is reasonable to conclude that readers with low self-esteem are less critical in their appraisal of the validity of reading content. In large-scale studies of self-concept, pupils with strong self-concept have been found to develop the most comprehension skill, at least when measured by standardized tests over a given span of time. This is more or less in keeping with the Rosenthal-Jacobson (6) theory of the self-fulfilling prophecy.

A second personality trait which has been shown to be related to reading comprehension is aggressiveness or hostility. Weiss (7) presented three types of printed content to three groups of subjects: first, very emotional content concerning the treatment of criminals; second, a rational statement containing factual data on the same subject; and third, a text which was a combination of the emotional and rational. The emotional content induced the greatest arousal of response on the part of the readers. Because Weiss had administered a personality inventory to the subjects, he was able to observe that the attitudes of the aggressive-authoritarian subjects were significantly more punitive than those not manifesting much of this tendency or trait. Some of Janis's (8) experiments seem to indicate that aggressively neurotic people are resistive to printed arguments.

Still another aspect of the affective life of the reader which has been shown to relate to reading comprehension is identification with peer groups. Riley and Riley (9) conducted a study of children's reactions to various mass media and concluded that reactions differ according to whether the child belongs to one or more peer groups. Ruth Berenda (10) discovered that peer group influence on children's judgment can be rather marked. In a pair of experiments she demonstrated that when confronted with the unanimous opinion of the peer group most children, and especially those from age seven to ten, agreed with the group's view.

A number of research workers have demonstrated that established biases and prejudices are very influential upon the comprehension of readers at various ages. One of the well known studies in this area is that of Helen Crossen (11). She sought to discover the relationship between students' attitudes towards a subject and their ability to read critically about that subject. She began by giving an intelligence test, a reading comprehension test and a two-pronged survey of opinions to each student. The survey was designed to probe students' attitudes towards Negroes on the one hand, and towards Germans on the other. Her subjects then performed on a two-section test of critical reading ability, one section of which contained material about Negroes; the other, of course, contained material about Germans. When student attitudes towards Germans and Negroes were compared with ability to read critically on these two subjects the following results were observed: The critical reading ability of the students who were favorably disposed toward a subject was not different from that of students who were indifferent to the subject. Students who were initially biased against Negroes were significantly less able to read critically about Negroes than were the students who were indifferent on the subject of Negroes. However, no such trend occurred with respect to students who were initially prejudiced against Germans. Crossen attributed this difference in response to the fact that the subjects had some first hand contact with Negroes who were easily identified visually, whereas Germans seemed much more remote to the pupils. From this logic she further generalized that "the more personal, immediate or intense the feeling, the greater the likelihood that it will prove a barrier between the reader and an accurate interpretation of the material to be read." Other studies by Kendall and Wolf (12), Cooper and Jahoda (13) and Cooper and Dinerman (14) have shown that prejudiced persons do not comprehend the printed word without distortion.

We might next consider the question, "How do readers protect their personalities—their egos—in reading situations?" One type of ego protection, of course, is through withdrawal, the avoidance of information which contradicts attitudes or biases. Lazarsfeld, Berelson and Gaudet (15) concluded that the majority of people who expose their thinking to political propaganda are already committed to one party or candidate.

Selectivity is another psychological process by which readers protect their personalities when confronted with reading material that might be somewhat threatening. When selectivity operates, the reader perceives and remembers either entirely, or at least best, those statements which agree with his biases. Manis and Dawes (16) presented two sets of context to some subjects. One set favored capital punishment; one was opposed to capital punishment. The materials were presented using the cloze procedure. No matter what percent of words were deleted, the subjects performed better when the content conformed to their pre-existing views.

Another means by which readers are likely to misinterpret the ideas that they encounter in reading in order to keep their egos unruffled is that of distortion—actually perceiving the author to have said what the reader wants to believe he said. Here again, Manis (17) has been one of the major experimenters. In one of his studies three groups of college students with varying attitudes regarding fraternities were given short statements about fraternities, half of which were attributed to authors of high prestige and half to writers of low prestige. After reading each selection the subjects tried to describe fraternities as the author had. The important observation is that the subjects were trying to paraphrase what the author had said about fraternities, including, of course, the author's emotional commitment. When student readers judged the high prestige articles, they distorted the authors' views in the direction of their own original attitudes toward fraternities.

Concerning these various adjustive patterns employed by readers, Pie-karz (18) has given us two generalizations: First, the more ambiguous a statement is, the more it is perceived, conceived and remembered in harmony with the reader's attitudes. Second, the more intense an attitude is, the more emotion is associated with it and the less subject it is to change.

Perhaps we are ready for a final question. Now that we have established that reader personality is a significant factor in reading comprehension we may ask ourselves, "What are the implications for the teacher of reading?" Again, it may be important to acknowledge that much of the research which has been cited in preceding paragraphs and which has shown relationships between reading comprehension and the affective state of the reader was not conducted specifically to aid the teacher of reading. In fact, much of it was performed under the auspices of advertising agencies which are motivated by goals almost diametrically opposite to those of the reading teacher. In addition, much of this research in communication psychology was not basically concerned with reading print as a means of presentation of information. Nevertheless, certain observations seem justified on the basis of what social psychology and related fields have demonstrated. First, the conventional skills approach to the development of reading comprehension does not touch upon some of the major sources of nonunderstanding. Second, reading comprehension is evidently a much more complicated process than the basic methodology texts indicate and must be reexamined in terms of the evidence available from the field of social psychology. Third, since there are some experiments which have shown that it is possible to teach pupils and students to resist or compensate for propaganda techniques in reading matter, probably academic instruction in the language arts and social sciences should include work in propaganda analysis, and certainly experimentation in these directions should be continued.

## References

1. McKillop, Anne S., *The Relationship Between the Reader's Attitude and Certain Types of Reading Response* (New York: Teacher's College Bureau of Publications, Columbia University, 1952).

2. Piekarz, Josephine A., "Individual Differences in Interpretation," Unpublished Doctoral Dissertation, University of Chicago, 1954.

3. Piekarz, Josephine A., "Attitudes and Critical Reading," in *Dimensions of Critical Reading,* Russell G. Stauffer, compiler (Newark, Delaware: University of Delaware, 1964).

4. Hovland, Carl, et al, *Yale Studies in Attitude and Communication,* vols. 1, 2, 3, 4, 5. (New Haven: Yale University Press, 1957 ff.).

5. Janis, Irving L., "Personality Correlates of Susceptibility to Persuasion," *Journal of Personality* 22 (1954): 504-518.

6. Rosenthal, Robert and Jacobson, Lenore, *Pygmalion in the Classroom* (New York: Holt, Rinehart and Winston, 1968).

7. Weiss, W., "Emotional Arousal and Attitude Change," *Psychological Reports,* 6 (1960): 267-280.

8. Janis, Irving L., op. cit.

9. Riley, Matilda White and Riley, John W., Jr., "A Sociological Approach to Communications Research," *Public Opinion Quarterly* 15 (1951): 445-460.

10. Berenda, Ruth W., *The Influence of the Group on the Judgments of Children,* (New York: King's Crown Press, 1950).

11. Crossen, Helen J., "Effects of Attitudes of the Reader upon Critical Reading Ability," Unpublished Doctoral Dissertation, University of Chicago, 1946.

12. Kendall, Patricia L., and Wolf, Katherine M., "The Analysis of Deviant Cases in Communications Research," in *Communications Research,* P. F. Lazarsfeld and F. N. Stanton, eds. (New York: Harper, 1949).

13. Cooper, Eunice and Johoda, Marie, "The Evasion of Propaganda: How Prejudiced People Respond to Anti-Prejudice Propaganda," *Journal of Psychology* 23 (1947): 15-25.

14. Cooper, Eunice and Dinerman, Helen, "Analysis of the Film 'Don't Be A Sucker': A Study in Communication," *Public Opinion Quarterly* 15 (1951): 243-264.

15. Lazarsfeld, P. F., Berelson, Bernard, and Gaudet, Hazel, *The Peoples' Choice* (New York: Duell, Sloan and Pearce, 1944).

16. Manis, M. and Dawes, R. M., Cloze Score as a Function of Attitude," *Psychological Reports* 9 (1961): 79-84.

17. Manis, M., "The Interpretation of Persuasive Messages as a Function of Recipient Attitude and Source Prestige," *Journal of Abnormal and Social Psychology* 63 (1961): 82-86.

18. Piekarz, Josephine A., op. cit., 142-143.

# The
# Early
# Years

Jean T. Kunz

# The Self-Concept of the Young Child as He Learns to Read

In our culture the young child approaches the formal project of learning to read when he is approximately six years old. During the few years he has lived, he has learned to handle his body, to speak a language, to find his way around his home and neighborhood, along with inumerable subtle learnings having to do with values and patterns of problem solving. He will bring all of his previous learning with him as he approaches the new challenge. The manner in which the child learns and the outcome of the attempt to read print will depend on the interaction between the child and the entire learning situation at school such as the teacher, the physical surroundings, the peer group, reading materials, methods of teaching, etc.

A review of how the self develops brings into focus the child approaching a beginning reading program. We can then discuss some of the research concerning the self-concept of the child in the classroom and the reading materials which can support the positive development of the self-concept of children.

## Interpersonal Relationships and Self-Concept

In the beginning, a child is aware only of his physical comfort and discomfort for he lives his life largely at a biological level. However, through the close, personal relationship with his mother and, perhaps, other nurturing adults, the relevant world gradually takes shape (1). As feelings, desires, goals, values, and ideas emerge, the behavior of the child indicates how he perceives, feels about, and thinks about his world and himself.

Before language and higher thought processes are well established, the conceptual value of self is determined (2). The significant people in the child's environment have put a "price tag" on him as they have fulfilled his survival needs. He senses whether they can increase or decrease his sense of helplessness; whether they can promote or diminish his sense of well-being. The child learns ways and develops capacities for meeting the expectations of the people on whom he is dependent.

The individual security of the significant people raising the child and their ability to give love rather than promise love, communicates to the youngster his worth and value as an individual. When acceptance and love at any price is sensed to be futile, the child uses his nuisance value to insure his not being ignored. It is more threatening to have no attention paid to him than to be punished. The young child accepts the assumptions and standards of significant adults, as he perceives them, without critical judgment and he does what he has to do in order to maintain the relationship.

Erickson states that the individual's physiological-psychological make-up—including intellectual potential, energy level, body shape, and temperament—are the basis for building a self-structure. The reciprocity or interplay that occurs between the child with his capacities and the significant adults with their capacities form the milieu out of which the child structures his concept of self (3).

As the child grows from infancy to toddlerhood, to preschool and school age, he is structuring a self-image out of the day by day life he lives. Individually, each child differentiates specific and somewhat stable characteristics of himself out of a phenomenal field. The structure of the specific and stable characteristics become the self-image (4). In time, the self-image is the child's guide to his behavior. He strives to maintain the image, for as long as he can function according to anticipation, he is relatively free from disturbing feelings of helplessness (5).

A child about three-and-one-half years old came into her new nursery school the first day to look around and become acquainted with her teacher. She was in the room only a few minutes when she asked the teacher:

"Where do you put the naughty children?"

The teacher replied, "You know, we don't have any naughty children in our school."

The child walked away, looked at the toys on the shelf and returned again to the teacher. Her face was tense, her voice determined as she asked again, "Where *do* you put the naughty children?"

The teacher stooped down to the youngster's level as she said, "Do you think we need a place for naughty children?"

"Yes."

"I wonder why?"

"Because, I'm one!"

Many times daily during the following weeks at school, the child would come to check with the teacher as to whether or not it was "naughty" to open the clay bucket, get on the climbing equipment if other children were there, etc. In the new setting, the child was not able to predict or anticipate the reactions of the adults to her behavior so she became very restricted and careful in what she did.

Hopefully, the child approaching a beginning reading program comes with a self-image which will allow him to enter into it with eagerness, confidence, and some degree of realism. The child who is behaving in such a manner will have the physical maturity and the experience and background necessary for successful reading. During the early years when much of the youngster's behavior was motivated by his physical maturation, "significant others" in his life reacted positively to his growth attainments. As the gradual shift from the force of maturation to the push for learning occurred, there were still adults who were willing and able to answer the child's constant questions, to adjust to his curiosity, to provide materials, equipment and time for him to learn skills, organize information, and develop ideas. To the educator this is the concept of readiness. The child, through his behavior, indicates that the essential conditions have been achieved so that he can learn (6). The self-image at this time is most pliable. Significant relationships can influence growth toward either a positive or negative self-concept as the child is working toward building skills necessary for reading.

Realistically, however, there will be children in every group who will come with privations of one kind or another—some severe, some slight. A youngster who has never felt a sense of being a trustworthy and able individual is not going to find the printed page exciting or challenging. It may be that some children came to school with such limited experiences that they have not learned the language necessary for reading print. One teacher took her students to see some cows and calves three different times before the children could give the animals labels. Even then the cows were horses and the calves were puppies.

Crow and colleagues (7) predict that by the early 1970s, one out of every two children under six in the United States will come from impoverished backgrounds. Children from a ghetto area often have low self-concepts and little or no sense of allegiance to authority, social order, or social institutions. The child's experience has taught him that his nuisance value is about the only way he has to make contact with significant adults. The teacher and the peer group are now significant others to the child and, positively or negatively, they will reflect back to him their perception of him. The expanded relationships within the school setting can enhance the child's sense of trust, autonomy, initiative, and industry, or they can intensify his feelings of mistrust, doubt, guilt, shame, and inferiority (3). The "price tag" placed on the child at this time is again dependent on the degree of personal security and adequacy felt by his teacher and his friends. When children are starting school the teacher is the bridge across which children relate to one another and to learning materials.

## The Teacher's Challenge

No two individuals have the same intellectual capacities nor do they have the same self-image. The challenge to a teacher is to plan and carry out programs for learning for every individual who comes into his class (7). For children from impoverished backgrounds, the beginning reading program may consist of building a broad background for reading through many first-hand experiences. The teacher may find it necessary to reach far beyond her basic reading series to challenge other children. You might respond that individual teaching is impossible. There are so many reasons why—classes are too large, it is too expensive, some children can't learn, administrators are not willing to provide materials, even the custodians will not tolerate moving the furniture. However, it is necessary to find a way to help every child learn if the social ills of the United States are to be remedied. If our democratic way of life is to be preserved, it is necessary to consider the social ills as they now exist in our society.

A close human relationship is the basis for all learning. The learnings which are of prime importance are the ones that influence behavior (8). The successful teacher is the one who strives to set the stage so that every child can feel the desire to learn, and not feel a responsibility for his own learning but for that of his fellow students. The teacher has a three-point goal in teaching. Such a teacher will be aware of 1) the student's self-image, 2) the skills necessary for reading, and 3) the subject matter being taught.

## The Self-Concept of Children in a Classroom Setting

On the premise that the self-concept is a learned structure growing mainly from reactions and comments made by others and inferences drawn by children out of their experiences, Staines (9) set up a study to investigate the possibility of teaching so that the self-concept would improve. Both experimental and control group were scholarship classes with highly rated teachers. The teacher of the control group had no awareness of the self-picture as an outcome of education and she made many more negative comments to children about their performance, status, and potential. Her students showed a significant decrease in certainty about self.

The teacher of the experimental group studied the self-ratings of her class and attempted to teach so that her students might positively change their feelings about themselves. There were statistically significant changes which occurred in self-traits.

Subject matter gains were slightly higher in the experimental group, but they were not statistically significant. Staines states that the self is a factor in all learning experiences and the development of self should become one of the major teaching aims for education.

Davidson and Lang (10) have examined how the self is influenced in a classroom setting by a study of the relationship between children's perception of their teacher's feeling toward them and the children's perception of themselves, academic achievement and classroom behavior. On all three measures there was a positive correlation. The investigators conclude that the teacher's feelings of acceptance and approval are communicated to the child and perceived by him as a positive appraisal. The teacher's positive feelings are the beginning of a circular reaction—the child achieves and the teacher's feelings cause the child to strive for further approval by behaving as a "good" student.

In an attempt to discover whether or not there were differences in the self-concepts of overachievers and underachievers in reading, Lumpkin (11) matched groups on chronological age, mental age, sex, and home background. Over-achievers revealed significantly more positive self-concepts, higher levels of adjustment, saw themselves as liking reading, and they were viewed positively by peers and teachers. The underachievers had low academic achievement measures, negative perceptions of self, showed a desire to be different from self as seen, expressed more feelings of conflict, and they were viewed by their teachers as having high problem tendency. The investigator concludes with confidence that in the group studied, the self-concept of the individual influences his behavior and may determine the direction and degree of his expression in academic work and social relationships.

Bodwin (12) found a significantly positive correlation between immature self-concept and reading disability. A study completed by Hamarchek (13) revealed a relationship between high intellectual and achievement self-images and reading age, mental age, and educational age.

Wattenberg and Clifford (14) set up an exploratory study to determine whether the relationship of low self-concept and reading difficulties was caused by poor self-concepts leading to reading difficulties or unfortunate experiences in reading undermining self-concepts. During the first semester in Kindergarten, ratings were obtained relative to 1) self-concepts, 2) ego strength, and 3) intelligence. Two years after completion of Kindergarten, the children were again measured and rated in self-concept and ego strength. Progress in reading was measured on the test for the book in which they were reading as prepared by the publisher. Generally, the measures of self-concept were the measures of mental ability. (The Detroit Beginning

First Grade Intelligence Test.) The authors recommend further study in this area.

The research of Perkins (15) indicates that a teacher's awareness of a child's self-image and the conscious reaching for enhancement of the self results in a general enrichment for more effective human relationships and living.

## Beginning Reading Materials and Self-Concept

There is a growing concern on the part of those preparing materials for the beginning reader to provide books and stories related to the child's life experiences. Reading materials must reflect an appreciation for and an understanding of language in the child's life. A child can experience a feeling of self-acceptance from the teacher when the reading materials presented to him reflect his life and his language. The creative teacher finds many ways of teaching and a variety of materials to use in a beginning reading program (16). In planning for the teaching of reading skills and enhancement of self, learning to read through experiences can be most effective (17).

A first grade teacher discovered soon after school started that she had a youngster who was not at all interested in reading. He was a polite, shy youngster who stayed to himself most of the time. She also found that he was in school daily until recess and then he was missing. Her concern for the child led her to try many ways to make friends with him and interest him in school and reading, but nothing seemed to work.

She enlisted the help of a sixth grade boy who was instructed to wander off with her charge when he left school—not to bring him back but to see where he went, what he did, where he stopped to look, and what he looked at. The older boy returned to report his findings. Rulan went into the foothills close to the school to look for lizzards. He was also interested in rocks and seemed to know a great deal about them. Once in a while he stopped to talk about the plant life on the hillside also.

The sixth grader became the teaching assistant in that he gathered specific information on lizzards, rocks, and plants for the teacher. The teacher wrote the stories and it was not long until Rulan was asking his teacher to write a story about how mountains were formed and what happened to Lake Bonneville. All the youngsters were eager to read the stories written for him and he was perceived by both teacher and students as the idea person in the room.

Another first grade teacher in a different location had a group of fifteen children who were not one bit interested in reading print. They had lived their total lives within a four-block radius where there was not much to see or experience which might relate to a beginning reading program. By listening to their conversation before and after school, on the playground, she learned that they talked about food a great deal along with some odd kinds of things. With her electric frying pan and a hot plate she started cooking in her room. If one cooks, one must read to find out how. Before too long, each of the fifteen students had a basic reading vocabulary. The word list included flour, sugar, salt, milk, stir, mix, etc. Soon there were stories about getting ready to cook. Through an individualized reading program, everyone was reading at least at grade level by May. School was a pleasure, the teacher a most significant person to the children. They arrived in the morning when she did and they left with her after school. Children can feel competent and valuable as individuals when they "know" they have some knowledge.

With the growing body of information having to do with self-concept and its relationship to behavior and learning, schools need to provide opportunities for experiences which will enable people to develop as individuals rather than stereotyped conformists. It is not only what a person knows; it is the way he feels about a situation that causes his behavior. Children need an education which will aid them in increasing their sensitivity to, and perception of, their own self-concepts and those of others. Teachers are indeed significant adults who can be instrumental in accomplishing this goal as they teach children the tools for reading.

*   *   *   *

"What is honored in a country will be cultivated there."

PLATO

## References

1. Stone, Joseph L. and Joseph Church, *Childhood and Adolescence* (New York: Random House, 1957), 456.

2. Anderson, Camilla A. "The Self-Image: A Theory of the Dynamics of Behavior" in *The Self in Growth, Teaching, and Learning.* Edited by Don E. Hamache (Englewood Cliffs, N.J.: Prentice Hall, Inc., 1965), 1–13.

3. Erikson, Erik H. "Growth and Crises of the Healthy Personality," in *Symposium on the Healthy Personality.* Edited by Milton J. E. Senn (New York: Josiah Macy, Jr. Foundation, 1950), 91–146.

4. Snygg, D. and A. W. Combs, *Individual Behavior* (New York: Harper Brothers, 1949).

5. Ausubel, David P. and Pearl Ausubel, "Ego Development Among Segregated Negro Children," in *Education in Depressed Areas.* Edited by A. Harry Passow (New York: Teachers College, Columbia University, 1964), 109–136.

6. Hymes, James L., Jr. *Before a Child Reads* (New York: Row Peterson and Company, 1958), 96.

7. Crow, Lester D., Walter I. Murry, and Hugh H. Smythe, *Educating the Culturally Disadvantaged Child* (New York: David McKay Company, Inc., 1966), 298.

8. Rogers, Carl R. *On Becoming a Person* (Boston, Mass.: Houghton Mifflin Company, 1961), 420.

9. Staines, J. W. "The Self-Picture as a Factor in the Classroom," in *The Self in Growth, Teaching, and Learning.* Edited by Don E. Hamache (Englewood Cliffs, N.J.: Prentice Hall, Inc., 1965), 404–423.

10. Davidson, Helen H. and Gerhard Lang, "Children's Perception of Their Teachers' Feelings Toward Them Related to Self-Perception, School Achievement, and Behavior," in *The Self in Growth, Teaching, and Learning.* Edited by Don E. Hamache, (Englewood Cliffs, N.J.: Prentice Hall, Inc., 1965), 424–439.

11. Lumpkin, D. D. *Relationship of Self-Concept to Achievement in Reading.* Ph.D. Dissertation. University of Southern California, 1959, 120.

12. Bodwin, R. F. "The Relationship Between Immature Self-Concept and Certain Educational Disabilities" in *Dissertation Abstracts* 19 (1959): 1945–1946.

13. Hamarchek, D. E. *A Study of the Relationship Between Certain Measures of Growth and The Self-Images of Elementary School Children,* Ph.D. Dissertation, University of Michigan, 1960, 210.

14. Wattenberg, William W. and Clare Clifford, *Relationship of the Self-Concept to Beginning Achievement in Reading.* Project of Office of Education, United States Department of Health, Education, and Welfare (Michigan: Wayne State University, 1962), 58.

15. Perkins, Hugh V. "Changing Perception of Self," in *The Self in Growth, Teaching, and Learning.* Edited by Don E. Hamache (Englewood Cliffs, N.J.: Prentice Hall, Inc., 1965), 449–453.

16. Austin, Mary C., Coleman Morrison, Helen J. Kenny, Mildred B. Morrison, Ann R. Gutmann, and J. William Nystrom, *The Torch Lighters, Tomorrow's Teachers of Reading,* Cambridge, Mass.: Harvard University Press, 1961), 157.

15. Lee, Doris M. and R. V. Allen, *Learning to Read Through Experience* (New York: Appleton-Century-Crofts, 1963), 153.

**James L. Hymes, Jr.**

# Teaching Reading to the Under-Six Age: A Child Development Point of View

The question of how much emphasis there should be on the teaching the child under six to read print has long been a bothersome one: a source of anxiety to parents, an argumentative question among educators. The old difficulties associated with the question are being heightened today as we move steadily toward the extension of public education downward. Once it could almost tacitly have been assumed that by "the under-six age" one of course meant the kindergarten child. Age five was as far down as schools dipped. Today, however, many public schools are serving four-year-olds in Head Start and Title I programs and in other programs of compensatory education. And as conservative a group as the New York State Board of Regents has gone on record as advocating public education for *all* children from at least three years of age on up. Startling as this may seem to some, even this bold statement must be put against the background of today's Parent and Child Centers of Head Start, serving children under age three, down to infancy, and their parents. The day may come when not only will our public schools serve three-year-olds, but the Three may look like an "old timer"! It is against this background of the inevitable extension of education downward that one must philosophically and psychologically today consider the question of teaching reading to the "under-six age." Today we have to think about the whole under-six age, not simply its topmost level of Five.

One answer has long been given to Fives that, if it has any worth, could probably apply as appropriately to Fours or Threes or Twos or any young age: We don't teach reading to the under-six age, *we teach reading readiness.* I have long found this a most unsatisfactory, unhelpful response, for Fives or any age. Teaching *reading* readiness? Does this mean that the nursery school and kindergarten also teach science readiness? And art readiness? And music readiness? Social studies readiness? Health readiness? The absurdity is self-apparent. The talk of teaching *reading* readiness, as the special approach to the under-six age, is gobbledegook. We either teach reading or we don't. We either teach science and math and the social sciences and art and music and language, or we don't. The reading readiness absurdity has led to exercises and drills and workbooks and seatwork which have been no friend to the field of reading, and certainly no friend to young children.

If we rule out "teaching reading readiness" as a possibility, what then? Our title today says: "A child development point of view." From the vantage point of one who tries to watch children, to stay close to children, to study children, to know a little of how they feel and how they think and how they see the world, the answer has to be: *Yes.* Of course! One has to teach reading to the under-six child. To the under-six five-year-old. To whatever under-six age we may have in school, or have in our homes. A child development point of view cannot lead one to say: No, don't teach ... postpone. It has to say: Teach, and teach as much as each child is comfortably, naturally, easily, rightfully ready for.

This answer of "Yes" underlies the whole nursery school movement in this country, now more than fifty years old. It underlies the whole kindergarten movement here, now more than a century old. Both are grounded in the observation that comes through so clearly as one watches young children: they are ready to learn. Parents seeking nursery schools for fours and threes have used different words: "He's into everything". . . . "We've run out of things to do." But however one says it, wherever one sees it, the fact is that the young child is a bundle of qualities which makes teaching him—reading (and science and math and philosophy and psychology and everything under the sun)—an inevitability.

This is a child full of curiosity, driven to touch and look and taste and ask. This is the child new to our world, smitten each moment by its wonders. This is the child dominated by one overpowering drive: to grow, to be big, to move from dependence to independence. This is the child who shows such gleeful bright pride in each new skill: "I can tie my shoes". . . . "I can climb to the top" . . . "I can write my name." With all this in his nature one *has* to teach as one lives with young children.

We come, then, to what is the central question: *How?* Too often, sadly, if the answer comes through, "Yes, teach the child under six," it is as if one had been given *carte blanche.* Anything goes! Here the smallness and newness and dependency of the young child militate against him. He cannot protect himself; he has to try to go along. And if "anything goes," he can be taken to queer places. The awareness of the young child's readiness, yea eagerness to learn, has to put parents and teachers into a stance of thoughtfulness and sensitivity. At least three considerations certainly must be kept in mind:

1) Yes, teach the under-six age to read *but teach it in a way that fits the child.*

We are talking about a special age. We have to keep reminding ourselves of that. These are five-year-olds (or fours or threes or twos). These are not eight-year-olds or twelves. There are qualities that stamp this age, in Head Start group or affluent suburb, at five or three, experienced, inexperienced, urban, rural—it is the age that counts.

These are all active children. They are moving. On the go. They are not good sitters, not good waiters. They are ready to learn to read any number of things but we have to have a way of teaching them that doesn't depend on their sitting down and shutting up.

These are all very egocentric children, every one of them, simply because they all are new, all just discovering themselves. They talk and think of "I" and "my." Our way of teaching them has to built on *their* lives, *their* concerns, *their* experiences. This is still where they live most keenly, in their own personal, private world. We will never touch all the eagerness they have to bring if our way of teaching is general, far-off, removed. This age, even more than their much discussed older brothers and sisters, craves relevancy.

This age craves the personal touch, too. Threes, fours and fives are old enough and ready to go to school and to be in groups. But once they get in school, a good school, they find warmth. Intimacy. Closeness. The best teaching of this age is done eyeball to eyeball, face to face, person to person. We have to have a way of proceeding that does not depend on their always being in a group.

These examples are perhaps sufficient to make the generalization clear: The way we teach has to fit the child. This is not the time or place to try to delineate all the special characteristics that mark this age, except to say: They are there. We have to look for them. We have to respect them and take them into account. We cannot simply plunge ahead, as if the nature of the child was of no importance.

But even this disclaimer makes it important to add one more characteristic of the age (albeit a characteristic not peculiar to this age). The way we teach has to fit *the* child. Each child. The spread of individual differences — in maturation, interest, need, background, ability . . .—is more impressive and more significant in this rapidly changing under-six age than at other stages in development. We speak of "Fives"—we have to for simplicity and speed. We speak of "Head Start groups"—we do for our convenience. We speak of "Fours." But we have to make ourselves remember: You cannot lump them. They always stay individual. And our way of teaching has to reflect this clear awareness.

2) Yes, teach reading to the under-six age *but teach it in a way that fits reading.*

Many of you, better than I, can say what is involved in this area of human experience. But let me suggest a few components that I suspect we would all agree to and accept.

Learning to read is a long, continuous story. It has slow beginnings. It has its peaks. But most of all it goes on and on. It doesn't begin in some one grade, it doesn't end in some one grade. Our approach to young children, as we teach reading to them, has to keep this time-perspective in mind. There *is* time. There has to be time. We must not panic or pressure as if time was running out.

Learning to read print is a complicated process involving many different aspects: memory, discrimination, language, attention-span, solid knowledge of reality. The list could be quite extensive. Our approach to young children must keep this wide scope in mind. Their hearing stories, for example, is a part of it. Their language, as they play, is a part of their learning to read. Their knowledge, as they take trips for example, becomes a part of their learning to read. We must not let the fact that we are teaching young children mislead us into thinking that learning to read print involves only a few, limited kinds of experiences.

Learning to read implies a variety of goals. We seek to build the technical skills so the activity is not a burdensome chore. We seek to build capacities for comprehension and for critical response so the activity is not a mechanical, meaningless performance. We seek to build a love of reading so that one not only can but one does! We must not let the fact that the children are young trap us into acting as if only the technical skills mattered. We must be pleased with gains in the direction of any of the goals. And if ever we have to choose, with the young and with the beginner, it would seem to make sense to be most sensitive to the feelings involved and the attitudes. A little love deepened may be immeasurably more significant than a little skill learned.

3) Yes, teach reading to the under-six age *but teach it in a way that fits the goals of general education.* Our target—under-six and over-six—is not to produce a reader but to help build a better human because now the child reads. Our way of proceeding ought to have as its end result a reader of print, yes but also: a prouder person, a freer man. A more creative human. Less docile, less hostile. A reader but a deeper-caring soul, someone more broadly aware, more open. . . . The fact that we are teaching young children to read must not make us callous to what liberal or general or humane education is all about.

A program that teaches reading to the under-six age in a way that fits the child, that does justice to the process of reading itself, and that is in tune with what education seeks can be a rich program. It can be a program full of choice, a program of freedom and of excitement. For the sake of teaching reading it can be a program of trips, of jobs and activities, of animals, of visitors, of creative experiences, of play.

Candor compels me to say, however: Almost always something goes wrong. In so many of the classrooms I visit, if the statement is "Yes, we do teach reading to the under-six age," I see a program that is narrow, not broader. I see a program where the children talk less, not more. I see a sitting, quiet program and not one where the youngsters are active. I see a program with store-bought materials, not a program growing out of the children's own activities and experiences, not one I would call relevant to them. I see almost always children brought together in groups and so seldom see the individualized and personalized teaching that I think is called for. I too often see programs where the pressure comes from the teacher, not the children. There is little evidence of love and joy and thrill on the children's part; there is much evidence of control and management on the teacher's part. It seems so often as if one had to produce followers or cows or sheep in order to produce readers.

It shouldn't work out this way but so often seemingly it does. When we consciously teach reading to the under-six child we forget to make our teaching fit the child and fit the field and fit our overall, long-range goals. It may be—one can hope!—that the admission of younger and younger children to our schools may force us to stop and think: Who is here? And what are we really trying to do?

**Ronald Macaulay**

# *Linguistic Diversity and the Elementary School*

Let us begin with an extreme example of linguistic diversity in the elementary school: the case of a child who enters school speaking only Spanish and unable to understand more than a few words of English. Clearly, such a child is going to have difficulty, in the initial stages at least, in adapting to this new situation. With a little imagination we can visualize some of his problems: he will have great difficulty in understanding what is being asked of him, particularly where any degree of precision is involved. He will also have difficulty in making clear what his needs and problems are. But this is only a crude picture of lack of communication. There is another important aspect of communication involved and that is that he may find it difficult to register the subtle linguistic clues by which we tell when someone is impatient, angry, really angry, and so on. The situation works similarly in reverse, for the teacher may not pick up the equivalent signals from the child. In such a situation it would not be surprising if the child should appear (and even act) more stupid·than he is, for his position is an unenviable one: A bewildered child in an alien world who cannot turn to his parents for help, since they may know little more than he does. It is a disturbing picture but thankfully it only applies to a tiny minority of the school population. Or does it? I am afraid the answer may be 'No.' I would argue that it applies in some degree to all those children who come from homes below the level that a sociologist would rate middle-class and who attend schools staffed by middle-class teachers. This may well be a majority of the elementary school population.

To understand why this may be so we need to look at the structure of language. Speaking a language is such a complex process that there is little or no room in it for random events. In fact, it is sometimes said that speaking is rule-governed creativity. Speech is creative because we can say things that have never been said before but it is rule-governed because (unless we are being deliberately perverse as a counter-argument) everything we say depends on some combination of internally stored rules. This applies to all levels of the language and includes regional, social and stylistic variations. In fact, in so far as each of us speaks consistently (and that does not mean in one style only) we do so because of a set of rules which circumscribe the kind of things we can say. On the neurophysiological level these rules must be related to complicated chains of muscle commands and this is one of the things that makes it difficult to speak differently from the way we normally do or to learn to speak a foreign language. In order to change our way of speaking we need to have a new set of rules and consequently new chains of neuro-muscular commands.

This means that we ought to be very careful about labelling certain forms of speech "mistakes." It is, in fact, very easy to define a mistake in speaking: a mistake is something we would immediately correct if we noticed that we had said it. We all make mistakes of this kind and frequently correct them. But we also often label as mistakes forms of speech that are not current among educated speakers and it is important to realize that these are mistakes of a different kind. The first kind of mistakes we can call "slips of the tongue" and the second "use of non-standard forms"; we all make "slips" but we do not all use "non-standard forms" and this is one of the sources of woe in the world. For it is often very hard for the speaker of the standard language to realize that those who use "non-standard forms" consistently are not merely making slips but that they have a set of rules which permit these forms. Thus when a teacher corrects a child who says *He don't,* she is not merely asking him to correct a slip or even to replace one word by another word, she is asking him to reorganize the set of rules by which this form was produced. In this case she is asking him to remove the auxiliary *do* from the class of modal auxiliaries such as *can, will, must,* etc. with which it has so much in common but which do not inflect for the third person singular of the present tense and put it in a class all by itself. This will affect the storage and ordering of the rules in the child's brain, so it is not surprising if the child does not immediately change his language habits and learn the form preferred by the teacher. The same is true of all levels of language.

Something of the same process is involved in understanding what is said to us. If we had to hear every detail of an utterance perfectly clearly in order to understand it then language would be a very inefficient means of communication because we would be forever asking people to repeat what they had just said. But, in fact, language is highly redundant so that if we even get about half of what is said or written we can usually understand it. And this is only because we know the language and have some idea, given a sound, letter or word, what is likely to precede or follow it. With a language that we know less well it becomes much more difficult.

Now it has not been clearly established how the process of understanding what is said to us takes place, but it seems likely that at some stage the same set of rules is involved as that used in the act of speaking. In terms of economy of internal organization this makes good sense, and there is some evidence that we hear speech sounds in terms of those we use ourselves. In general, it is probably true to say that we can understand someone who speaks like us better than someone who speaks differently.

This may seem of little relevance to the situation in the elementary school, apart from those children who come from homes where Spanish is spoken, but the point I wish to make is that such children are only extreme examples of a much more widespread language problem. All children whose language differs significantly from that of their teacher are going to have some difficulty in understanding. This difficulty may be obscured by the fact that it is very hard to know whether someone has understood what you have said. It is much easier to notice misunderstanding when something incongruous follows your remarks, but teachers who assume understanding in the absence of clear evidence to the contrary may be taking a big risk.

How likely is it that many children misunderstand? I think it is fairly likely that all children misunderstand part of the time. Piaget's experiments demonstrate the difficulties children have with abstract concepts, and we have all had the experience of a child using a word confidently a number of times and only later asking what it means. I think most adults (including many teachers) would be surprised how much of their speech to children is not really understood.

Of course, you may say: it depends on what you mean by "really" understood, and that is exactly the point. We can all communicate quite effectively on a very crude level in certain contexts by gestures and facial expressions, but language is a much more delicate instrument than that and "really" understanding involves responding to some of the subtleties of expression and not just the general trend of the remarks.

To what extent can we assume misunderstanding on some level? The answer is clearly related to the amount of "correction" the teacher feels compelled to make in the child's language. Every time the teacher says (or even thinks) it is wrong to use a certain sound, word or pattern in a given situation there is some danger of misunderstanding. The differences between one dialect and another are not merely differences in individual items but differences in systems, and so it is not surprising that "corrections" do not necessarily bring immediate improvement, and likewise presumably do not help understanding much. In fact, if the "corrections" are based on a mistaken view of language (which I fear may sometimes be the case) then they may add considerably to the child's confusion. What is more, misunderstanding is cumulative so that those who are confused at the beginning are less likely to see things clearly at a later stage. And this is reflected in tests of various kinds in later life as well as in the comparative dropout figures for lower-class and middle-class children.

Perhaps I have said enough about the point I am trying to make: that linguistic diversity may be more than a matter of aesthetics, and in fact a real source of inequity for many people. If this is so, what then can be done, especially at the level of the elementary school? I wish I could give a useful answer but I do not know one and I do not believe that anyone has found the answer. One reason is that we simply do not know enough about the language of the children who are entering the elementary schools.

It is not enough to say 'Let us be tolerant of the lower-class child's language' because this may be depriving him of the means to intellectual development. On the other hand, it is apparently not very realistic to say 'Let us teach all lower-class children the language of the middle-classes' because that has been tried for many years, and while a certain proportion of the working-class succeed in learning this new language, the majority manifestly do not.

The one thing I am sure of is that the elementary school teacher cannot know too much about her own and the children's language. And by this I do not only mean she should know all the difficult words in the dictionary, or rare literary devices such as inversion, or the subtleties of the difference between a colon and a semi-colon; least of all do I mean what Thorstein Veblen called "As felicitous as an instance of futile classicism as can well be found, outside of the Far East . . . the conventional spelling of the English language" (1).

No, what I want the teacher to know is the nature of the system that underlies her speech and how it differs from the speech of the children she teaches. This cannot easily be found in books, and so I would like the elementary school teacher to be trained to observe the speech of the children she teaches so that she can at least have some insight into their problems and avoid adding to their confusion. I would also like her to know as much about the structure of English and methods of teaching its patterns as she would need to know if she were teaching foreigners who were learning English as a foreign language. (In a sense, this is what the elementary school teacher is doing since the language the children speak IS a foreign language, and moreover, as someone has pointed out, it is a language which we as adults can never learn.)

Finally, I would hope that the teacher would follow the golden rule of teaching and look at the results of her language teaching. If we assume, as we must, that the teachers are intelligent and well-meaning and that the children are intelligent and curious (i.e. normal), and yet the results are by and large unsatisfactory, then we must conclude that there is something wrong with the system. It may be, as Bernstein has suggested, that "the methods and problems of teaching need to be thought out almost as though middle-class children do not exist" (2). And if that is so one of the first places we must look is at language.

## References

1. Thorstein Veblen, *Theory of the Leisure Class,* Chapter 14.
2. Basil Bernstein, "Social class and linguistic development: a theory of social learning" in A. H. Halsey et al. (eds.), *Education, economy and society: a reader in the sociology of education,* New York, 1961, 306.

Margaret E. Smart

# Piaget, Language, and Reading

The need to develop educational programs based upon empirical evidence increasingly has drawn educators to the work of Jean Piaget. Although his primary purpose has been to trace the development of human intelligence, educators have found his studies highly significant for their purposes. The evidence Piaget derived from the ingenuous questions he raised about man's knowing has provided us with a new conceptual framework from which to view children's mental development and in turn, from which to plan educational programs more appropriately matched to the diverse needs of children.

This discussion is limited to: 1) outlining some of Piaget's notions concerning the development of symbolic representation which seemingly have relevance for planning a language arts program for young children, and 2) suggesting classroom practices which seem to be appropriate in light of Piaget's studies.

## Symbolic Representation

Symbolic representation is an integral piece of the cognitive puzzle Piaget has attempted to solve. Although it assumes its place in the overall framework of developing intelligence, it may be precisely identified and studied as one sub-stage among other sequential stages in the child's development of representation. Not surprisingly has Piaget distinguished stages and sub-stages of representative activity which coincide with his stages of cognitive development. Consequently, we find symbolic representation belonging concurrently to the periods of egocentric representative activity and of intuitive thought.

Since this crucial period in the development of representative activity approximates the years between four and eight, it is a time closely associated with the beginning school years when the child has his first encounters with formalized training in symbols and signs. How, then, does the child develop the ability to present reality?

Although the beginnings of representation are found within the sensori-motor stage, its development is continuous across the many years of childhood. Ultimately it is included within the framework of operational, reversible thought (approximately 12–14 years).

The function which gives rise to symbolic representation is described by Piaget as:

> The ability to represent something (a signified something: object, event, conceptual scheme, etc.) by means of a signifier which is differentiated and which serves only a representative purpose: language, mental image, symbolic gesture and so on (1:51).

By the second year of the child's life five behavior patterns appear which, Piaget (1:53) tells us, "imply the evocation of an object or event not present and which consequently presuppose the formation or use of differentiated signifiers." These five behaviors, appearing almost simultaneously but in an increasingly complex order, are: 1) deferred imitation, 2) symbolic play, 3) drawings or graphic images, 4) mental image, and 5) language.

Each behavior may be traced separately through its successive stages of development yet all five are interdependent and interactive. Briefly let us consider each.

*Deferred imitation.*    For Piaget, imitation is closely associated with representation. "Since representation involves the image of an object," he (2:5) wrote, "it can be seen to be a kind of interiorized imitation, and therefore a continuation of accommodation."

Gradually children are able to defer imitation behaviors to times when models are absent and thus to build adaptations of reality. During this period of egocentric representative activity imitation develops spontaneously and often unconsciously because the child is unable to distinguish between himself and "out there." Not until about seven or eight does imitation become deliberate and, for Piaget (2:72) "takes its place in intelligence as a whole."

Two observations of Piaget's (2) concerning imitation seem particularly significant. First, imitation is always a continuation of the child's understanding. Secondly, only models held in high regard are imitated.

*Play.*    Play is considered by Piaget to be the counterpart of imitation and indispensable to children's affective and cognitive equilibrium. He explained:

Play transforms reality by assimilation to the needs of the self whereas imitation . . . is accommodation to external models. . . . [Thus play is] essentially assimilation of reality to the self without coercions or sanctions (1:58).

Through play the child adapts actions to his needs and develops personal meanings and understandings.

It is even possible to trace the child's representational and social development through Piaget's sequential play categories, but a comment must suffice for each.

1.  There is *exercise play* wherein newly acquired skills are repeated again and again either for the pleasure derived from the repetition or for the affirmation of the skill.
2.  In *symbolic play* the child constructs his own symbols and adapts them to his own needs.
3.  When the child can *play games according to rules,* he has moved from "symbolization centered upon the self" (1:77) towards a more objective socialized point of view of reality. Such behavior usually emerges about six or seven.
4.  *Games of construction* appear about the same time as games with rules. Now children can actually construct and build models as representations of their mental images.

*Drawing or graphic images.*   Piaget (1:63) considered drawing similar to "symbolic play in its functional pleasure and autotelism and like the mental image in its effort at imitating the real."

Representations of reality begin to appear with the child's first attempts to put meaning into his drawings. In this respect drawing and spatial development are inseparable. An examination of his drawings enables us to understand that the child first draws what he *knows* long before he draws what he actually *sees.*

*Mental images.*   This form of the symbolic function Piaget (1:69) described as "a signifier or symbol which gradually emerges as internalized imitation." He tells us that the young child's mental images are limited "to evoking sights that have been perceived previously" (1:71). Thus, it is clear that understanding must precede the formation of mental images.

*Language.*   The child acquires his language in a social setting where the rules and meanings of the linguistic system are pre-established; therefore, he learns his language through verbal imitation.

Through Piaget's detailed analyses on how language functions for the young child (3) we may gain new insights into the child's developing thought. For instance, until about seven years approximately 50% of the child's spontaneous language is a monolog. Such language accompanies, reinforces, and supplements actions. Although he may be speaking within a social environment, in reality he is organizing his ideas and internalizing images through his oral expressions. When we expect children to be silent most of the school day, are we not inhibiting their development of representational thought?

A second instance of the limitations of intuitive thought is reflected in the children's use of social language. Children asking such questions as: "Where is the green crayon?" "Where did he go?" "Are we going to play ball?" illustrate how their thought is centered on the specifics of the here and now. Even "why" questions do not represent a concern for true causal relationship. An example of this is found in the response of a five-year-old whose mother asked him why the fish stayed in the fish bowl rather than on the ground. "Because," he replied, "he's afraid of the cat."

Do we distinguish between the evoked and spontaneous language of children? Do we analyze the classroom setting in which each occurs? Alas, it is relatively simple to evoke language from children. If we are not careful, we may not be counterbalancing this with enough time for the all important spontaneous language to develop.

## Implications for a Language Arts Program

From Piaget's notions concerning the development of symbolic representation the following ideas seem to be relevant for planning a language arts program for young children.

1.  The development of the symbolic function is fundamental to later developmental patterns. Thus, time must be provided for children to internalize representations of their world through imitation, symbolic play, drawings, and language.
2.  Classrooms which enable children to internalize their experiences and adapt reality provide unpressured opportunities to:
    a.  increase their mental storehouse of ideas through meaningful field experiences.
    b.  manipulate a wide variety of objects and materials and to discover what they can do with them through their own actions.
3.  All forms of imitative expression such as art, music, dance, mime, language are integrated into the daily program.
4.  At least half of the day is spent in small groups (4). The following advantages of small instructional settings more than offset the difficulties encountered in organizing the room for such instruction.
    a.  Language is developed in conversational and meaningful groups.

    b.  The teacher easily hears what the children are saying, can elaborate their ideas, can raise questions to extend thinking, and can clarify any misconceptions.

    c.  The teacher, provided with this continuous feedback, may modify and adapt the language arts experiences to the immediate needs of the individual.

    d.  The setting is an invitation for children to express their own ideas.

5.  Child-prepared charts, graphs, murals, and child-authored books reflect the daily interests and activities of the classroom. An over-emphasis on teacher-prepared paper and pencil tasks limits not only the child's explorations but also the range of choices he may have to learn.

6.  The linguistic setting is such that children build associations between their speech and print. The teacher, indicating the high value he places on the children's ideas, encourages them to talk about their ideas; willingly records their language, and uses such recordings as a necessary part of the reading program.

7.  The teacher accompanies oral directions with descriptive actions thereby facilitating the child's language and concept growth.

If we accept Piaget's ideas, then classrooms for young children become centers of activity where questions are asked, ideas are exchanged, problems are solved, experiences are recorded, and reading follows as an important but natural sequence.

## References

1. Piaget, Jean and Barbel Inhelder, *The Psychology of the Child* (New York: Basic Books, 1969).

2. ———*Play, Dreams, and Imitations in Childhood* (New York: Norton, 1962).

3. ———*The Language and Thought of the Child* (New York: Meridan Books, 1955).

4. Smart, Margaret E. "What Piaget Suggests to Classroom Teachers," *Childhood Education* (January 1968), 294-300.

John Downing

# The Implications of Research On Children's Thinking for the Early Stages of Learning to Read

If *reading is the process of making discriminative responses,* then it is important to add that, for such responses to lead to successful reading, the discriminations must be relevant. Petty (1), for example, observed that children, "who paid too much attention to detail, which was often irrelevant," had more difficulty in learning to read than children, "who saw words as wholes." Thus, if we make full use of our capacity to discriminate we may become slaves to the particular. In order to make discriminations we have to learn to neglect irrelevancies. Indeed, in an early experiment on thinking by Moore (2), it was found that irrelevances were "not merely neglected, but. . . . positively cast aside." In determining which differences really make a difference we learn essentially to *categorize,* and as Bruner, *et al.* (3) say, "category learning is one of the principal means by which a growing member of society is socialized." Bruner, *et al.* (4), believe "that virtually all cognitive activity involves and is dependent on the process of categorizing."

In this discussion, we shall not be concerned with that topic which is often found on programs of reading conferences—"How to teach children to think." Instead, interest will be focussed more on the problem, "How do children think, and what must adults do to adapt their approach to the child's modes of thinking?" Children's thinking is a topic strangely absent from standard textbooks on the psychology of reading. I cannot hope to fill that gap in this short paper. What I hope to do, rather, is to show how psychological research on children's thinking suggests a need for reconsideration of some current practices in our schools. While I may not be able to satisfy you with answers, I hope that my brief review of some of the interesting findings of research on children's thinking will provoke many questions and problems. Perhaps further discussion of these questions may give us a glimpse of needed changes in educational practices.

## Children's Thinking About Reading Is a Vital Factor in
## Their Learning to Read

Important research on this question has been conducted by Reid (5) in Scotland. She used a kind of focussed interview method which was designed to stimulate spontaneous comments about reading by 12 children, aged 5, in their first year of school. They were interviewed three times, approximately 2, 5, and 9 months after beginning school.

The results showed very clearly the enormous difference between the child's thinking about reading and the approach of the adult to the same subject. Most significant of all, for these children reading was a "mysterious activity, to which they come with only the vaguest of expectancies." In the first interview, the children had almost no idea what activities reading consisted in, nor did they know its use or purpose.

Reid also found that these beginners were very confused about the technical concepts involved in reading. They did not understand such terms as "word," "letter," "number," "sound," and the confused manner in which they employed these terms often caused still further confusion. For example, one girl declared she was "past reading" (she had completed the readiness materials), and wrote her name as BA∃LR (Balfour). She said she "learned it on her door" and it "begins with three." Numbers were often confused with letters, and letters were often called "words," *e.g.,* *"It's* (the word—'have') got an 'e' on the end. It should only have three words instead of four words being there. You go to sound it out and you hardly know what to say. It's like a different word."

Reid's research is very thought-provoking. One finds numerous connections from her interview records to the more general theoretical accounts of children's thinking by Piaget and Vygotsky, and one may anticipate that it will be a launching pad for more research of this open-ended and intensive type. But, for practical purposes, Reid's report has an immediate implication for the reading teacher—*don't assume that the child thinks about reading in the same way that you do!* We ought to know this already on the basis of the more general theories of children's thinking. Piaget, for instance, showed long ago that the logic of the child is quite different from that of the adult.

But, more specifically, can teachers help children to find their way out of this lack of understanding of the total activity of reading and its technical concepts? Reid seems to believe that there should be some "fostering of the understanding of classification, order and regularity," and she recognizes that successful progress seems "to depend on whether or not a child had at his disposal the vocabulary which would help him to grasp the various schemata which even elementary discussion of language involves." However, in two footnotes, Reid makes it clear that she is not advocating merely an emphasis on labelling or naming, *i.e.,* the verbal aspect only of the basic concept. For example, she states explicitly "that the teaching of the letter names is not being advocated as a part of early teaching of reading," and refers to her previous research (6) which showed the "considerable" danger of confusion with the phonemic sounds.

This brings us to a second very important implication for reading teachers arising from research on the psychology of children's thinking.

### Verbalized Rules May Be An Ineffectual Way of Modifying Children's Thinking

Firstly, research has shown repeatedly that the verbalization of rules is *not necessary.* Rules may be effective without their being formulated. As Cherry (7) has shown, "the user of signs need not know the rules." Thus, from the economic point of view, it would seem better to give our time and attention to providing experiences which will lead children to attain the concepts rather than to their verbalizing about them. Furthermore, children normally and naturally progress from the *use* of concepts to their verbal forms; and not *vice versa.*

For example, Piaget's (8) research led him to conclude: "a child is actually not conscious of concepts and definitions which he can nevertheless handle when thinking for himself," and (9) "verbal forms always evolve more slowly than actual understanding."

This fact was most clearly brought out in an experiment by Hunter and Bartlett (10) on children's thinking. Their subjects had to solve a problem in which boxes had to be opened in a serial order. Children even younger than five were able to solve the problem, but *could not say* how they knew which box to open. "I know how 'cause I do" was a typical explanation. Hull's (11) well-known experiment on concept formation led him to conclude that ability to define was often a very poor indicator of the functional value of a concept. It can be concluded with certainty from these several researches that children can form and utilize a concept without verbalization.

What is far more serious from the practical reading teacher's point of view is that, although the ability to verbalize about a concept seems to develop naturally *after* experience in using it, *the fact that a child can verbalize about a concept is no guarantee that he can utilize it in his thinking.* An interesting example of this can be found in the research on road safety propaganda conducted in England by Belbin (12). She found children's verbalizations about road safety films correlated poorly with their behavior on the road. Children who scored highly on their ability to recapitulate the road safety propaganda were less likely to put it into action in safety behavior. Whereas, those who showed poor verbal recall of the propaganda tended more often to incorporate the safety rules into their actual behavior. The parallel case in reading is well known: the parroting of sounds to letters without any understanding of their reference to the real world—"barking at print," as it has been called. Belbin's research suggests that such barking at print can have negative rather than merely neutral effects in learning. The effects are even worse if such meaningless "barking" becomes habitual. Some other research on human thinking indicates how this may happen.

## Appropriate Orientation to the Task is Vital in Learning to Read

Goodnow (13) researched the differences in behavior when people are oriented towards problem-solving or "gambling" type behavior. She noted that in problem-solving the goal was 100% success, whereas in gambling it need not necessarily be so. One can succeed as a gambler without having to know how to win *every time.* Bruner *et al.* (14) show that in a gambling situation "all-or-none" behavior can pay-off quite well. For example, if the task is to discriminate between "b" and "d," and "b" occurs 70% of the time and "d" only 30% of the time, betting on "b" 100% of the time does pay off at least 70% of the time. This particular example may be applied to a great many real-life situations in the task of learning to read.

Now, if the child becomes confused as to the purpose of the reading task, he may give up hope of solving the problem (and surely we must admit that it is a highly complex one for the beginner in learning to read). Then he may no longer treat reading appropriately, as a problem-solving task, but instead as a gambling task, using "all-or-none" type responses. For instance, barking at print may be such a response—"maybe I can never get an A or B, for all the skills, but at least I'll get one for word recognition," might be his attitude. But, it is important to note that treating the task as a gambling one, and responding to it by "all-or-none" behavior occurs without the individual being consciously aware of the perception of the task or his response in these terms.

Perhaps a better example would be in children's writing. If children are inappropriately oriented towards learning to write they are likely to produce stereotyped "all-or-none" responses in their compositions. Confusion about the purpose of writing often arises through teachers' insistance on correct spelling, correct letter formation, or writing between the lines on lined paper. The real purpose of communicating creative ideas may be lost if children see the situation as a gamble in which it is safer to put your bet on the words you can be sure to spell correctly and write neatly.

In learning to read, therefore, children need to be oriented towards it as a problem-solving task. But, again, we cannot guarantee this by more verbal instructions. A gambling orientation results from the conditions under which the child is working. If conditions are such as to cause him to give up hope of solving the problem, then his thinking behavior will be based on a gambling strategy, and many inappropriate responses may become chronic.

### Concrete Experience and Opportunity for Experimentation is the Fundamental Basis for Concept Development in Learning to Read

It has been shown that verbalized instructions, explanations, or models for imitation are liable to misfire in numerous ways. The alternative is to fit our educational aims and methods of securing them to children's natural ways of thinking. In attempting this, the central fact from the research of the two outstanding theorists on children's thinking, needs to be kept constantly in mind. Piaget and Vygotsky confirm each other's finding that the progression is from concrete experience to concept formation and that the ability to verbalize about concepts develops out of experience in using them in thinking.

It is not the purpose of this paper to describe in detail the kinds of classroom activities and organizations which have been developed on the basis of Piaget's and Vygotsky's research findings that point to this need to begin with concrete experiences. An excellent description has been provided in a recent article by Featherstone (15). His report is based on a survey of many classrooms where a wealth of opportunities is provided for those concrete experiences and experimentation which are the only sure and certain foundations for the later development of abstract thinking. A delightful account of an intuitive application of these principles can be read in Sylvia Ashton-Warner's book, *Teacher* (16). In another discussion I have described the methods derived from these theories which are being applied in one of the several different i.t.a. programs now being used in British and American schools (17).

The fairly recent translation into English of Vygotsky's (18) great work on children's thinking in Russia, which modifies and extends Piaget's theory, is of immense importance for the improvement of classroom practices. It is extraordinary (and sadly so) that books giving ignorant and erroneous accounts of Russian educational theory and practice have actually led some American educators in just the reverse direction. Russian educators do recognize a reading problem, but they do not see its cure in putting the clock back to the "good old days" of formal synthetic phonics and the McGuffey Readers. Vygotsky finds that "the tremendous lag between the school child's oral and written language" is caused by "the abstract quality of written language." Indeed, he singles out phonetic analysis as being a typical example of the abstract thinking involved (19). The certain way to prepare children's thinking for these abstract tasks is, as Almy (20) puts it, "An environment that provides the child with many opportunities for varied sensory and motor experiences. . . . So, too, is the presence of people who talk *with* (not merely to or at) the child, people who read and write and who share these activities with children."

It may be obvious, but perhaps it should be stated explicitly. The implications of all these researches on children's thinking themselves imply strengthening the principle of fitting our teaching to the individual differences of children. The principle of equality in education should mean that every child has an equal right to be educated *according to his own individual differences in aptitude and ability. If children's thinking is taken into account, the need for individualization of our teaching becomes more important than ever.*

In summary, research on children's thinking tells us these important facts about the way we need to improve our teaching of beginning reading. We must adapt our approach to the child's logic, which is quite different to ours. Reading print is an abstract task often far removed from previous life experiencing. Guiding a child toward the discovery of the purpose and processes of reading cannot be achieved by simply telling. Rich and individually motivating activities with accompanying language experiences provide the only sure foundations for the development of those thinking abilities which are essential for the problem-solving basis of learning to read (21).

## References

1. Petty, M. C., "An experimental study of certain factors influencing reading readiness." *Journal of Educational Psychology* 30 (1939):215.

2. Moore, T. V., *University of California Publications in Psychology,* 1 (1910): 2.

3. Bruner, Jerome S., Jacqueline J. Goodnow, and George A. Austin, *A Study of Thinking* (New York: John Wiley and Sons, 1956), 231.

4. *Ibid.,* p. 246.

5. Reid, J. F., "Learning to think about reading," *Educational Research* 9 (1966): 56–62.

6. Reid, J. F., "A study of thirteen beginners in reading," *Acta Psychologica* 14 (1958):295–313.

7. Cherry, C., *On Human Communication* (Cambridge, Mass.: Technology Press of Massachusetts Institute of Technology, 1957).

8. Piaget, Jean, *The Language and Thought of the Child* (London: Routledge and Kegan Paul, 1926): p. 79.

9. *Ibid.,* p. 203.

10. Hunter, W. S., and S. C. Bartlett, *Journal of Experimental Psychology* 38 (1949): 558–567.

11. Hull, C. L., "Quantitative aspects of the evolution of concepts," *Psychological Monographs* 28 (1920): No. 1.

12. Belbin, E., "The effects of propaganda on recall, recognition and behavior," *British Journal of Psychology* 47 (1956): 163–174 and 259–270.

13. Goodnow, J. J., "Determinants of choice-distribution in two-choice situations," *American Journal of Psychology* 68 (1955): 106–116.

14. *Ibid.,* 193.

15. Featherstone, Joseph, "The Primary School revolution in Britain," reprint of three articles in *The New Republic,* Washington, D.C., 1967.

16. Ashton-Warner, Sylvia, *Teacher* (London: Secker and Warburg, 1963).

17. Downing, John, "Self-discovery, self expression, and the self-image in the i.t.a. classroom." Claremont Reading Conference, *32nd Yearbook* (1968): 123–30.

18. Vygotsky, Lev Semenovich, *Thought and Language* (Cambridge, Mass.: M. I. T. Press, 1962).

19. Of course, Vygotsky's *Thought and Language* is now over 30 years old in Russia (though only 5 years old in its English translation). However, these principles have been followed through in later work in Russian educational and psychological research. For example, there are the more recent writings of Elkonin.

20. Almy, Millie C., "Young children's thinking and the teaching of reading." In Frost, Joe L. (ed.) *Issues and Innovations in the teaching of Reading,* (Chicago: Scott, Foresman, 1967).

21. Editor's note: This article is the review of the literature on this problem which led up to Dr. Downing's own research on children's thinking in learning to read. His findings are given in the following research reports: John Downing, "Children's concepts of language in learning to read," *Educational Research* 12 (1970): 106–112; and "The development of linguistic concepts in children's thinking," *Research in the Teaching of English* 4 (1970): 5–19.

Lois Fair Wilson

# The British Infant School:
# A Model for Early Childhood Education

> It takes a lot of courage to teach this way. *(a headmistress)*
>
> Children become responsible for their own actions. Children can learn to become independent. *(a teacher)*
>
> In an integrated program you can do everything and by the end of the year children have so much more. *(a teacher)*
>
> I like to work this way. You can have more fun with the kids. *(a teacher)*
>
> If I don't know each child well, then I know the school population is getting too big. *(a headmistress)*

Such comments are among some of those made to us by British educators during a recent visit to England where my husband and I visited primary schools in London, Dursingham, Chertsey, and in Leichestershire County.

My first acquaintance with the British primary schools came from reading a series of three articles by Joseph Featherstone published in *The New Republic* in the early fall of 1967 (1, 2, 3). In these articles Featherstone describes the educational reforms which he labels as "a revolution in British primary education." Because of the discovery of these and, subsequently, other articles describing innovations in British primary education, my husband and I arranged to talk to British educators and to visit in primary schools as a part of an educational research project in Western Europe.

The British primary school is an institution organized for children between the ages of five and eleven, or if there is a nursery class, three and eleven. The school is divided into separate infant and junior departments.

123

The infant school includes children from five through seven in age. The junior school includes the eight to eleven age group. Recently, eight-year-olds have been included in some infant school programs. Each department has its own head teacher and is housed in a separate building or separate floor if both units are included in the same building.

The number of children attending an infant school averages around 240. The average number attending the junior school is three hundred. Thirty-five to forty children are found in most classrooms. Most classes have one teacher although in some situations auxiliary teachers move from room to room to assist in the classroom setting. The head teacher continues in the role of teacher and moves in and out of classrooms serving as another adult available to help children.

Certain areas in Britain have become identified as exemplary in reflecting modern school programs. Schools in these areas tend to provide direction and models for change throughout the nation. Many of these schools have been visited by American educators who have written about their observations. (Please see references 4 through 17.) Such reports continue to appear in current professional journals.

Interest and concern about the British primary school revolution appear to be increasing on the American professional scene. British educators are serving as resource personnel in workshops and study groups throughout the United States. National and regional conferences concerned with curriculum and learning have included sections dealing with the British primary school. Educational study tours to Europe include scheduled visits to British primary schools. Some groups are scheduled only in the British Isles, spending the entire period learning more about British education.

The growing interest of American educators in the development of British primary programs appears to be influencing the pattern of some school programs in the United States. Several of the present Follow-Through models recommended to follow Head Start are based upon the British Infant model (18, 19). In recommending changes in elementary education in the United States, Charles Silberman presents a case for the new British primary schools as a desirable alternative to present classroom learning conditions (20). The labels of "open classroom," "open school," and "open education" used in describing modern English schools appeal to a growing number of American educators as a way of providing a learning climate relevant for young children.

*Open education* is a phrase used to describe what otherwise might be termed "free day," "integrated day," "integrated curriculum," "informal classroom," "developmental classroom," or the "Leichestershire model." Ronald Barth and Charles Rathbone state that "open education has its immediate roots in England" and that "it is a way of thinking about children, learning and knowledge" (21).

The *integrated day* may be described as a school day which is combined into a whole and has the minimum of scheduling. Within this day
there is time and opportunity in a planned educative environment for the
social, intellectual, emotional, physical, and aesthetic growth of the child
at his own rate of development.

Individualization is a natural product of an environment where children are free to move to centers containing a variety of learning materials
which stimulate interest and assist children in finding answers to their
questions. A fascinating account of the development of the concept of the
integrated day is presented by Mary Brown and Norman Precious in *The
Integrated Day in the Primary School.* In the introduction they state, "Here
there is an integration of the child's experience and learning which may be
within the framework of an integrated week or even within the whole of the
child's life in primary education" (22).

State schools in England are identified as the tax supported schools
which most children attend. Compulsory education begins at age five. Five
year olds might join other five year olds in a single classroom with one
teacher or might become a part of a larger grouping of five year olds with
team teachers. Often they would join a group including sixes and sevens
who had been together the previous year.

In one of our visits we saw four rooms for five year olds with different
kinds of materials in each room, such as paint, clay, books, sand, floor
blocks, Wendy house (home center), and materials for water play. Every
morning each child chose the room in which he wished to begin. He was
free to move to another room whenever he chose to do so. The four teachers
decided which rooms they would be responsible for each day. In the hall,
separating these rooms, was a table with milk. Throughout the morning we
saw one or more children stop at the table and serve themselves. More than
one head teacher stated that since children's nutritional needs differed, milk
was available throughout the morning as not all children were ready for or
needed milk at the same time.

*Family grouping* is the term used for vertical or multi-age grouping.
Family grouping has been most common in infant school organization but
is now appearing in junior schools. In an infant school where family grouping occurs, a child may remain in the same class, with the same teacher,
for the whole period of his infant school life. Entering with a few (perhaps
five to eight newcomers) a child joins a class which already contains ten to
twelve children of six years of age and ten to twelve children seven years
of age. If a child does not seem to be developing in one classroom setting,
the head teacher may place him in another with a similar physical environment but containing other children of various ages serving as peers and
models.

Ridgeway and Lawton describe family grouping in the primary school as giving children a valuable sense of security and stability. They suggest that the teacher develops a deeper quality of insight into the all-around development and character of the children which springs from two to three years of close and intimate association (23).

In our visits to infant schools we saw family grouping, integrated programs, and integrated days. We saw children learning to read, to write, and working with numbers. We saw children working alone or in small groups, in measuring, weighing, estimating, and computing. We saw children recording their findings in individual math booklets. We saw children writing stories or developing reports in individual writing booklets. We saw children painting, engaged in art activities, using tools and lumber, building with blocks, tending pets and cooking. Ongoing science projects and investigations were in evidence. Children moved around the room freely interacting with others.

There was little organized activity for a whole class to do together other than a religious assembly required by law in which the total school participates. Even that period is changing. In many schools head teachers have chosen to make this a time for children to come together to share class activities, to talk together about special events or concerns, or to enjoy a special program together.

Upon entering classrooms it sometimes took time to locate the teachers in them. Teachers moved about the rooms, sitting with groups of children to help as needed, listening to children read, answering questions, supplying the spelling of words for writing, talking to children and helping students with their projects.

Many hallways were used as extended classrooms where children painted, measured, developed large murals, maps and graphs. Tables were available for collections of shells, seeds, and plants. Carts with cooking and science materials, available to several classrooms, were often stored in the hall. Stoves for cooking were available in most infant schools.

In an assembly room in one of the schools in Leichestershire County, we saw a number of shops or businesses set up by children of each class group; a grocery store, a card shop, a barber shop, a bakery, a florist shop. The head teacher explained that on certain days all children moved into the area to work in their establishments as a market day, to buy and to sell. Later, each class decided how to improve its own enterprise. A sale, a special, a closeout with hopes of opening a new business became important aspects of planning for the next business day. Here children learned to use play money for counting and making change, as well as learning about profit and loss.

Throughout our visits we found the rooms fairly noisy. American writers indicate that such rooms reflect a noise level higher than many American principals or teachers would allow. With as many as thirty-five to forty in some classes rooms are crowded. Children's voices, sounds of blocks, water play, and the sound of moving chairs and equipment, all reflected the noise of children's involvement in active learning.

Activities are set for a limited number of children. Around the room are tables for different kinds of activities: art, reading, writing, mathematics, science. The mathematics tables have number lines taped down each side which children use as they learn to count and reason mathematically. Buttons, beads, a collection of things to count, sort, classify and label are available at the mathematics area. Usually each classroom has measuring sets for dry and liquid measuring, weights and balances. A rich variety of materials is available for learning basic mathematics concepts. Some of these materials are commercial, some are teacher made. This description is more fully developed in Joseph Featherstone's presentation of "The Primary School Revolution in Britain, Schools for Children," *The New Republic,* August 2, 1967.

Practical application of mathematics principles is stressed rather than formal arithmetic. The British publication, *Mathematics in the Primary School* (24), and the Nuffield Mathematics booklets (25) provide teacher help and direction for meaningful activities. Work cards or directional cards are placed in the math center by the teacher and are used by children to provide guidance for the mathematics work for the day whether it be estimating, measuring, weighing, graphing, or practical computation relating to ongoing projects. Children record their findings in their own math booklets which also serve as a record of their work.

Our visits included a range of British infant schools and they all reflected the same kinds of open programs described in both American and British literature. How common such programs for young children might be throughout Britain still remains a question. In the preface to *Teaching in the British Primary School,* Vincent Rogers indicates that about twenty-five percent of Britain's primary schools fit the model described in this book. Perhaps, he states, forty percent can be described as quite traditional. Nevertheless, he concluded, twenty-five percent is a significant number of schools, when one looks at the total size of the educational enterprise in Britain. Even more significant, he feels, is the obvious movement toward this kind of education among the schools not included among the twenty-five percent (26).

*Children and Their Primary Schools,* Volumes I and II, more commonly known as the Plowden Report, is one of the most comprehensive on the British primary educational reforms. The study for the Plowden Report began in 1963 when the Central Advisory Council for Education (England) was asked by the Minister of Education to consider the whole subject of primary education and the transition to secondary education. Volume I includes the findings and recommendations of the Council. Volume II consists of accounts of surveys and research commissioned at the request of the Department of Education and Science (27, 28).

The Plowden Report indicates the major bodies of research dominating primary school program development are associated with the theories of Baldwin, Isaccs, Luria, Bruner, and, in particular, Piaget. The report considers their research as setting the "ground plan in the growth of intellectual powers and the order in which they are acquired."

Piaget's research influenced recommendations included in an earlier report of 1931 on the status of education with recommendations for future change. This report, known as the Hadow Report, was the force influencing the Education Act of 1944 which drew attention to the importance of the environment as a major learning factor. Schools were empowered to provide an environment in which children could grow imaginatively as well as intellectually.

The Plowden Report, published in 1968, emphasizes the value of the relation of learning and experience with the concrete in the school environment. The report interprets the application of Piaget's theories to learning by stating:

> One of its most important conclusions is that the great majority of primary school children can only learn efficiently from concrete situations, as lived and described. From these situations, children acquire concepts from every area of the curriculum. According to Piaget, all learning calls for organization of material or of behavior on the part of the learner, and the learner has to adapt himself and is altered in the process. Learning takes place through a continuous process of interaction between the learner and his environment, which results in the building up of consistent and stable patterns of behavior, physical and mental. Each new experience reorganizes, however slightly, the structure of the mind and contributes to the child's world picture. Piaget's thought which influenced the 1931 Report and our own, is not easy to understand. It is almost impossible to express in other than technical terms. Although he is not primarily an educationalist, his work has important implications for teachers. His observations of the sequence in the development of children's concepts are being tested on samples of children in many countries and these tests are tending to confirm his main findings. Much more investigation is needed on the extent to which the school environment and the guidance of teaching provided by teachers can accelerate children's progress. The effect of social expectations on the way children learn also calls for study. Nevertheless Piaget's explanations appear to most educationalists in this country to fit the observed facts of children's learning more satisfactorily than any other (29).

For a more detailed analysis of the use of the implication of Piaget's research in the development of experiences in the English primary school reference is made to Leonard Marsh's sensitive report on British education, *Alongside the Child.* (30) Marsh analyzes the stages of thought as developed by Piaget with implications for learning. He places significant value on the relation of language and the role of the teacher in helping the child to develop and use appropriate language to accompany the activities in his daily school life.

Celia Stendler Lavitelli, an American educator, applies Piaget's theory of cognitive development to the kinds of education possible for young children in the United States. In an analysis of contrasting views of early childhood education she describes the British infant school as a positive force influencing program development in the United States. She begins her description by stating, "A movement that does recognize the value of play is attracting considerable attention on this side of the Atlantic at the present time is that of the British Infant School"(31). She compares the British infant school to the child-centered nursery schools in the United States. The difference she feels is that there is more emphasis upon cognitive learnings, and more materials provided in British schools that will encourage cognitive learning. The structure of the British school and choice of activities provide for more opportunities to acquire concepts in math, science, reading, and writing skills. Vertical or family grouping, open-ended materials, and the choices available to children free them to use the environment as they wish.

In considering the focus on informality, open-endedness, discovery, and freedom in the modern British schools, questions such as these might be asked: "Is this possible in classrooms in the United States?" "What really makes the difference in learning for the young child?" "What difference does the role of the teacher make in the kind of learning environment provided for child interaction?" "With the increased emphasis upon testing and accountability dare we allow open programs to develop?" "What are our alternatives?"

Under the present pressure to produce results we might stop to ponder the significance of the Chinese proverb included on the title page of the first volume of the British Nuffield mathematics material:

I hear, and I forget
I see, and I remember
I do, and I understand.

## References

1. Featherstone, Joseph, "The Primary School Revolution in Britain, How Children Learn," *The New Republic* (September 2, 1967).

2. ———, "The Primary School Revolution in Britain, Schools for Children," *The New Republic* (August 19, 1967).

3. ———, "The Primary School Revolution in Britain, Teaching Children to Think," *The New Republic* (September 9, 1967).

4. Barth, Ronald, "Teaching, the Way It Is, the Way It Could Be," *Grade Teacher* (January 1970).

5. ———, "When Children Enjoy School, Some Lessons from Britain," *Childhood Education* (January 1970).

6. ———, and Charles Rathbone, "The Open School: A Way of Thinking About Children, Learning and Knowledge," *The Center Forum* (July 1969).

7. Cazden, Courtney B., *Infant School* (Education Development Center, Newton, 1969).

8. Cohen, David K., "Children and Their Primary Schools: Vol. II," *Harvard Educational Review* (Spring, 1968).

9. Cook, Ann, and Herbert Mack, "The British Primary School," *Educational Leadership* (November 1969): 140–143.

10. Featherstone, Joseph, "Report Analysis of Children and Their Primary Schools," *Harvard Educational Review* (September 1969): 317–328.

11. Gross, Beatrice, and Ronald Gross, "A Little Bit of Chaos." *Saturday Review* (May 19, 1970): 71–85.

12. Horn, Solomon, "Reading Activities in English Primary Schools," *The Reading Teacher* (October, 1969): 23–26.

13. Hull, W. P., "Leichestershire Revisited," *Occasional Paper #1* (Education Development Center, Newton, 1969).

14. Rogers, Vincent R., "English and American Primary Schools," *Phi Delta Kappan* (October 1969): 71–75.

15. Ulin, Donald S., "What I Learned from the British Schools," *Grade Teacher* (February 1969): 100–103, 194–197.

16. Villet, Barbara, "The Children Want Classrooms with Chaos." *Life* (April 11, 1969): 50–56.

17. Weber, Lillian, "English Infant Schools," *The Center Forum* (New York, July 1969): 8–12.

18. Armington, David, "A Plan for Continuing Growth," *Follow-Through Program Approaches* (Washington, March, 1962).

19. Cawthorne, John, and Kenneth W. Haskins, "The Morgan Community School Follow Through Program," *Follow Through Program Approaches* (Washington, March, 1962).

20. Silberman, Charles E., *Crisis in the Classroom* (Random House, 1970), 208–264.

21. Barth, Ronald, and Charles H. Rathbone (No. 6), op. cit., 1.

22. Brown, Mary, and Norman Precious, *The Integrated Day in the Primary School* (London, 1968).

23. Ridgeway, Lorna, and Irene Lawton, *Family Grouping in the Primary School* (London: The Trinity Press, 1968).

24. School Council for the Curriculum and Examinations, *Mathematics in Primary Schools* (London, 1966).

25. Nuffield Mathematics Project, *I Do and I Understand, Beginnings (1), Mathematics Begins (1), Pictorial Representation (2), Computation and Structure (2) (3), Shape and Size (2) (3)* (W. R. Chambers and John Murray, 1967).

26. Rogers, Vincent R., *Teaching in the Primary School* (Collier-Mcmillan Canada, Ltd., 1970), p. x.

27. Department of Education and Science, *Children and Their Primary Schools, Volume I: The Report* (London, 1967).

28. ———, *Children and Their Primary Schools, Volume II: Research and Summary* (London, 1967).

29. ———, (No. 27) op. cit., pp. 192–193.

30. Marsh, Leonard, *Alongside the Child: Experiences in the English Primary School* (Praeger Publishers, 1970).

31. Lavitelli, Celia Stendler, *Piaget's Theory Applied to an Early Childhood Curriculum* (American Science and Engineering, Inc., 1940), 20–24.

R. Van Allen

*Bring Your Own: An Invitation to All Children to*
*Bring Their Personal Language to School*

Give me your tired, your poor,
Your huddled masses yearning to breathe free,
The wretched refuse of your teeming shore,
Send these, the homeless, tempest-tossed to me:
I lift my lamp beside the golden door.

From *The Collossus*
by Emma Lazarus

By the year 1876, the United States of America had achieved already —in 100 years of history as a nation—a reputation of broad acceptance which inspired the people of France to give us a memorial, the Statue of Liberty. Emma Lazarus wrote the fitting message which I have just read, a message which continues to have meaning today as we seek to conquer new frontiers through education and creative living.

The masses came to our shores seeking refuge from oppression and deprivation. During the succeeding almost 100 years they have found that religious oppression and physical deprivation is closely akin to what is coming to be called "educational deprivation." Generation after generation of some of our families has failed to move into the mainstream of American society, not because there were no jobs or any opportunities, but because they were unprepared to do the jobs which were available. They have lacked the skills which our society had hoped to provide through its public schools. Many *have* succeeded! But too many have failed. Simple literacy as conceived and implemented in most of our common schools has passed too many children by. Fortunately, we have not given up our hope for freedom for all. We still value what is inscribed on the Statue of Liberty, but we are beginning to say in many ways that what is said there is not enough.

132

Today a new memorial is being erected across our nation. In thousands of communities across America there is an open invitation to

—the culturally different

—the language disadvantaged

—the economically deprived

—the retarded

—the handicapped

—the academically talented (but often ignored)

—and in some places the *poor in spirit*

to join in the mainstream of American life in meaningful and satisfying ways.

We are saying to children and to adults in new and creative ways, "Bring what you have, limited as it may seem to you and to us. We are now prepared to accept you as a learner if you want to learn. We are ready to adjust our school curriculum and our instructional materials in a thousand ways to meet your varying needs. We are willing to listen for clues which will help us individualize instruction for you, and we are willing to wait for personal commitments from you to guide us into next steps in the great adventure of learning. *Bring your own language! It is good enough for a beginning!*

"We are ready to help you learn to talk about anything you can think about or anything which interests you.

"We know how to write anything you can say and can help you learn to write it by yourself.

"Anything we write we can read to you, and we can help you learn how to read anything you can write.

"After you can read the things you can write, we will help you to read what other people have written for you to read.

"As you read the stories, books, and poems of many authors, you will be influenced by their ideas and their language to such an extent that your own thinking and your own language will reflect that influence.

"With basic tools of reading and writing you can enter into the mainstream of American education and gain a measure of personal freedom which is forever denied those who cannot communicate their own ideas effectively and interact with the great ideas of the present and past."

For thirty-three years the leadership of the Claremont Reading Conference has been issuing this kind of invitation to *all* the children of *all* the people. With tenacity this leadership has held to certain truths as the rights of all our children:

—that they should be helped to make discriminating responses to their total environment, not just the world of print;

—that the resources of all professional persons in a community should be integrated into educational efforts;

—that no uniform material or standard method will meet the wide range of needs in any given learning situation;

—that no administrative organization is sufficient in itself to assure success for every child;

—that "instant remedies" have never had enduring effects;

—that every teacher needs professional and personal preparation in order to view each child and diagnose his needs;

—that the precise efficiency of industrial assembly lines has never proved to be an efficient way to deal with human beings;

—that the multitude of materials which suggest that education can be acquired by learning answers to questions which can be printed and distributed to the learners is no substitute for a sensitive teacher.

As I have attended the Claremont Reading Conference for the past ten years, I have been challenged to re-think the *truth for me* about the place of

—basic textbooks

—ability grouping within the classroom

—self-contained classrooms

—*sequence of skill development* as a valid way of thinking about the reading curriculum

—remedial classes

—use of standardized tests to determine individual needs and abilities

—use of workbooks for follow-up activities in reading and language instruction

and dozens of other well-worn and time-tested ideas which have come to be accepted by those of us who fail to make discriminating responses to the educational environment in which we live and work.

As I have searched out the *truth for me* over the years, I have come to view reading instruction as an act of raising levels of sensitivity of each child to the world in which he lives. With this simple and broad definition of reading, I am able to invite every child, regardless of whether his language is fluent or faulty, into our classrooms on an equal basis. This is because my goals are not those of achieving uniformity, but goals of leading each child to

—see things he has never seen before;

—hear things he has never heard before;

—have deeper feelings about himself and others;

—observe something unusual in the usual things around him and to say usual things in unusual ways;

—look at something ordinary and see something extraordinary in it;

—discover new meanings in his surroundings;

—heighten imaginations to include the delights of songs and stories;

—express ideas in many ways—through talking, painting, writing, singing, dancing, acting;

—build language power which provides a great reservoir of words to express ideas clearly and beautifully;

—enjoy studies of English as a language;

—embrace as one's own, ideas and language of great authors.

Are such goals feasible? Can they be implemented in classrooms with a wide-range of abilities? Is it possible to conceptualize reading instruction within a rationale that values divergent-type thinking as much as it values convergent-type thinking? Can *any* teacher join the host that is now saying, "Bring your own language—what you have. I'll accept *it* as much as I accept *you* as a person?"

The answer to all the questions is "YES." Numerous studies have followed wide-spread exploration of what we now call a language-experience approach in reading instruction.* These studies have validated much of what was believed to be true about reading instruction which uses as a basic framework a statement of twenty language experiences which centered in school districts in San Diego County, California, and which have been reported from time to time at the Claremont Reading Conference since 1956. As described in recent publications, including *Language Experiences in Reading, Level I,* the framework forms a rationale for the selection of activities and materials which contribute to a balanced development of communication skills and attitudes (1). These language experiences can be viewed as having three major emphases with sub-topics under each:

*Studies sponsored by the U.S. Office of Education which include a language-experience approach: San Diego County, California, Mr. William Kendrick, Director; Colorado State Department of Education, Denver, Mr. Roy McCanne, Director; Oakland County, Pontiac, Michigan, Dr. Harry Hahn, Director; University of Pittsburgh, Pittsburgh, Dr. Donald Cleland, Director; University of Delaware, Newark, Dr. Russell Stauffer, Director.

*Group One:* Extending Experiences with Words

1. *Sharing experiences*—the ability to tell, write, or illustrate something on a purely personal basis.
2. *Discussing experiences*—the ability to interact with what other people say and write.
3. *Listening to stories*—the ability to hear what others have to say through books and to relate ideas to one's own experiences.
4. *Telling stories*—the ability to organize one's thinking so that it can be shared orally or in writing in a clear and interesting manner.
5. *Dictating words, sentences, and stories*—the ability to choose from all that might be said orally the most important part for someone else to write and read.
6. *Writing independently*—the ability to record one's own ideas and present them in a form for others to read.
7. *Authoring individual books*—the ability to organize one's ideas into a sequence, illustrate them, and make them into books.

*Group Two:* Studying the English Language

1. *Conceptualizing the relationship of speaking, writing, and reading*—the ability to conceptualize, through extensive practice, that reading is the interpretation of speech that has been written and then must be reconstructed, orally or silently.
2. *Expanding vocabulary*—the ability to expand one's listening, speaking, reading, and writing (including spelling) vocabulary.
3. *Reading a variety of symbols*—the ability to read in one's total environment such things as the clock, calendar, dials, thermometer.
4. *Developing awareness of common vocabulary*—the ability to recognize that our language contains many common words and patterns of expression that must be mastered for sight reading and correct spelling when expressing one's ideas in writing.
5. *Improving style and form*—the ability to profit from listening to, reading, and studying the style of well-written material.
6. *Studying words*—the ability to pronounce and understand words and spell them correctly in written activities.

*Group Three:* Relating Author's Ideas to Personal Experiences

1. *Reading whole stories and books*—the ability to read books for information, pleasure, and improvement of reading skills on an individual basis.
2. *Using a variety of resources*—the ability to find and use many resources in expanding vocabulary, improving oral and written expression, and sharing ideas.

3.  *Comprehending what is read*—the ability, through oral and written activities, to gain skill in following directions, understanding words in the context of sentences and paragraphs, reproducing the thought in a passage, reading for detail, and reading for general significance.
4.  *Summarizing*—the ability to get main impressions, outstanding ideas, or some details of what has been read or heard.
5.  *Organizing ideas and information*—the ability to use various methods of briefly restating ideas in the order in which they were written or spoken.
6.  *Integrating and assimilating ideas*—the ability to use reading and listening for personal interpretation and elaboration of concepts.
7.  *Reading critically*—the ability to determine the validity and reliability of statements.

Teachers who use this rationale in the selection of activities and materials do not make the recognition of words or portions of words a crucial issue in early reading experiences. Rather, they see in this rationale an opportunity to invite children to mature their language as they

—tell something on a purely personal basis through talking with whatever language they possess, painting to express any idea they may possess, writing in ways that are meaningful to them, and saying things in any way so that people share their ideas;

—talk with others about topics of current interest, agreeing and disagreeing, liking and disliking, accepting, and rejecting, altering ideas and prior information, and building interests in pursuing a topic further;

—listen to the way hundreds of authors say things through stories, books, and poems, and be influenced to increase the ways to express personal ideas;

—tell stories heard and ones which are composed out of real experiences or imagination;

—add words, phrases, and sentences to paintings and drawings;

—experience the thrill of authorship of many books which contain their own ideas—written and illustrated;

—study the language we call English—its alphabet, its sounding patterns, its idiomatic expressions, its modification systems, its phonetic systems, its variety of sentence patterns;

—recognize that all persons who speak English use many of the same words they use when they talk and write;

—adjust their style and form in writing as a result of hearing and seeing the many ways people say things effectively;

—expand their vocabulary daily as they listen, read, and observe;

—gather impressions, general ideas, and details from what they hear, read, and observe;

—lift their soul and mind into flights of fancy with great authors;

—relate the experiences of authors to their own experiences—joy, sorrow, anger, bewilderment, facts, fiction, dreams, achievements, hope for a better world.

This invitation may appear to be a long one, but it is a simple one; it may appear to require wisdom, but it requires much more of faith and lovingness than of wisdom; it requires much more of self-commitment than of lessons completed.

Each person, alone, must develop inner resources with which he can make choices about himself and reading. Choices may become automatic, but they have been made—or a lifelong experience with reading or a lifelong struggle against reading. To be able to read and not choose reading may be a far greater tragedy than not being able to read at all. Positive attitudes generated by acceptance and involvement of one's own language and success in using that *improving language* day-by-day and year-by-year is to assure for each of us *reading beyond literacy!*

## References

1. Allen, Roach Van and Claryce Allen, *Language Experiences in Reading, Level I* (Chicago: Encyclopaedia Britannica Press, 1966), 6–7.

# Vision
# and
# Listening:
# Seeing
# and
# Hearing

Peter L. Spencer

# Reading, the Visual Process

*Varied Concepts of the Reading Process.*    The Claremont Reading Conference has presented, illustrated, and applied through the years a more tenable conception of the reading process than is customarily considered. The usual idea of reading conceives of it as being a special type of learned behavior which is used mainly, if not exclusively, when one is responding to visual stimulation by means of printed words. This conference considers that such a narrow and restrictive notion of the reading process is psychologically unsound and educationally inadequate. Throughout its history this conference has identified reading as being the perceptual process which occurs whenever one experiences any kind of sensory stimulation and makes an adaptive response thereto.

*We read many things.*    Printed words normally activate a reading behavior, but so do spoken words, gestures, and innumerable other sorts of stimuli. Hence, restricting the consideration of reading to a single type of stimulation distorts one's ideas of the process and of its occurrence and functioning in human behavior. Everything of human concern will be read. But, it needs to be read in perspective. The relationships among various applications of the reading process need to be recognized and utilized advantageously.

*Reading is done with each of our sensory processes.*    It is important to recognize that the visual process is merely one of the many sensory processes with which human reading is accomplished. Furthermore, it seems highly improbable that any human sensory process ever operates singly. We are equipped with many sensory processes. They complement each other. Each contributes its special part to a common perceptual (reading) process wherein sensory impulses are given meaning and significance. It is entirely proper within such a setting to "read the visual process" in an attempt to determine its nature and its uses.

*The visual process is activated by Light.* The visual process is adapted to stimulation by a very narrow band of energy waves which we call *light.* The boundary lines separating this light-band from other energy waves are determined more by the nature of our visual receptors than they are by the nature of the energy pattern of our environment. The variability of the energy waves of our environment appears to be continuous. We are equipped by nature to sense only limited portions of that continuum. However, by ingenious use of instruments we have learned how to contact waves beyond our native sensitivity and to use them in our reading. For example, the waves which transmit our television communications, x-rays, infra-red and ultra-violet are commonly used to produce "readable" phenomena.

*Reading the light stimulus.* Reading the visual process may reasonably begin with the reading of the light stimulus which normally initiates the process of seeing. Since there is a range in the quality of light extending from violet to red, inclusive, we should expect to find visibility affected by variations within that range. Visibility or "seeability" is dynamically affected by them. Most of us have experienced striking changes in visibility under stimulation by so-called "black light" (ultra-violet radiation). Certain objects which appear very drab and unattractive when viewed under ordinary light become brilliant and beautiful when viewed under ultra-violet "light." In like manner some of us have noticed the difference in visibility of an auto when viewed under sunlight and when seen under mercury-vapor illumination. There are many interesting and important aspects of visibility as it is affected by chromatic factors. While it may be strictly a matter of visibility the whole question of chromo-therapy is properly included under reading the light source. However, space does not permit its being discussed here.

*Most visual reading is done by reflected light.* By far the greatest amount of visual stimulation is accomplished by reflected light, and not by light directly from a luminous source. The sun is, of course, our greatest source of light. However, little is seen by viewing it directly. Since man has become able to produce light from sources under his control, he does have a problem in the use of *direct lighting.* A striking example of this is the use of head lights on automobiles. The riders behind those lights view things only by *reflected light.* But, the people and animals upon whom the light is directed see it in a far different manner. While viewing the light only as reflected produces comfort and clarity of sight, those who must view it directly are often discomforted and even blinded by it. Surely, this is an aspect of reading the visual process which needs to be better understood and more effectively utilized for the sake of safety on our roads.

*Conflicting light sources give trouble.*    There are many other aspects of this phase of visibility which need educational consideration. We shall mention one which is all too often ignored or improperly treated. It is the matter of classroom illumination. Proportionately too much concern is commonly given to the amount or intensity of light which is present in the room and too little concern is given to how that light actually affects the sight process. For example, in visual reading the eyes are affected by the light which is *reflected from the target source.* This may be quite different from the amount of light which falls upon that target. Some targets *absorb* a large amount of the light which strikes them. Hence, very little is *reflected* for use in seeing. Other targets *reflect* light in such a manner that glare is produced making the discrimination of the details of the target difficult, if not actually impossible. It is important that we be concerned with the amount of *usable* light which is reflected from the target to the eye of the seer.

The eye may be and all too often is affected by other light than that which the target reflects. This may and often does greatly increase the effort needed to see the target. This condition prevails in far too many classrooms. It may be due to light coming through the windows or to improper place-ment or functioning of the luminaries. It is not uncommon to experience bright light within the field of sight and in opposition to the light which is being reflected from the target of regard. This obviously unhygienic visual situation is far too prevalent in visual reading situations. The discomfort experienced and the extra effort expended in visually reading under such circumstances dynamically affects that process. The elimination of glare and of conflicting directional light stimuli could add much to the effective-ness of the light stimulus for visual reading. These simple illustrations are sufficient to indicate that there is need to read better the light stimulus which makes visual reading possible. It is light which initiates the visual reading process. It can be used effectively or otherwise.

*Characteristics of the target affect its readability.*    Of course, what is sighted is the target which light reveals. All targets occur as figure-ground relationships. Part of the act of visual reading is that of determining what the target is. This requires that the situations as sensed be structured and that the target of regard be differentiated from the rest of the situation within which it occurs. Obviously, this structuring process is not solely a function of the light stimulus. It is also a function of the nature of the target itself. The mere act of sensing may be identical for a poorly revealed target and for one that is clearly and readily structured. But, the readiness with which reading is done is certainly facilitated by the clarity of the target pattern.

*Clarity of structural pattern of target is important.*    Disregard for the inherent or structural qualities which facilitate the target's being visually sensed is distressingly common in our society. One illustration of pressing importance is targets naming the streets in our cities. The poor readability of street name-signs is so evident and so freighted with potential hazard that one wonders at the common tolerance of the condition. With modern transportation there is need to see and to read readily the name of a street at least a full block distant. There is pressing need for, at least, comparable visibility in this regard at night. Does anyone know of a community which is equipped with such readable signs?

*Visibility of targets often obstructed.*    The sight of street signs and of other things to be visually read is often obstructed by extraneous objects such as poles, shrubbery, other signs, etc. If we were truly concerned for the visual reading of essential traffic guides, we would apply what we know regarding readability and thereby make life on our streets easier and more secure.

*Targets should be both visible and readable.*    The structural pattern of a visual target should be readily sensed. Extensive study of this matter as regards the format and typographical aspects of printing have been reported. Such factors as the size and shape of letters, spacing between letters, words and lines, contrast between print and the paper on which it is printed and numerous other aspects of this concern have been investigated. However, the findings have all too often been disregarded. A case in point is the license plates for automobiles. Since much of the reading of such things needs to be done rapidly and under poor visibility, one would suppose that care would be exercised to pattern them to facilitate accurate reading. However, it is extremely difficult to determine whether the letter O or Q is used in many of the new California license plates.

*The target and the light source which reveals it are peripheral to sight.* While we have not treated exhaustively the peripheral aspects of the visual process we have tried to point out their importance and to call attention to the fact that they are commonly ignored or improperly used. If we wish to perform visual reading efficiently, there certainly is need to attend to the matter of adequate lighting and to the providing of readable visual targets.

*The eye is the visual receptor; the organ of sight.*    There is need to distinguish clearly between mere sensitivity to light and the process of visual perception. As Edgar Dale has pointed out, the major function of education is that of "changing mere sensitivity into sensibility." That the process of producing "sensibility" is not perfectly and positively correlated with sensory efficiency is readily evident. However, this does not imply that sensory efficiency is not important. It does indicate, that more than sensory efficiency is involved in visual reading.

*The process of seeing has kinesthetic aspects.*    As mentioned previously, it seems doubtful that any sensory process operates wholly independently of other sensory processes in our body. This is well illustrated in the operation of the sight receptor.

The eyeball contains two sets of muscles which are of major importance in producing acuity of sight reception. These are the sphincters which control the pupillary opening and those which operate the lens. There are also external muscles which are attached to the eyeball and which form a suspensory net within which the eye rests. These are the muscles by means of which the eye is aimed at the target and held steady for a fixation or moved in pursuit as the case may be. Reading the eye as the receptor of light and the organ of sight entails among other things consideration of the operation of these muscle systems.

*The sphincter muscles are mainly controlled automatically.*    While the performance of the sphincter muscles which control the pupillary opening is probably not directly modifiable through learning, there certainly is need for reading it. Unless the pupillary organ is functioning properly sight will be impaired. Many have experienced this when ocular practitioners have placed drops in their eyes causing the pupils to dilate. Others have noted the same effect indirectly by observing how photographs may be affected by too little or too much light. Note the care with which the skilled photographer measures the light conditions and adjusts the camera mechanism to cope with it. Comparable noting and adjusting is normally accomplished intuitively in human seeing.

Dilation of the pupillary opening may be produced systemically by means of certain drugs or other toxic factors. The resulting impairment of the sight process may be a matter of concern. Reading the pupils of the eyes may reveal to the observer some important information concerning the fitness for visual reading. Thus we sense another facet to the message normally implied by the statement, "Every teacher should become pupil conscious." Seers also need to realize that their eyes are affected by their body states.

The sphincters which control the operation of the lens serve to adapt the focal length of the eye as an organ of sight. While these adaptive adjustments are largely controlled intuitively, there does appear to be a considerable potential for learning as well. The matter of facile adjustment for seeing far and near targets is extremely important for many visual reading tasks. There is need for providing for systematic development of this ability.

*The external muscles are largely controlled by the voluntary system.*    The major function of the external muscles is that of turning the eye so that it is aimed at the target of regard. *This is no small matter!* When one realizes that the pupillary opening is commonly small, and that the image for printed words should fall upon an area about as large as the head of a common pin, the matter of properly aiming the eye commands respect. The matter of holding the eye in proper position for seeing as well as that of moving it either in pursuit movement or the saccadic action used in reading printed words is not a simple task.

*Muscles are response organs.* Muscles are reactors. They do what they are told to do. Hence the matter of producing the requisite neural instructions to produce effective movement of stabilized fixation is one of primary importance. Difficulties in performance with eye movements are more likely to be due to improper neural controls than they are so-called "muscle imbalances." Learning how to see is an important educational accomplishment.

*Sight is not the same as Vision.* It is important that we distinguish between the process of visual reception (sight) and the process of visual perception. Sight is semi-peripheral to vision. Sight initiates the visual process. Sight is "what goes on in the eyes" and what the eyes send on to the brain. Vision or visual perception is what the brain makes of the sight impulses together with comparable impulses from other sensory processes, from memory images, and from the seers purposes and personal characteristics. Visual perception is a creative process. It is not a mechanical one. Efficient seeing assists that process but it does not determine it.

*Metabolism factors in the visual process.* The holistic principle that the body functions as a whole is an important one to recognize. The neural processes need to be fed and cared for just as does any other function of the body. Recent emphasis upon the functional metabolism of the synapse has great significance for visual reading.

*Facile recall is essential for efficient reading.* It appears that the nervous system has a built-in provision for memory. Whatever is experienced apparently leaves its impression. But, tapping that impression for use when it is desired is not so readily assured. We need to find ways in which "to put handles on" memories so that they may be brought effectively into perceptive use. Knowing something which one cannot recall is disturbing and is not helpful.

*There is need for the development of the field of EDUCATIONAL OP-TICS.* The field of visual sensing and its related processes has been studied from many points of view. Much is known concerning the physics of optics, somewhat less is known of physiological optics, still less is known of psychological optics. But the field of Educational Optics which has to do with developing efficient seers and efficient visual perceivers is far behind the other phases of this knowledge. The education profession has been remiss in not attacking this aspect of reading development more effectively. Reading the visual process has not received the attention that it needs. However, much more is known about it than is currently applied. Efficient visual performance is an educational accomplishment. It is not an endowment. It is a development which must be achieved by systematic learning and practice. There is need for a VISION EDUCATION program at all levels of our educational offering.

Andrew Wilkinson

# Listening and the Discriminative Response

The context in which listening is to be discussed here is one in which the study of linguistics—and perhaps even more, the advent of the tape-recorder—have had a considerable effect on our thinking about the spoken language. We recognize there is no such thing as correct English or, to put it less dramatically, we recognize that there is no one correct form of English appropriate for all occasions; there are many types of spoken language and many types of written language. The context, further, in which listening is being discussed, is one in which the study of psychology and child development has made us aware of the fundamental importance of the spoken language for the growth of the human intellect and personality; and of the secondary function of the written language in this process. The implications in this connection of the findings of linguistics and psychology for education are deep and wide reaching.

However, these implications are only slowly making themselves felt—in Britain at any rate. Education is gradually breaking away from literacy as the only base; and by literacy of course we understand not just elementary reading and writing of print, but the disciplines acquired through, and developed on them. The spoken language has been neglected. There are of course historical and cultural reasons for this; they explain but do not justify. The neglect is to be discerned clearly when one comes to try to talk about the spoken language; vocabulary for even elementary features of it is lacking. One finds oneself referring to an 'illiterate speaker' as though it were his ability to read and write that one were commenting upon. Investigating speech at the University of Birmingham in England we in our research team found we had constantly to devise terms. There was even no term for the central concept—speaking and listening. We offered the word *oracy* as a parallel to literacy, with the adjective *orate,* and the opposites *inoracy* and *inorate.* Not to have a word with which to think about a concept may mean that the concept is not thought about. This has been particularly apparent in curriculum construction where syllabuses in the language arts have predominantly concerned one reception skill, reading, and one production skill, writing. This term oracy will be used in what follows.

### Register and Situation

The kind of interest in the spoken language which has been developed in recent years is not one which would have found approval in that age which refined our language, nor of that great non-relativistic linguistic philosopher Samuel Johnson. There is a magnificent passage in the preface to the great dictionary in which Johnson defends some of his omissions:

> That many terms of art and manufacture are omitted, must be frankly acknowledged; but for this defect I may boldly allege it was unavoidable; I could not visit caverns to learn the miner's language, nor take a voyage to perfect my skill in the dialect of navigation, nor visit the warehouses of merchants, and shops of artificers, to gain the name of wares, tools and operations, of which no mention is found in books; what favourable accident or easy enquiry brought within my reach, has not been neglected, but it had been a hopeless labour to glean up words by courting living information, and contesting with the sullenness of one, and the roughness of another (1).

Johnson could not, or would not 'court information', words of which no mention is found in books did not really interest him—they would probably be "sullen" or "rough" or "low" or "bad" or "barbarous"—to quote but a few of the terms of disapprobation he uses in the dictionary. Now the modern linguist is out to do the opposite—to "court living information." The "miner's language", the "dialect of navigation," the words of trade and industry interest him greatly. In the U.K. the grammar and lexis of the miner's language or of navigation, would be called the *register* of mining, or the *register* of navigation. This word *register* corresponds to some extent to the American use of "code." But the word register is not confined to the languages of trade or profession. The definition needs to be amplified by J. R. Firth's words:

> Effective action and good manners require appropriateness of language in situational context. This leads to the adoption of the notion of restricted languages. The social person collects a varied repertory of interlocking roles without conflict or serious disharmony. Such an integrated personal-

ity makes for personal and social responsibility and stability. For the purposes of linguistics such a person would be regarded as being in command of a constellation of restricted languages, satellite languages so to speak, governed by personality in social life and the general language of the community (2).

We may define *register* as the variety of English appropriate in a particular situation; appropriateness being judged by its acceptability and its effectiveness in communication.

Language implies situation. A typical language situation is one in which there is an Addressor and Addressee, there is a Subject of some kind, and there is a Context in which they are functioning. All these factors influence the language used. Today I am the Addressor, you are the Addressees, my Subject is listening, and the Context is this hall. My whole set and past history, and my present purpose, influence my language. It is influenced by my attempt to communicate with you, the assumptions I made about you, and your reactions; it is influenced by my Subject. There are certain words I must use in talking about listening, and they must be used exactly rather than loosely; it is influenced by the Context—this hall, these numbers, this occasion—it must have a certain formality; whereas if I were talking to any one of you, even on the same subject, over a glass of beer, my language would be modified accordingly.

That there are differences between the spoken and written languages is often remarked on. But in the U.K. at any rate, the implications of this are by no means realised, and educational behaviour is based on the dominance of the written language. It is necessary for my argument that I should glance briefly at some of these differences.

In a story called 'High Dive' by L. P. Hartley, the owners of a small circus, who find their audiences dwindling are delighted to find a young man who offers to dive 40 feet into a tank 8 ft long by 4 ft wide by 4 ft deep. Naturally they ask him to demonstrate. Here is how Hartley describes the scene:

> He was too tall to stand upright on the platform. The awning brushed his head. Crouching and swaying forty feet above them he swung his arms as though to test the air's resistance. Then he pitched forward into space, unseen by the manager's wife who looked the other way until she heard a splash and saw a thin sheet of bright water shooting up. The man was standing breast high in the tank. He swung himself over the edge and crossed the ring towards them, his body dripping, his wet feet caked with sawdust, his tawny eyes a little bloodshot.*

*From *The Collected Stories of L. P. Hartley* (copyright © 1968), Hamish Hamilton, London.

Now that is a clear direct written style. But if the circus owner was describing the incident to some friends, he'd be much more likely to do so like this:

> well this chap was tall/too tall to stand up properly/head touching the canvas/so he er crouched down/there he was/right up in the roof of the big top/know it do you/some height that/ crouching and swaying about a bit/he er swung his arms as though he's er—as though he's testing the air to take his weight/ know what I mean/then he dived as if he'd got the whole Pacific Ocean under him/terrifying/I really thought he'd bought it/Ethel daren't look/she looks the other way puts her hands over her eyes/until she hears a splash/water coming up all round/light catches it/and there he is standing in the tank/ water up to his chest/well he climbs out and comes across the ring to us/hair plastered down/dripping wet/not very steady/ reminds me a bit of a sea-lion crossing the ring/sawdust caking his feet/yes and his eyes/he'd got yellowish eyes you know but they were a bit bloodshot by then/

The differences between the two versions are interesting. The grammar is different. In the written version there are six sentences. In the spoken 28 groups of words. The circus owner is creating language while speaking it; the shorter sentences are an indication of this creative activity. They also function as a help to the listener in following him. The pauses and hesitations, stablisers like er and mm, are necessary springboards. They precede the more exact word, the more vivid utterance. Again the spoken sentences are not constructed according to the rules of written grammar; sometimes they have no verbs, sometimes several as several ideas come out urgently:

> She looks the other way puts her hands over her eyes

The number of words in the written version is about 100, in the spoken version it is about 170. This is largely because of the greater redundancy in the spoken language. The circus owner subconsciously stresses the important points. In the written version we are told once that the circus owner's wife didn't watch; in the spoken version three times:

> Ethel daren't look, she looks the other way puts her hands over her eyes

If a message comes through on ticker-tape it comes through once—you can always re-read it; but if it comes through the air you can't. So we build in redundancy.

> Red leader to red fox. Return to base. I say again, return to base.

Another difference we might comment upon is in the spoken pause. The reciprocal features, which have no parallel in the written version. The speaker sends out echo-soundings "know it do you", "know what I mean", "you know". The question he is asking here is the same as that the pilot asks.

> Red leader to red fox, red leader to red fox. Are you receiving me? Are you receiving me? Over.

Of course many of the enquiries the circus owner gives in this connection will be visual; just as the signals the listeners may give him back may be visual; looks of interest, boredom, nods, eyes wandering; though of course they may answer. Whatever the signals he should adjust his utterance accordingly. Speaker and listener are bound in reciprocity. In a sense the listener creates the language of the speaker.

This analysis will be referred to later. For the moment let us turn to the educative aspects of oracy.

## The Teaching of Oracy

Any training in oracy must start with situation. Let us consider first the *production* of language—speech. Much speech work in the past has been carried out in isolation, as though "good speech" had an existence apart from the circumstances in which it occurred and the communication it had to make. Much of it further has been carried out in separate departments of speech, or at least in separate speech lessons. In the U.K. we are seeing it as inseparable from English and from drama, and indeed from the other subjects in the curriculum. Where the elements of the speech model as described above are present, when the Addressor is present, with something to say, to an Addressee or Addressees in a particular Context—when these elements come together they produce that tension which calls forth speech. If I speak to you you must answer, if you speak to me I must answer —or contract out by being exposed as rude or ignorant or tongue-tied. The speech situation is a compulsory one. And the teachers task is the creation of a variety of compulsory situations, both for speech and writing. In these speech and writing grow and develop.

To turn from production to reception—to listening. In education students spend a great amount of time listening. Wilt (3) examined the classroom time spent by 530 elementary school children at all levels and found they were listening for 57½ percent of it, a daily average of 2 hours 38 minutes. Surveying the communication time of college students Bird (4) assigned 42 percent to listening, 25 percent to speaking, 15 percent to reading and 18 percent to writing. These figures would seem to imply the silent students with only the teacher saying very much. One might think that with such an amount of practice students would become fairly proficient at listening. But research suggests that this is not the case (5). There would appear to be several reasons for this. One is that the sheer weight of words causes students to switch off, the teacher being unaware that the span of attention of even the ablest is limited; another is we listen best when there is a compulsory situation—when we are expected to answer, as in a conversation, reply as in a discussion—this is a reason why group work is becoming more popular as a means of learning; another is that the students have not been taught to listen; another is that the lesson or lecture may be conceived in a written rather than a spoken mode. More consideration needs to be given to listening, the conditions under which it best functions, the question of training it, and the nature of the material it is appropriate to listen to.

## The Testing of Listening

In order to do this it is necessary to turn to the investigations which have previously been carried out on listening. Every worker in this field owes a considerable debt to the work of Nichols and particularly of J. I. Brown and G. Robert Carlsen, whose famous Listening Comprehension Test of 1953 (6) was a pattern for later work. Brown and Carlsen drew up a taxonomy of listening skills which they classified as receptive and reflective skills. Receptive skills were associated with accuracy in listening— ability to keep related details in mind, ability to follow all directions. Reflective skills on the other hand were the ability to use contextual clues, to recognise organisational elements, to select main as opposed to subordinate ideas, and the relationship between them, and the ability to draw justification inferences. (This itemisation is given by Pratt (7).)

As was mentioned this test has been very influential. But subsequent investigators tend to have been psychologists or research workers interested in "skills" and mental factors. The culmination of this line of work comes with the Australian, Spearritt (8) who in 1962 published his factorial analysis of listening comprehension where he isolates a separate listening factor related to I.Q. but distinct from it. But what these investigations have lacked on the whole is an interest in language and the essential accompaniment of it, an interest in situation. Many test items used are fragments.

A different kind of limitation, however, and a more serious one, lies in the type of language used in many listening tests. It is written language read aloud. The fact might well explain Lindquist's comment in 1959 (9) that there was no evidence that a listening comprehension test measured anything different from a silent reading test.

It is now proposed to speak of the work in listening which is going on at the University of Birmingham. We believe that the material of a listening test should be spoken material and we are able to contemplate this because of course we have tape upon which to record it, a facility which was not available to the earlier workers in the field—all their tests had to be read aloud, with a consequent loss of reliability. The use of tape and objective type answers means that it is possible to standardise it and create listening norms for various ages of student in a way which was not possible before. We have a brief from a funding body, The Schools Council, to create measures of listening comprehension throughout the secondary age range.

The speech model outlined earlier enables us to discern certain areas of interest. About the Addressor we may make certain deductions—his business, his class, his status, his age. We may ask what his purpose is— to display, to deprecate himself, to affect the listener by informing, instructing, entertaining. We may consider what sort of a person he appears— positive (friendly, secure, appreciative, uncritical), negative (unfriendly, withdrawn, deprecating, critical) or "evaluating" moving between cautious and enthusiastic, balanced and extreme, fair and carried away, reasonable and emotional. We may ask similar questions about the Addressee—and in addition questions like, is he willing to accept the intentions of the Addressor, is he seeking clarification? The relationship between these two is of particular importance; who is superior, who talks most, is this dialogue friend to friend, older to younger, stranger to stranger, expert to layman, teacher to taught, lecturer to audience, broadcaster to listener or viewer? Further, we may consider the Subject—what are the main points, what are the subsidiary, what is stated, what is inferred, what is hypothetical and what is actual? The Context will be of interest. Where are the speakers? What is the occasion? Are the objects they speak of present or absent? And, finally, we may consider the language itself—what is the register, is the language literal or metaphorical, how functional is the phonological content?

## Some Suggestions for a Listening Comprehension Test

It will be clear from the foregoing what kinds of elements would seem appropriate to the present speaker in a test of listening comprehension. The emphasis would be on the language, which would be the spoken language. In this way it would be hoped to draw on some of the skills which have been considered important in previous tests.

*Prediction.*    There is however one skill which has not formed a part of previous tests, and which might seem important in understanding the spoken language. That is prediction. We often interrupt people because we know from what they've said what they are going to say. We often finish their sentences for them. But equally important is a kind of post-prediction which enables us to understand what people have said before in the light of what comes after. Thus in the following brief conversation we suspect that the sentence of the second speaker is wrong when we hear it, but since any sentence can be a reply to any other, we cannot be sure until we have heard what follows. The problem sentence will be indicated by a bell:

A.  Where did you go for your holiday?
B.  Grandfather clocks are quite expensive.
A.  Yes, I enjoyed Guernsey too.

The conversation would obviously have gone like this:

A.  Where did you go for your holiday?
B.  Guernsey, and enjoyed it very much.
A.  Yes, I enjoyed Guernsey too.

By taking the recording of an extended genuine conversation, and ringing a bell against sentences which are either right or wrong, it is possible to detect the predictive and post-predictive ability of the students.

For the rest it would seem that a test of listening might profitably concentrate on language—on for instance a piece of classroom exposition, in which questions are asked on Content; on Phonology, as a quite distinct oral feature; on Register, and on Relationship as expressed through language.

*Content.*    A content test might consist of a passage of classroom exposition say, or a conversation, and questions would be asked about the main points of information and understanding.

> Well, I want to tell you where I went this weekend. I went to the Green Chapel. You know, the place where the Green Knight and Sir Gawain are supposed to have met in the old poem we read. You remember the story, don't you, how King Arthur and his knights were feasting one New Year's Eve, when all of a sudden there galloped into the hall a Green Knight. He was a huge man and he was dressed all in green, and his beard was green and his hair was green and the trappings of his horse were green, and he flung himself off his horse and he proposed a most strange party game. Now this game was that one of the knights there would cut his head off and that then, in return, a year hence, he, the Green Knight, should cut that knight's head off. Everybody got that?

Further questions might be asked—did the listeners already know the story, what was the attitude of the narrator towards it, in what relationship does the narrator stand to his audience, and so on. The justification for such a test would seem self-evident.

*Phonology.*    A further test would be one of phonology—the differences brought about in meaning by a differing pronunciation of the same words. Some taxonomy such as Halliday, *Intonation and Grammar in British English* (10) is useful as a background, but provides no guide to the degree of occurrence of particular features. The investigator has to use his ears and his judgment. Here is an extract from such a test. A husband and wife, John and Helen, are in a restaurant:

| | |
|---|---|
| HELEN: | You can't be hungry in a place like this. |
| JOHN: | I can be hungry anywhere. Oh come on, have something. Some coffee. |
| HELEN: | All right, some coffee, but I'm really not hungry you know John. Must be the car. |
| JOHN: | Yes, I'm sorry. I think there must be some fumes coming from somewhere. |
| NARRATOR: | Does the husband now think his wife is hungry? |
| JOHN: | Yes, I'm sorry. I think there must be some fumes coming from somewhere. Waiter. |
| WAITER: | Yes, sir. |
| JOHN: | A pot of coffee for two please. And a grilled steak. |
| WAITER: | Very good sir. |
| JOHN: | Hope they don't take long. It's still about 100 miles drive after this. |
| HELEN: | Let's spend some time here. We haven't got to be there tonight after all. Let's put up somewhere here. |
| JOHN: | No, we haven't got to. |
| NARRATOR: | Does the husband feel they should get there tonight? |

From our preliminary tests it looks as if younger students and less-able students are missing out on common intonation features. They are taking statements literally. If this finding is substantiated it may provide an important reason for them not learning—the teacher's language may be simple in vocabulary but its intonation may be too sophisticated for them.

*Register.*    A good deal has been said about register. To ask students to recognise registers is largely a waste of time. A single word is often sufficient to provide a 'register marker' and thus to give the game away. But to ask them to detect breaks in register is a more difficult and a more valuable exercise. It has similarities to a literary study of style. Registers may be differentiated by all kinds of polarity—formal/informal, literal/metaphorical, technical/non-technical, archaic/modern, written/spoken, technical/other technical, public/private, personal/impersonal, naive/critical, and so on. Here are a few examples. The test is to detect an inappropriate phrase in the passage.

Station Announcer (two-tone bell): The 8:15 from Wolverhampton, going forward to London Euston at 8:35, has been diverted to Platform 8. The train has been reported 20 minutes late but I think it will be less than that. Will all passengers waiting for this train on Platform 3, proceed as soon as possible to Platform 8.

Well, I'd been spoiling for a fight for quite a bit. He'd kept niggling me, you know, always on my back. So I thought, right matey, you just wait till the bell rings. And yesterday was the big day. Seconds out you might say. I'd always said I'd pull no punches and I didn't. I let him have it straight from the shoulder. He looked stunned. He went dead pale. Then he began to bluster and shout. He was getting the worst of it all right. The old ref had to step in.

(Mood music). Silver birch trees, delicate saplings, slim, delicate. Caressed by sun and wind. Delicate lady, slim, delicate, laughing lady. Slim, delicate, lovely lady. Be like her, eat Slim-line Biscuits. You'll become, if you're lucky, slim, delicate.

We are going to continue our study of the kidney today. You remember that the main functions of the kidney are urine formation and maintaining an adequate water salt balance. I've got a diagram here showing the position of the kidneys in a sheep. As you will note the mutton and offal have been removed and the kidneys are lying in the dorsal region of the body cavity. Can you pick out the ureter leading from the kidney?

The first, a personal phrase "I think it will be less than that" into an impersonal train announcement; the second a literal use of language "The old ref had to step in," amongst metaphorical; the third a critical phrase "if you're lucky," in the naive advertisement; the fourth a breach of technical vocabulary—mutton and offal—in a biology lesson.

*Relationship.*    Finally, and perhaps the most important, would come relationship. Here is a brief scene between a teacher and a pupil:

| | |
|---|---|
| HELEN: | Can I have a word with you Mr. Johnson? |
| MR. JOHNSON: | Certainly Helen. |
| HELEN: | Well, what I wanted to ask you about was this math exam. Do you think I've got a chance in it? |
| MR. JOHNSON: | Well, it depends on the questions that come up. You seem to be good at arithmetic but your geometry isn't so good, is it? |
| HELEN: | You think I'm terrible at geometry then? |
| MR. JOHNSON: | Oh no, I wouldn't say that. |
| HELEN: | Well I do try hard. I spend hours trying to solve some of those problems. |
| MR. JOHNSON: | Yes, I'm sure you do—it's just that you're a bit erratic at times. |
| HELEN: | Erratic? I wouldn't have thought that. |
| MR. JOHNSON: | Well you are a little you know. |

| HELEN: | I sometimes have difficulty with one or two of those theorems but otherwise I always thought I was pretty steady. |
| MR. JOHNSON: | Well. |
| HELEN: | I've got pretty consistent marks. |
| MR. JOHNSON: | Well the piece of homework this week, that wasn't very good was it? |
| HELEN: | Oh, there was a special reason for that: I just couldn't get interested—wasn't feeling like it for some reason. |
| MR. JOHNSON: | You did a good piece of homework last week, but what about the homework before that? |
| HELEN: | Oh well, I was away when you set it and I did some of the wrong questions. |
| MR. JOHNSON: | Well, you could have come and seen me and found out. |
| HELEN: | Well, I didn't have time. Anyway, geometry! |
| MR. JOHNSON: | You've proved my point. |
| HELEN: | What point? |
| MR. JOHNSON: | That's what I mean by erratic; doing some things well, some things badly. |
| HELEN: | You can't really blame me for that. |
| MR. JOHNSON: | Oh, who can we blame then? |

The sort of questions which one would ask would be of the kind: what motive the girl has for seeking the interview—does she want to know the truth, or does she want only reassurance; does she accept her teacher's criticisms or does she attempt to excuse herself; how sensitive is the teacher to her feelings at the beginning; is he more, or less, reassuring at the end. And so on.


## The Place of Listening in Education

It may now be useful to draw the ends together and to make some kind of statement about the place of listening in education.

(a) Tests of listening obviously have their place, both normatively, and diagnostically. As has been argued, a test of phonology may reveal under-functioning in some students. But although this paper has described these tests this has been done principally to demonstrate a particular kind of interest in language, the spoken language. The crucial question is whether training in listening should go on in language arts courses.

(b) Training in listening has been given considerable attention in the research. It has been demonstrated by numerous studies that it can be trained over an experimental period, but there seems no evidence whether the gain is permanent or not. Three aspects can be discerned in the courses of training which have been used: the necessity for attention and appropriate set; the ability to perform certain operations—separate main from subordinate ideas for example; and the ability to recognise certain crude signposts—"the first thing," "all of a sudden," "after this," "there is still another thing" (11). Such training might be useful. But the crucial factors in listening would seem to be the motivation of the students and the interest of the material. As mentioned above, research seems to indicate that people perform "badly" in listening tasks. But this may be as much a comment on the task, e.g. a lecturer's performance, and the nature of his material, as on the students. And, of course, the trend in education is for less "set piece" lessons and lectures and more for reciprocity in discussion.

(c) The type of listening comprehension which would seem to be profitable in education is not one that can be separated out under such a heading as training as it would be part and parcel of a language arts course in oracy and literacy. It would be a study of the English language in its wide variety of uses, and through it of people and their relationships and their social context. The thinking for such a course would be informed by linguistics but far removed from the toying with and mumbling over bones which linguistics seems to stand for in some courses. The discriminating response should be developed on material as rich in life and experience as the sound or video tape-recorder can make it. And if (*pace* Johnson) this means "visiting caverns to learn the miner's language" or "taking a voyage to perfect one's skill in the language of navigation" then in effect such must be undertaken. We must "court living information," "glean up words" rejoicing in the "sullenness of one and roughness of another" (12).

## References

1. Samuel Johnson, *A Dictionary of the English Language,* London, 1755.
2. J. R. Firth, "The Treatment of Language in General Linguistics," *The Medical Press* 19 (August 1959).
3. M. E. Wilt, "A Study of Teacher Awareness of Listening as a Factor in Elementary Education," *Journal of Educational Research* 43 (1950): 625–636.
4. D. E. Bird, "Teaching Listening Comprehension," *Journal of Communication* 3 (1953): 127–30.
5. See for instance P. E. Vernon, "The Intelligibility of Broadcast Talks," *BBC Quarterly* 4 (1950): 206–12; W. A. Belson, "Topic for Tonight: A Study of Comprehensibility," *BBC Quarterly* 2 (1952); R. G. Nichols, "Factors in Listening Comprehension," *Speech Monographs* 15 (1948): 154–163; and J. J. Brown, "The Construction of a Diagnostic Test of Listening Comprehension," *Journal of Experimental Education* 18 (1949): 139–146.

6. J. I. Brown and G. R. Carlsen, *The Brown-Carlsen Listening Comprehension Test* (Harcourt, Brace & World, 1953).

7. E. Pratt, "Experimental Evaluation of a Program for the Improvement of Listening," *Elementary School Journal* 56 (1956): 315–320.

8. D. Spearritt, *Listening Comprehension: A Factorial Analysis,* A.C.E.R. Research Series No. 76 (1962).

9. E. F. Lindquist, Review of Brown-Carlsen Listening Comprehension Test and STEP Listening Comprehension Test in *Fifth Mental Measurements Year Book* (Ed. Buros) (Highland Park, N.J., The Gryphon Press, 1959).

10. M. A. K. Halliday, *Intonation and Grammar in British English* (Mouton, The Hague, 1967).

11. M. K. Hollow, "Listening Comprehension at the Intermediate Grade Level," *Elementary School Journal* 56 (1955): 158–161.

12. My thinking has been influenced by discussions with colleagues in the University of Birmingham; I am particularly indebted to Mr. Leslie Stratta of the School of Education, and Professor John McH. Sinclair of the Department of English.

# Helen Kennedy

# *Problems in Aural Reading*

Most of those attending the first Claremont Reading Conference in 1932 could recall the first time they heard a radio or saw a sound motion picture. Television was a name rather than an instrument to most of us. And while the old gramophone or phonograph was a familiar instrument, the tape recorder with all of its modern uses was not yet in our everyday vocabulary. Other changes have occurred which are as closely related and just as miraculous. Mastoiditis was a major cause of hearing difficulty, yet in a recent issue of the *Reader's Digest* there is an advertisement sponsored by a group of prescription drug manufacturers which comments concerning this problem: "In 1933, some 5,400 cases were reported in New York City alone. In 1956—only 50. Today the mastoid operation is so rare that most young doctors have never seen it." So with these advances in the understanding and use of sound and of antibiotics, today's teacher is more likely to find a transistor radio than a hearing aid attached to the receiver button seen in the ear of her students.

When we consider reading as the process of making discriminative responses we realize that in speaking of aural reading we are limiting our consideration to the making of discriminative reactions in response to sound or more precisely to audible stimuli. It will be well then for us to review briefly the nature of the stimulus—sound, the receptor mechanism—the ear, and most important the numerous factors involved in interpretation of the various stimuli.

I

A pure tone has two characteristics—intensity and frequency. These are usually illustrated by sine waves in which the height of the wave indi-

161

cates the intensity and the closeness of the waves, or the number of the waves in a given space, indicate the frequency. For example:

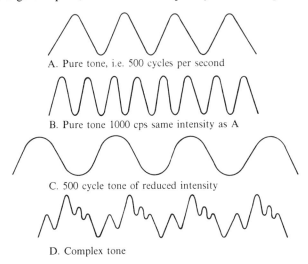

A. Pure tone, i.e. 500 cycles per second

B. Pure tone 1000 cps same intensity as A

C. 500 cycle tone of reduced intensity

D. Complex tone

An illustration frequently used is that of tossing a rock into a pond and watching the circles of waves. The height of the waves thus illustrates the intensity and the number of such waves passing a given point in a specified length of time indicates the frequency. The units of measure applied to sound waves are the decibel (dB) for the intensity and the cycles per second (cps) indicating the frequency.* On radio or television sets we find a "volume" control to increase or decrease the intensity and a "tone" control which either amplifies or attenuates the high or low tones. It should be noted that the tone control does not change the frequency of the sounds; it merely makes certain parts of the range more or less intense. Of course, most sound is not pure tone but rather a mixture of various frequencies at different intensities. The mixtures are referred to as complex sounds.

In this paper we will be primarily concerned with speech sound. These sounds are complex and are limited to a small part of the range of sound which is generally thought of as audible. As in all other factors which might be considered when the human is involved, there are great individual differences in the range of sounds which are heard comfortably. In general it may be said that the human range of audibility is from about 20 Hertz or Hz to an upper range of perhaps 32,000. In relation to intensity the range between the least intense sound which can be heard and the most intense which can be tolerated is about 140 decibels. In the higher and lower frequencies the range is much less. Speech sounds occupy a very small part of the range. Although there is not complete agreement with regard to the

*The term *Hertz* (Hz) is currently (1971) being used rather than *cycles per second.*

range of English speech sounds, the range is generally held to be from about 250 to 6400 Hertz or Hz with an overall intensity range of 28 decibels. The range, of course, varies with the speaker.

Without reviewing the old differences of the physicist and pyschologist, it will suffice to say that we are considering that sound is generated by anything causing motion within any media. In thinking of speech we naturally think of the sound waves which result from the control of the stream of air passing through the human vocal mechanism. There was a time when sound was thought of as being primarily transmitted through the air. Now, of course, the understanding of the transmission of sound is the subject of much research and to many of us, the present day knowledge is phenomenal. There seems to be no limit to the new understandings and uses of sound. However, many of the present day uses are not those employing the range of audible sound which is our point of concern.

## II

Before we discuss the factors which make speech sounds intelligible, attention should be given to their reception. The normal channel for reception of sound waves is through the outer ear and the middle ear and thence to the cochlea or inner ear. The function of the outer ear is the collection and the channelizing of the sound against the tympanic membrane (ear drum) which is the separating wall between the outer and middle ear. When the sound waves hit the ear drum, it vibrates in accordance with the intensity and the frequency of the stimuli. The movement of the tympanic membrane causes the movement of the ossicular chain of three little bones, the malleus (hammer), incus (anvil), and stapes (stirrup), within the middle ear. The foot-plate of the stirrup in turn fits into the oval window which opens into the cochlea and hence the sound is transmitted via the fluid in the cochlea to the hair cells in the basilar membrane. These hair cells connect with the nerve fibers which transmit the impulses to the auditory centers in the brain. Obviously, this description, as also that of sound waves, was greatly simplified. The process of transmission and conversion of sound waves into nerve impulses is complex but fascinating.

It is not until the impulses have been transmitted to the brain that the individual even becomes aware of the presence of sound. Just as the various parts of the ear serve different functions in the collection, conversion and analysis of the stimulus, so different parts of the brain have their hierarchy of function. These three phases are frequently termed perception, recognition, and recall. When speech reaches the area of auditory preception, it is perceived as sound but nothing more. "The perceived sound is then referred to the area of Wernicke in the superior temporal convolution where it is recognized as language, distinguished from all other kinds of sounds and noises. The sounds recognized as language are referred to the area of recall where the particular combination of speech sounds is interpreted and clothed with meaning."* But even then correct interpretation is not assured. Interpretation is dependent upon many factors. These include accurate reception and transmission of the stimuli, the experience of the individual with these stimuli and the meaning he has given to them, the context in which the sounds occur, and the state of the organism at the time the stimuli are received, perceived, recalled, and hence interpreted.

The question of how the sound is interpreted is our chief concern. However, there are various things which may interfere with a correct and adequate stimulus reaching the perceptual area. First, we must concede that the stimulus may be inadequate. As teachers we would probably prefer not to admit that our speech may be less, far less, than correct. At this time the reference is not meant to include such things as the grammatical constructions, though obviously they are very important, but just the matter of the correct pronunciation of words. Foreign accents, regional variations, articulatory problems such as a lisp, and careless speech habits all fall into this category. Speech also may be inadequate in the sense that the stimulus may be weak. Even though properly produced with adequate force there may be interference in the transmission. It may have to travel too far, there may be interfering structures through which it must pass, or there may be conflicting stimuli reaching the receiver at the same time. If the sound is being transmitted mechanically there may be loss in the transducers or in the transmission system itself.

If it is assumed that a correct and adequate stimulus reaches the ear, consideration must then be given to the losses which may occur in this part of the transmission system. When there is some interference in the transmission of the sound waves either in the outer or the middle ear, the resultant loss of hearing is termed a conductive loss. Usually this loss most seriously limits the transmission of the low frequencies. In such instances, a hearing aid is both useful and easily fitted, and surgical procedures are effective. Perhaps the most common cause of such a loss is nothing more complicated than the accumulation of wax in the ear canal or some other form of obstruction which may occur when something is put in the ear. Some otologists have quite a collection of beads, beans, erasers, etc., which they have removed from the ear canals of children. Interference in the function of the ossicular chain will result in a similar type of loss. Such problems have been receiving far more attention since mastoiditis has responded to control by use of antibiotics. Several surgical procedures have come into more common use in the case of otosclerosis and the repair or substitution of ear drums.

The mechanism of the cochlea is so complex that when difficulty occurs in that area, repair is not yet feasible. The same may be said of the

---

*"Introduction to Aphasia," motion picture produced by The Veterans Administration.

impairment which occurs in the eighth nerve. In fact, only recently has there been a differentiation of losses occurring in the cochlea and eighth nerve. In each instance the loss is primarily in the high frequencies. A differential diagnosis relating to recruitment is becoming better recognized as distinguishing between a cochlear and nerve loss. Such a differentiation is helpful in the fitting of hearing aids. Since hearing aids merely amplify sound, they may be just as useful in these losses as in the conductive losses, provided they can be fitted comfortably. However, it is in the instances of reduced annoyance threshold that a major problem occurs in the successful fitting of the hearing aid.

Even when the stimulus is adequate and there is no interference in the transmission, there will be definite differences in the required intensity of sounds for them to be recognized as present. These receptive differences are related to age. That there is a decrease in auditory acuity associated with advancing years has long been recognized. It is well known that such differences begin to appear in the high frequencies when one is in his thirties. They gradually become more severe during each of the succeeding decades. As the loss progresses, it becomes more pronounced in the high frequencies and gradually extends lower and lower into the frequency range.

The factor which has not been well recognized is that hearing is developmental. The young child hears less well than the child several years his senior. Hearing in the middle range of frequencies, 1000 to 4000 cycles per second, is more acute in the six-year-old than either the lower or higher frequencies. The acuity increases throughout the range tested until about the age of fifteen. The greater increases occur at the low and high frequencies, especially in the highs. After the age of fifteen the gradual decrease in hearing noted above begins. There also appear to be definite sex and laterality differences associated with the maturation of hearing (1).

### III

Attention should now be turned to the consideration of how these various factors affect aural reading. It has already been stated that aural reading is the process of making discriminative responses to sound. For the purposes of this discussion our concern is with speech sounds or more accurately the spoken word. It has been necessary, then, to consider the adequacy of the stimulus pattern, its reception and its transmission to the brain. Whenever there is interference or a breakdown in the transmission of the stimulus, the pattern reaching the interpretative center of the brain will be inadequate and the reading rendered more difficult if indeed possible at all. If there is a general hearing loss, the type of pattern received would be similar to that which would occur if the stimulus were weak. In certain types of hearing problems there will be selective interference with the speech patterns just as there can be selective interference when poor amplifying equipment is used. Such losses can be demonstrated with the use of filters which will reduce or even eliminate the transmission of given frequencies. A rough equivalent visual pattern is represented by the following:

> u   i e  it to  ay the   e i  of thi   di  cussion is the   uc  e     ul
> re  eption  and  under  tanding  of    ound    timuli.  A  ba  ic  con
>   ideration  is  how   ome  lo   e   e   ect the  e   ort  of  li  tening.
> Mi  con  eptions  and  di  belie    con  erning  the     eriou  ne     of
> hearing lo   es is di   icult   or me to ac  ept.*

This represents how an individual with a high frequency loss might hear the following paragraph if several high frequency sounds were "filtered out."

> Suffice it to say the thesis of this discussion is the successful reception and understanding of sound stimuli. A basic consideration is how some losses effect the effort of listening. Misconceptions and disbelief concerning the seriousness of hearing losses is difficult for me to accept.

Even though the stimulus pattern is correctly received at the perceptive level of the brain, there are many factors which still may affect the adequacy of the aural reading. There may, of course, be a breakdown in the transmission within the brain. The sound pattern may be received at the perceptive level but if there is a lesion in the area of Wernicke, the ability to recognize language will be impaired in that these sounds will not be distinguishable from other sounds. The area of the brain concerned with meaning of spoken words is in the second and third temporal convolutions. Damage occurring in this area usually in the left hemisphere of the brain will result in the individual being unable to comprehend the significance of spoken language.

When it is remembered that aural reading is a psychological process, it will be recognized that no two persons will "hear" exactly alike. Each individual interprets the sounds he receives as being of a given pitch and loudness. We usually think of pitch and loudness as representing given frequencies and intensities. But no one person can ever really know what any other person "hears" when he says that the sound is of such and such a pitch or loudness. In fact, under certain abnormal conditions, an individual may perceive the same tone as being of an entirely different pitch or being much louder when received through one ear and nerve pathway than

---

*In the original chart the letters which are here omitted were printed in red. By using a red which is not too intense, the red letters will be blocked out completely when covered by a piece of red cellophane.

through the other. On one occasion, I tested a musician who identified one tone as almost one full octave higher when it was heard with one ear than when he heard it through the other ear. Loudness differences are more frequently recognized than the differences in pitch.

With the recognition of these differences in the aural reading of pure tone what then must be expected in the aural reading of words? Each person necessarily reads into each word the meaning or meanings which he has developed based upon his experiences. No two people can ever have the identical experience nor can any person ever exactly repeat an experience. Every interpretation is made upon the basis of the accumulated experience of each individual with all that this implies concerning the emotions, the expectations, and the prejudices of the person at the time. This is but another way of saying that one does not read aurally with one's ears but with one's mind.

The fact that there is more to aural reading than accurate reception and transmission of an adequate stimulus word is evidenced by some of the research on "intelligibility." Much of this work was initiated in the Bell Laboratories in their concern for the improvement of telephone circuits. Such tests were also used for testing the acoustical properties of such things as theaters. In these situations trained "listeners" were used. As I recall reports of early work in the testing of telephone equipment, a "listener" might have been trained for as long as two years before being used in the test situation. Such training was in receiving and recording phonetic syllables composed of an initial and terminal consonant and an internal vowel. Similar work continues today in the evaluation of the reception of word stimuli under adverse conditions relating to background noise.

## IV

Since it appears that there are factors other than "hearing" which affect the "intelligibility" of the word, investigation into these factors is in order. The impetus for the present report is nearly twenty-five years old. At that time (1941) various hearing problems were being studied in relation to children's reading of printed word symbols. Using the consonant-vowel-consonant format a test was developed which consisted of both words used with great frequency and those used infrequently. This test was dictated to a group of eighth graders. It was noted that most errors occurred with the less familiar words. The type of error made seemed to be the substitution of a common word for the unfamiliar one. Later a similar list was made for use in demonstrating this condition to college classes. Gradually the test was more carefully made and recorded for these demonstrations. The results of six administrations of the recorded test are to be considered here.

The test consists of forty-eight words taken from the Thorndike and Lorge Teachers Word Book of 30,000 Words (2). Each word was selected on the basis of the pattern of an initial and terminal consonant sound and an internal vowel. The test design called for half of the words to be selected from among the most common words in the count—the AA designation. These words, which we shall call "familiar," occur at least one hundred times in each million words of the count. The other twenty-four were taken from the list of words which "occur less than one per million but more often than once per four million." These we shall refer to as "unfamiliar" words. Insofar as possible they were chosen so that each consonant sound would occur in both the initial and the terminal position. When a sound can be used in only the initial or the terminal position, as for example "h" and "ng" respectively, it was used twice in that position. Several errors occurred in the dictation but are not significant in relation to the major findings to be reported here.*

In making the taped test, the writer dictated in the manner recommended for the administration of the Phonetically Balanced lists used in clinical tests for the hearing of speech. The recording was made with an Ampex 600 tape recorder which permitted the careful monitoring of the intensity of the test word. The monitoring phrase used was: "Now write the word _____." The test instructions included on the tape are:

> This is a test of hearing. It is not a standardized hearing test but one that is designed to illustrate a particular point. Forty-eight words will be dictated with sufficient time allowed for you to write each word. Spelling is *not* important. If you do not know how to spell the word, write it phonetically. May I repeat: 'Spelling is not important' so write what you hear as you hear it.

One group was a mixed graduate and undergraduate class in education. Three groups were in reading workshops at Claremont Graduate School. Two groups were students at San Fernando Valley State College. One San Fernando group was a freshman psychology class while the other was an undergraduate education class. Ages were not obtained for any group. One group of 75 students heard the tape played at an intensity level which they said was comfortable and easy to hear. These shall be referred to as the "high" intensity group. Another group of 101 heard the tape at a lower intensity level. These shall be referred to as the "low" intensity group. Sound levels were not measured during these tests. The intensity level of

---

*In rechecking the material while preparing this report, three errors have been found. "Boat" and "pause" appear in the test when the words should have been "vote" and "cause." These mistakes result in the "v" and "k" sounds being omitted in the initial position and "b" and "p" occurring twice. The word "mouth" which should have been dictated as the noun was given as the verb resulting in an unequal distribution of the two "th" sounds. In the first two errors the substitute words are in the AA cagegory of familiarity. However, the last error mentioned removes the word from the "familiar" category by our definition.

the test words presented to the two groups at San Fernando Valley State College was approximately 70 db. Very little variation occurred in the different test positions in the room. These groups of thirty-four and thirty-five shall be referred to as the "70 db" group. It is my impression that this is a slightly higher intensity than was used in the "high" intensity groups.

Auditory acuity data were not obtained for any of the students. It was assumed that most had normal hearing although several students at Claremont indicated that they had some hearing loss.

Each student wrote the words as he understood them on sheets of paper numbered from 1 to 48. The number of the test item preceded the monitoring sentence. Subsequently, the student was given an answer sheet from which he corrected his own paper. He was then asked to record exactly his errors on the answer sheet. Each paper was carefully reviewed and in some instances errors noted by the student were not allowed because the spelling seemed to indicate that the word had been heard correctly but that the student was not familiar enough with phonetics to recognize it as phonetically correct. Omissions were also noted. In one instance a door was banged so that the students seated near it had not heard a word. In this set of papers the word is treated as an omission.

The test for Claremont and Los Angeles State results were examined in relation to several different problems including errors made with different intensities of presentation, familiar versus unfamiliar words, initial versus terminal consonants, certain high frequency sounds, and the most frequently found type of error—namely, the substitution of a familiar word for the unfamiliar. The San Fernando results were used to verify the findings with regard to the familiar versus the unfamiliar words.

In Table 1 data are presented showing the number of incorrect responses made with each of the familiar and unfamiliar words. The breakdown also permits comparison of the groups with regard for the intensity levels of the presentations. The lower section of the table shows both the percentage of responses which were not correct and the percentage of the incorrect responses or omissions occurring with each type of word.

From these results it is easy to see that both the intensity of the presentation and the familiarity with the word contribute to its intelligibility. As has been indicated, sound level measurements were not made at the time of the Claremont or Los Angeles State College tests. However, with the two groups designated as "low," the intensity of the presentation was definitely lower than for the two groups designated as "high." The two classes designated as "low" had almost the identical percentages of error of 17.6 and 17.4. There was a slightly greater difference between the two "high" classes. Their percentages of error were 11.3 for the class of sixty-six students and 12.5 for the smaller class. When one applies the test of independence to the correct and incorrect responses for the "high" and "low"

## TABLE 1.

*Incorrect Responses Made with Familiar and Unfamiliar Words by the Different Intensity Groups.*

|  | Familiar | | | Unfamiliar | | | Total | | |
|---|---|---|---|---|---|---|---|---|---|
|  | Low (75) | High (101) | 70db (69) | Low (75) | High (101) | 70db (69) | Low (75) | High (101) | 70db (69) |
| Possible Resp. | 1800 | 2424 | 1656 | 1800 | 2424 | 1656 | 3600 | 4848 | 3312 |
| Incorrect Resp. | 224 | 141 | 54 | 1050 | 1063 | 597 | 1274 | 1204 | 651 |
| Omissions | 0 | 3 | 0 | 3 | 23 | 0 | 3 | 26 | 0 |
| Total Not Correct | 224 | 144 | 54 | 1053 | 1086 | 597 | 1277 | 1230 | 651 |
| % Not Correct | 12.4 | 5.9 | 3.3 | 58.5 | 44.7 | 36.0 | 35.5 | 25.4 | 19.7 |
| % of Incorrect | 17.5 | 11.7 | 8.3 | 82.5 | 88.3 | 91.7 | 100.0 | 100.0 | 100.0 |

groups, a chi-square of 107.3 is obtained. To be significant at the 1 per cent level, a chi-square of only 6.635 is needed.

As was noted earlier, the two classes tested at San Fernando Valley State College were given the test words at approximately 70 db. When the test of independence is applied between the errors made by one class with familiar words and with the unfamiliar words missed by the other class, the resulting chi-square was 305. Again a chi-square of only 6.635 is needed to be significant at the .01 level.

It is interesting to note that the freshman class of thirty-five students made only twenty-one errors with the familiar words but a total of 301 with the unfamiliar. The somewhat older group in the education course made thirty-three errors with the familiar words and 296 with the unfamiliar. These findings may suggest that some hearing loss is beginning to appear in the older group. In the younger group one student made seven mistakes with the familiar words, one made two, twelve made one and the remaining twenty-one made no such mistakes. One of those making no mistakes with the familiar words missed nineteen of the unfamiliar. One student made only two mistakes with the unfamiliar words while fifteen made at least ten. In the older group the lowest number of mistakes with the unfamiliar words was four while thirteen missed at least ten. The greatest number of mistakes with the unfamiliar words was thirteen. Nineteen made no errors with the familiar words, seven missed only one, three missed each two and three, one missed five and another six.

Tables 2 and 3 present a further analysis of the mistakes made by the "low" and "high" intensity groups. Each mistake was noted with reference to whether it occurred with the initial and/or the terminal consonant. No effort was made to summarize the data for the vowels since the students were not trained to record their responses phonetically. Table 2 presents the findings for all consonants with regard to position. Obviously, there are more incorrect responses involving the end of the word than the beginning. However, these differences are less pronounced with the unfamiliar words than with the familiar. By comparing the data in Tables 1 and 2 it is interesting to note how relatively few mistakes involved both the initial and terminal sounds.

According to Fletcher (3), most speech sounds as observed in the air have two frequency regions of prominence; sometimes there are three such regions but seldom only one. In his chart of the "Combined Characteristics of the Fundamental Sounds of Speech," (4), we note that there appear to be three sounds with only one fundamental frequency. These same three sounds, "f" as in fish, "s" as in save, and "th" as in thing, are high frequency sounds of relatively low intensity. The combination of all of these factors would lead one to suspect that these sounds would be more difficult to hear than the other consonants. Consequently, these sounds were subjected to special study the results of which are presented in Table 3. It is obvious tht when these sounds occur in a terminal position, they are frequently misunderstood.

The consideration of errors would not be complete without some mention of the kinds of errors made. Because it had been noted that the eighth graders had frequently substituted a familiar word for one which was unfamiliar, the mistakes made by the "high" and "low" intensity groups were reviewed with this in mind. To summarize these findings, it may be

## TABLE 2.

*Incorrect Responses Made in the Initial and Terminal Positions.*

|  |  | Familiar | | Unfamiliar | | Total | |
|---|---|---|---|---|---|---|---|
|  |  | No. | % | No. | % | No. | % |
|  | Initial | 55 | 3.1 | 490 | 27.2 | 545 | 15.2 |
| Low Intensity | Terminal | 188 | 10.0 | 621 | 34.5 | 809 | 22.5 |
|  | Total | 243 | 6.5 | 1111 | 30.9 | 1354 | 18.8 |
|  | Initial | 23 | .9 | 342 | 14.0 | 365 | 7.5 |
| High Intensity | Terminal | 124 | 5.1 | 756 | 30.9 | 880 | 18.2 |
|  | Total | 147 | 3.0 | 1098 | 22.7 | 1445 | 14.9 |

## TABLE 3.

*Incorrect Responses Made with Three High Frequency Sounds*

|  |  | Familiar | | Unfamiliar | | Total | |
|---|---|---|---|---|---|---|---|
|  |  | No. | % | No. | % | No. | % |
|  | Initial | 13 | 5.8 | 41 | 18.2 | 54 | 12.0 |
| Low Intensity | Terminal | 116 | 57.6 | 177 | 78.7 | 293 | 65.0 |
|  | Total | 129 | 28.7 | 218 | 48.4 | 347 | 38.5 |
|  | Initial | 2 | .007 | 22 | .07 | 24 | .04 |
| High Intensity | Terminal | 58 | 19.2 | 188 | 62.1 | 246 | 40.6 |
|  | Total | 60 | 9.9 | 210 | 34.7 | 270 | 22.3 |

% Indicates percentage of possible responses which were incorrect.

said that 96 per cent of the mistakes made with the unfamiliar words resulted in a common word being substituted for the less familiar word. Even with the familiar words 92 per cent of the mistakes resulted in the presentation of a common word.

To allay the suspicion that the mistakes may be a direct result of the dictation in the preparation of the tape, it should be noted that a number of different responses were given for each of the test words which was missed frequently. This is true both with the familiar as well as the unfamiliar words. For example, the word "chief" was one of the familiar words most frequently missed. There were nine different responses among the 48 mistakes. "Cheat" accounted for thirteen, "cheap" for twenty-four, "cheek" and "cheese" for three each. The other five occurred only once. With the unfamiliar words more than half had at least five different errors. There were proportionately more different errors as there were more incorrect responses.

In attempting to analyze the errors it seems possible that there was some carry over from the unfamiliar words. This was particularly noted in the first part of the test. Answers appeared that could not be interpreted as a hearing error—a logical substitution of one sound for another—but, in fact, would have been logical perhaps for the previous unfamiliar word.

In conclusion we may say that aural readability is dependent upon many factors. The stimulus pattern must be clear. The receptive and transmission systems must be adequate. Even when these conditions are met, words unfamiliar to the reader are very likely to be misunderstood. The error most likely to occur is the substitution of a familiar word for one which is unfamiliar. The substitutions are more likely to involve the end of the word than the beginning, especially when low intensity-high frequency sounds are involved. Is it any wonder that the small child is heard to pray: "Lead me not into Penn Station" or in Sunday School to join the choir in singing: "Bringing in the sheets, bringing in the sheets."

## References

1. Helen Kennedy, "A Study of Children's Hearing as it Relates to Reading," *Journal of Experimental Education* X (June 1942): 238–251. See also: Helen Kennedy, "Maturation of Hearing Acuity," *Laryngoscope* LXVII, 8 (August 1957): 756–762.

2. E. L. Thorndike and V. Lorge, *Teachers Word Book of 30,000 Words* (New York: Bureau of Publications, Teachers College, Columbia University, 1944).

3. Harvey Fletcher, *Speech and Hearing in Communication* (New York: D. Van Nostrand, 1953), 10.

4. *Ibid.,* 87.

# On
# Methods
# and
# Materials

Hubert C. Armstrong

# What Price Standards?

## Introduction

I should like to say at the outset that this is a biased presentation. I am inclined to favor reading in most of its forms, but with reservations. Ever since I learned to read I have held a mild contempt for those who read better than I do—a weakness I trust you will tolerate. Another bias which I feel I must confide in all honesty is that I have a deep suspicion that interesting reading is not too desirable—for one thing it might be spicy.

Of course, there are other reasons for being skeptical of interesting reading. It keeps children from doing work around the place—such as bringing in the wood, cleaning the lamp chimneys, and feeding the chickens. Worse still, it sometimes prevents them from doing their school work. For instance, a boy in a nearby school district got an unsatisfactory grade in social studies because instead of studying his social studies textbook he had been reading *The Folklore of Capitalism* to his parents—a thing hardly forgivable at the age of eight.

But there are powerful and even more cogent reasons for my bias against interesting material. Book companies have made millions out of uninteresting reading—and making money is not to be taken lightly. An example of supposedly uninteresting reading is that famous tome entitled *Dick and Jane.* It has enthralling sentences like, "Look, Jane, look," and I believe a few startling comments were made about Dick, too. For years I thought these statements would hardly warrant interpretation in depth. Very recently, however, I discovered that the context of this book was quite salacious, and that it ran the risk of being banned or burned at the stake. I read in the paper that Dick was only a pseudonym . . . and that the true name was Tarzan . . . and that the unexpurgated edition read, "You Tarzan, me Jane." It was then and only then that I saw clearly that what appears to be dull and pedestrian in meaning is but a thinly veiled disguise of the most intriguing and exciting of children's literature.

In spite of the title of this talk, which was spoken in a careless moment, I am for standards—especially low standards—for then so many people can reach them. In fact, I have found an inverse relationship between the altitude of standards and the number of children who can benefit from them —the higher the standard, the fewer who attain it. Since this often makes for feelings of conflict, jealousy and rivalry—not to mention work—I propose that we set standards so high that no one can reach them. In this way we can have both high standards and that tranquility of mind that comes with surrender in the face of the impossible.

But we must leave these fantasies. I used to be an educator, but now I am an educationist, a promotion I hardly envisaged years ago when my salary was but a pittance. Pittance, by the way is derived from the word "pit" meaning in the hole, or in the red, or more commonly, to be in debt.

## I

When a mother takes her son to get a new suit, the tailor needs nothing more than a tape measure to obtain a proper fit. He is not at all concerned with what the boy has been, and little indeed with what he may become. As educators we, too, endeavor to fit the boy. But, since we do not have as accurate a measure as the tailor's tape, we veer a little toward the World War I army technique of fitting overcoats. I am sure there must have been more than one size, for the supply sergeant would glance at the recruit and select a coat from a certain pile. To the casual observer, however, it appeared that small men had long coats and tall men had short ones—an optical illusion, perhaps.

If a mother takes her son to the doctor for an annual checkup, she expects something quite different than she does from the tailor. She wants to know whether the boy is healthy and growing as he SHOULD. The doctor does not merely consult a table of height and weight averages, and inform the mother that her son is too tall or too short. True, the doctor, as does the mother, considers the characteristics of the general population for that age and sex. But he also considers family traits. The doctor will consider the extent to which the boy has suffered from pathologies and his reaction to them. He will ask about diet, sleep, and daily routine. Depending on the history of that child, he may take specimens for laboratory analysis. Finally the doctor comes up with an assessment of the present status of the child as measured against a criterion of good health and of normal growth for that child. He does not interpret individual differences as pathological *per se.* He expects individuals to differ. He is not like the philosophy student who, after graduation, wrote the philosopher Bergson, "At last I have come to accept nature." To which Bergson replied, "You'd better." The point I wish to stress is that individual differences are not an indication of abnormality. The physician uses the concept of pathology to distinguish the normal from the ill. He must, therefore, know both the nature of individual differences and the nature of health and of specific pathologies.

We in education have been a little schizophrenic with respect to this matter. On the one hand we not only acknowledge individual differences but pride ourselves on investigating them. But, on the other hand, when it comes to school learnings we fall back upon the concept of *grade standards* as the criterion of expectancy. This you recognize as the army overcoat theory of excellence. For the average man it works, for the small man there is no trouble—just cut the sleeves off; but for the oversized man—well, let's just say he doesn't photograph well in winter clothing. The strange logic of this view is that while children differ in most ways, they should not differ in school work; but if they do not differ, they should differ above and not below the average. That is to say that the optimum lies somewhere between the median and the maximum, while the pessimum lies anywhere below the average.

There are two basic reasons for our dilemma. One lies in our concept of the curriculum and instruction, and the other lies in our homage to tests and averages. Let me discuss each of these briefly.

Curriculum is a term applied to what we intend that children should learn. It is an ought—what ought to be. Instruction refers to the means we use to put it across. Learning is the net result. The aptitudes, interests and motivations of the learner are omitted from the formula, as are the cultural variations among our people. We seem to have made the assumption that children learn what they are taught—a cordial compliment to ourselves but hardly supported by an investigation of our product. We must face the fact that the less apt learn far less than we teach while the most able learn much of our curriculums before it has even been presented to them—a most unflattering thing to dwell upon, and a most unfortunate trait of the bright child. For example, I once had as a "case" a boy whose I.Q. was 204. He displayed an average 10th grade level of accomplishment when he was only nine years old and in the 4th grade. What was far more disturbing was the fact that he could answer correctly without paying attention to the teacher. Everyone was worried about this boy—a very sad case indeed. To return to the point, what we may expect of a given youngster cannot be determined from the curriculum, the methods of instruction, textbooks, home-work, parental aspirations or midnight oil. The nature of the individual besets us as the confounding factor at every turn. May I suggest at this point that it is the *intra*-individual, as well as the inter-individual differences that we are forced to adopt as a criterion of expectancy. But more of that in a moment.

Faced with the fact that individuals differ, and also with the fact that schools seem to increase individual differences rather than diminish them, what do we do? We test. Now a test is a list of items so chosen as to be successfully passed by some but not all of the population tested. It is constructed to measure individual differences. It is really a rubbery tape-measure without a zero point—that is, if it is a fairly good one—but sometimes it is no better than a device to sort pupils in their order of size, or to be more precise, in serial sequence of academic magnitude.

But tests have four major faults. I will only mention three of them and comment on the forth.

The first difficulty is that standardized tests do not necessarily test what is taught, except that there are certain similarities between the school systems in which the tests were standardized and the school systems using the tests. Such tests are especially made for the middle part of the population and they are even poorer measures of what is taught to children who deviate very much from the average.

The second fault is that standardized tests place a premium on recognition rather than recall. The latter is a higher level of learning.

The third problem is that tests yield data on inter-individual differences with little or no evidence of intra-individual differences.

The fourth fault lies in norms and in how we have used norms to obliterate measures even of inter-individual differences. A norm is nothing but an average. An average, by the way, has been defined as the result one gets when one foot is in the oven and the other in the ice box.

It is easy enough to understand the meaning of the average score for the fourth grade or the tenth. In normalizing tests however, every score is translated into an average at some age or grade level. Thus the scores for the fourth grade students become averages of grades 2, 3, 4, 5, 6, 7, 8, and all points in between. In doing this we have sacrificed the usual measures of scatter and thus of inter-individual differences. Since the differences between grades are neither linear nor equal, except possibly within a narrow span in the elementary school, it is nearly impossible to interpret age or grade norms when these refer to grades other than the one tested.

An additional problem is this. An average is a statement of the IS— the central tendency of existing conditions. It is not an ought.  It is not what should be. Furthermore, we cannot determine the OUGHT from the IS. We cannot, for example, determine the criterion of good health from the average state of health of the population, nor the desirable amount of delinquency from the current rate, nor the wished for peace of mind of the administrator by the mean number of grains of aspirin he takes, nor the desirable level of achievement in reading by the average score on a reading test.

What I have tried to say up to this point is that we cannot use either the curriculum nor tests to determine the level of expectancy for *any* given individual student. The best we can do is to compare his deviation scores on a variety of tests. In short, the problem is to arrive at a level of expectancy for each child, expecting that individuals will differ, without falling into the error of assuming that the then existing level of achievement should be what it is.

I wish to propose three ideas. The first is that we explore the nature of normal, healthy development within the range of individual differences; second that we adopt the concept of *learning pathologies* which may be detected and treated educationally; and third, the idea that each child provides within himself a criterion of expectancy for language potential. I want to develop the third idea for the field of language in detail here. This view is offered with research evidence in the hope that we may be able to avoid the error of setting standards to the average, to the grade level, or to the curriculum. The able child need not be paced to the average, nor the slower to the modal, nor the few to the many.

## II

The research I am about to report extends from the late 1930's to the present. It falls into two broad categories. The first of these was a period of discouraging results. The second, a period of exciting results.

Let me summarize briefly the first period. Some of you may recall the Adolescent Study conducted at the Institute of Child Welfare at the University of California in Berkeley, and supported by the Rockefeller Foundation. For a period of three years, beginning in 1935, I conducted a project in that Study to determine the relationship between vision and the ability to read. We used virtually every measure of visual abilities available at that time—three one-hour examinations by a university optometrist, Stanford batteries of achievement tests, Binet Tests, all the Telebinocular materials including experimental cards, measures of the accommodation-convergence reflex, and some 700 photographs of eye movements taken while reading. There were nearly 80 variables in all. Suffice it to say that the results were negative. Many measures were highly unreliable, and most of the 300 correlations between the ability to read and visual functions were so low that prediction was little above chance. But there was one exception.

The relation between the ability to read and the Binet M.A. was high, and between the vocabulary test on the Binet and Reading age it was still higher. This certainly was not a new discovery, but it led to rethinking our hypotheses about reading.

In our work with vision we had been exploring the relation between a *peripheral* function and printed word reading. But the Binet measures were of *central* nervous system functions. This was a clue to the hypothesis that the ability to read printed symbols was a central rather than a peripheral function. This suggested that the semantic element, understanding, was of more import than the sensory media. Then came the notion that the spoken form of language is the primary carrier of meaning. It was Dr. Herbert Stolz, as I recall, who stressed this point. As a result of emphasizing the central nervous system functions, the role of spoken language and hearing and the patterns of speech of the linguistic community to which a child is a member, we began to look into the patterns of development of the several modes of language: listening, speaking, reading and writing. Two of these are passive or receptive: listening and reading; and two are active or productive: speaking and writing. Of the two receptive modes, one is mainly auditory and the other visual. Both of the active, productive, modes require both central nervous system activity and complex motor patterns.

Is there any way of putting this complicated puzzle together?

We began searching for evidence wherever we could find promising bits of data. Mental tests were analyzed and vocabulary tests examined. I must omit much that was fascinating, but let me point out the first two most promising leads. When the Binet vocabulary and M. E. Smith's(1) studies were graphed by age levels they seemed to make sense. The two studies together made it appear that auditory vocabulary development was a straight line—a linear, arithmetic function in which the size of vocabulary was directly related to age. (Vocabulary in this sense refers to the ability to give *word meanings* to spoken word forms.) So far as I know there is no evidence that school influences spoken vocabulary either way—up or down—although either view might be hypothesized.

Vocabulary as we speak of it here refers to a sample of a large number of words in a designated parent population. It does not refer to a selected group of words that is convenient to use. By using a random sample of terms from a large word population, *e.g.* a dictionary, estimates may be made of "total" vocabulary. I should digress here for about an hour to discuss the complexities of estimating "total" vocabulary. I shall not, you will be delighted to hear. But permit me this: vocabulary estimates vary with the size of the dictionary sampled, with the mode of presentation, and obviously with the definition of the term "word." Since we are concerned with the relative sizes of vocabularies in the auditory and visual modes, we will not be in error if we use the same list as a baseline in both instances. But this is ahead of the story.

The second promising lead was a study by Hockett (1938) (2) in which he had determined the number of different words in elementary school readers at various levels. The median vocabularies (different words) of books ranging from pre-primers to 4th grade readers was as follows: 69, 276, 565, 1022, 1625, 3500. Note that vocabulary size approximately doubles each time. These data refer to books rather than children, but it led to the second hypothesis, namely: that reading vocabulary grows geometrically.

If this hypothesis were supported, we should number 'reading' grades differently as 1,2,4,8,16 rather than 1,2,3,4, etc. Furthermore we should expect to find a time when the auditory and visual vocabularies were approximately equal. I wondered at what age this would normally occur. I asked teachers. There were many guesses, but most of them said it would be at about 5th grade. At that time I was supervising about 20 teachers of remedial reading. We tried out the hypothesis in the teaching-clinical situation first. The basic idea was simplicity itself, namely: that we would expect a child—a boy in most cases—to be able eventually to learn to read at least as well as he understood *spoken language.* Situationally it would mean that if a father left a note for his son instructing him to feed the cattle and open the weir in the irrigation ditch, but found the work undone because the boy could not comprehend the note, he would know without the benefit of statistics, I.Q's, mental age, or anything else that language in written form did not get the message across to the boy. Now suppose the father said the same thing to his son, whereupon the boy said, "Oh, that's what you want. I understand." The father then knows that one of two things is true: either the boy has a specific reading difficulty, or, he may not have had time and opportunity to learn.

This concept applied in the clinical-remedial situation meant that if a child read through his ears better than he did through his eyes that he could improve his visual reading. The criterion of need for aid in visual reading of printed symbols was ability to understand spoken language better than visual language. Of course, we had mental tests too—usually Binets—and much other information, but the criterion of expectances was basically, that child's level of understanding language in auditory form. You'll be interested to know that the average rate of gain for 800 children over a two-year period was 2.4 times normal. The intelligence of this group was normal. The mean I.Q. was 100.2 and the spread was about what you would expect in a normal population.

But this clinical-remedial experience was far from solid confirming evidence that the hypothesis was correct. An experimental investigation was needed. This I did as my doctoral dissertation (3). A random sample of ⅓ of the children in grades one to eight in two Massachusetts schools was given auditory and visual presentations of the Binet Vocabulary List. This was the first time, to my knowledge, that both auditory and visual modes of presentation were obtained from the same vocabulary material. The results of this investigation of about 200 elementary school children confirmed to a surprising degree the hypotheses that auditory vocabulary growth was an arithmetic, straight-line function, and that the visual vocabulary developed in a geometric fashion.

One of the most interesting aspects of this study is that visual vocabulary correlated with "reading age" (with chronological age controlled) .88, or to an extent that is approximately as high as the reliability of the reading test itself. Thus it was possible to measure not only a child's expectancy in printed word reading but also to approximate his ability to read at the same time, and without the need of a so-called mental test. (Parenthetically, I would like to point out that the usual group mental tests are often worse than useless as measures of mental ability of children who have not learned to read printed symbols as well as the spoken word, for it is their facility with the printed word that constitutes a ceiling for their performance.)

Now let me propose for your consideration and invite your cordial interest in the proposition that the public schools employ criteria of EX-PECTANCY as well as one of ACHIEVEMENT . . . in addition to that OF GENERAL APTITUDE. To do this would require that both auditory and visual vocabularies be measured ON THE SAME SCALE, a scale based on a sample of a large word population. The ability of each child to comprehend the meaning of vocabulary presented to the EAR would be taken as the criterion of his *THEN* level of expectancy or potential in reading.

The results of such an additional measure would provide us with a new yardstick based on INDIVIDUAL *potential.* We should find, without doubt, that the STANDARD thus arrived at, would be above any of the bases we now use, to wit: age norms, grade norms, or mental age. We would have an objective, individual criterion for adjusting our sights. For the gifted it would be higher and for the less apt it would be lower than the averages we now use. We could take into account both individual differences and STANDARDS of EXPECTANCY.

Should such criteria be employed we would then be in a position to develop what the field of medicine has already accomplished. We could develop normal patterns of growth in reading printed symbols—and other fields of language—so that we might anticipate the ages at which there would be essentially no difference between auditory and visual modes of presentation. We would be able to assess linguistic maturity in these two modes of language. As far as data now indicate, this would be at about the end of the elementary school period, but for some children it would be as early as the end of the second grade.

Of equal importance we would also develop a concept that is still in its very infancy—the idea of what constitutes pathologies in language learning. These pathologies may be native or induced by improper teaching, or both. But this is a whole field that would require far more time than is now at our disposal.

Let me point out in closing that I have said almost nothing bearing upon auditory language development as it is influenced by culture, or about speech and spoken language, or about writing and spelling. These, too, fit into the theory of linguistic development. Let me propose the hypothesis that maturity is that stage in which the mode of presentation or expression is not a deterrent to intellectual potentials nor to the understanding of human linguistic communication.

## References

1. Smith, Madorah E., "An Investigation of the Development of the Sentence and the Extent of Vocabulary in Young Children" (Iowa City, Iowa: University of Iowa Studies: Child Welfare, III, No. 5 [1926]), 1–92.

2. Hockett, John A., *The Vocabularies and Contents of Elementary School Readers,* California State Department of Education, Bulletin No. 3 (May 1, 1938), 104.

3. Armstrong, Hubert C., *The Auditory and Visual Vocabularies of Children,* Unpublished Doctoral Dissertation, Stanford University, 1953.

# H. Alan Robinson

# *Reading and Realism*

These are grave days for education. We must be very concerned with the situation surrounding us, educationally, socially, economically, politically. We as teachers have not been trained for the situation today; and we are not, as I view it, training new teachers to face that varied environment. I hope we can make some changes. This is what this paper is all about.

I have already used the following quotation in another paper, but its grave timeliness and appropriateness necessitates my utilizing it again to set the stage for my comments.

> At exactly 5:13 a.m., the 18th of April 1906, a cow was standing somewhere between the main barn and the milking shed on the old Shafter Ranch in California, minding her own business. Suddenly the earth shook, the skies trembled, and when it was all over, there was nothing showing of the cow above ground but a bit of her tail sticking up. For the student of change, the Shafter cow is a sort of symbol of our time. She stood quietly enough, thinking such gentle thoughts as cows are likely to have, while huge forces outside her ken built up all around her and—within a minute —discharged it all at once in a great movement that changed the configuration of the earth, and destroyed a city, and swallowed her up. And that's what we're going to talk about now; how, if we do not learn to understand and guide the great forces of change that work on our world today, we may find ourselves like the Shafter cow, swallowed up by vast upheavals in our way of life—quite early some morning (1).

There is one unalterable fact in education—probably only one circumstance we cannot change—that is that the students are ever present in the

186

classroom. Sometimes, some teachers seem to wish that the students would disappear, except for a certain few, so that they might impart their knowledge without interference from the learner. This is particularly true in many graduate schools. Scholars feel they have a job to do, and students get in the way. No matter, in whatever school you wish to think about, the learner is there. Too often the learner has been treated as part of a struggling mass, an amoeba. We have allowed the form to change slightly, but we are afraid it will reproduce itself in different forms.

We have talked about individual differences to the point the term is hardly more than a cliche. Still, in most of the situations I have had the opportunity of viewing across the country I note, at the elementary school level, three struggling amoebas, three lesson plans for the three group method. I think it is about time we abolished it. Or at the secondary school level, I see most often one large struggling amoeba, and at times it seems as though it is a paramecium unable to alter its form. We appear to be a great distance from what we talk and write about when we say we must evaluate the strengths and needs of individuals. To make matters worse, we keep on evaluating with instruments which are faulty. We talk about the flaws, but little has been done to remedy them. We even make use of the tests we call faulty which provides us with such scores as 4.3 or 7.2, and upon this faulty basis we believe we have permission to do some kind of grouping we call "homogenous." We do know there are many other methods for evaluation, but we have done little about clustering the methods of evaluation together in a systems approach to diagnosis. Obviously, this is a direction in which we need to move, but teacher training programs, both before, during and in and out of the school situation, are not coming to grips with a systematic, valid, diagnostic approach to learning which will help us build programs for individual students. One single formula is not adequate. A formula is not what we need; we have many formulas. We need a strong conceptual framework for looking at individual strengths and weaknesses. And obviously we need to diagnose both strengths and weaknesses. We cannot treat an educational diagnosis as if it were comparable to medical diagnosis. In medicine if there is a need, the weakness is found, the treatment is given, and hopefully, the patient lives. In education we must find the strengths as well as the weaknesses because we defeat the learner by putting our focus exclusively on his weakness. In medicine the focus on weakness may bring the results. In education it often increases resistance and lowers ego development.

In addition to faulty diagnosis through the use, in my opinion, of formulas of diagnosis which supposedly should apply to each student, we have also maintained the myth that once we teach a skill in a particular context the learner will make it a part of him from that point on and will be able to use it anywhere. In believing this we have disregarded the large body of psychological literature which has shown us time and time again, that transfer of learning does not take place automatically. Nor does it take place easily. It may take place for the gifted or highly motivated learner; it often takes place if the environment in which it was learned is identical to the environment in which it will be used. For most learners, however, much help must be given in dealing with a skill in specific situations. We have also believed that if we teach a skill in using one type of discourse—such as narrative—it will automatically be usable in another type of discourse—such as expository.

For example, in a typical beginning reading program we are not teaching students how to cope with a variety of materials they must read in the curriculum; rather, we are teaching a literature program. We give students, in the main, much narrative material and through it, attempt to plug in all the skills we think a student ought to possess. In reality, many of them are very unsuitable for teaching through narrative material. Grasping main ideas, as one example, is very difficult to teach in literature. I am not sure it can be done at all except with isolated passages written in an expository vein. Still, we have produced materials including a vast array of workbooks, to go with them, based on the notion that children are learning what we teach. And so, we work with the skill in the workbook, we present little bits of additional material, and we train pupils to manipulate inconsequential if not unrelated bits of information. Very often we teach pupils to match titles on a workbook page to paragraphs without really giving them independence in grasping the main idea on their own. If we really wanted to help them grasp the main idea wherever they found it, we would have to build a very careful program using a variety of kinds of discourse so that they would be able to cope with the skill throughout the materials across a school curriculum.

What I am really saying then is that a reading program cannot be any one small part of a school day dealing with one small set of materials. I even question the seemingly accepted concept that a specific reading skill is the same when it is used with one type of material as it is with the other. We have assumed, as we have talked about grasping the main idea, that this is the same whether it is used with materials in physical science, in social studies, in mathematics. We need research studies in each curriculum field to look into the differences as well as the similarities of the specific skills we have called comprehension or study skills in reading, to see how they apply to the specific disciplines. Perhaps such studies will lead us to a readjustment of our ideas about the component parts of specific reading skills—or at least the labels we have given to those skills—if there is any validity to the idea that reading skills either change in nature or are altered by the discipline for which they are put to use. Then we need to be concerned with the reading program at every level as a vast network or array of skills, attitudes, and capacities which students can learn throughout the curriculum to apply to whatever materials are facing them during their lifetime of schooling.

It must be our credo that reading is indeed a process or processes, *that indeed it is not a subject.* Reading cannot stand alone in the curriculum; we cannot pride ourselves on an excellent reading program if it makes little or no contact with everything else going on around us. Reading has no content of its own. Reading depends upon the content fields for its life.

Let us relate some of the problems already mentioned to the terms "developmental" and "remedial" or "corrective" reading programs. When I visit a school or school system I usually ask for a definition of the reading program. At the elementary level, most of the time, I get the response that it is a particular basal reader system. At the secondary level I am often told that they have a program that is taught to certain groups of students during certain periods of the day. Much less frequently do I hear that the reading program is based on objectives set up by the total school community, that the school community is concerned with all kinds of communication throughout the curriculum, and that they have chosen particular procedures and materials to use in specific situations with specific learners.

The developmental reading program is meaningless if it fails to help students deal with the needs surrounding them now. A remedial or corrective program is of limited value if it only focuses on a group of skills to be learned. Too often the remedial program is dichotomous from the rest of the program. I have seen such programs as separate little situations, set aside from the ongoing curriculum, having little to do with it. Much of the time when I speak with remedial reading teachers in such programs, I find they were much happier when they were in the classroom, when they were on a par with classroom teachers and not set apart from them. Too often the environment for corrective or remedial work has not been prepared carefully through the endeavors of a total staff, and the classroom teacher feels that the remedial teacher just has a lighter load.

I am not sure that remedial reading situations as I have viewed them in many parts of this country and in other countries, are very effective. Not that they don't help some students; but I think they could be much more profitable. How much more profit to students would there be if we looked at the cliche, "take a child where he is," and considered it to be a little more than, "take him at beginning fourth grade level, if he measures fourth grade level on the standardized test." By taking him where he is must we not mean, "let's work with this learner in terms of his present environment," meeting his curricular demands as well as his personal-social needs. If, then, there is a "remedial reading room" it should house tape recorders, listening posts, television, and opportunities to do much in the way of all of the other communication areas, so that the student weak in working with specific reading skills might get some help through other modes. But most important of all, he can have help in meeting the reading demands surrounding him by using some of the workbooks and other reading skills development material to help develop these reading skills. Most important of all though, he would have help in meeting the curriculum demands surrounding him —he would be helped to cope to some extent with the materials now facing him in the classroom.

The remedial teacher has no business working only with a set of separate materials that have little to do with the ongoing program in the school. "Taking a child where he is" does not mean keeping someone who is in the tenth grade reading at a fourth grade level for fifty minutes per day for three days a week while the rest of the time he sits in a tenth grade class looking at tenth grade material. He needs the help of the teacher in the remedial situation with those tenth grade materials. He can manage much more intelligently with that kind of guidance even if he is reading at a so-called fourth grade level. He can get help at looking at topics, in reading pictures, diagrams, and individual sentences, and in learning how to go to the questions and finding answers. He can get help through other modes in developing an experience background and in enriching his knowledge.

Obviously the whole program would be more potent if the remedial reading teacher could go to the classroom teacher and say "we've got to do something about adjusting materials. We've got to have many different kinds of materials, not just books, but many other kinds of reading materials. And such materials should be at a variety of levels dealing with content related to the experiential and curricula needs of the students. The emphasis should be placed on the acquisition of ideas through skill development, not on the acquisition of skills alone." The classroom teacher needs help as well in differentiating assignments, especially if he cannot get a variety of materials. Even if there is only one textbook, a teacher can learn to differentiate assignments so that poorer readers have things to do with which they may cope.

If we are going to build a sound reading program we must be concerned about curriculum change. If a reading program is to be integrated into the total curriculum, this means, obviously, the curriculum is to meet the needs of the students. We have attempted to adjust basal readers and trade books in that segment we call our reading program, but we have not progressed very far in adjusting to the kinds of materials. Although most retarded readers, with guidance, can learn to cope at least in some limited way with the materials about them, there are obviously some very poor readers or non-readers who need what might be called "basic help."

Very often with these new readers we have started with a word list to build up their sight vocabulary. I am not sure that this is the best kind of help—this single word identification level, per se. I think we can probably do more by concentrating at least on the sentence level so that the communication is more meaningful. With these readers language experience approaches are probably desirable, but I would certainly not restrict it to just the story experiences of students. Such approaches can also reflect exposition and can be used to develop expository sentences and paragraphs. I am reasonably certain that youngsters who come from linguistically deprived backgrounds would be better off without books in the classroom for quite a while before they turned to alien language structures. Our use of language experience approaches should not only permit children to bring out their feelings, but to feel fully accepted in the classroom by the teacher and by their peers.

A language experience approach, both for linguistically disadvantaged children and others, would force us to look at the materials we introduce so that the transition from the spoken words familiar to the children to the printed words might not be a major obstacle. Teachers must not be just manipulators of materials. They must be selectors and producers of materials that will meet the needs of the individuals in their classrooms.

There is, of course, no such thing as any one language. Language is not stable; it is not absolute. It changes. And we should be willing to listen to many kinds of languages. In fact, as teachers, we speak many kinds of languages. We have a language we most often speak in school, but we very often speak a different one at home. The student needs to learn to feel free in the classroom, to use both the language he knows best, and the other kinds of languages that are needed for specific types of situations. One of the grave difficulties is that he does not meet this when he comes to the printed word. The teacher needs to fill in these gaps. Somehow the student needs to realize that people not only speak in different ways, but write in different ways, and one of the reasons for his going to school is to learn how to broaden his understanding of the various ways of communicating. He will learn best not by having someone say to him that there are different kinds of languages, but by the attitude he finds in the classroom in relation to language. In other words, certainly in the early stages of learning, and certainly when new subjects are being introduced, more emphasis needs to be placed on language and language development than on a single process growing out of language, such as reading print. Granted, it is important for students to learn how to read in given disciplines, but this reading will be a much easier task if it has been preceded by careful guidance in the language of the discipline. Such emphasis on language development means that all teachers, teachers of specific subjects in the high school as well as generalists in the elementary school, need to have training in language development. Part of their education program needs to consist of learning about our language, its strengths and its limitations. Reading methods courses alone are not sufficient. Prescriptions, manipulations of materials, and formula-following result often from a lack of understanding of our language.

In approaching reading realistically, it is also especially important that we learn to evaluate carefully and systematically. Obviously, we want to look at current reading research dealing with new programs. We want to look at such research cautiously and be sure that innovations are not just accepted because something new resulted in better scores on standardized tests than something old. When innovations purport to be successful and this success is based on improvements in reading scores, we need to look further. Gates has said,

> . . . any device which is of great value for certain children is typically mediocre or futile and frustrating for others. A method which is best even for a large majority of a class may be unsuitable for the rest. . . . I hope that as you observe the reports of future research you will remember that, even when the "experimental method" surpasses the "control" method by a wide margin, the way in which the experimental procedure confused and confounded Johnny and Fred and Mary and Peter is concealed in the mass scores, however high the reliability of the averages may be (2).

In other words, if i.t.a. is being used in a particular situation, with enthusiasm, and if at the end of the experiment the median score in that class is higher than it is in the other class (without even thinking about any other controls), what about the Johnny and Mary and Theresa and Tom who scored at the lower part of the experimental group? What do we know about them? What procedure would perhaps have been better for them? We may have found an approach successful for some students, but at the same time, we may not have found what approach is best for others. Our research efforts and our evaluation of research must look very carefully at the individual within the learning situation.

I have already suggested several ways of making reading more realistic. I have talked about the need to put real emphasis on the individual student and teach through his strengths to his weaknesses. I have suggested that we cannot count on the transfer of learning to carry our total reading program across the curriculum. I have also suggested that the total reading program really should be integrated with the total curriculum and not just considered one isolated part of it. I have questioned the remedial and corrective reading program as it is found in a number of settings, and have suggested that it not be divorced from the rest of the program in a school. I have shown concern for the materials we use and placed emphasis on language development and language experience approaches. I have also indicated that reading research and our evaluation of innovations ought to consider the individual's success rather than the group's success.

In light of the factors already discussed, there are three developments which hold promise for providing optimum opportunities for individual learners: 1) the instructional materials team, 2) broadened concepts of the term, motivation, and 3) systems approaches.

A most important way of providing the best opportunity for optimal learning, and to achieve full integration of the reading program within the curriculum, is to establish an instructional materials team in every school. This team needs to be trained fairly broadly and know something about each of the disciplines. If the team does not have enough information about a particular discipline, there must be a planned way for the team to get further information. Teams should work in collaboration with the classroom teachers to develop and stock suitable materials for the particular students in that particular school. In addition to many kinds of excellent commercial materials now available, we need these kinds of assistance to teachers. It is in this way the school can make contact with the environment of the student.

The instructional materials team approach not only results in producing materials related to the pupils' environments, but also helps in meeting the needs of particular objectives and goals. In fact, an instructional materials team can even help to develop more realistic goals. Reading in this context has an immediate payoff.

We must also broaden our thinking about motivation. However, at certain stages in the lives of certain learners it may be much more functional to concentrate on concrete goals achieved through extrinsic rewards. A linguistically disadvantaged youngster may very well learn to read a sentence that says, "I get a piece of candy," when he knows he will get the piece of candy, than a sentence that has little meaning for him but promises some far-flung abstract goal.

Approaches to diagnosis and instruction in teaching reading may eventually become possible through systems networks. A system is an integrated cluster of techniques where a variety of modes are capitalized on so that individual learners may benefit from that combination of learning strategies most suited to their own modes of learning. Optimistically, an instructional system could take care of the many individual needs in a particular classroom, school or school system. Hopefully, such a system might play a role in integrating the processes of communication throughout the content of the total curriculum.

Nonetheless, if reading instruction and indeed instruction in all communication capacities is to be realistic—that is, meeting the demands of the learner—we need to make changes in our teacher education programs. There are, as I see it, three levels of teacher education—the inspiration level, the discussion level, and the involvement level. We have used level one and some of level two with very little of level three. The inspiration level may be effective at the beginning stage or at one or two singular places in a training program, but it certainly cannot stand by itself in changing the learner. The second, or discussion level, provides a slightly better situation. At this level small groups of individuals come together to talk about problems as they perceive them. The third, the involvement level, is used much less frequently, probably because it means the concentrated work of a small group who must participate until change takes place. Industry uses this approach extensively. Education seems fearful of it.

In-service programs should be conceptualized as on-the-job training as conceived of in industry. A faculty should be studied for its strengths and weaknesses in terms of the problems to be solved. The training program should then be set out in order to help solve problems by filling in on the weaknesses of the faculty. In-service programs should be offered throughout the school day. Such programs will more nearly meet the real needs of teachers if they are held at the involvement level. This means that there should be a specific, workable problem, that the teachers have to deal with, and the group should be small. The result should be changed behavior. In-service courses should not be given for salary increment; they should be part of the job. Teachers should be paid for learning as well as teaching. Pre-service training and graduate training at the college and university setting also needs to be strengthened. It is, of course, impossible for a training institution to do the whole job. In-service education must always be a part of the function of a school system. There must be a continuity between pre-service and in-service. But it does seem obvious that the teacher-trainer is not equipping the teacher to deal with the present circumstances in the classroom. Unfortunately, too many college professors are able to verbalize without having been in a classroom setting recently. It is probably necessary for us to develop a two-way street when we speak of educational consultants. It is fine for the college professor to be a research consultant to the school or school system, but the professor needs a consultant from the schools as well. In order to have an effective program of pre-service training, we need to have good teachers and advisors from the schools look at the college course of study and tell us what is really going on. We also need to get into the school and look for ourselves. Courses need to be altered to deal with the times.

Teachers need to be helped to think so they may get students to think. University and college students must learn more and more to help educate themselves. College instructors should be resource persons, stimulators, process developers. Emphasis must be placed on thinking if we are to get students in our classrooms throughout the nation to think. Controversial materials of all kinds should be introduced into the classroom so that students may think, evaluate, select, discard, retain.

Realistic reading instruction can be achieved and maintained if faculty members and community members will help set concrete as well as abstract goals for their learners in *their* situations. There is no reason why teaching procedures and materials used in instruction should be the same from one situation to another. Programs must be tailored for need—for realistic need.

In his "The American Scholar," Ralph Waldo Emerson stated: "Meek young men grow up in libraries, believing it their duty to accept the views which Cicero, which Locke, which Bacon, have given; forgetful that Cicero, Locke, and Bacon were only young men in libraries when they wrote these books."

Teachers and teacher trainers, accepting of new ideas and yet cautious of evaluating each, are still faced with the unalterable fact—those students sitting in the classroom. They need aggressive teaching in tune with the reality of their environment. They need to learn how to learn and how to communicate. They cannot settle for an education of approximations. They cannot wait for tomorrow. And, perhaps more important, they cannot and must not be cheated by an educational system unequipped, unready, and all too frequently unwilling to change.

## References

1. Don Fabun, *The Dynamics of Change* (Englewood Cliffs, N.J.: Prentice-Hall, Inc., 1961), 1.
2. Arthur I. Gates, "Characteristics of Successful Teaching of Reading," in *Reading: Seventy-five Years of Progress* (H. Alan Robinson, ed.). (Chicago: University of Chicago Press, 1966), 19.

Harry F. Wolcott

# The Ideal and the Real World of
# Teaching Reading*

Anthropologists frequently make a distinction between two aspects of cultural behavior: the real world of actual behavior—what people *do*—and the ideal world of normative behavior, what people *say* they do or say they *ought* to do. Neither world is actually less "real" than the other. The kind of sharing of behaviors and expectations which comprises the way of life of a group of people—their culture—depends as much on shared notions of what *ought to be* as on shared perceptions of what *is*. At the same time, in every culture there are paradoxes between the real and ideal. These paradoxes themselves are of varying magnitude, now humorous or mildly ironical, now presenting the individual with important alternatives, now providing him with options that find him behaving in ways antithetical to the very goals he is trying to achieve.

The cultural anthropologist, in attempting to provide what Clyde Kluckhohn referred to as a "mirror for man," seeks to present man with a way of looking at his own behavior so he may better come to understand it. As an observer of human behavior, and typically as an outsider to the group he is studying, the anthropologist frequently provides a new perspective simply by identifying paradoxes in a given cultural system. His purposes in studying any cultural behavior are to describe and to analyze it. His research is not necessarily focused on the paradoxes or discrepancies between the real and ideal in a cultural system, but neither does he ignore the inevitable contrasts once they have been identified. No group of humans has ever worked out perfectly integrated patterns of behavior where there

*This paper is an abridged and revised version of a longer paper, "The Ideal World and the Real World of Reading: An Anthropological Perspective" (Bloomington, Ind., ERIC Clearinghouse on Reading, in press). The author wishes to acknowledge the editorial assistance of Norman Delue in the preparation of the present version.

is no conflict or strain, where there is only one course of action possible in every conceivable social situation, and where real and ideal behavior correspond perfectly.

Here, I have taken an anthropological perspective in examining five aspects of the teaching of reading. I have sought to identify contrasts between the ideal world—what we say is going on or what we want to believe is going on in the reading classroom—and what is actually going on there.

## The Ideal and the Real World of Expertise in Teaching Reading

First, consider the teacher as an expert in reading instruction. *Ideally,* we like to think of those teachers whose work includes the teaching of reading as professionals possessing a specialized body of knowledge regarding this area of instruction. Many aspects of the teaching of reading contribute to the idealized image of the teacher of reading as an expert. For example, parents seldom have specific and accurate information about what goes on in classrooms, yet they share a long tradition when they attribute their child's reading progress to the competence of his teacher. Adults have forgotten how they themselves became readers. Lacking evidence to the contrary, most of them regard their reading ability as a happy consequence of their early schooling.

The ideal of achieving expertise in teaching reading is supported by the existence of a formal and extensive body of literature, by a proliferation of courses at the university level in the methodology and problems of teaching reading, and by the presence of specialists who make reading instruction their life work. The field of reading has its own journals, its own professional associations, and its own high priests. To someone outside the reading "establishment" these aspects of reading are known *about,* rather than known, but they help to reinforce faith in the efficacy of the experts and in the knowledge base from which they work. For the aspiring teacher, initiation into the role of reading teacher reinforces a faith in the existence and power of a specific body of knowledge and professional performance. As long as instruction in how to teach reading remains at the theoretical level —that is, the lecturer talks about it rather than does it—a teacher-to-be may feel that he really *is* mastering how to teach reading. Or at least he may sustain the belief that a definitive body of research literature on reading does exist, even if it is beyond his immediate grasp. Consider the level of expertise pertaining to reading instruction implied in the following questions taken from a test given to students enrolled in a university course on the teaching of reading in the elementary school:

1. Name the five word attack skills and follow each with an adequate illustration.
2. Name in proper order the steps listed by Dolch for the teaching of skills.
3. Give three reasons why consonants should be taught before vowels.
4. Why is "sounding out words" not reading?
5. Should sounds be learned first or words? Defend your answer.

A student from whose paper I extracted these questions received full credit for the following answer to the question, "What purposes do word attack skills serve and how many should be used?":

> They aid in learning to say new words. They should be used as part of other methods to teach reading, thus maintaining a balanced approach.

In discussing his reaction to the reading methods course and to this test the student said to me, "To tell you the truth, I didn't get just a whole lot out of that course. I got a D on this particular quiz, which was on a phonics book. Needless to say, I didn't read it." [Needless to say, this student was not considered the most promising candidate in his teacher-training program.]

*In reality,* the teaching of reading combines a disparate mixture of art and science based heavily on tradition, seasoned with a constantly changing complement of mildly innovative devices, served in an aura of crucial significance, and almost guaranteed some degree of success by the fortuitous element of maturity. Children today spend so long in school that the majority who do learn to read may do so as a result of sheer exposure rather than as a result of instruction. The critical question is: Do children learn to read *because of* the skill of their reading teacher, with the *assistance of* that skill, or *in spite of it?*

Consider this latter possibility—that children learn to read, for the most part, independent of the instructional activities of their teachers. No one, as far as I know, has attempted to study the plausibility of this important question or investigated what may sound like a strange complement to it: Could we ever prevent a child who wanted to read from learning to do so?

Suppose we explore the idea that the process of learning to read is independent of our efforts at instruction. We might compare the role of the reading teacher with some other culturally assigned role for which desired consequences appear to be independent of the role performance believed to cause them. In all cultures we recognize certain behaviors and roles which are associated with and believed able to influence important consequences, although we usually find it easier to identify such behaviors and roles in other cultures (e.g., the couvade, shamanistic curing, or rain dancing) rather than in customs common in our own society (e.g., observing superstitions, praying for the sick, or "keeping our finger crossed").

For purposes of analogy, let us explore a comparison between the reading teacher and a rain dancer. What insight do we have about human behavior under circumstances where highly desirable outcomes, like getting a needed rainfall or acquiring the ability to read, may occur quite independently from our immediate efforts to produce them?

In this analogy assume a similar seriousness of purpose for the rain dancer or the reading teacher. Although each deals with a phenomenon we are here considering to be outside of his control, neither entertains the possibility that his efforts, when properly executed, do not effect a significant influence. The rain dancer carefully repeats every part of his traditional performance exactly the way it was taught to him—to neglect any one aspect is to invite failure based on the possibility that *this* was the crucial gesture, the right thought, the essential sequence, or the proper timing of the performance. It worked last time; it will work again. When an apprentice is to learn the dance, he must learn it perfectly, for who can say which element can be ignored or slighted in the total ritual as it has traditionally been performed.

Like the rain dancer, the reading teacher solemnly performs a complicated ritual, introducing skills and drills in a traditional sequence. This is how I taught reading last year. My pupils learned to read. Therefore, this is how I am teaching reading this year. Apprentices to whom future responsibility in performing the ritual is to be trusted are carefully instructed and their apprenticeship is closely supervised to assure the mastery of practices essential to the ceremony.

Apparently there is no single *best method* for teaching reading, there is no guaranteed approach or foolproof set of materials. When teachers are called upon today to explain (or defend) their own classroom approach, they seem inclined to rationalize their instructional procedure because of its *lack of dependence* on any one approach. Like the rain dancer, the reading teacher recognizes a host of elements that are potential contributors to the total performance and each receives its due. New methods are often only shifts in emphasis as we become excited over the potential of certain aspects of the ritual, such as phonics, to the neglect of others, like "sight words."

Why are non-readers such a threat to teachers? If learning to read occurs independently of teacher effort, we can speculate that non-readers threaten teachers because teachers are unable to show any results with them in spite of their efforts. If teachers actually had the expertise they are purported to have, then they could help. As it is, the existence of non-readers suggests a lack of teacher expertise, just as an extended drought may lead to suspicion about the effectiveness of the rain dancer. The success of teachers of remedial reading would seem to controvert this point except for the fact that some remedial teachers using the "worst" methods are said to get good results anyway, an indication that social factors, like a change of surroundings or a decrease in peer influence, may be more critical than the techniques employed.

Instead of maintaining the generally accepted idea that *teachers can teach children about reading,* our exploration of learning to read as a phenomenon relatively independent of instruction might lead us ultimately to hold that *reading teaches teachers about children.* It is the child's presentation of himself as a reader which provides the basis for the teacher's assessment of the child's intellectual capabilities. The teacher judges his pupils by how well they read, and we find a self-fulfilling prophecy in which past performance determines future expectations. The child constantly presents an intellectual image of himself to the teacher, providing the teacher with an informal, essentially intuitive rating of the child within the particular classroom. The child's performance on formal standardized tests, tests which are inevitably related to or dependent upon reading skills, is taken by the teacher as further and more conclusive evidence of academic potential because it is validated by the aura of scientific measurement. To illustrate with case study material, consider the effect of test results on the attitude of this teacher working in a oneroom school with Indian pupils of low reading ability. In November, before formal testing, he wrote:

> I have some bright students and I mean it. I have some who are average and I have some that are just plain stupid—let's face it, you'll find this in *any* school.

Two months later, after administering a standardized test, his reaction was:

> I have just finished giving all the second through seventh graders I.Q. tests. WOW! Now I know why I usually had the feeling of beating my head against the proverbial brick wall! I have out of eight students tested, only one I.Q. over 76!! They're all of the near-idiot caliber. God! I was bowled over. Then I figured out their respective mental ages and this was just another shock wave!!—even my 13-15 year olds have mental ages of 10!! How can you stop from lowering your own bloody standards after reading results like this (1)?

Instead of asking himself what might be *wrong with the test* for these particular pupils, the teacher let the test results tell him what was *wrong with his pupils.* When official standardized scores failed to sustain his more optimistic intial assessment, his confidence in the ability of his pupils to learn diminished. Occasionally the situation is reversed and pupils perform better than their teachers anticipate. When this happens, teachers absolve themselves of their error in assessment by applying the curious label of "overachievers" to their pupils.

Learning to read has never been an elective activity in school. Like most other rights guaranteed for pupils, the newly heralded "Right to Read" program disguises as a right what the schools hold to be their clearest mandate in the formal training of the young: They Shall Read! Regardless of whether pupils are necessarily helped by special programs and concentrated attention to reading instruction, receiving such instruction has never been optional at school. Nonreaders have always been the target of an endless barrage of teacher effort and teacher concern. A student who is living with reading failure is apt to find attendance at school an unrewarding experience. Research supports our suspicion that reading-disabled pupils show more maladjustment than pupils making normal progress.

The purpose here is not to argue that teachers have no effect on the process of learning to read. I do suggest, however, that there is a lack of clear and convincing evidence about the effectiveness of what it is that teachers do in class that contributes to the process of reading. The vast and sometimes frighteningly ambiguous body of research in reading is curiously biased to the study of the teaching of reading rather than to the study of learning to read.

## The Ideal and the Real World of Classroom Literature

As another aspect of the ideal and real in the teaching of reading, let us examine classroom reading as a window to the world. *Ideally,* we think of reading as providing pupils a vicarious way to explore and experience their world. *In reality,* the picture of the world presented to children through the books available to them in school is a carefully screened one. Martin Mayer commented in his book *The Schools,* "Hemingway's *Old Man and the Sea* has been seized on gleefully . . . there is no s-e-x in it." His observation calls attention to only one of many facets of human life purged from the content of classroom reading. The content of those books which filter past the zealous watch of parent-censors, chary administrators, and placating teachers is not threatening to adults but neither is it exciting reading for pupils. The basal readers are usually criticized for being the worst of the lot. Mayer gave this candid reaction to the basal readers:

> The books are stupid and dull; despite all the grandiloquent claims to the contrary, they are regarded everywhere simply as "books for learning to read," not as books that anybody who already knows how to read might be interested in looking at. They are written in the flattest and deadest imaginable style, and the conversation in them are embarrassingly unlike the speech of children or adults (2).

I do feel, however, that the oft-maligned "Dick and Jane" have taken more than their fair share of criticism for being the reason for the absence of genuine literature in the classroom. Taken to represent basal readers in general, "Dick and Jane" are criticized for providing an insipid non-literature, for representing only the middle-class, and for representing an unrealistic picture of American life. As to the first criticism, that they are non-literature, one can ask: are they intended to be contributions to literature? The answer is that they are not. They are instructional media developed on the basis of the hypothesis that learning to read is an accumulation of discrete skills which must be presented in an orderly sequence.

The second criticism—that the readers deal exclusively with people and experiences typical of the middle class (and therefore, the argument goes, lower class or ethnically different children cannot identify with the characters or relate their own experiences to the reading material), may be warranted (3), but it leads us to a too-simple conclusion. The problem lies not in the readers themselves, but with the total orientation of public schools to a middle-class way of life. While it is fashionable to criticize the readers for showing how life is fun in a smiling, fair-skinned world (4), this argument draws our attention to the minor faults of the basal readers and diverts us from an awareness of how *everything* connected with schooling tends to be middle class. The basal readers are no more middle class than the teachers, the curriculum, the architecture, or the daily time schedule. Basal readers are designed for volume sales. The content is a compromise to wide appeal; the demands of the market preclude the possibility of providing stories and characters with whom all students can identify. Recent efforts in developing multiethnic readers seem to have resulted essentially in substituting one socio-economic or ethnic class for another.

The point that basal readers portray an unrealistic picture of American life has a leavening footnote. Suppose we accept the criticism that classroom literature provides a carefully screened picture of the real world and recognize that the basal readers epitomize the consequences of content screening. What picture do they present of American life? Otto Klineberg posed the question in his critique of the basal readers: What if a visitor from Mars tried to reconstruct a picture of life in America solely from the content of the readers? What kind of picture would he have? He concluded that the picture would be one of all-white (mostly blonde) happy, friendly Americans, North European in origin, going pleasantly about their work with a minimum of frustration and in a setting peopled by gentle and understanding parents, doting grandparents, cooperative neighbors, and warmhearted strangers. Certainly the authors of the readers have succeeded in utilizing innocuous content in complying with the public school tradition of avoiding controversy. But the picture that our mythical Martian gets is by no means a haphazard selection of non-controversial traits and episodes.

Rather, the basal readers provide an excellent normative statement of American life: all the nagging problems of the real world are gone—there is no violence, no injustice, no hunger or poverty, no sickness, no pollution, no overcrowding; there is leisure time for travel and fun; and, most important to American norms, there is no problem regarding differences because, in the normative world of the readers, the differences themselves are gone. There are no ethnic minorities, there are no lower classes, there are not even any old people except a still-spry set of grandparents keeping up a few acres in the country. A realistic picture, no; a reflection of American norms, definitely. We would only hope our Martian is enough of a social scientist to recognize that the image of American life as presented through basal readers is a utopian one.

## The Ideal and the Real World of Reading for Fun

Next, consider the place of fun and work in classroom reading. *Ideally,* reading is pleasureful. We eulogize its excitement and satisfactions. Books are written telling us how to provide reading experiences for young people that will lead them "one step at a time up the ladder of reading enjoyment." An outsider might be led to believe that the sheer joy of reading supplies all the motivation necessary in the reading classroom. One might assume naively that the dominant activity in the reading class is pupil reading, and that the only other activity occurs during those moments of instruction when the teacher attempts to improve the specific reading skills of the pupils.

*In reality,* the reading class, like every other period of the school day, is dominated by the spectre of our work-ethic culture which dictates that because reading *is* fun—as it is for at least some students—it must be both meted out and, especially, earned.

Classroom reading confronts the work ethic morality with a curious problem. In the work ethic, one is ultimately rewarded for his efforts—a man *earns* his rewards. The sequence itself is important. First the work, then the pleasure that derives from it. The traditional approach to classroom reading reverses this proper order—the pleasure of reading a story precedes the "follow-up activities" which earn it. The reward for classroom reading is almost inevitably some class assignment of a non-reading nature (e.g., writing a book report, completing a fill-in assignment, or, in primary grades, drawing a picture about the story). That such assignments are work, or at least the classroom equivalent of it, is clearly reflected in the names given to the activities: "reading work," "workbook," "seat work" (or, as it is more deprecatingly known, "busy work"); it is also reflected in the comments one hears from teachers during the reading class: "Have you boys back there finished your reading work?" or "Some children are doing a nice job of reading today."

To avoid the risk of having the pleasure precede the effort, some teachers treat both the reading of a story in a basal reader and the follow-up assignment as reading "work." This work must be completed in order to earn the reward of "fun" reading of a book of one's choice or at a specially designated "fun" reading place within the classroom such as a "library table" where magazines can be perused without the penalty of a subsequent assignment.

## The Ideal and the Real World of the Reading Period

Now look at the role of the classroom teacher during the reading period. *Ideally,* the teacher's role in the reading class is an instructional one concerned primarily with helping pupils improve necessary reading skills. *In reality,* while the reading period may well be the busiest one of the classroom teacher's day, the portion of the teacher's efforts immediately related to teaching skills in reading is small compared to the time devoted to the management of the entire class, to rituals of the reading class such as "motivating" the reading of a new story or hearing a story read aloud, and to maintaining classroom traditions like pursuing quiet, practicing manners, and keeping everyone busy.

The reading classroom is busy for the teacher in part because one of its objectives is to free time for instructing a few pupils while other pupils carry on independently at tasks sufficient to keep them occupied (intellectually, if possible) without having to interrupt the teacher for assistance or approval. An analogy might be drawn between the teacher during the reading period and an organist playing a giant console intent on keeping every key playing for the maximum amount of time. One consequence of a preoccupation with keeping every pupil or key occupied is that the theme or continuity may have to be sacrificed to do so. Quantity of teacher-pupil interaction is substituted for quality of instruction. Primary teachers, for example, are delighted when they can report after the reading period, "Today I heard *everyone.*"

One of the remarkable things about many teachers during the reading class is the contrast between the concentrated attention they require of their pupils and their own diffuse attention which seems to enable them to "catch" anything going on anywhere in the classroom. Let me illustrate with a few specific examples, in this case the remarks made by a primary grade teacher during one brief reading period and recorded by a student observer:

Stay in your seat until I call you. I'm not going to call you for a minute. You have some reading to do.

Polly, do you have a pencil that's not yours?

There's a little bit too much visiting. If you're visiting, I don't think you're working.

Boys and girls, don't tell the words. These stories have some words we need to figure out ourselves.

Ann, you have your *other* workbook to do.

Let's get your papers from yesterday out. Those playing checkers are fine. The rest of you, let's get something to do. Hurry, I'm waiting.

If learning is proportional to the time and emphasis given by the teacher, then the reading period in this classroom served as a vehicle for teaching many lessons, most of which were more concerned with classroom behavior than with reading behavior. The actual role of the teacher provided little opportunity for or evidence of the teacher acting as an instructor unless the teaching of reading is as simple as naming the words a child cannot read. Yet the reading period was a busy one for the teacher being observed, and she demonstrated success in keeping the period a busy one for most pupils. There is a great deal of skill required to keep children in a classroom occupied, but the skill is of a different order from expertise in teaching about vowel sounds, dipthongs, or initial consonant blends.

## The Ideal and the Real World of Learning About Reading

Last, let us look at the possibility of unintended consequences in the teaching of reading. *Ideally,* what the teacher intends for the pupil to learn in the reading lesson, as in any lesson, is what the pupil actually learns. *In reality,* the lesson as a teacher intends it is never exactly the same as the lesson perceived by a learner. Pupils perceive many simultaneous lessons at once. Some of these lessons are intended by the teacher; others are not (5). Let me suggest three potential unintended consequences of the teacher's efforts in the reading classroom.

The first unintended consequence deals with the narrow concept of "reading" as used in the formal setting of the school. At the extreme, one finds pupils so accustomed to receiving a classroom assignment to read a story and then complete a subsequent reading-work task, that any variation in this procedure is likely to be considered by pupils to be non-reading, even when the non-reading activity may consist of reading a book of one's own choice completely free from any subsequent assignment. Thus the reading classroom may come to be associated with the narrowest expectation of what constitutes reading rather than with the wide context in which adult reading takes place. Similarly, the pupil who "learns" in school that he is a poor reader may overcome his school-learned self-concept and find pleasure in adult reading if he discovers that it is not like classroom reading. It is also possible, however, that he will eschew reading because of the kind of reading to which he was exposed in school. The suggestion here is that the child who continues to read as an adult may do so in spite of, rather than because of, the reading experiences of the classroom. This is hardly the intent of the teacher.

Second, consider the unintended consequence of making the reading period a time of pupil dependence. Because reading is such a uniquely individual activity, it would seem to lend itself to pupil independence. The whole purpose of reading instruction is, after all, to develop each pupil's reading skills so that he can "attack" new words independently. Much is made of independent reading habits and of providing pupils with "independent seat work."

A critical examination of what actually goes on in the classroom reveals that while independence may be a stated objective of the reading program, the organization of the classroom typically generates dependence instead. The factors which contribute to this unintended consequence are in part due to the very nature of classrooms as groups rather than individuals assembled for instruction. As the number of pupils increases, the teacher's estimate of the appropriate level of difficulty for independent work becomes increasingly a compromise between assignments too easy for some pupils and too difficult for others. Too-difficult assignments lead to greater pupil need for help. Too-easy assignments lead to other classroom problems for the teacher, problems both of pupil output and of pupil behavior. Teacher dominance in either aspect leads back to dependence on the teacher. Perhaps these are the very problems which new computer programs are designed to ameliorate. I have not had an opportunity to observe such programs in action. I do know that in my community computers are not applying for teaching jobs in the elementary schools.

Some of the teacher's activities during the reading period actually *preclude* reading rather than nurture it. To a certain extent the reading classroom can be viewed as a plot against reading. We have already discussed how classroom traditions restrict the scope of material which is acceptable as reading. We know that few teachers can resist the temptation to chastise pupils who appear to be doing "escape" reading. Teachers also restrict the output of certain *kinds* of classroom reading, often restricting the reading of those very materials which have been identified as possessing the power to turn pupils into readers. As one of reading's "high priests" once explained to me, the stories or programmed exercises in any sequential series are "like vitamins—they must be taken regularly to do any good, but you don't take them all at once." The adult logic here may be sound, but perhaps children take a different perspective: Here is a book that is supposed to help me learn to read. If I can only read one or two stories a week, learning to read will take forever. If I read it now, I will be a better reader sooner. In my own teaching I can recall the day when the slowest reader in my class—a boy, naturally—took from my desk the next harder book in the reading series in which he was reading, carried it home, and read it—all in direct violation of my instructions. For some unexplained reason, immediately following that incident he made a noticeable gain in his classroom reading.

There are additional ways in which teachers reduce the amount of reading that is done in the reading period. The assignment of non-reading tasks and teacher talk are two examples of such "plots" against reading.

By "non-reading assignments" I refer to those "follow-up" activities assigned in the reading period which may require or develop other useful skills but which minimize or ignore reading. I have already suggested the influence of our work-ethic culture on reading: because reading is pleasurable, it must be earned by some show of effort. Reading effort, however, is difficult, if not impossible, to assess directly, and the assessment of reading effort must be based almost solely on what we charitably describe as "related activities" for evaluating pupil performance. Thus classroom reading leads almost inevitably to subsequent non-reading tasks. At the extreme, it is reading itself that is excluded from the reading classroom, and we find teacher and pupil attention diverted to making puppets to act out stories, to doing and correcting word puzzles and worksheets, or to preparing a chart of standards for giving an oral book report.

Teacher talk is a more subtle "plot" against reading, in part because we expect teachers to talk in class, and in part because we tend not to differentiate between pupil reading and teacher talk about reading. Teacher talk is actually institutionalized as part of the formal reading lesson, both in "motivating" stories and in explaining follow-up assignments. In her analysis of the teacher's manual accompanying one widely-used beginning reader, Jeanne Chall found that a teacher who dutifully followed the manual in guiding the pupil's reading of a story would ask *one question for every seven words read by a pupil* (6).

Reading is a quiet, individual activity. Talk precludes reading, particularly if it is directed at the reader, yet the quantity of teacher talk in class is not necessarily diminished during the reading period. Excessive teacher talk can follow several patterns. My observations in schools suggest that some teachers do their greatest amount of talking in their attempt to maintain pupil quiet during reading periods. Some teachers make a comment of praise every time a pupil completes a turn at oral reading; others repeat each sentence or even reread aloud the entire selection that a pupil has just read.

One of my students observing a first grade classroom during a reading lesson once attempted to record all the comments made by the teacher. Although he recorded neither pupil comments nor pupil reading, the extent of the teacher's comments are sufficient for reconstructing the essence of the lesson. Here are some excerpts from his notes:

> Ride, bunny.
> Do you recall this word?—Ride?
> Bunny, bunny.
> That's very nice John; keep reading.
> That's very . . . Let's turn to the list of words.
> No that's—okay.
> Next row, John.
> And the last word—fine.
> You go back to your desk, I want to talk to Mark about some words.
> John, you'd better take care of your work.
> Mark, do you know *this* letter?
> Mark, do you know *this* letter?
> Mark, do you know *this* letter?
> Those letters make Tom's name.
> He likes to ride—third letter r-i-*d*-e.
> Those letters, r-i-d-e, together, make ride.
> What's the name of the boy? Uhhuh [yes].
> What does he do?
> Mark, what does Tom like to do? Right!
> When we look at this word, what does it mean?
> Let's see if we can read a little bit more about Tom and ride.
> What does this sentence mean?
> What is it, Ann?
> Let's be looking at these words, Mark.
> Good.
> Read it again, Mark—Good
> Remember the name of the boy?
> Very nice, Mark.
> That's how we do our reading.

## Conclusion

The purpose of this discussion has been to look at some contrasts between the ideal and the real world of the teaching of reading and to suggest how teachers live with and perhaps even perpetuate paradoxes for their pupils as readers. In some ways it would appear that the teacher of reading unintentionally works against the accomplishment of the very objectives he seeks to realize. While the teacher cannot remedy all of reading's paradoxes, he can analyze those practices in his own classroom which either facilitate or minimize the amount of reading his pupils do. He can examine his own attitude about reading. He can make explicit for himself how he regards classroom reading: Is it fun; work; skill-building; means or end? He can examine whether the organization of his reading program helps him to accomplish his purposes, and whether he inadvertently allows or even fosters unintended and perhaps undesirable consequences as well.

The discrepancies between the ideal world of reading and the real world of reading are a social fact which need cause no undue teacher anxiety. We do assume, however, that the reading teacher may want to be conscious of these discrepancies and aware of how they reflect broader aspects of classroom and community culture. To the extent that his behavior as a teacher may thwart the very purposes he wishes to achieve with his pupils, then the teacher may wish to take an analytical look at his own classroom behavior and ask of himself: What are my pupils *learning* about reading? Is that what I want to *teach* them?

## References

1. Harry F. Wolcott, *A Kwakiutl Village and School* (New York: Holt, Rinehart and Winston, 1967), 90–91.
2. Martin Mayer, *The Schools* (Harper and Brothers, 1961) (New York: Anchor Book edition), 212.
3. Marilyn Collier, "An Evaluation of Multi-Ethnic Basal Readers," *Elementary English 44* (February 1967): 152–157.
4. Otto Klineberg, "Life is Fun in a Smiling, Fair-Skinned World," *Saturday Review* February 16 (1963): 75–77.
5. CF. Harry F. Wolcott, "Concomitant Learning: An Anthropological Perspective on the Utilization of Media," in Raymond V. Wiman and Wesley S. Meierhenry (eds), *Educational Media: Theory into Practice* (Columbus, Ohio: Charles E. Merrill Publishing Company, 1969), 217–247.
6. Jeanne S. Chall, *Learning to Read: The Great Debate* (New York: McGraw-Hill Book Co., 1967), 253.

**Malcolm P. Douglass**

# *Does Nongrading Improve Reading Behavior?*

Any response to the question raised here depends foremost upon reaching some commonality of meaning for the term "nongrading." The most widely agreed upon assumption today is that the term *nongrading* means a form of grouping having as its central concern the gathering together of learners on some basis of similarity (or homogeneous quality) either in achievement, measured intelligence, "maturity," eagerness or willingness to learn, or some combination of these characteristics or qualities.

The graded school, long cursed, wherein children are grouped primarily according to the year of their birth, came into existence in the 1840's in Quincy, Massachusetts. However, hardly a generation of experience led to the first of what has become a legion of attempts to ameliorate the "problem of teaching" presumed to grow out of having children with the diverse talents, interests, and capabilities observed, even among youngsters of a similar chronological age. That first systematic attempt at homogeneous grouping was to take place in St. Louis under the guidance of its superintendent, W. T. Harris, in 1867. The historical fact of the matter is, of course, that the age-graded school has prevailed along with the notion that *homogeneity within grades is a desirable, and achievable, educational objective.* "Nongrading," then, has occurred almost totally within the context of school grades. Most recently, however, the concept has been applied to children enrolled in two or three different grade levels. Still, the central theme in the vast majority of instances where "nongrading" is said to be taking place is that of grouping children "homogeneously" either in ability, capacity for learning, or achievement.

It is not the purpose here to recount the various "nongraded" mutations proffered over the past century—reviews are available in the literature of education (1). But it is perhaps worthy of note that the post-Sputnik era has been sprinkled as no other period of educational history with a variety of terms that connote some sort of shift away from that old bugbear, the "lock-step" age-graded school. I give you as exemplars such catchy terms as *team teaching, continuous progress,* The Dual Progress Plan, The Appropriate Placement School, *flexible scheduling, developmental age,* the *levels system,* The Trump Plan, *cross-age teaching, multi-grade* and *inter-age grouping* and, among the very latest of entries, Teachability Grouping.

When one scratches the surface of any of these plans or schemes, it becomes immediately apparent that the vast majority of them are, in fact, variations albeit frequently more sophisticated ones, of Harris' St. Louis venture into homogeneous grouping. The basic presumption pervading most plans lies in the belief that like children, when grouped together, will learn better than if un-like children are so grouped. Since the school is, at least on the surface of it, oriented above all else toward achievement, it is not surprising that the major criterion for grouping children is some blending of measures of achievement. Thelen, taking a somewhat abysmal view of the social role of the school in the American culture, asserts that another value, segregation, is the not *in*deliberate result of various grouping plans. He asserts that, since homogeneous grouping practices segregate children by socio-economic class, children are also being taught

> what to expect of themselves and of each other as denizens of that place in society. They are also trained for some degree of tolerance or sympathy toward groups at other levels. The reason for separating bright children is to indoctrinate them to expect that they will go to a university; hold top jobs in industry, research, or business; live in suburbs [etc.] . . . This is what parents of the upper class groups probably desire—a reinforcement of family expectations for the child. (Lower class parents do not come to school, so their voices are not heard.) (2)

Be that as it may, we may note that, as the pressures for greater achievement generally have mounted in the period since Sputnik I was placed in orbit, elementary schools in the United States at least have responded by becoming increasingly active in seeking ways of regrouping children according to some criterion assumed to lead to improved school performance, particularly in reading. Note, for example, that virtually all of the terms proferred above, claiming to be departures from the conventional mode of grouping, i.e., by age, have been given birth since 1957! I say that such departures "assume" there will be greater growth in learning. Yet, what do we really know concerning the effect of these manipulations and their relationships to learning improvement? Are the assumptions validated by research? My remaining comments will be directed toward an evaluation of the data at hand with particular reference to the problem of improving abilities in reading printed words and in terms of language performance in general.

Studies of the effects of grouping practices on children divide into two major groups: those occurring prior to 1940 and those reported within the past half dozen years (3). Interest in studying these questions nearly died out completely in the period intervening between the Progressive Era and that of the post-Sputnik decade. Of the studies conducted during the period from about 1920 to 1940, most can be severely criticized for methodological errors or omissions. They are characterized by failure to develop, or at least report clearly, the research design and method of analysis; most were conducted over such a short period of time that the reliability of the instruments used, even then a serious handicap to any study in this dimension of schooling, prevented definitive analysis of the data. Of course, research sophistication—when compared with that of today coupled as it also is to fantastic instrumentation—was hardly up to anything more. Strangely enough, however, the findings of that period generally conform to the extremely complex studies that have been going on here and abroad in more recent years. These highly complicated studies, where data have been treated in every conceivable form and relationship, leave one wishing that the basic test instruments available for our use had been as remarkably developed as the machinery employed to worry out every possible meaning that might be imbedded in them.

In general terms, then, we find ourselves with no dearth of data about the effects of various kinds of grouping procedures, not a few of which would very comfortably fit within the general meaning contained in the rubric, "nongrading." The literature is, as well, now elevated to an international level, although the reports are yet exclusively tilled from the Western World (primarily the Scandinavian countries, England, The United States, Canada, and Australia) (4). In an analysis of these studies, both old and new, several generalizations are now warranted:

1.  Taken as a whole, the findings of studies into the effects of grouping practices that meet minimal standards of objectivity present a most ambivalent face. There is no clear advantage for such grouping procedures or practices over the traditional forms of school organization, i.e., the graded pattern. It is also generally true that within any particular study, ambiguities in findings tend to arise that are inexplicable within the framework of the data provided or the hypotheses governing the study.

2.  Where differences are obtained in favor of nongrading (in this case, some form of achievement or ability grouping), those differences tend to disappear over time. That is, where scores beyond those expected accrue within the first year of the study, the benefits seem largely to disappear two years or more hence (5). A number of the studies that report favorable results for such groupings were not extended beyond a few months or a year

—leading one to wonder whether the number of favorable reports would have remained in that category had such studies been conceived on a truly longitudinal base. In the case of reading behavior, at least, the disappearance of favorable attributes might be explained by the fact that such grouping usually removes artificial ceilings that are imposed by the materials in common use in classrooms. Everyone is aware of the schism existing between all grades, and particularly between grades existing in different school units. "Seventh grade reading materials," for example, are much less likely to find their way into a conventional sixth grade classroom than in one where high ability readers are re-grouped for reading instruction. The research strongly suggests, even so, that the initial gain re-grouping these children may bring about is dissipated in a very short time (6). And, for those children in the low end of the achievement scale, those whom everyone worries about so constantly, no apparent benefit is realized. Indeed, in a study by Goldberg, Passow and Justman, the treatment group containing the broadest range of ability appeared to be "somewhat more effective for all pupils than any of the combinations of narrower range patterns" (7).

3. In those studies reporting benefits to children in "nongraded" situations, a consistent trend can be identified indicating that those most likely to find advantage are children in the high group. Middle or "average" children and those in the low group are least likely to benefit, apparently. Still, the data are, as indicated, full of ambiguities that cannot be explained. Thelen notes, for example, in response to the questions inevitably arising when it is observed that the results of homogeneous grouping are inconsistent that, "as a matter of logic, if a factor is influential only sometimes, we are justified in concluding that this factor is irrelevant, and this difference is due to another cause" (8). Another reason that self-contained and so called nongraded plans show no differences might be that we very likely may be testing the same thing. Why is it safe to assume, in other words, that achievement or ability groupings across grades secures any different effect than achievement grouping within grades (the predominating pattern in 90 to 95 per cent of all self-contained classrooms in the country)? It is Goldberg's contention, however, that advantage goes to the child no matter what kind of grouping he may be in, when the teacher knows what he is doing and/or when the materials used in teaching are especially appropriate (9).

4. Another morass of confusion is presented in noncognitive matters —the affective domain, if you will. Attitudes of self, feelings of one's own worth as a person, sometimes categorized as *self-concept,* present a highly variable picture. In Goldberg's study the self-estimates of high ability children seemed to increase when low ability children were present (10). Borg found an initial benefit accruing to segregation of high ability children in self-attitudes. However, this advantage tended to dissipate over time. While self-attitudes of low group children appeared to favor heterogeneous or

random grouping practices in Borg's study, these children showed remarkable improvement in sociometric status when grouped homogeneously (11). The sociology of the classroom, regardless of the intellectual task at hand, may be the most relevant explanation of these results.

5. Attitudes of parents, teachers, and children toward various forms of nongrading fly in the face of the ambiguities and ambivalencies present in more objective research. Generally speaking, each group is strongly supportive of nongrading, perhaps for different reasons, but nonetheless supportive. Attitude research is less well developed as a tool for discovering educational truths, and so there is much testimonial available and little objective evidence. For the most part, however, teachers and administrators believe that some form of grouping that reduces the range of achievement or ability in some dimension or another also reduces the problems of teaching. Consequently, it is generally held to be true that children benefit because the teacher is more effective under such circumstances. Goldberg points out rather brutally that, lacking such objective evidence, one can only conclude that grouping "can become harmful when it lulls teachers and parents into believing that because there is grouping, the school is providing differentiated education for pupils of varying degrees of ability, when in reality that is not the case." She points out, as well, that grouping "may become dangerous when it leads teachers to underestimate the learning capacities of pupils at the lower ability levels. It can also be damaging when it is inflexible and does not provide channels for moving children from lower to higher ability groups and back again either from subject to subject or within any one subject as their performance at various times in their school career dictates" (12). However, the implicit assumption that reading is a "subject" may invalidate these observations, especially in the latter instance. Perhaps a measure of good will toward the school and its attempts to educate children is the most important evidence available to us in the data supporting nongrading practices emanating from parents and children. These groups support such practices, for the most part, indicating that the school is actually viewed as having the welfare of children in mind and that any change from past practice must, by definition, be an improvement!

6. Increasingly, researchers are commenting upon the self-fulfilling prophesy as the determining factor in the matter. Foshay, in remarking that ability grouping may well be "selective deprivation," is striking at this question (13). That is, we live up to the expectations of those around us, to the circumstance we find ourselves in; and in schools, we tend to perform in a manner commensurate with the expectations of teachers, parents, and peers. In studies conducted in England, where the term is *streaming* rather than *ability grouping* or *nongrading,* comparisons made between upper and lower streams illustrate this point. Children so studied perform not in terms of ability measures but according to expectations. Thus, the child in the

lower stream tends to perform increasingly less well while his counterpart in the upper stream excels (14). Gradually, over the years, the one youngster achieves in school, the other does not. Surely, the expectations of teachers, the social climate of the instructional circumstance, and the socio-economic status of children are combining to bring about success or failure, regardless of the conditions that are said to be crucial in teaching and learning: namely, as Goldberg avers, the methods of the teacher and/or the materials available to him. It can at least be said that our present level of ability to convert our knowledge of the reading process into practice in the classroom apparently makes this true. That one will or will not succeed is in the woodwork —the circumstance itself is prelude to the effect.

Whether we like it or not, then, it appears we must conclude with Goldberg that "grouping arrangements, by themselves, serve little educational purpose" (15). The response to our original question must be that nongrading as it is conventionally viewed, holds no future for us. But there are some threads emerging from the studies on grouping, and from other sources that might give a different meaning to the idea of nongrading, at least in terms of developing facility for the processes of printed-word reading. The basic idea is contained in a statement by Macdonald, when he asserts, in his criticism of the U.S. Office of Education studies in beginning reading programs, that "it is perhaps time to drop our parochial methodological approach to conceptualizing instruction and social relationships within the classroom, and to examine the process of learning to read in the context of the socialization process. For example, such questions as the following may be more productive avenues of investigation: What social conditions are necessary for the free and flexible development of language behavior? What status and role perceptions and competencies need to be internalized for language learning?" (16) As one reviews the research in grouping, particularly with respect to the notion of the self-fulfilling prophesy, and data on self-concept and sociometric status, support for this contention begins to emerge. And as we look to recent pioneering work in studies of the growth and development of language in children, and the contributions of the anthro-linguists to our understanding of the relationships of language to culture and thought, further evidence supports another conception of what we might wish to mean by nongrading than that commonly accepted today (17).

Consider, for the moment, such interrelated ideas as these. The nature of the reading process is distinctively different from what we normally term "subjects" in the school curriculum. Because there is no "structure" to reading as there is to a discipline of knowledge such as mathematics or science, existing outside of the learner, identifiable and, potentially teachable as such, learning to read print poses fundamentally different problems to both teacher and learner. Reading abilities evolve in ways that are unique to individuals, are highly personal and intuitive; they continue to defy those who would approach problems of instruction and learning in this arena from a highly logical vantage point. If there were a structure to the reading process similar to that of the disciplines of knowledge, then we would not find ourselves immersed in seemingly endless arguments over what is the best or most appropriate method of instruction and over details of the sequence of knowledges and abilities that lead to success in reading print. Truly, every person follows his own pattern; reading print is not merely the sum of its parts, learned incrementally. It is a highly creative process, learned in large measure intuitively, its development intimately a part of the entire socialization process; it is truly more than the sum of its parts. Reading is, then, not a subject in the school curriculum, to be taught didactically. It is simply a process very much like speaking or listening that is best learned in a fashion similar to ways we learn to speak or listen, by actually participating in the process. More of that, however, in a moment.

The anthro-linguist indicates to us that we should never forget that language, the basic form of communication, provides the primary means by which we think. Reading print, as a part of language, is therefore truly *thinking* above and beyond anything else. He demonstrates that the manner of thinking varies by examining differences in language from one culture to another, and how language and culture are interrelated. The learning circumstance must be one that stimulates thinking and reading as, beyond anything else, a creative act. Conversely, we can readily see that language also provides a window into the child's (or adult's) innermost being. The quality of his thinking is observable through the language he uses or in the uses he makes of language. What, then, is the effect of situations that emphasize the negative side of learning—that are overabundant in criticism of the students' capacities for language—for thinking? Obviously optimal learning is tied to the social circumstance (the feelings of worth generated in the classroom) since a positive feeling of value (or its negative counterpart) grows primarily out of the interpersonal relationships of the individual as he engages with others in various forms of communication—or language. Can we expect maximal growth when "classroom practices, saddled by outmoded and ill-conceived directed reading activities presented and represented by stereotyped basic reader programs, violate these principles?" (18) If there are doubts about the effect of ability or achievement grouping between classes, what conclusion would one be forced to draw about the creation of "nongraded" circumstances *within* classrooms—an almost universal phenomenon in the elementary schools, at least? What are the fundamental or qualitative differences between this form of achievement grouping and that organized on a school-wide basis? Comparative studies of the effects of such in-class groupings are not available except as one might "read into" the studies cited here and the equally conflicting reports of studies of individualized, self-selection, and experience approaches to reading.

Linguistic inquiry also reveals the close relationships between the language functions. Loban's research clearly indicates that a child whose oral language is advanced will in all likelihood be an advanced reader of print. These interrelationships are observable for each of the four basic verbal language functions of reading, writing, speaking, and listening (19). Awareness of these conditions strongly suggests that learning to read print is supported, in fact enhanced, by opportunities to grow in the other language functions, dependent as all future language growth is upon the development of the basic functions of listening and speaking. It is quite clear that the child whose speaking and listening capacities are poorly developed, for example, will be hampered in reading print and in writing, regardless of how much instruction is pumped into the situation at that end of the language scale. The "reading program" is therefore as big as the curriculum of the school, and more, because its base rests in the first few years of life, before the child comes to school and upon continuing out-of-school experiencing. Clearly this must be so since much of the child's language growth subsequent to his entry into school occurs without reference to schooling *per se.* It is in this earlier period that the initial listening and speaking vocabularies are established, the pronunciation system firmly completed, and most of the grammatical forms (for good or ill) acquired. Of prime importance in our consideration here are the teachers of this language upon whom we *must* base the processes of schooling. The child learns from those people around him in every day living. In virtually every culture, the mother is the primary source of these earliest and, as it turns out, highly permanent language learnings. She provides the model for the child. In a circumstance that is characterized primarily by love, warm acceptance of the child's efforts to re-create the language of his culture, and individualized instruction, where failure is not considered possible, the youngster makes tremendous, almost unbelievable growth in his language capacities. Although we change the rules on him when he comes to the classroom, seeking to teach each of the verbal language functions separately, logically, as subjects in the curriculum, in groups that for the most part recognize at best only three or four levels of achievement, the facts of language learning and the conditions under which real growth might occur are ignored. The early nongraded instruction of the family and immediate neighborhood is put aside in favor of approaches that demand, frequently before the child is capable of it, excursions into logical thinking, analysis, and synthesis. It is little wonder that, when early reading instruction makes such impossible demands on children's thinking, in social settings that are alive with the conditions for "selective deprivation," the fruits of our educational efforts are, as any high school teacher will tell, "schools . . . literally overrun with students who cannot read above the fourth grade level" (20).

If the social circumstance is as powerful as Macdonald, Thelen, Yates, and others report, if growth in language is unique to individuals and learned largely through models, and if the language functions are truly interrelated, with reading and writing abilities emerging from and related to the oral and aural language abilities, we might postulate a circumstance for nongrading that would in fact cause reading behavior to improve, or at least to improve more by design than presently appears to be the case. Rather than developing classroom and school circumstances that segregate children by ability or achievement, one would seek instead to work with children in groups that represent the social realities of their world. Rather than organize boys and girls so that there is only one model for language learning—the teacher, with his textbook—deliberate steps might be taken to provide a wide variety of models in the classroom. This would mean that children grouped for instruction in printed-word reading would be chosen deliberately to represent a variety of levels of ability and achievement, especially at the primary levels. Finally, the interrelationships of language functions signal the all-important recognition that reading and writing programs must be based upon the child's own oral and aural language abilities, and cannot be taught separately from one another.

Thus, we pose a nongraded elementary school classroom composed of many age, achievement and ability levels, where growth in language behavior recognizes the fact that reading, like listening, is a silent act accomplished only by individuals, where each learner follows his own unique growth pattern. In this multi-age classroom, the teacher has "come out from under the basic reader yoke" (21); the widest variety of materials are available and used. In such a circumstance there is no place for groupings that tell a sizeable number of children that they are inadequate individuals because they are no longer in a social situation that has built into it years of invidious personal comparisons. Such a circumstance also has the power within it to allow each child to grow toward maturity in reading and writing in an accepting, warm, and individual way—not unlike the family setting where the first steps in language learning took place so successfully. Children grow up in our culture able to speak and listen effectively *in their own society.* Why is it they are failing in so many instances to develop their power to read print and write their own language? Could it be that we have been trapped by our past, condemned to repeat our errors because we have not considered the nature of language, its growth characteristics, and its highly personal intuitive nature? Have we, in continuing to teach "the language arts" (including reading) as subjects in the curriculum, built social systems within our schools, *and within our classrooms,* that have been grossly at variance with the realities of child growth and development and the manner in which language growth can best be facilitated? Have we done what we should have done to provide the very best base for expanding the power to think? Can we dare to think about nongrading in this very different context?

## References

1. See, for example, Lawrence F. Cremin, *The Transformation of the School* (New York: Alfred A. Knopf, 1961); also Chapter 2, "Antecedents of Team Teaching," by Judson T. Shaplin, in Judson T. Shaplin and Henry F. Olds, Jr. (eds.), *Team Teaching* (New York: Harper and Row, 1964). The latter chapter contains useful references to detailed accounts of various plans.

2. Herbert A. Thelen, *Classroom Grouping for Teachability* (New York: John Wiley & Sons, 1967), 30–31.

3. An excellent resume of a large number of studies conducted in the United States at both the elementary and secondary levels is contained in Walter R. Borg, *Ability Grouping in the Public Schools* (Madison, Wis.: Dembar Educational Research Services, Inc., 1966). See especially pp. 12–15.

4. The most comprehensive review of recent research both in the United States and elsewhere is contained in Alfred Yates (ed.), *Grouping in Education: A Report Sponsored by the Unesco Institute for Education, Hamburg* (New York: John Wiley & Sons, 1966).

5. Findings in Borg's study typify the situation here. See: Walter R. Borg, *op. cit.*

6. In a recent study of the effectiveness of the "Joplin Plan," one of the most widely known schemes for regrouping children according to reading achievement, no significant differences were noted in comparisons with traditional groupings for either high or low achievers. See: Roy M. Carson and Jack M. Thompson, "The Joplin Plan and Traditional Reading Groups," *The Elementary School Journal* LX (October, 1964): 38–43.

7. Miriam L. Goldberg, A. Harry Passow, and Jospeh Justman, *The Effects of Ability Grouping* (New York: Teachers College, Columbia University, 1966), 71. This study is reviewed in Alfred Yates, *op. cit.,* 212–215.

8. Herbert A. Thelen, *op. cit.,* 30.

9. Miriam L. Goldberg *et al., op. cit.*

10. Ibid., 101ff.

11. Walter R. Borg, *op. cit.,* 92.

12. Miriam L. Goldberg *et al., op. cit.,* 168.

13. Ibid., v.

14. This effect is most clearly demonstrated in an extensive longitudinal study reported by Alfred Yates, *op. cit.,* 199–202, of a study by J. W. B. Douglas, "Streaming by Ability." The full report is contained in Douglas' *The Home and the School* (London: MacGibbon & Kee, 1964).

15. Miriam L. Goldberg, *et al., op. cit.,* 169.

16. James B. Macdonald, "Research in Review," in *Educational Leadership* 23, 6 (March 1965): 443.

17. For example, consider the following milestones in our developing understanding: Benjamin Lee Whorf, *Language, Thought, and Reality* (New York: John Wiley & Sons, 1956); Edward T. Hall, *The Silent Language* (New York: Doubleday & Co., 1959); and the work of other anthro-linguists who demonstrate as well as discover relationships between language and culture or such studies of the growth of children's language as: L. S. Vygotsky *Thought and Language* (Cambridge, Mass.: Massachusetts Institute of Technology, 1962); or Walter D. Loban, *The Language of Elementary School Children,* Research Report No. 1, The National Council of Teachers of English, 1963.

18. Russell G. Stauffer in "Time For Amendment," The Reading Teacher 20, No. 8 (May, 1967): p. 685.

19. Walter D. Loban, *op. cit.*

20. B. Frank Brown, *The Appropriate Placement School: A Sophisticated Nongraded Curriculum* (West Nyack, New York: Parker Publishing Company, Inc., 1965), 104.

21. Russell G. Stauffer, *op. cit.*

**Jeannette Veatch**

# Sign and Significance: The Jabberwock Rides Again

You may well wonder what the Jabberwock has to do with the field of reading. Let me read you the whole poem and then tell you how I see it fitting into the picture.

### Jabberwocky

'Twas brillig, and the slithy toves
    Did gyre and gimble in the Wabe
All mimsy were the borogoves
    And the mome raths outgrabe.
"Beware the Jabberwock, my son!
    The jaws that bite, the claws that catch
Beware the Jubjub bird, and shun
    The frumious Bandersnatch!"
He took his vorpal sword in hand:
    Long time the manxome foe he sought—
So rested he by the Tumtum tree
    And stood awhile in thought.
And, as in uffish thought he stood,
    The Jabberwock, with eyes of flame
Came whiffling through the tulgey wood
    And burbled as it came!
One, two! One, two! And through and through
    The vorpal blade went snicker-snack!
He left it dead, and with its head
    He went galumphing back.
"And has thou slain the Jabberwock?
    Come to my arms, my beamish boy!"

**221**

Of frabjous day! Callooh! Callay!
    He chortled in his joy.
'Twas brillig and the slithy toves
    Did gyre and gimble in the wabe:
All mimsy were the borogoves
    And the mome raths outgrabe (1).

As you know, this is a poem about nonsense. In fact, it raises nonsense to quite a high literary level, and the Jabberwock is slain, killed dead, among much rejoicing. Now, I propose that we apply a SIGN to the Jabberwock, and then discuss its SIGNIFICANCE.*

To me, the JABBERWOCK is nothing more or less than the commercialization of the field of reading; the gadgetry, the materials, the machines, the hardware of all sorts. To the extent the gross aspects of commercialization are nonsense, it is Jabberwocky. The SIGN then is the profit motive and the SIGNIFICANCE is that excessive commercialization is interfering with the proper education, in its highest sense, of our young.

"Beware the Jabberwock, my son!" says to me "Beware of all of the materials that exist for the major purpose of making money." Note that word, *major.* It is an important emphasis. My point is that the vast majority of materials are manufactured first for profit and second for their educational purposes. Great is the rejoicing when educational professionals come up with ideas that are both educational AND profitable. The sickness that is now so obvious on all sides in American society comes, in some part, from the sickness within the majority of classrooms in our nation, with the seemingly inescapable dependence upon inanimate materials, particularly the children's texts, in every conceivable aspect of the curriculum.

As I would show that most materials are interfering with the best education of our young, let me define the word "commerical." I mean it to describe those materials that are intended for use, if sales would allow, by every child, in every school, all over this nation. As it is patently impossible for single pieces of material to perform such a monumental task, the hard sell must take place.

Obviously there are few things that do not make money for the manufacturer. Chalk yields profits, chalk boards yield profits. So do paper and pencils as do the most beautiful of all books, the trade books. In the case of chalk and paper, the profits are small. In the case of trade books, the numbers are so extensive that it is difficult for any one of them to be used by every child in every class in the nation. Trade books are the best of children's books. They exist on charm. They dare to take their chances in

*The special theme of the Claremont Reading Conference at which Professor Veatch presented this talk was *Sign and Significance.*

the market place. The good ones will sell in the tens of thousands. The poor ones fall by the way side in sales. This is the way it should be. Monopoly capital has no place in the realm of childhood. Yet it is here. It has been here for decades, and unless we expose its terrible consequences it will continue to exist.

## Dangers to Democratic Principles

Eisenhower, it must be recalled, issued a warning in the last days of his presidency against the danger to freedom, democracy, and our way of life inherent in the military-industrial complex. I am only a professor, but I hope this audience will not deny me the right to take a leaf from Mr. Eisenhower's book and warn, in just as serious terms, that our way of life, our society's happiness, is in desperate peril from the tidal waves of educational material and hardware that inundate our teachers at all levels, in all parts of the country.

One month after his resignation as President of San Francisco State College, Robert Smith spoke on the Bill of Rights. I quote from his text:

> Our society and our educational system has managed . . . to teach increasing numbers of its young the antithesis of democratic concepts . . . (the) massive failures in the nation's efforts to measure up to, and live by, its humane ideals, provide an ample context in which the young learn at the gut level the antithesis of democratic principles. Educational institutions contribute their share to these baleful outcomes. I believe that young, fanatical totalitarians are increasing in number and rapidly gaining in sophistication and capacity for liaison and alliance and disruption. . . .

The sickness in this country is too wide spread. The role of the schools is too prominent in producing this sickness. We have no more time. Tax monies are involved here, and some kind of controls, some kind of checks are necessary. The extent of inane, non-educational, expensive, gadgetry suggests that there is more than innocence abroad in the land.

Nor are the manufacturers really to blame. They have consistently said that they will fill a marketing vacuum, if it can be proven to exist. I am sure that is true. But I cannot help but wonder why they are dragging their feet at filling the overwhelming dearth of trade books, the best of books, in the nation's classrooms. It is strange that manufacturers do not move more quickly into this wide open market. I think they will, but not until the monopoly of basal texts in all fields is truly broken. And that is our job. We are the professional educators. We must clean our own house and expose the nonsense that is being foisted on the American school child. I propose to proceed with the job.

It is tempting to go more deeply into the totalitarian personality and how it develops, but others must take over that task. This Conference deals with reading, and I have been asked to interpret in my own way the continuing theme of the Claremont Conference: "Reading is the process of making discriminative responses." The sign of the Jabberwock is the profit motive that interferes with rational, relevant education. And the field of reading is the worst offender in the whole curriculum on this point. It is the most material-ridden and irrelevant of all.

Materials pour from the manufacturers. We claim to be interested in reading achievement. Note that the *Stanford Primary Battery* correlates .95 with the vocabulary of five of the big selling basal primers. This, I submit, is professional incest.

> " 'Twas brillig and the slithy toves . . ."

For the truth of the matter is that materials are not the answer at all. The secret to good education is what happens between human beings, the teacher and the child. Yet, producers of educational materials have been, and still are, in a state of alarm over a practice called "Individualized Reading." This is the only practice, in its original, self-selective conception, that has nothing to sell in a single package. Yet the basic idea was and is so frightening, so powerful, to vested interests that efforts to mechanize individualization, to package it, are still going on. Anything, it would seem, except a child and his teacher sitting down together to talk about a book the child has chosen, because 1) he likes it, and 2) because it is just right for him.

You see, materials are the answer to nothing, educationally speaking. But teachers have been trained to panic when they are not provided. It is quite possible that American elementary children can be taught all of the reading, writing, math, etc. to the peak of their ability, with no children's texts *whatsoever* available. Teacher's texts, yes. But not children's texts.

> "And as in uffish thought he stood,
> The Jabberwock, with eyes of flame
> Came whiffling through the tulgey wood
> and burbled as it came."

Well might the commercial interests whiffle through the tulgey wood. I am using my vorpal sword in the only way I know how. For my vorpal sword is belief in the educational strength of one human being teaching another; human to human, and the inanimate relegated to a very minor, ancillary position.

## The Sword Cometh

Using the sword in this way, we might start with those machines called "Controlled Readers" available under several manufacturing labels. The theory, once the verbiage of the manual is stripped away is that if the retarded reader's eyes look at moving words (with occasional pauses, often unrelated to the meaning of the phrases involved), then by some magical operations, those same eyes will be better able to deal with honest-to-goodness reading in some book somewhere. Even the Old West gambler knew that the hand was quicker than the eye because the eye can see NOTHING when it is moving. So an enormously expensive machine is bought by the sickening thousands to do a job it can never possibly do.

## Film Strips Instead of Books

Another twist of the sword might be made in the body of the machines that have a film strip, with story and pictures, which is read over ear phones from a central tape. Each child, isolated in a booth, is supposed to keep turning the picture in order to keep up with the story. A more major indictment of the wreckage caused by traditional materials can hardly be imagined. Such children have been taught to hate books so much that it takes an expensive gadget to revive—if it works—an interest in reading. It would be funny if it were not for the spectre of the Jabberwock overhead. Profit making. ANYTHING except good books for children. ANYTHING except contact with a human being with whom you might exchange thoughts about reading.

## Mis-used Hardware

The sword should also swing a bit, although perhaps not so vehemently, against the misuse of some hardware such as the overhead projector. In a city near Phoenix I have seen classroom after classroom, with chalk boards covered with—you know—flowers—"Welcome to Spring," and other such slogans and decorations—where the teachers are teaching, of all things, penmanship, on the overhead. I have seen dozens of times when teachers were screwing up their faces deciding how their marker was going, when the chalk board beckoned by their side. Put it down to my being of the older generation. I just hope that the public never catches on to how we are squandering money on misused hardware. If they do, we will all be out of a job.

## An Analysis of Some Materials

Let us take some developments and see how they might be analyzed. A recent workshop on a systems approach to communication in Phoenix hit the front page of the local paper thusly, and I quote in part:

> Donald E. Miller, assistant superintendent of schools in San Mateo County, California said a "systems" approach to problem-solving in education would improve communications in school districts.
> Miller . . . offered an 18-page paper on the "systems" approach which contained the following sentences:
> > "The (systems) concept has been expanded, . . . and . . . validated as a meaningful logic construct through its historical use and subsequent appraisals."
> > "These early scientists explored every available method and means which might aid them in their attempts to conceptualize interrelationships among complex phenomena and enable them to integrate these interrelationships into a systematic body of knowledge."
> Mrs. Pauline Dorsett of Tempe, a first grade teacher . . . and president of the Arizona Classroom Teachers Association, was asked by a reporter what she thought about the two sentences. "Why, I think the two sentences are just fine," she said. "Conceptualize is a great word" (2).

So much for systems analysis. You take it. I don't want it.

> "Beware the Jubjub bird, and shun
> The frumious Bandersnatch."

## Individualized Prescribed Instruction

There is the Oakleaf Project in Pittsburgh in which highly structured programming is being carried on. Dr. Louis Bright, at a conference in Mesa, Arizona, in describing how children could proceed at their own pace thru unit after unit of programmed material, with the privilege of skipping that which they already knew, nevertheless confessed: "We don't do very well with creative communication." This is precisely the problem with Individualized Prescribed Instruction. It freezes the child and teacher into an Orwellian pattern of mechanized uncreative lessons. In another center for Individualized Prescribed Instruction, The Rocky Mountain Educational Laboratory, this paragraph appears in their material:

> . . . It is planned that a series of specific learning episodes are to be developed to help the child overcome his specific deficits. Certain clusters of checked remedial procedures which *the classroom teacher can select from until one is found to work best with a given child* . . . [Italics added]

This, I believe, is a gross prostitution of the concept of individualization. It is materials' centered to the ultimate degree. I suggest that if such practice becomes nationwide the current turmoil in our schools will be child's play. Or we will have an elected totalitarian government that will spell the demise of democracy as our founding fathers conceived of it.

## An Analysis of Some Current Programs

Let me analyze some more programs on the market in terms of their educational and social validity. For example, take the visual perception materials. At this moment there are doctoral studies at the University of Southern California and perhaps elsewhere that demonstrate the ineffectiveness of these materials and activities. They not only do not improve reading, they don't improve visual perception. Sidney Shnayer reports a study at Chico where children, pre-tested by the *Frostig Test,* then subjected to the program as described in the manual, were found to do worse on the *Frostig Post-Test!* Patently, what has physical movement to do with the process of gaining meaning from a printed page? Oh, I know, the process of left to right is a physical progress. Yet Klausmeier states:

> Research on rigidity and set in problem solving shows conclusively that when an individual experience repeated success in solving problems with a certain method or instrument, he clings to that method or instrument *even when it is inappropriate for solving new problems for which other methods and/or instruments are appropriate* (3). [Italics added]

In short, one learns to read by reading, and not by identifying differing shapes and sizes of non-words to teach word recognition, or to hope that movement from left to right in a non-reading situation will lead to progression from left to right in a reading situation. The transfer of training is nil, as the efforts to validate all perceptual materials is rapidly proving.

## The Role of the S-R Bond

Not surprisingly, at the root of such commercial systems is the Pavlovian strategy of stimulus response. The behaviorists are the enemy and, perhaps more than any other group in education are responsible for the hatred of learning in this country. Behavioral psychology was most certainly used by Hitler and Stalin for the subjugation of their peoples. Many of the less violent techniques are prevalent in many classrooms today, however innocently and unknowingly they are used.

For example, one technique to subjugate the masses to the will of authority is monotonous repetition. All I have to say to illustrate how prevalent monotonous repetition is in American classrooms is to quote.

"Oh, Oh, Oh.
Look, Look, Look."

Another strategy for totalitarian methods is that of forceful interrogation. We have the Bereiter and Engleman example gaining ascendancy so that it is one of the four accepted programs for national *Follow Through* funding. Who here has not heard their classic lesson? THIS IS A CUP! SAY IT! THIS IS A CUP!"

While there is certainly something to be said in favor of not boring children by yelling at them in contrast to the teachers who demand deathly stillness, nevertheless, this program is an extreme expression of totalitarianism, and is so admitted, with pride, by the authors (4).

Another technique to enforce unquestioning obedience is that of the seeming logical syllogisms. That is, if something SEEMS logical then it must be so. For example, the teaching of sequence in the manuals of the basal readers is presented over and over again. That is, children should know the plot of a story. Therefore to know it, they must be trained in the proper sequence of the story. This, of course, completely ignores the automatic understanding of a story's plot by children who are captivated by the story. In short a poor story needs its sequence taught. A good story's plot sequence is learned automatically.

Further strategies can be found in the isolation of human beings from each other. "Sit in Rows." "Do not look at each other's papers." The list goes on.

You will notice that my vorpal sword has not even drawn blood from the most vulnerable commercial materials of all—the basal readers and their workbooks. This has been a subject of attack by others than myself. I remember some lovely articles on the matter around 1948 and 1950. To this day, there is no research evidence of educational validity of basal readers and their omnipresent workbooks. One child called one publisher's efforts "The Unthinkables." Over and over there have been attempts to prove the worth of these materials. But, alas, the Jabberwocky rides again. They exist only because of his sign.

## The Directed Reading Lesson

Let us take the most prevalent reading practice there is: the directed reading lesson. It is straight S-R bond behaviorism, as are all materials that require a response as stated in the manual. The directed reading lesson begins with Step #1 called "Developing Interest." Briefly, the merit of the teacher's performance depends on how she can persuade children to become interested in the story chosen for the day. How does this persuasion take place? By charm—"This is a very exciting story, etc.," by force—"I want everyone to turn to page 10," or by guilt, convincing the child that he SHOULD be interested in this material. In short, every aspect of "developing Interest" is a form of obedience training. The American Kennel Association does it better. But obedience training is not education.

The remaining steps of the Directed Reading Lesson are designed to drill, by repetition of course, so that the desired material will be learned. Not that the child will learn to think, mind you, but that he will learn the material. This audience is surely sophisticated enough to know that monotonous repetition is a tool of the brainwasher. So teachers proceed through succeeding steps of this practice: #2, anticipating problems; #3, reading silently; #4, reading orally; and then #5, doing follow up exercises. Of course, the monotony of the tasks are such that each teacher must again resort to persuasion, charm guilt and/or force to secure concentration to the task—more obedience training.

### Non-Meaning "Reading"

Another interesting piece of material is to be found in the teacher's manual accompanying Lippincott's *Basic Reading Series,* page iv. I quote:

> . . . So reading must be the process of turning these printed symbols into sounds. The moment we say this, however, someone is sure to ask . . . "But what about *meaning?* So you propose to define reading as mere word calling, without regard for meaning?" *Yes, we do.* [Emphasis mine]

This type of statement could be found in many places, and particularly in manuals for commercial phonics systems. What is so wrong about it? It is wrong because it makes no sense to the learner to make meaningless sounds. When a child is asked to do something that makes no sense to him he must be conditioned to trust the authority. Conditioning is obedience training. Instead of conditioning a child to reality, to relevance, to sensibleness, he must be conditioned to accepting meaningless symbols, slogans, catchwords, jargon. "Can Dan fan man" certainly fits in that category. Nonsense, non-words, mumbo-jumbo must, sooner or later be turned into sense. So why do it *senselessly* in the first place? There are many, many similar kinds of printed offerings. As such approaches are deeply rooted in the S-R bond, I think there must be a connection to our young totalitarians. The schools do have some responsibility, I do believe.

## Boxed Individualized Materials

There is another commercial program long on the market, called SRA Individualized Reading boxes. As most of you know, it is composed of a series of folders purportedly to be of graduated difficulty. Its virtue is that children may proceed through the folders at their own pace. This is true of all programmed material. But its vice is that it teaches children that reading is only for the purpose of answering questions. But whose questions? The child's? Of course not. The questions are the product of the developer of the material, as are all of the questions to be found in workbooks in teacher-made exercises. Endless questions. None of them are from the inner being of the child.

## Inquiry

Yet, we know from studies of totalitarian societies that the one activity that cannot be tolerated, if a given population is to remain under the sway of an authoritarian regime, is open-ended, freely asked and answered questions. Democracy cannot exist without inquiry. But teachers often mistrust the child's study skill and intention so that they fall into the trap of questioning him on the content of what he is studying. He is not allowed to examine the philosophical aspects of what he is reading. He must answer what the material wants him to answer. He cannot inquire independently. Study of Pavlov's dogs showed that all of the conditioning, ingrained laboriously into the animal, broke down when the dog's master came into the room. We know prisoners of war become "*un*brainwashed" after months of effort if, by chance, they hear just one word from the "outside." American textbooks are built upon a systematic, rigorously planned, graduated program of question asking, and rarely are those questions genuinely the child's. Only the individual conference approach allows inquiry.

## Humanistic Learning

I cannot close my presentation on such negativism. I insist that it is easy to teach FOR democracy if we only avoid S-R bond obedience training as educational method. We must teach so that learning is instantaneous, as it is with Sylvia Ashton-Warner's key vocabulary. We must avoid monotonous repetition, as in a self-selection program of reading and, most of all, we must encourage the process of unfettered inquiry—wherever it may lead. The development of thought units comes from within the child. Skills are not a thing apart. We learn *through* experience, not, as Skinner erroneously states, *from* experience.

Learning words in order to read is backwards. Learning sounds in order to learn words is a further step backwards. We read in ORDER TO LEARN WORDS. We write in ORDER to learn sounds. Involving children in learning must necessarily involve working with whatever it is he wants to express. We must perfect ways of getting him to want to verbalize —not what we want him to say—but what *he* wants to say. It may be that the manufacturers, after all, can provide us at a profit with pieces of equipment that encourage children to say what *they* want to say. What is better for that, of course, *outside* of a living, breathing, warm teacher, than a tape recorder and a microphone?

But the answer lies, for democracy's sake, in human interaction.

> One, two! One, two! And through and through
> The vorpal blade went snicker snack!
> He left it dead, and with its head
> He went galumphing back

The Jabberwock should not ride any more. Or we, as a democratic society, are done. The sign of the profits that interfere with education must be the significant fact for the decades to come. Whether or not you agree with me is not the point. The point is on the health, the sanity, the human values of our society.

## References

1. Lewis Carroll, *Through the Looking Glass.*
2. *Arizona Republic,* February 2, 1969.
3. Herbert J. Klausmeier, *Psychological and Classroom Learning.* Mimeographed.
4. *This Magazine Is About Schools* (Fall 1967): 96.

**Patrick Groff**

# *Culture and the Single Textbook*

Culture is how human beings live in society, the standards of conduct by which their behavior is regulated or judged. "The culture of a group is its standardized behavior, values, and products evolved through time and sanctified as tradition" (1).

Culture passes to successive generations many things: technologies (the atom bomb), ideas (religion), values (racial superiority), and social systems (representative democracy). All these affect man's physical appearance, his physiology, intelligence, thoughts, and overt behavior. Culture, then, is the proper domain of linguists, anthropologists, historians, biologists, sociologists, and certainly educationists.

It is obvious, too, that culture can be pleasant or cruel, accepting or prejudiced, just or unjust, fear evoking, or excitingly attractive.

The purpose of the following discussion aims to inspect more precisely why we have chosen to teach the way we do, and, specifically, why we have chosen to do it with the so-called basal reader. What have been the cultural relationships of culture and the single text? What effect will this past practice have on how we adjust the teaching of reading to the cultural demands of the future years?

## The Blue Back Speller

Let's trace this heritage back historically as far as the Blue Back Speller (*The American Spelling Book*). This phenomenal publishing enterprise by Noah Webster was begun in 1783. By 1837 the text had sold fifteen million copies. As late as 1880 it was still claimed to be the best seller besides the Bible. "No other secular book," according to Commager, the famed historian, "had ever spread so wide, penetrated so deep, lasted so long." While Webster was vainglorious, "a creature not of reason but of sentiment," he so clearly perceived the structure of the emerging American culture with its central drive for nationalism and need for national pride, that he could say with little contradiction that his text was published so as to "promote the honor and prosperity of the confederate republic of America" (3).

But these moral and patriotic readers by Webster also set a cultural model for the dozens of other series of readers that were to follow. Webster labored not to teach a common language but to inculcate an American one. His text was designed:

> to extirpate the improprieties and vulgarisms which were necessarily intro-
> duced by settlers from various parts of Europe; to reform the abuses and
> corruption which tincture the conversations of the polite part of Ameri-
> cans; to render the acquisition of the language easy, both to American
> youth and foreigners; and to render the pronunciation of it accurate and
> uniform by demolishing those odious distinctions of provincial dialects
> which are the subject of reciprocal ridicule (4).

### Changes in the Twentieth Century

Webster and his successors reigned until sometime in the eighteen-eighties when a new movement, to last for some thirty years, began to shape itself in the field of reading instruction (5). The nation now had the time to turn its attention to different, if not greater, matters than nationalism, namely, its cultural advancement. No longer was it necessary to create a common history and its attendant legends. It was no longer necessary to see the school as an engine of nationalism, as had Noah Webster.

It followed that the *first* influence or emphasis in reading material for the young in the 20th century would reflect this change in the culture of the society. Literary appreciation and interest in the finer aspects of writing, and the development of permanent interests in classical writing, obviously would enhance this different stage of culture evolution. Such became the major content of the readers.

The *second* impressive influence in this century upon education proba-bly was the scientific movement which can be dated roughly from 1910. Almost the first to fall under the blow of scientific inquiry was the great emphasis naturally given to oral reading in the previous literature readers. From the first standardized reading tests (1915), oral reading showed weak-nesses in both speed and comprehension. Moreover, as we have seen, the content of readers had since grown out of the narrow nationalistic lines set by Webster. Reading was seen increasingly to have other purposes than to develop patriotism.

Indeed, with the advent of the great emphasis upon silent reading of this period came another change in the content offerings of the readers. From previous largely literary offerings, children now (after World War I) were given content "largely of factual and informative selections" (6), about practical life situations. It was felt that this type of material, rather than literature, would be what the child would eventually want to read outside of school. Society, it was felt, demanded this. This advent of experimentalism and the scientific study of the reading act, represented by the new standardized tests, did not hinder the growth or status of the basal reader, however. Indeed, the text seemed to flourish under its protective mantle. For now the basal reader could more perfectly defend its right to eminence in the field of reading materials by its insistence that it was not only traditionally good, but now scientifically good, as well. The science of reading became its handmaiden, to be used when it appeared to enchance the marketability of the product, or to be jilted whenever it proved theoretically embarrassing or economically impractical.

The *third* great change in reading instruction in this century useful for our present analysis was the attempt to individualize reading instruction in the 1920's and 1930's. The NSSE 1925 Yearbook was on this subject. It is not so remarkable that such reports were made considering the evidence the new standardized tests had given about the variability of pupil achievement. What is of special pertinence to our discussion is the way in which the basal reader was able to counteract this first really critical challenge to its hegemony.

The approach that attacked the basal reader approach in the 1920's would have children select the material they would read in terms of their own interests or needs, to read it for their own purposes and at their own particular speeds. For, indeed, the critics of the scientific basal reader movement were saying American society had accomplished, but all too well, what had been Noah Webster's dream. In producing a startlingly industrialized and technological culture within the space of a century, the materialistic forces of the culture, they felt, had obviously won out over the more creative and individualistic facets of life. It was insisted that "In more than one hundred years of systematization of the national educational scheme, the materials and activities of the school have not only been largely aloof from, indeed foreign to, the institutions and cultures of the American people, but they have failed equally to provide for maximal child growth" (7). Thus, the "mutually interactive group life" wrought from the industrialized culture demanded that instruction in reading be child-centered, activity oriented, and individualistic in its methodology.

To fight against this threat that the reading program would change to one in which children would learn to read by reading from many sources, the basal reader found it necessary to shift ground. The answer to the challenge seemed to lie in the rather simple expedient of expressing for itself broader objectives than it had hitherto claimed. "No one type of instruction was given an exaggerated emphasis overshadowing all others, as had been true in preceding periods" (8). Too, the editors of the basal reader were quick to sense and consider the criticisms given to the practical content readers. They sensed the time had come to build in some possibilities for greater attention to creativeness and imagination, and to the child's current and changing interests.

## The Viability of the Basal Reader

In spite of the seemingly great support the activity reading movement of the 1920's and the 1930's could garner from the culture, the fact that during the depression years greater consideration was given to the importance of the individual than ever before, that the arts and literature were receiving more support from the federal government, and the fact the country seemed in the mood to accept radical and creative changes, the basal reader weathered this storm of contention and emerged relatively unscathed.

The remarkable vitality of the basal reader to this point can be attributed to several interrelated and yet individually identifiable causes:

1. The phenomenal success for the Webster texts implied that schools found these materials very useful. The pattern of a reader had been so deeply engrained since Webster in the thinking of teachers and supervisors of reading that critics of it were not to be trusted.

2. The textbooks were not unresponsive to the changes in the culture. The textbook companies were obviously run by vigorous and shrewd editors who made many attempts to accommodate the textbook to the changing times. Without making their product look too unfamiliar, around 1925–1930 they "updated" the books in several ways: a brighter color for the covers of the readers and the addition of colored pictures. They now used dull paper, a bolder and larger type, vocabulary control, and heavy repetition—all the things that are seen in today's reader. In fact, very few, if any, basic changes have been made since 1930.

These editors were also quick to exploit the reserve of highly potent but low paid talent that lay in the minds of college professors. They induced these otherwise public servants to use their spare time to produce the readers in the forms that were marketable, at least, if not in keeping with the principles of progressive education. The penurious college professor jumped readily at this bait, and was paid handsomely in many instances for his work. This college professor-author, in keeping with economic traditions, could justify this private activity as protection for society against the dangers of the preparation of the basal reader by the centralized state or federal educational systems.

3. The readers were little challenged by the typical reading authority employed by the influential city school districts. Teachers' guides and courses of study in reading seldom, if ever, broke away from the structure of reading set by the basal readers. Instead, these materials continued to be slavishly derivative of either the college texts on reading (often written by the authors of the basal readers) and the interpretations of reading research made in these books, or in the teachers' manuals of the basal reader.

4. Most importantly, the basal reader seemed to fit the cultural needs of the classroom teacher. Let's accept for our argument what Landes says about teachers (9). They tend to disparage themselves and are very conscious of their image or public stereotype, social status and prestige. Teachers tend to separate themselves from the mainstream of their community. They become unaware of the many social forces shaping the child, forces that are not represented in the reader. They generally are susceptible or sensitive to praise or criticism, but often in unusual ways. A child who does not learn to read well is "felt by teachers to act unfairly toward them, almost by deliberate intent." The words used by the teacher for the child who fails in reading support this idea: low motivated, slow learner, remedial case, underachiever, problem child, language handicapped, uncooperative, member of the low reading group, and later on, non-academically oriented. This teacher, convinced of his cultural inferiority, finds it difficult to challenge the authenticity or validity of the seemingly well-designed basal reader or to contradict its impressive list of expert authors. This teacher also finds it is too risky, too big a chance of further loss of personal prestige, to break away from the authority of the reader. For if the child does not read, the teacher can blame the authority. In other words, the basal reader becomes the scapegoat for what it considered a failing act by the teacher. "I didn't fail," says the teacher. "The reader failed. It needs revision." Or, "I need a new one."

This teacher also recognizes that the reader represents middle-class culture, albeit in rather anachronistic or dogmatic terms. "Shouldn't," the teacher asks, "all children be taught to accept the middle-class ethos, ethics, and mores? Aren't we trying to get all children middle-classed?" For the teachers who are unaware of the middle-class cultural pattern they follow, the readers present a subliminal recognition of the culture pattern. The writers of the readers carefully planned this juxtaposition; it is not accident it occurs so readily. These middle-class teachers worry if they are not fulfilling a supposed cultural commitment to teach a polished or standardized conduct system. The readers give reassurance they are.

Finally, the basal reader does nothing to frustrate, annoy, or embarrass the teacher. It does not present cultural dilemmas for which open-value judgments of a controversial or subjective nature will have to be made. The teacher is not put into a compromising position. To this purpose we notice the basal reader never deals with the gutsy issues of birth, death, poverty, sex, hygiene, comparative religions, racial problems or prejudice, family instability, the decay of the city, etc. This fits the cultural expectations of teachers who have become teachers just so they may be removed from the competitive cycle of the salesman, the emotional issues of the social worker, the life and death visitations of the nurse, the materialistic orientation of the loan officer, etc.

As Barton and Wilder report, "Apparently, teachers are committed to the notion that they are professionals who should be free to decide how to teach in their own classrooms, but when one considers their heavy dependence upon basal readers, this commitment to professionalism and autonomy appears to be an expression more of ideology than of reality" (10). What teachers do when they accept the basal reader as "absolutely necessary" is to admit inwardly that schools are essentially bureaucratic structures, and the teacher's role in the system is largely that of a functionary.

## The Progressive Education Movement Dies

The *fourth* impressive effect on reading instruction was not, as it might be guessed, that the teaching of phonics was dropped in the 1930's, later to be recovered. As Smith makes clear, the 1925–1930 readers used the same intrinsic phonics methods that do the varieties of series we see forty years later (11). Nor was the most momentous event the rise of the reading readiness movement. Both of these aspects can be subsumed under a broader event, the Progressive Education Movement. It was the death of this movement to which we now turn our attention. Founded in 1919, the Progressive Education Association was highly involved in the notion of individualized reading instruction. However, by the late 1930's the movement was fragmented, in a dying state in the 1940's, to finally succumb in the 1950's with Sputnik as its gravestone.

With the demise of the PEA went an overwhelming victory for the basal reader, since the progressive movement called for teaching the child to read in ways radically removed from those proposed in readers. It is easier, it was felt, for the child to learn to read by asking him to behave like a mature reader than doing something else, even though the something else may be more closely related to reading. Reading, then, became the act of conveying meaning. The progressivists were not preoccupied with isolated word analysis obviously. They were concerned not with the training in the mechanical use of a particular set of materials, but instead in training the intellectual utility of many or all materials available or usable. They did not approach the task of reading piecemeal, but rather with the language arts curriculum as a whole in mind. Some believed that a corrupted middle-class culture had arisen, and that was what was largely given in the basal readers. Essentially, the basal reader to them was a manufactured commodity that grew increasingly downward toward tawdry cheapness, humdrum standardization, and crass uniformity. While maintaining a pretentious morality by avoiding sensationalism and sordidness, it lulled its audience into an insensibility toward real problems.

To reverse this trend, the progressivists believed that reading should be essentially concerned with making children aware of the facts, opinions, and values with which they were being bombarded so they could question them and finally make judgments about their significance. They would agree with Huxley that "Children should be taught that words are indispensable but also can be fatal ... begetters at the same time of all superstition, all collective madness and stupidity ..." and that "never have misused words —those hideously efficient tools of all the tyrants, warmongers, persecutors, and heresy hunters been so widely and so disastrously influential ..." (12).

Why did this movement in reading fail? Cremin (13) gives the best answer in *The Transformation of the School:*

> The attack on the life-adjustment movement was no isolated phenomenon; it came rather as part of a much larger crisis in American Education that had been brewing at least since the early 1940's. There were, to begin, the prosaic problems of buildings, budgets, and enrollments created by the war; few schools had been built since 1941; teachers had deserted the profession in droves; inflation was rampant; and the first of a flood of 'war babies' began to enter the elementary grades as early as 1946. Then, too, there were the multifarious difficulties associated with deepening public concern over communist expansionism at home and abroad. And, finally, though perhaps less visible, there were the voracious demands of an expanding industrial economy for trained and intelligent manpower.

The general reason, then, for the demise of progressivism in reading instruction was the general turning toward conservatism in post World War II social thought. The PEA had not kept pace with the need to accept the responsibility for transmitting the technical knowledge that was rapidly expanding. Too, some of the reforms that the PEA called for (not, unfortunately, in reading) had been achieved. The tragedy of the matter, however, was that the progressive movement was not criticized in terms of the principles it had tried to defend: initiative by citizens, progress in an open society, personal happiness, an attempt to make the scientific world liveable, and the elimination in the school of the inconsequential, stupid, misleading, or unnecessarily difficult.

Predictably, the demise of the progressive movement did not hurt the basal reader if we can believe one of its advocates: "The criticism by laymen probably had three good effects: it caused school people to examine their present methods more carefully; it stimulated the interest of parents and other laymen in reading instruction; it offered motives and opportunities to school people to explain the research, psychology, and philosophy on which present methods are based. So in this situation, as is often the case in other situations, even criticism caused reading [read: basal readers] to move forward" (14).

That the trend to conservatism in the U.S. after World War II, the beat-the-Russians mentality of school critics, proved of little threat to the basal reader is believable. The reader, of course, is a conservative product of a conservative industry. Its conservative orthodoxy was supported, too, in the college textbooks on teaching reading of this period. One could search in vain in them for a discussion of the activity reading curriculum or individualized reading. Too, the overall similarity of the organization and content of these books at this time was amazing. It was as if all the prospective teachers in the country were receiving a reading course exclusively designed for basal reading.

Such absolutism was destined to bring on reactions, however. Consequently, by 1960 there appeared a revival in the interest in individualized reading in the country. While this became a most popular topic in educational journals and at meetings of reading teachers, while all save a few of the new reading textbooks on teaching reading had something favorable to say for the approach, and while the new evidence on individualized reading indicated it to be a safe alternate to basal reading, it is doubtful that many teachers have actually turned to its use (15).

## Present Challenges to the Basal Reader

The *fifth* and latest important aspect of cultural change affecting reading has been the concern over teaching this skill to the economically poor child, or as he is commonly referred to, the culturally disadvantaged, deprived, or different. It is because of this concern that the greatest protest of cultural origins have been made against the basal reader so far. This criticism points out and confirms the fact that the life of the children in the readers is far removed from that of the culturally different child. The CD child has never experienced the life portrayed in the new, clean, orderly, suburban homes in these books, with their close parental supervision of children and their numerous pets, toys, trips, and friendly, helpful relatives and neighbors. In the reader there is no observable poverty nor its humiliating effects. Father, in these readers has a well-paid, white-collar job, and maintains a dominant, respected role in the family. Everyone speaks standard American English. No personal tragedy nor conflict mars this ideal setting. The scene is laid in a segregated neighborhood of white people of North European origin and appearance, where obviously no Negro is allowed to reside. Here is perpetuated the myth of Negro invisibility. The overall effect is to strengthen the ethnocentric attitudes of the white child while at the same time making the Negro reader see himself as an outsider or as inferior.

The basal reader has responded somewhat to such criticism of late but has only offered simple solutions to the profound handicaps one finds in using these materials with CD children. Through a "color-me-brown" technique, certain characters of the originally all-white readers have been introduced as members of the minority race. The appearance of creating an integrated society is given, but what has been turned out so far is simply a statement that middle-class Negroes and middle-class white families enjoy the same activites, and that children of these families will willingly play together. The real problems of race integration have accordingly been carefully avoided. The Negro child can realize how inaccurate such a portrayal is of his actual condition in the ghetto; the white child, equally segregated, may judge such a situation to be a fantasy. What such a story must involve to be worthwhile, for example, would be an instance of a colored family moving into a white neighborhood and how mutual friendships between the races grew out of this relocation. Or the story might depict the actual evidence of segregated ghetto living and leave some suggestions as to its remedy.

The problem of racial integration is far from the only cultural reality the basal reader must face in the future if it is to justify itself as the material with which reading is to be taught. The cultural facts of life the reader can no longer avoid with impunity must include:

1. The decay of the center city.
2. The rise of the teen-age culture.
3. The destruction of traditional sexual ethics.
4. The statistics of crime and mental disorder.
5. The increasingly paternalistic and dictatorial state and federal governments.
6. The status of international relations.
7. The conflict between the private and the social good.
8. The danger mass democracy will pull culture down to the lowest common denominator of the masses.
9. The crisis in divinity: Is God dead in a scientific world?
10. The state of invention and technological advancement. What will be the place of formal education when knowledge will be accumu-

lated in electronic banks and transmitted directly to the nervous system by means of coded electronic messages, or when closed-circuit television replaces the filing cabinet and bookshelf? All we need to do, says one experimenter in this field, is to find the input terminals in the human brain and the necessary code. To him the total teaching machines obviously are no more alarming than the pop-up toaster or the automatic phonograph. The human engineers are planning even more. They suggest selective breeding and other planned genetics for long-term intellectual improvement or drug therapy for short-term acceleration in learning.

Basal readers will face extinction from what *Life* magazine (January 27, 1967) calls the "computer as a tutor." In Palo Alto, California, children are learning to read at computer terminals, each of which is equipped with a teletypewriter keyboard, cathode-ray tube, earphones, and projection screen. These children listen to instructions through the earphones and following given instructions, write with a light-pen on the cathode-ray tube of the terminal. The really slow learners are branched off by the computer into a sequence of corrective drills. The computer stores up multitudinous facts about each child's responses so that the program can be adjusted to his individual learning style and so that redundant, misleading, or too difficult material can be avoided, so that a precise sequencing of the materials is possible. (The hardware industries: IBM, RCA, Litton, GF., Xerox, Raytheon, etc., are so sure of the financial prospects of this procedure that they and many other companies are buying up the software publishers: Random House, American Book, Silver Burdett, etc.) The major proposition of the computer-learning movement is that the machine teaches the child to read; the teacher instructs him in how best to use this ability and to think critically about it. The teacher becomes an intellectual and mechanical troubleshooter, a computer manager. The only catch seems to be a financial one: *Life* reports the first grade program in Palo Alto cost 1.5 million; the textbooks necessary to teach the same number of children the same thing over the same time would have cost $180.

The basal reader faces other challenges from the electronic technology. The most interesting theorist among those who proposed the decline or demise of books as the central learning tool or source is Marshall McLuhan. In two of his books, *Gutenberg Galaxy* (16) and *Understanding Media* (17), he believes not only that books are obsolete or that their content is simply impertinent, but that they have had an overall harmful effect on mankind.

In stating his belief that "the American stake in literacy as a technology or uniformity applied to every level of education. . . . is totally threatened by the electronic technology," McLuhan sees himself "in the position of Louis Pasteur telling doctors that their greatest enemy was quite invisible and quite unrecognized by them" (18). In reaching this conclusion, McLuhan has identified what he considers the four critical areas in the intellectual and social status of man, those of:

1.   illiterate tribalism,
2.   the invention of the phonetic alphabet,
3.   the era of the movable type, which we are still in, and
4.   the era into which we are fast moving: electronic technology.

At present Mcluhan feels we are about as far into the electric age as the Elizabethans were into the age of movable type. And, he believes the advent of the alphabet and movable type transformed an oral, tactile, tribal togetherness into the present specialized, fragmented society characterized by visual perception, the use of logical, sequential organization and a fixed point of view. The printed book, by translating all human experience into the visual, linear, sequential form of written sentences, has tended to alienate man from deep involvement with his environment and proves destructive of the democratic ethos. Man finds, unfortunately, that he cannot cope with reality until it is processed into the linear, mechanical order of print. Electronics technology, McLuhan feels, will take us back to the rich oral-aural world, the one structured by myth and ritual, with its communal and sacred values. The electronics technology will liberate man from the impoverishing effects of print since it demands participation. It will restore man to harmony with man. The very portability of the book is attacked. It allows man to feed his intellect in isolation from others, thus introducing an undesirable individualism. The uniformity and repeatability of alphabetic print strengthens a mechanistic thinking. The alphabet thus is the "Africa of the mind."

Television, on the other hand, is tactile and tribal because:

1.   it lacks definition (is difficult to make out), and thus forces participation;
2.   it is preliterate, and
3.   it is an extension of our central nervous system.

Television gives children a taste for experience in depth, but in images of low visual definition—which forces them to extend their own powers to fill in what is missing. Modern children come to reading with all their senses alerted by TV, to find that print rejects all but one, the isolated and stripped down visual faculty.

Moreover, McLuhan believes the social effects of a medium is more important than the cognitive content of the medium. Thus, the "medium is the message." For instance, it is not what TV does that counts. It is the fact that TV displaces reading and reintroduces the communication of preliterate societies. It provides us with an extension of not one sense organ, as reading does, but of the sense structure as a whole. Consequently, "the next logical step would seem to be . . . to bypass language in favor of a general cosmic consciousness which might be very like the collective unconscious." Speechlessness "could confer a perpetuity of collective harmony and peace."

What is the future of the basal reader in the face of these astounding cultural challenges, and the attacks both actual and theoretical from the emerging technology? In the past the basal reader has found that minor adjustments to cultural change have been enough to satisfy its users. Whether such toleration will be the case in the future seems in serious doubt, however. There seems little from the history of the basal reader that would lead one to believe it has the capacity to adjust to the massive modifications in traditional life that are presently taking place. Nor does it seem it will be able to compete with the computer in a race to teach the child to read in the shortest possible time. The question is, how much longer will we accept its contention that it provides the reading environment best designed to develop reading abilities for the child, in as short a time as possible, with the reading content that engages him in an intellectually respectable way with the real world and the important problems of life?

Finally, we must agree not to summarily dismiss such theorists as McLuhan. Considering these troubled times, if giving up books would ensure universal peace and goodwill, who would not gladly make the exchange?

## References

1. Landes, Ruth. *Culture in American Education* (New York: John Wiley, 1965), 37.

2. Webster, Noah. *American Spelling Book* (New York: Teachers College, Columbia University, 1831), Preface by Henry Steele Commager (1962), 5.

3. *Ibid.,* 4.

4. *Ibid.*

5. Smith, Nila B. *American Reading Instruction* (Newark: International Reading Association, 1962).

6. *Op. cit.,* 72.

7. Rugg, Harold, and Ann Shumaker. *The Child-Centered School* (Yonkers-on-Hudson, N.Y.: World Book, 1928), 12.

8. Smith, Nila B., *op. cit.,* 198.

9. Landes, Ruth, *op. cit.*

10. Barton, Allen H., and David E. Wilder. "Research and Practice in the Teaching of Reading: A Progress Report," in *Innovation in Education* (Matthew B. Miles, editor) (New York: Teachers College, Columbia University, 1964), 384.

11. Smith, Nila B., *op. cit.*

12. Huxley Aldous. "Education at the Nonverbal Level," in *Revolution in Teaching* (Alfred de Grazia and David A. Sohn, editors) (New York: Bantam Books, 1964), 70–71.

13. Cremin, Lawrence A. *The Transformation of the School* (New York: Alfred A. Knopf, 1961), 338.

14. Smith, Nila B. "What Have We Accomplished in Reading?" in *Revolution in Teaching* (Alfred de Grazia and David A. Sohn, editors) (New York: Bantam Books, 1964), 282.

15. Barton, Allen H., and David E. Weldon, *op. cit.*

16. McLuhan, Marshall. *Gutenberg Galaxy* (Toronto: University of Toronto, 1962).

17. McLuhan, Marshall. *Understanding Media* (New York: McGraw-Hill, 1964).

18. *Ibid.,* 17–18.

**Augusta Baker**

# Beyond Literacy: Pinfeathers or Wings in Children's Books

I am happy to be with you tonight since I owe a great deal to California. Four Californians have given me strength and support in my world of books: Frances Clarke Sayers, whose 1937 paper, "Lose Not the Nightingale" was characterized by Anne Carroll Moore as the most important paper ever read before an audience of librarians. Here was a magnificent plea in behalf of the imagination. Then, there is Lawrence Clark Powell, a true bookman, famous for his glorification of books in these days of data processing, information retrieval, and other automatic mindstuffers. Next Rosemary Livsey, who has spent her professional life bringing together children and good books, who has been an inspiration to children's librarians throughout the country—and who is my friend. And then, Hildegarde Swift, whose books have helped me bring understanding to children and adults who are questioning all men are brothers.

It was Frances Clarke Sayers who introduced her children's librarians to a great scholar, a man of Letters, an eloquent and masterful teacher—Paul Hazard. I remember that introduction for Mrs. Sayers read aloud from *Books, Children, and Men.* As we listened we realized that, at last, children had a great spokesman. He cried out for them. "Give us books, . . . give us wings. You who are powerful and strong, help us to escape into the faraway. Build us azure palaces in the midst of enchanted gardens. Show us fairies strolling about in the moonlight. We are willing to learn everything that we are taught at school, but, please, let us keep our dreams."

Are we giving our children books that will build azure palaces or are we giving them factories that will grind out "learning" from morning to night? Have we declared war on imagination, beauty, dreams? Albert Einstein said, "Imagination is more important than knowledge." I am particularly concerned today because I hear talk, all around me, about what to give the child. The voices do not say, "give him wings" but rather, they say, "give him pinfeathers. Give the bright child more information because he needs to be practical, he needs unimaginative knowledge." What are the problems of the inner city? Consult the city records to find out more about the sewage system. These are his assignments. Cram his mind with facts and figures—stifle his soul. And then, that poor, newly-discovered child—the culturally deprived, the disadvantaged, the socio-economically handi-capped, the slum child. Don't dare let him stretch to a piece of fine litera-ture. Let us get busy and write books that will have limited vocabulary, short sentences, familiar surroundings (the slums?). Books that he can read without the least bit of strain; books with which he can identify; books about his own way of life—the hard, dirty, noisy city. If you were a slum child, would you want to stay in that world forever? If you had a bright, inquiring mind, would you not want to let it roam without restraint? If you had difficulty with words and language, if you were a non-reader, would you want to be confined to the dull, unimaginative world in which you already find yourself? If I were a slum child I would want to be brought up from my morass. I would want my intellect strengthened and challenged, for, make no mistake, these children have intellect. They have not had the kind of stimulation and environment which we associate with an affluent, middle-class society, but they have imaginations, aspirations, and the seeds for successful living.

These are all children trying to be just plain children while we are busy planning different childhoods for different categories of children—the gifted, the normal, the disadvantaged. Granted that there is a necessity for a certain amount of planning in various areas, it might be of greater worth to remove some of the mediocrity, false standards and overstimulation to which children are exposed and encourage them to be children. Francis Thompson, in his essay, "Shelley," wrote of Shelley's childlike quality when he answered the question: Know you what it is to be a child? He said, in part, "It is to be so little that the elves can reach to whisper in your ear; it is to turn pumpkins into coaches; mice into horses; lowness into loftiness; nothing into everything, for each child has its fairy godmother in its own soul." In our plans for the knowledgeable child, are we forgetting the fairy godmother in his soul?

In 1937, nearly 30 years ago, a young librarian was sent by Anne Carroll Moore, one of the great figures in the world of children and books, to work in a slum area in Harlem. A children's librarian, Priscilla Edie Morton, trained her and convinced her that children do respond to well-written books and that it is the moral obligation of every adult to introduce all children to great books. She and I, for I was that young librarian, used every technique to bring together children and books—reading aloud, story-telling, book talks, reading clubs, were but a few. No one had told us about the limitations of a slum child so he was fair prey. We gave him un-adapted, full length stories. They had long words, long sentences and long thoughts. Yes, he often struggled with the words but it never dawned on us that he shouldn't. I suppose that we were ignorant for we had not heard about vocabulary control. We gave these children Howard Pyle's *Robin Hood* because we loved the roll of the "thee's" and "thou's." We gave them fantasy. "Alice thought she had never seen such a curious croquet-ground in all her life; it was all ridges and furrows; the croquet-balls were all live hedgehogs and the mallets live flamingoes, and the soldiers had to double themselves up and stand on their hands and feet, to make the arches." We gave them *Wind in the Willows,* Arthur Ransome books, folk tales, poetry, as well as Negro history. Out of that ghetto and world of books came such people as James Baldwin, Langston Hughes, Kenneth Clarke, and others. Many people of stature and substance were "library boys and girls" who came from this depressed environment. In many cases they were there because of the restrictive, racial pattern of segregated housing. It would not have helped them if we had restricted their children's world.

They reacted differently to books since no two children react alike. We read from Langston Hughes' *The Dream Keeper* (1) . . .

Prayer

I ask you this:
Which way to go?
I ask you this:
Which sin to bear?
Which crown to put
Upon my hair?
I do not know,
Lord God,
I do not know.

We took our Boys' Reading Club to see and hear Maurice Evans in Shakespeare's "Hamlet." We talked about Shakespeare and his times before we went to see the play.

Some of our children reached for the books and clutching them tightly, went home to read more. Others could not read these words and so they directed me to "read it again!" And I read—again and again, and again!

Today in that same library nearly 30 years later, we are giving the present generation of slum children the same basic food for their minds and souls. We are giving them good books. Sometimes we falter. We doubt the wisdom of our course as we are bogged down in methodology, educational theories and practices. We wonder if we have lost step with the world. Are we old-fashioned traditionalists? Then, Annis Duff, out of her concern, asks, "What of the books that are full of wonder and enchantment, full of poetic fire and imaginative power and spiritual wisdom? Can it be that this kind of literature has diminished in value for the young? Or is it that we grown-ups are encouraging a situation in which realism takes the place of reality in our children's reading? Are we so intent on developing the average child that we forget that every child is special? Have we outgrown the belief that 'the child is father to the man, and that minds nurtured in richness in childhood will never lose their power to gather up richness through the whole of life'." We hear these words and we know that we shall continue to give the Harlem children the best.

I would like to mention, in particular, two types of literature which have proven most effective to me, in reaching all children. Over the years I have shared poetry with all kinds of children and they have been consistently responsive. True poetry—not jingles and rhymed words—will open a new world for the child. Many people have tried to define poetry but it has eluded every effort to confine it in a definition. Poetry is the pattern of life—the inner life of mind and heart, and the outer life of the world about us. The true poet combines, within himself, truth and imagination and he creates sharp, clear, and moving images. The child enjoys poetry. He loves repetition and rhythm, joyous lyrics, martial strains which set his feet a-tapping just as a Sousa march will do.

We must share poetry with our children and the best way is to learn how to read it well. When a child listens to poetry he is becoming accustomed to words in an unfamiliar arrangement, or order. Many times he is being introduced to strange and new words so that his appreciation for language is deepened at the same time that his imagination is being stretched. Fortunate is the child who is introduced to Mother Goose when he is a little one. Some years ago Annis Duff wrote a book *Bequest of Wings.* It is as timely today as it was when she wrote it. It is a sharing of family responses to books and in it Mrs. Duff tells how she sang and recited Mother Goose rhymes and poetry to her children before they could speak but she instilled in them a love for music, rhythm and the sound of words, the measured movement of their cadence.

It is not imperative that children understand all of the meaning found in a poem. We do not have to dissect and crucify the poem. As I look back on my own school days I wonder that I love poetry as I do. The entire class memorized a long poem and then recited it in unison with great good spirit and gusto. Then with a sharp knife and scalpel, the teacher dissected it, word by word, thought by thought. It was punished and tortured until very little enjoyment of it was left. Fortunately, today's child is not exposed to this and we are aware of what Coleridge meant when he wrote, "Poetry gives much pleasure when only generally, and not perfectly, understood."

I like Emily Dickinson's description of what poetry was to her. "If I read a book and it makes my whole body so cold no fire can ever warm me, I know that is poetry. If I feel physically as if the top of my head were taken off, I know that is poetry. These are the only ways I know it. Is there any other way?"

Do we, today, still shy away from books of fantasy and fairy tales? In 1931, Coward-McCann published a collection of articles and reviews written and edited by Anne Carroll Moore. It was called *The Three Owls: Third Book.* It has long been out of print but it is well worth searching for in our second hand book stores. Paul Fenimore Cooper had just published a highly imaginative story: *Tal: His Marvelous Adventures With Noom-Zor-Noom.* Miss Moore was struck by the magical quality in this book and so she asked this great-grandson of the famous novelist to write a little article about the child's imagination. He did and he called it, "On Catching A Child's Fancy." Let me give you just two paragraphs.

> Every child has a fancy, and every child likes to have his fancy caught. No matter where the catching of it may lead, the child will follow. He will run and stumble, get up and run again, with the same eagerness with which he will give chase to a soap bubble over a rough and furrowed field. Once his fancy is caught, everything is fun. Catch it in his work, catch it in his play; and it will bring about more wonderful changes than any magician's wand. In many ways it is a child's most valuable possession, for through it he gets his greatest pleasures. However, valuable as it is, he never hoards it up nor keeps it to himself. He carries it openly, begging to have it caught. And to those who can catch it and hold it the child gives freely of this heart.
>
> Varied as its uses are, the real value of fancy lies in its imaginative qualities. Fancy is to the imagination what the seed is to the tree. Let it lie in barren ground and it will not grow. But nourish it and care for it through the years and it will grow into imagination, as dear a possession for the man as fancy is for the child. He who lacks imagination lives but half a life. He has his experiences, he has his facts, he has his learning. But do any of these really live unless touched by the magic of imagination? So long as the road is straight he can see down it and follow it. But imagination looks round the turns and gazes far off into the distance on either side. And it is imagination that walks hand in hand with vision.

Facts are facts, and fancy is fancy; and there is room in the world for both. Each is important and there is no reason why they should not be in peaceful co-existence.

Permit me to make one more digression. You know, by now, how strongly I feel about the child's right to have beauty and truth. Yet, I am not in the clouds. We are in a changing world—a rapidly, spinning one and the child must keep abreast with the changes. Therefore his diet must be a balanced one and he has a right to know about life as it is today. He sees it on television, he hears about it over the radio and through adult discussion in the home. He knows what it means to have an alcoholic parent; he is torn apart when his parents separate from each other; he knows poverty and filth. He knows the pressure of the gang—and he knows it early in life.

"What are you going to do now, Rufus?"

"About what?"

"Going to join a gang, aren't you?"

Curtis hesitated—"I've been thinking about joining the Little Warriors."

Rufus and Curtis are in *Durango Street* by Frank Bonham.

Books that face up to today's problems and discuss them with frankness and good taste are needed but they, too, should have quality in writing. They should not be moralistic tracts nor should they be rewritten reports of a social worker. The child who has developed discriminating taste will not touch such contrived books—not with a ten foot pole.

> *Story of the Negro,* by Arna Bontempts
> *Mary Jane,* by Dorothy Sterling
> *South Town* and *North Town,* by Lorenz Graham
> *Snowy Day* and *Whistle for Willie,* by Ezra Jack Keats
> *Two is a Team,* by Jerrold Beim
> *The Empty Schoolhouse,* by Natalie Savage Carlson
> *Jazz Country,* by Nat Hentoff

All of these books are good, exciting books that have been touched with the author's own imaginative creativity. No do-gooders or missionaries are here. These are men and women who have a story to tell and who tell it well. These are the books which touch the heart of every child, which strengthen his fancy, extend his horizon, bring him truth and beauty. These are the books from which the stuff of life comes. They are the heritage of all children—black and white, advantaged and disadvantaged; readers and non-readers—ad infinitum. It is our responsibility as parents, librarians, educators, to listen and act as the children plead, "Give us wings—not pinfeathers but strong, powerful wings that will take us soaring over the ordinary, the mundane, the silly, empty, pedantic books that paralyze our souls, that stifle our young hearts, that crush our imaginations. Please—let us keep our dreams."

## Reference

1. Langston Hughes, *The Dream Keeper and Other Poems,* Helen Sewell, illus. (New York: Alfred A. Knopf, 1937).

# Kenneth S. Goodman

## *Comprehension-Centered Reading*

Reading is a process by which a person reconstructs a message encoded graphically by a writer. Like all language activities, reading has as its central purpose, effective communication of meaning. In the full sense, comprehension is the only objective of the reader. To the extent that he has this end continuously in view he is reading; to the extent that he loses comprehension as a goal he is doing something other than reading: saying sounds, naming words, manipulating language. This alone would be enough to justify the claim that instruction in reading must center on comprehension.

But there is an even more basic reason why reading instruction must be comprehension centered. Language does not exist apart from its relationship to meaning. Now this meaning is not a property of language—the sounds or ink blotches have no intrinsic meaning. Meaning is supplied by the reader himself as he processes the symbolic system of language. As a user of the language he relates language sequences to experiences and conceptual structures. He cannot get the message unless he can process the language. But neither can he process the language unless he has the relevant experiential-conceptual background to bring to the particular task. I can't read a technical treatise on nuclear physics: I'm disadvantaged; I lack the background. But I do well at reading even highly technical material where I have strong interests and relevant cognitive structures. Meaning, in short, is both output and input, in the reading process. Unless the teaching of reading is comprehension centered the very nature of the task is changed from reading to something other than reading.

That's my basic message. The rest of my discussion will be 1) an attempt to support this view, and 2) an attempt to explore its implications.

## Building Reading Instruction on a Sound Theoretical Base

My view of reading instruction I must warn you is built on a strong theoretical base which has been continually tempered by plunging it into the reality of real people reading real language.

I am convinced that, to build effective reading methods and materials, we must (a) understand the reading process (b) know what it is that proficient readers do (c) get clear in our minds what reading is for (d) understand how people become proficient readers: that is, how reading is learned.

My research has been devoted to describing what readers do when they read material new to themselves and deriving from that a theory and model of the reading process which in turn can be applied back to predicting, categorizing, and describing what people do when they read. I am fully aware that each day thousands of teachers are confronted with millions of learners who must be taught *now* and that the educational assembly line cannot be shut down until basic knowledge is available on which instruction must be based. But I am convinced that the quest for that basic knowledge must be pursued.

The alternatives are visible in the old and new solutions to the reading dilemma in current vogue.

At the risk of setting up straw men I'd like to characterize these approaches.

1.  There's the *butterfly collector* approach. Most relatively effective reading teachers and clinicians are butterfly collectors. They have large collections of bits and pieces, and gimmicks that work with some children some time. And every so often they add a new butterfly to the collection making a mental note as they do so that one day they must organize that collection. But they never do and they are unable to build on knowledge or put it in a form that can be transmitted to others.

2.  Some solutions to the reading problem are neat, sequential, behaviorally stated *stairways to nowhere.* Assumptions are made about what readers must do or know or existing materials are searched for bits and pieces and gimmicks and these are stated as behavioral objectives. Early results with such approaches are always impressive since 1) the readers already could do a lot of the things they're taught and 2) evaluation is through tests composed of items that are just like the instructional materials. But the stairways never get the learner to that glorious behavioral valhalla in the sky because to complete the stairway the entire reading process would have to be understood and that process would have to be amenable to sequencing into neat behavioral steps. And it is not so amenable.

3. Other programs are derived from diligent and rigorous *trial and error*. Try method A, book A, system A against method B, book B, system B, discard the poorer and use the better. Then proceed with C, D, etc. Or keep changing your procedures until you get better results. While the latter is practical advice for a teacher the teacher will certainly need some criteria for determining how to change. How long would we have waited for a cure to polio if we were depending on testing any proffered method against any other or making sporadic and intuitive modifications in existing treatments? How in fact can you achieve major innovations in solving any problems through trial and error, however rigorous?

4. A rather homey solution to the reading problem is one I call the *chicken soup approach*. Phonics is liberally served up to all like chicken soup on the assumption that it might help and it couldn't hurt. Unfortunately it can hurt some learners.

5. Finally there is the *systems approach*, recommended as a solution for everything (so why not reading). If we are confused let's organize our confusion systematically. This approach was pioneered by the Department of Defense (affectionately known as the DOD) and has demonstrated its utility in the solution of such problems as the Viet-Nam war. In the aero-space industry problems are solved through systems approaches at no more than three to ten times their original projected cost. There is however an adage which has found its way into even the Pentagon: Garbage in, garbage out. Reading problems will apparently not be solved simply by broadening the scope of the DOD and renaming it the Department of Education and Defense (DEAD).

Fortunately many children have the internal resources to surmount all obstacles we place in their way and to learn to read anyway. For this fact we should be grateful though it confuses research since children can apparently learn in spite of their instruction rather than because of it.

## The Reading Process

There *is* a process of reading with certain essential characteristics regardless of the nature of what is being read or even the language and orthography in which it is printed.

Reading, like listening, is a receptive psycholinguistic process. Language in its graphic form is the starting point. The reader brings to the text his knowledge of the language. As he reads there is an interaction between language and thought processes such that the reader moves from a language encoding of meaning to meaning itself.

Though the sensory modality involved is visual, the reading process is only incidentally visual since even what the reader thinks he sees at any point is only partly what he sees and partly what he expects to see. On the basis of the language structures he controls, the reader is constantly predicting what he will see. He samples from the available cues of the graphic display using language strategies he has developed to select only those cues which carry the most information. He arrives at hypothetical, tentative choices (guesses), as he reads, checking them against his predictions and the grammatical and semantic constraints of which he is aware. Then he needs only enough subsequent information to confirm or disconfirm his prediction.

Reading printed words then is a spiral of predict, sample, select, guess, and confirm activities. The reader has strategies for these activities. *The proficient reader uses the least amount of information to make the best possible first guesses.* He also has an effective set of strategies for checking the validity of his guesses. Simply, he asks himself whether (a) they produce language structures as he knows them and (b) they make sense. Finally he has a set of strategies for correcting when he realizes that he has been unsuccessful.

Reading is *not* an exact precise process of identifying each letter and then each word and then each sequence. Such a process would be not only inefficient since all information need not be processed, but it would be ineffective as well, because readers would be distracted by the excess of graphic and phonic information and would be less able to integrate it with the syntactic and semantic information they must process to deal with the text as language.

No single cue or system of cues in fact is useful in reading unless it is processed in its relationship to all other cues in a natural language setting. Language is *not* a salami which can be sliced as thin as one wishes with each slice retaining all the essential qualities of the whole. When language is broken into sounds, letters, words, or even phrases what results is something other than language. Language must be understood *in process* as it stands in relationship to its use. It must have structure and there must be meaning for it to be language.

A word needs to be said about context in reading. There are in reality two contexts: one is syntactic, the language structure. The other is semantic: the meaning or message. These are interdependent. In fact it is not possible to have meaning without grammar; but readers use both contexts. Let us remember that the reader is not ultimately concerned with naming, recognizing, or identifying words but that his concern is comprehension. Reading programs have been word centered for too long. The reader does not use context simply to identify words, rather he uses all cues in relationship to all others to reconstruct the message.

## The Reader as a User of Language

Because reading instruction was disconnected from its language base for so long the most important resource children bring to the task of learning to read has been underestimated or ignored. That resource is their highly developed language competence. Beginners in reading are already highly skilled in using language. They are able to communicate their needs, thoughts, and reactions to the world to others by encoding them in language and producing speech. They are able to understand messages from others by processing the surface phonological structures of speech, inducing the underlying language structures and reconstructing the meaning.

Any limitations on the child's ability to function as a listener in his own community are experiential and conceptual and not primarily linguistic.

All of this is of enormous use to the beginning reader. His task is to learn to induce the underlying language structures from *written* language. As long as he is confronted with graphic material which is real and meaningful (as opposed to fragmentary, artificial, and/or non-sensical) he can utilize his language competence. If, however, the meanings require more semantic input than he can provide then the task becomes nonsense for him. He must in fact be able to know whether the message he is reconstructing makes sense.

To give the child beginning to learn to read his native language full credit we must differentiate between language competence and language performance. Too many studies of child language have equated the two assuming that what children *do* in language is the same as what they are capable of doing. That can be put another way; we have confused behavior with the competence that underlies it and makes it possible. In studying vocabulary, for example, we have assumed that we could judge its breadth by listing the words used by a child in a given situation. Vocabulary, however, is highly contingent on a particular individual's interest *in,* background *for,* and willingness *to discuss,* a particular topic under particular circumstances. We have been quite willing to accept the conclusion that boys are less competent linguistically than girls at school and pre-school ages because in fact girls perform better on typical research tasks. It is at least as likely, however, that under different conditions that favor boys they would perform better than girls.

We must learn to relate linguistic performance to a theoretical understanding of language competence in order to interpret the former and gain insight into the latter.

Frequently we interpret particular language performance as indicative of lack of competence where in fact it indicates quite the opposite.

The pre-schooler who says "I taked it" is showing mastery of a basic pattern for indicating past tense, not sloppy speech. Similarly, the beginning reader who reads *home* for *house* in *The dog had a new warm house,* is showing a high degree of reading competence, not a lack of word recognition. A child who says *horse* for *house* in the same sentence is not showing a lack of phonics generalizations so much as he is having some difficulty in using them in language context. A key to his competence will be whether he corrects [himself] if his reading is not comprehensible.

The goal of reading instruction is not to change reading behavior but to expand the reader's competence in comprehending written language. Behavior, at best, is a shadow image of that competence.

Perception as it functions in language is very much misunderstood. Every language user learns two things as he learns the language: 1) What to pay attention to 2) What not to pay attention to.

Each language uses only a small number of the ways that sounds may differ as significant distinctive features. The user of language must learn to note those significant features. If he did not also learn to ignore nonsignificant differences he would be constantly distracted. The unitary symbols of any language are perceptual rather than real units. Features may vary widely within the units but language users will ignore the differences. But minor differences *across* the boundaries must be noted. This is true for written as well as oral language. A reader comes to treat *A* and *H* as different though they are very similar and  **A**, ɑ, *a*, *𝒶*, **a**, as the same though they are very different.

We tend to treat performance on "auditory discrimination" tests as indicative of linguistic incompetence when it really shows how well the child has learned to screen out differences not significant in his own speech (pin, pen for example).

Speakers of low-status dialects are repeatedly misjudged as linguistically deficient by teachers and researchers because their language behavior does not match an expectation model. But difference and deficiency are not the same. All children, normal in the broadest sense of the word, have a high degree of language competence to bring to learning to read.

## The Purposes of Reading

There is a romance that surrounds the purposes of reading that obscures its most vital functions and exaggerates others.

Written language develops in human societies when they become so complex that communication must be carried on over time and space and not merely on a face-to-face basis. Writers may seek to communicate messages to people whose ears they can not reach. They may preserve messages for the later use of others as well as themselves.

The basic reason for existence of competence in written language for an individual in a literate society is to cope with the everyday experiences in his culture which employ written language. He must read signs, follow written directions, fill out forms, read his mail.

Written language is the basic (though not exclusive) medium of literature. But one can function in literate society without reading literature. Minimal functioning with no reading competence at all is much harder.

Putting the purposes of reading in proper perspective it would appear that instruction should be built around what I choose to call situational reading, the kind that is so universal in a literate society that it is incidental to life itself. Situational reading, by virtue of its constant impingement on the life of children is self motivating. Many an American five-year-old can recognize five kinds of peanut butter and twice that many cereals by their labels. Four-year-olds quickly learn to know which door says "Men" and which one says "Ladies."

Once it is learned, reading can, of course, be used in pleasure seeking activities as in the reading of comic books or other literary works.

It may even be used in learning. But I must point out that in situational reading the meanings are either well defined by the situational contexts or within the conceptual grasp of the learner because they relate to recurrent experiences. Both the reading of literature and reading to learn move out and away from the learner and his immediate world.

Language grows in direct proportion to the experiences and conceptual growth of the learner. But there are limits on the leaps he can make. To gain new knowledge or concepts in reading requires considerable relevant semantic input. Bormuth's work indicates that unless a reader can score fairly well on a comprehension test over material *before* he reads it he will learn little from the reading.

Particularly in the elementary years, where skill in using written language lags well behind oral language competence, reading to learn has severe limitations. That suggests that reading should support or even follow learning in school rather than become its basic medium. A defensible cycle would be first to do, then to discuss, then to read, and then to write.

*Textbooks* are, by design, difficult reading tasks. They deal with many concepts unlikely to be known to the learners; the lower the level the more superficial they are likely to be. That doesn't necessarily reduce the comprehension problem since instead of treating a few topics in depth they treat many, bouncing along without developing any semantic context well enough to give the struggling reader much to go on. Many teachers have the mistaken notion that the textbook's function is to teach *for* them and that each child should be able to read and learn from a text written for use at his grade level.

If the focus is kept clearly on comprehension teachers can sense some of the inherent difficulties children encounter in reading school texts. Particularly teachers will need to realize that vocabulary, in and of itself, is seldom the key problem but that the profusion of new concepts, the special ways that language is used, the reading tasks that are particular to each area of study are all major sources of problems.

Vocabulary can develop, in any useful sense, only in close relationship to experiences and concepts. It is the ideas that need introduction before reading. New vocabulary is only of value as it is needed to cope with those ideas.

Even the grammar of language used in mathematics texts, science texts, and social studies books varies. Though all are rooted in the same grammatical system the special uses of language in each field require structures which may be unique to the field or uncommon in other areas. Conditional statements in mathematics involve rather unusual structures somewhat different than conditional statements in science.

Recipes are special language forms which require special strategies to adequately comprehend and use them.

Even the reading of literature requires strategies for dealing with language that have special characteristics. In the situational language which is basic, the reader can depend on it to be predictable. Writers of literature tend to avoid common predictable structures, forms, and vocabulary and to seek novel and hence unpredictable ones. Further, each writer establishes a style of language all his own. The language of Hemingway is not that of Steinbeck.

If learners are to develop the competence to comprehend a wide range of reading materials they must then develop general reading competence to handle other kinds of language. They will also have to see purposes for themselves to make the development of such competencies necessary.

Intrinsic motivation in reading is simply a matter of wanting to get the meaning. That is true whether the form is a sign on a wall, a set of directions for assembling a model airplane, a comic strip, a chapter in a text or a short story.

Motivation which is extrinsic, such as grades, rewards, punishments, may lead to acceptable behavior which does not in fact represent the underlying reading competencies sought. Too many readers can answer questions acceptably over reading materials they do not comprehend. If so they have learned not to read but to behave acceptably.

## Teaching and Learning Reading

It should be apparent that I am advocating organizing reading instruction totally around advancing comprehension. Each instructional activity should, in fact, be screened on the basis of whether it contributes to comprehension. Any skills or strategies should be developed within the quest for meaning in which the reader should be continuously engaged.

Relevancy is not a vague proposition in selecting reading materials. Since meaning is both input and output in reading, materials must be closely related to the background, interests, and experiences of particular learners.

To be comprehensible the language *at every stage of instruction* must be real language which is natural to the learners.

With the focus on meaning pupils will be able to move toward the integrated use of all cue systems in reading.

Throughout this discussion reference has been made to comprehension strategies. Strategies are general patterns readers develop for utilizing the varied kinds of cues available to them in reading print. The term "skills" has come to mean an isolated, or isolatable, bit of knowledge or technique which a reader uses. Such a term is inappropriate for describing what a proficient reader does (hence what a pupil must learn to do) since no such skill could be used invariantly in dealing with *actual* written language. In fact the reader's strategies must be flexible enough to allow for the changing relative importance of cues and cue systems in relationship to each other in given tasks.

In reading a recipe, for example, the difference between *2t baking powder and 2T baking powder,* is the difference between success and failure of the recipe's use. But a cook who understands the function of baking powder and who is experienced would recognize the improbability of a reading error almost immediately. Semantic input serves, then, as a safeguard on graphic or phonic miscuing.

It is only when the focus is on comprehension that the relative importance of cues becomes clear and useful strategies may emerge.

Readers need a set of initial strategies for coping with varied reading tasks. They need a set of related, but somewhat different strategies for testing the acceptability of their reading as they proceed. And they need still another set of strategies for correcting and recovering meaning when they recognize that they have miscued.

Some strategies will be general for all reading tasks. Others will be utilized for special kinds of reading.

## Uses and Misuses of Reading

With the focus on comprehension certain key misconceptions about the uses of reading become apparent.

The "By the third grade" myth is very popularly subscribed to. Many teachers believe that if a child can't read "by the third grade" he is doomed to school failure. This belief comes from a strong tendency to make written language the main medium of instruction much too early and much too completely. No child can read and comprehend material that assumes concepts and experiences that he hasn't had. When this is compounded by a limited control over the reading process (as compared to listening) he is very much at a disadvantage. Reading to learn must be used much more carefully at all levels of instruction. It will be most successful after initial learning has taken place.

Many secondary teachers use a "here, read and learn" approach. They assume that the text is the teacher, that the pupil is fully able to learn through reading and that their own role is to test, evaluate and grade. Such a view is untenable. The text can be a component in the learning process only if it is used in relationship to experience and oral language. Further, the teachers must work with their pupils on developing and extending their comprehension strategies to deal with the texts.

Particularly, teachers must ask themselves how much semantic input is necessary to make it possible for the reader to produce semantic output from a reading assignment. The answer to that inquiry will suggest how the pupils may be prepared for the task as well as whether the task is fundamentally appropriate or inappropriate.

Both the acquisition of the reading process and the effective use of that process depend on the reader and his teachers seeing comprehension as the continuous objective at all times.

# Helen Fisher Darrow

## *Reality, Morality and Individualized Reading*

Reading achievement test scores don't seem to tell us much about the effectiveness of individualized reading procedures—except to say that children who experience individualized reading do as well on achievement tests as those who experience more traditional grouping plans. A number of research summaries confirm this (1).

Perhaps the major value of such research to date has been the refreshing challenge made to presumed faith in sequenced reading materials. We know that children in classes of thirty or more need *not* be saddled by what Russell Stauffer calls "outmoded and ill-conceived directed reading activities presented and re-presented by a stereo-typed basic reader program"! In the all too typical schools, he asserts, the minimal parrotlike demands placed upon children actually deprive them of opportunity to think in relation to reading, including knowing why one reads what he reads and knowing what one expects to attain through his reading (2).

Someone not interested in individualizing reading, of course, could easily express the research results another way: Children don't do any better, so why bother! However this leads to a larger question, one which Sam Duker calls the *real* question: Does individualized reading lead to the accomplishment of the aims of reading instruction? He notes that despite the millions of words devoted to the subject of reading, it has not been easy to determine what these aims are (3). If reading aims do in fact continue to be obscure, then arguments comparing methodologies become absurd, as James MacDonald suggests: What moral difference, says he, does a three-month gain in reading achievement mean in the long run anyhow (4)? It seems time now to move toward a far more fertile area of exploration—*the usefulness of individualized reading for promoting humanistic or moralistic values,* formerly referred to as *democratic values.* Malcolm Douglass, in a review of research on reading improvement in the nongraded school, notes that optimal language learning, including reading, becomes closely tied to the social situation, especially the interpersonal relationship arising as individuals communicate with each other in a variety of language functions. Here reading functions not as a subject, but as a language process like speaking and listening. In this sense the reading program becomes as big as the curriculum of the school (5).

## Some Realities of Individualized Reading

Are the experiences which children have during individualized reading truly as big as the curriculum of the school? What seems needed is better awareness of what goes on during individualized reading periods. In some attempt to get at the question, we interviewed 87 children, ages 7-14, random sampled from seven classrooms where teachers professed to be engaged in individualized reading from "a little bit" to "very much" (6). The data gathered generated several discoveries, perhaps overlapping:

1. *Children recognized individualized reading to be a matter of an informal setting* rather than formal—informal in the sense of children freely moving around, engaging in a variety of interactions, with the teacher somewhat obscurely in the background, as opposed to a formal arrangement of children all seated and facing the teacher.

Most children interviewed stated that they usually talked with other children during reading time; they usually worked with other children or could do so if they wished. Mutual-work activities ranged from art production efforts to directing plays, conducting skills games or doing a workbook page with mutual aid. Talking activities ranged from "stuff about school" and deciding "where to sit while working together" to discussion of reading interests or making schedules for reading activities. Some individual comments follow:

> We talk about projects we want to do; or talk about whether the story we read was good or not. (13 year old.)
>
> We talk about sharing books in small groups or with a friend in class. (12 year old.)
>
> We talk about planning plays or debates or reports on authors, characters, and things like that. (11 year old.)
>
> Jimmy and I decided about what we were going to do and who was going to draw what. We're making stuff to put on the bulletin board. (9 year old.)

These same children indicated they did not engage in such talk the previous year (when they had three-group reading). They gave such reasons as:

> There was nothing to do that needed talking over.
>
> Teacher told us what to do as we left the reading circle.
>
> Teacher didn't feel we knew enough to talk things over.
>
> All we done was read and my teacher wouldn't even let us tell children words.

2. *Children recognized individualized reading more clearly as a matter of open regulation and open structure with minimal controlling imposition by the teacher* than as a situation calling for closed regulation, closed structure with maximum controlling impositions by the teacher (7).

The majority of children stated that they usually had choices to make during the reading period; they described their choices specifically, ranging from what to read, when to read, where to read, and what to do about reading to choices of activities related to art, language and other curricular tasks. Choices included whether to work alone or with others, whether to "do what someone else is doing" or not; there was even the choice to "fiddle around" that day "if you wanted to." Activity choices ranged from 31 in a classroom where the teacher had indicated "very much" individualized reading was going to 7 in a classroom where the teacher indicated just "a little bit." Children listed filmstrips, tapes, stories to read, stories to write, making movies, sculpturing, conferencing, developing dioramas, creating mosaics, conducting debates, planning interest centers, sharing books, going to the school library, etc. One child said: "We have such a large variety of things to do; we can do them almost any time we want to; we can do any project we want to; we can even read a scientific book if we want to." Contrast this remark with one from a more restricted classroom: "The teacher lets you pick a book when she is busy."

3. *Children recognized reading to be a matter of variability and personal satisfaction* rather than a matter of uniformity and "the thing to do." When queried about what they had done in "yesterday's reading period," children's answers usually varied from individual to individual except in those classrooms where there was only "a little bit" of individualized reading. In the latter instances, children answered identically: These children when asked what they planned to do "tomorrow" did not know, said the teacher had not told them yet or guessed it would be the same. "You see," explained one of the guessers, "that's what we always do day after day." In the classrooms where individualized reading occurred "very much" children described explicitly what their plans were, including these by some 10 year old children:

I read *Dwight Eisenhower* and *Huckleberry Finn*, then worked on a play today. Tomorrow I'm going to keep reading and make a report.

I read *Mouse* and *Motorcycle* and made something today. Tomorrow I'm going to make a book jacket for it and then go to the library and select a new book—fiction.

I worked with a friend today on a special report on Canada. Tomorrow I plan to share my book with someone.

We tried to make a tape discussion about a poem today, but it didn't work out too good. Tomorrow I'll do a page in my workbook and read in my library book.

I was checked out today. I did one phonics sheet, one Reading for Meaning, checked some work from my workbook and looked for a book for a puppet play. Tomorrow I'll do some work in my workbook and try to find a book for puppet play.

I read *Lord of the Flies*, illustrated my book, and made of book of homonyms. Tomorrow I'll continue the book and write another chapter to the book I'm writing.

While almost all the children interviewed registered high satisfaction with their reading periods, those from restricted classrooms gave their reasons in terms of liking to read and enjoying the work which the teacher gave. These children, when asked what they thought reading was, tended to describe it as "something we learn."

Children from more highly individualized-reading classrooms expressed satisfaction with their reading period in terms of appreciation for the variability offered; the majority of these conceived reading as "learning, getting information, getting pleasure or being able to live someone else's life."

## Some Moralities of Schooling

If what these children said is a bit of reality, what can be said about morality; first, the morality of schooling, and second, the morality of individualized reading as an aspect of schooling?

Several years ago at the University of Wisconsin, a Conference on Moral Dilemmas of Schooling was held where some direct questions were posed: Are our schools a desirable place for the education of human beings? Do schools embody in practice the revered humanistic values of our culture? Are the schools, in short, essentially moral enterprises? Conferees pointed out that if we are to function morally in schools, we should be concerned with moral terms like *justice, service* and *vitality.* These should be viewed not by intentions so much as by consequences of results (8).

Harold Taylor earlier charged that in reality the family for better or worse had already transferred responsibility to the school for sustaining morality; but the schools have avoided the responsibility by simply picking up existing social values however immoral they may be: approval, material reward, popularity, etc. Our schools, he said, have failed to treat children as ends in themselves, thus leaving a great gap in their development (9).

Sidney Hook calls the moral dilemma an inevitable phenomenon because human beings live with multiple not single ends. With the number of ends available we are inevitably confronted with the haunting problems of which end, and which means for which ends. Both kinds of decisions require laborious work not only in checking ends in light of other ends which seem to have validity, but checking alternatives in terms of consequences of means used (10).

Philip Phenix in his own examination of such ends suggests a few to be most prized and valued in the decades ahead. Among them are: *Intelligence*—valuing man as a thinker with capacity to decide and to judge; *creativity*—valuing man as a producer experiencing work and play as a single joyous activity while being aware of beauty and good taste; and *conscience*—valuing man as a responsible being who respects others as individuals, who ignores unreal lines of social class, academic class and so on, but recognizes man's responsibility to man (11).

*Individualized Reading as a Moral Affair.*    To apply these moral terms and values to the field of reading, we might accept them as reading goals desirable for human integrity (12). We would then need to look at individualized reading as a means. Does it actually result in achieving the ends which we prize and value?

First, we might conjecture some conditions which should appear in the classroom, and then attempt to relate those desirable conditions to actual consequences. At any rate let us try:

*Conditions A:* The teacher should be in a position to listen to the child's view of the world and make adjustments to individual demands and interests without having to sacrifice the individual to the group or vice versa. Such conditions would appear to be *just* and the value of *conscience* would seem to be dominant.

*Consequences:* The informal setting provided by individualized reading as seen by children *for real* permitted a high degree of interaction and two-way communication channels between children and children and teachers in fluid arrangements defying rigid class groupings. To the degree that this occurs, it appears likely that *individualized reading becomes an effective means for establishing justice in school life and for enhancing the* value of conscience where man feels a responsibility for his fellow man and acts upon that feeling.

*Conditions B:* The teacher should be in a position to place the child, not the material nor the method, in a dominant position and accordingly enable him to function as a consumer, not a victim of education. Such conditions would appear to *serve* the child during the school hours and to demonstrate the value of *intelligence.*

*Consequences:* The wide variety of materials for learning and the degree of choice-making provided by individualized reading, as seen by children *for real,* permitted the child to function as a judge weighing alternatives to action and as a decision-maker. To the degree that this prevails it appears likely that *individualized reading becomes an effective means for establishing service to children in school life and encouraging the value of intelligence to be demonstrated in action.*

*Conditions C:* The child should experience renewed energy for learning and living for its own sake, thus enabling the child to function as a maker. Such conditions would appear to render the reading period as a *vital* part of the school day and to promote *creativity* as an operational value.

*Consequences:* The diminution of teacher control coupled with the expansion of individual control over what occurs during the reading period as seen by children *for real* permitted each child to function with a sense of individuality and destiny, freely integrating subjects into enjoyable work-play experiences. To the degree that this prevails it appears likely that *individualized reading becomes a basic means for nurturing vitality in the school life of children and nourishing the value of creativity* where children produce their own creations with an eye for beauty.

In summation, it seemed as though the children we interviewed called out to us: "Classrooms where individualized reading occurs (and to the degree that it occurs), are in reality learning centers where morality ranks high." They also seemed to say: "When you adults fulfill your moral obligations to provide for us during school hours *a life-encouraging environment,* you will help us identify with ourselves and with humanity in general." Reading is indeed at least as big as the school curriculum.

## References

1. Patrick Groff examines 33 studies in "Comparisons of Individualized and Ability Grouping Approaches to Teaching Reading: A Supplement," *Elementary English* 41, 3 (March 1964): 238–241. Other reports include: Rodney Johnson, "Individualized and Basal Primary Reading Programs" in *Elementary English* 42,

8 (December 1965): 902–904; Dorothy Talbert and C. B. Merritt, "The Relative Effectiveness of Two Approaches to Teaching of Reading in Grade V" in *The Reading Teacher* 19, 3 (December 1965): 183–186. The latter gives further references to other researches.

2. Russell Stauffer in "Time for Amendment," *The Reading Teacher* 20, 8 (May 1967): 685.

3. Sam Duker, "Needed Research on Individualized Reading," In *Elementary English* 43, 3 (March 1966): 220.

4. James MacDonald reflects deeply upon the state of present research in reading in "Research in Review: Thoughts about Research in Schools," *Educational Leadership* 23, 6 (March 1965): 443.

5. Malcolm Douglass, "Does Nongrading Improve Reading Behavior?" in *31st Claremont Reading Conference Yearbook* (Claremont Graduate School, 1967): 178–190.

6. Some original research conducted with teachers participating in a workshop on "Innovations in Individualized Instruction," Thousand Oaks, 1967. Information was gathered by teacher aide-interviewers using picture sketches, open-ended questions and item-selection techniques.

7. Marie Hughes' study of teacher behavior dealt with the tendency of teachers to control children intellectually through such means as teacher functions of regulation and structure. Teacher control of who did what was considered closed regulation; control of what was going on was called closed structure. For further details see: *The Assessment of the Quality of Teachings: A Research Report* (U.S. Office of Education Cooperative Research Project No. 353, 1959), 60 ff.

8. A summary of Dwayne Huebner's paper is found in Millard Clements and James MacDonald, "Moral Dilemmas of Schooling," *Educational Leadership* 23, 1 (October 1965): 29–30.

9. Harold Taylor, "What the Family Isn't Teaching," *Saturday Review* (May 18, 1963): 19.

10. Sidney Hook, "Does Philosophy Have a Future?" in *Saturday Review* (November 11, 1967): 21–23. Another helpful discussion on the problem of means and ends is Ernest Bayles', "John Dewey on Morals and Values," in *Teachers College Record* 68, 8 (May 1967): 654–659.

11. Philip Phenix, "Values in the Emerging American Civilization," *Teachers College Record* 61, 7 (April 1960): 358–365. Also see: Clark Moustakas, "Essential Conditions in the Development of the Self," in *Children and Today's World* (Washington: ACEI, Bulletin 19A, 1967): 39–49. The article also includes some basic references for this point of view.

12. The entire issue of *Educational Leadership* 24, 5 (February 1967) is devoted to discussions of reading in relation to humanized education under the theme of "Reading: Claims and Proof."

R. Van Allen

# The Language-Experience Approach to Reading

A sense of urgency surrounds the question of improving reading in-struction at all levels of the school program. For some educators this is a new concern, but for most of us it is not. It is one which has been the all-consuming interest and focus of activities of some of our most prominent educators and most dedicated professional societies. But today's heightened public interest presents new opportunities for answering this question with new positive action. The challenge to improving reading instruction opens doors for rethinking our present approaches and requires that in reading instruction, as in all other areas of human endeavor, more effective pro-grams must be developed. School programs are dealing with the *human* resources of our society—resources which are so precious and essential to survival that we cannot risk the possibilities of *intellectual servitude* any more than we can risk the possibilities of *physical servitude* as a result of not doing our best. This means that reading instruction must result in more than pronunciation of words, the reciting of phonetic or grammar rules, the verbatim parroting or rote memory of passages, and the completion of pencil and paper activities which are selected and administered by the teacher. Reading instruction must result in more than blind following of the printed page. Reading from its very beginning must be an integral part of a meaningful, useful language experience. At all times it must remain in its natural relationship to the other communication skills of listening, speak-ing, and writing.

A danger to society which is far greater than the fact that all children read the same book is the danger of uniform responses to ideas. Uniform, blind thinking is the dream of leaders in authoritarian societies. The con-trasting dream of a democratic society is that reading instruction will serve to develop thinking individuals—

—who are critical of sources, definitions, and assumptions

—who are prepared to select from the many sources available those which serve the situation best

—who choose a wide variety of reading materials for leisure time activity

—who view reading as a means of communicating ideas, ideals, aspirations, and flights of fancy

—who contribute to the storehouse of reading materials by recording their own thinking on topics of deep concern and personal pleasure

For many years some of us have felt that a reading instructional program with broad goals which are related directly to effective living in a democratic society could be achieved. We have worked diligently to identify some of the obstacles and to enlist the help of classroom teachers in trying out new approaches. One of the results of this effort is the beginning description of an approach to reading instruction which has come to be identified in the San Diego County Reading Study Project as the *language-experience approach.* The name has evolved as a result of the main focus of effort on the part of the researchers in the project—the effort to identify the language experiences (listening, speaking, reading, and writing) which are essential tools of communication for effective participation in a democratic society. Briefly stated, the language-experience approach is one which brings reading and other communication skills together in the instructional program. In this approach there is no way, or any need, to distinguish between the reading program and the development of listening, speaking, and writing skills. This "togetherness" of the development of skills makes possible the continuing use of each child's own experience background and thinking as he grows toward reading maturity. More than other approaches which have been described at the classroom operational level, the language-experience approach uses the thinking of individual children as the basis for skill development. As each child matures, he conceptualizes reading in a rationale which might go something like this:

What I can think about, I can talk about
What I can say, I can write
What I can write, I can read
I can read what I can write and what other people can write for me to read.

From the earliest days of school each child is encouraged to share his ideas with others through the use of words and pictures. With repeated opportunities for creating stories and for writing stories with teacher help, children begin to develop writing vocabularies and are able in an amazingly short period of time, to write their own stories independently. Soon each child's ability to express his ideas in writing is limited only by his ability to create ideas.

## Comparison of Common Goals in Reading

Whether a teacher is using the language-experience approach or any other well defined approach, there are many common goals as far as the development of a balanced reading program is concerned. To achieve these common goals, each approach has a plan for developing a basic sight vocabulary and competence in using a variety of word recognition skills, of providing a wide variety of reading materials, of integrating the various communication skills, and of developing a genuine desire to read.

*Developing Basic Sight Vocabulary.*    A common goal of all plans or approaches is to help each child develop a basic sight vocabulary. In most plans the selection of the vocabulary to be developed is on a basis of high frequency in our language. Material is developed which repeats each word a sufficient number of times for most children to recognize it at sight.

In the language-experience approach the idea of the highly controlled vocabulary for beginning readers is rejected as being invalid. The development of a basic sight vocabulary is deemed to be an individual matter and is governed to a great extent by the *oral vocabulary* of the learner. From oral expression the next step is writing, or recording the oral language. This is done by the teacher or the child according to maturity and ability. Recall, or reconstruction of the written language (reading), is a third step in the sequence of developing basic sight vocabulary.

Early recognition of words of high frequency in our language is a natural result of repetition which cannot be avoided in a productive environment. Each child gradually gains a sight vocabulary of common words in our language, but at the same time he gains a personally tailored sight vocabulary which is functional for him and which reaches far beyond the words which are selected for other reading programs. Ceilings are lifted for all children.

*Phonics Instruction.*    Among the word recognition skills which are developed in all successful reading approaches but treated differently in the language-experience approach is phonetic analysis. Phonics instruction is a necessary and natural part of the language-experience approach, but it is developed from a "say it" to "see it" sequence rather from the "see it" to "say it" sequence of other approaches.

We have known for a long time that there is a closer relationship to phonics and writing than to phonics and reading. The application is necessary and immediate. The desire to create stories and do independent writing provides a powerful motivation to acquire skills of selecting the correct symbols to represent the sounds of oral language. The phonics learnings take place in their natural setting and have immediate application. They are applied to the real language experiences of each child, including skills in listening, speaking, and word recognition and spelling.

*Materials for Reading.* The problem of providing appropriate reading material for each child in a given classroom has been and is a source of real concern for a teacher or administrator who knows anything of learning processes. Within a given classroom there may be a son of an English professor and one of a migrant farm worker. Both have good ideas. Both have information. Both have self-motivation to share their ideas and information with others. But the information shared will probably be quite different and the quality of oral language might be poles apart. Between these two children of extreme contrasts in experience and language development there is a wide range of differences among the other children at any grade level.

What materials will the teacher use to help each child conceptualize reading as a record of oral language? What material can be selected which will be of interest to the wide range of individuals? How can a teacher have enough materials which are not too difficult for some and too easy for others?

As I read the professional books on reading instruction these points are labelled as essential for success in learning to read—materials which are related to oral expression, interesting and easy!

Maybe you have tried using materials which have been developed with a very limited vocabulary. They are easy for some, but they are ridiculous in terms of their relationship to oral expression and interests of children. This is especially true at the beginning levels where the concocted materials are devoid of any real meaning or interest. There is no story, no message from an author, absolutely no similarity to the oral language of the children who are learning to recognize the words.

The language-experience approach features children as authors with unique language abilities, with wide interests, and with individual vocabulary control built in. In the process of dictating and writing their own ideas, children learn to recognize enough words that they can read what other people have written with little or no systematic instruction.

Some people might say that oral language of children is so far advanced by the time they start to learn to recognize the symbolic forms of words that anything they would dictate or write would be too difficult. But analysis of reading material shows little evidence of any attention to what makes a sentence easy or difficult for a child to read. It is quite possible that the choppy, unnatural sentences of present-day pre-primers and primers are more difficult to read than more natural sentences might be. The experience of teachers who emphasize authorship in their classrooms bears this out.

To the extent that children perceive themselves as authors—producers of reading materials—they are interested in interacting with the products of other authors. First, they are interested in knowing what other authors in their class have produced and from there their interests expand to encompass the whole world of authorship. Their interest and their basis of selection of books is not that they can learn *how* to read if they read a given book, but that the author has something to say. Reading of whole books becomes a natural desire and a natural language experience of children. They assume responsibility for selecting their own material; in fact, self-selection of materials is mandatory in the language-experience approach. Many books must be in the environment—books that have been produced by the children and books purchased and brought into the classroom, books from the public libraries and books from home. Books must be selected with a wide range of difficulty, a wide range of interest and information, and a wide variety of literary forms. The success of the language-experience approach depends on the development of a balanced program of production of reading materials and the use of increasingly varied reading materials.

*Motivation for Reading.*    Motivation for reading is stimulated through the child's realization that his oral language expression, based upon his own experiences and thoughts, can be written and read along with reading the thoughts and ideas of others. This is quite different from approaches where children are motivated to read by being helped to see the relationship of their own experiences to the story selection to be read.

*Integration of Communication Skills.*    Teachers who use the language-experience approach do not attempt to distinguish between reading development and other communication skills—listening, speaking, and writing. In fact, a time for writing might be looked upon as a most profitable experience for developing word-recognition skills for reading. The *how to read* part of the program is integrated with other aspects of skill development—spelling, writing, listening to stories, and telling stories.

*Classroom Organization.*    Classroom organization must be adapted to serve an approach which does not require regular reading periods and follow-up activities each day for every child. Organization, materials, and facilities must be provided for a strong emphasis on production of materials. To accompany this emphasis must be adequate materials for children to select a variety of reading materials for information, recreation, and skill development. The program is incomplete until there is provision for sharing, discussing, and interacting of ideas, thoughts, and concerns of children in the class with the ideas, thoughts, and concerns of good adult authors.

*Evaluation of Pupil Progress.* A program based on the gradual maturing of language experiences of children must be evaluated on a broader base than that afforded by standardized reading tests. Ability to express personal ideas in oral and written form is a continuing expectancy. Comprehension and interpretation are judged as reading skills. Growth in depth of thinking, clarity of expression, sentence sense, and correct spelling are revealed clearly as children write on their own. The teacher has multiple clues of progress in skill development and creative thinking which are not present in many reading programs.

## Concepts Which the Teacher Holds

The language-experience approach is dependent on the evolvement of a conceptual framework more than on certain methods or materials. Teachers and supervisors working in the program establish a pattern of thinking which guides them in the selection of activities, experiences, materials, and evaluation. This conceptual framework helps teachers establish goals for teaching which interrelate reading instruction with instruction in other communication skills. Some of the concepts which a teacher must hold in order to work within the spirit of the language-experience approach were identified by teachers participating in the San Diego County Reading Study Project. Briefly stated, they are:

1. As a basis of reading, the child should gain the feeling that his own ideas are worthy of expression and his own language is a vehicle for communication.
2. The basis of children's oral and written expression is their sensitivity to their environment both within the classroom and in the world at large.
3. Freedom in self-expression, oral and written, leads to self-confidence in all language usage which includes reading skills.
4. Children's oral expression may be stimulated and strengthened through paintings, drawings, and other graphic art or sound symbols.
5. The child's own thoughts may be used as the main basis for development of instructional reading materials.
6. There is a natural flow of language development in children. This flow proceeds in the following steps:
   a. The child's oral expression is stimulated and strengthened through art expression.
   b. Children's written expression flows easily from their oral expression.

      c.  Motivation for reading follows easily from the child's see-
          ing his own language in written form.

      d.  After reading his own language in written form, the child
          moves "naturally" into reading the written language of
          other children and adults.

7.  Numerous activities, experiences, and devices are used to provide
for interaction of children such as sharing experiences, discussion
experiences, listening to stories, telling stories, dictating, developing word recognition skills, making and reading books, developing basic sight vocabulary, expanding individual vocabularies,
writing independently, choosing reading as a leisure-time activity, using reading as a study skill, and reading as a process of
thinking and interacting with an author.

8.  Utilization of the child's own language as a basis of reading
instruction results in a high degree of independence in writing
and reading.

One might continue indefinitely to describe an approach to reading
which is built upon a base as broad as the language experiences of the
children we teach. The future development of the approach will not depend
on what is said here, but rather on the changing role of reading in enriching
the lives of children, in facilitating learning, in promoting good citizenship
and in strengthening each child's concept of himself as a contributor of ideas
to an emerging and growing society.

Wilhelmine Nielsen

# Twenty Language Experiences Which Form the Framework of the Experience Approach to Language Arts

Over the past several years, teachers and administrators in San Diego County have worked to develop procedures for facilitating what has been called an Experience Approach to the Language Arts.* The first detailed descriptions of this approach resulted in the development of a list of twenty specific elements which could be said to characterize it in classroom practice. Gradually, this list was refined and reorganized under three major categories: 1) converting experiences to words, 2) studying the words themselves, and 3) recognizing words and relating them to experiences. One end product of this attempt to define and clarify what is meant by an Experience Approach to the Language Arts was the production of a filmstrip in which each of the elements was pictured and explained. In the material which follows, an attempt has been made to describe in words, employing the framework used in that filmstrip, these twenty characteristic elements which can be found in classrooms where teachers have developed successful programs utilizing this approach to language learning.

## Converting Experiences to Words

*1. Sharing Experiences.* Through the experiences children have during their pre-school years they acquire a vocabulary meaningful to them. When expressing an idea in conversation, they select the words which have meaning to them. It makes sense to start this writing-reading process with the words children understand.

*Under the leadership of R. Van Allen, formerly Director of Curriculum Coordination, San Diego County Schools, and presently Professor of Education, University of Arizona.

In general there are three ways in which we share experiences with each other: through conversation, pictures, and writing. The young child shares his ideas through conversation.

A kindergarten child may need some concrete object to talk about. This is why we encourage children to bring animals and toys to school. Sharing experiences orally assists both child and teacher. The child refines his ability to express ideas and increases his vocabulary, and the teacher becomes acquainted with the child's "understanding vocabulary."

After expressing ideas through conversation, the child progresses to communicating through pictures. The child has something to say and he discovers he can say it by pictures.

After expressing ideas through conversation and pictures a child is ready for written expression. In the initial stage this takes the form of dictation. A child may talk about an experience, paint a picture which describes it, and then dictate his story to the teacher who writes down what he says as he observes her.

*2. Discussion Experiences.*    We progress from the one way communication of sharing to the two way interaction of discussing experiences. A child may read his story, add information and answer questions from the group. In the process the group becomes actively involved rather than merely assuming a passive role.

*3. Listening to Stories.*    As a child learns to contribute to a discussion, he needs the skill of listening and relating what he hears to his past experiences.

As the teacher reads an interesting story in a dramatic way, the children become active listeners.

At the listening center children can enter another world where head sets reduce outside distractions. Commercially prepared records and tapes are available or the teacher may prefer to prepare tapes which meet specific needs.

*4. Telling Stories.*    This activity involves more than just sharing a personal experience. Using a doll or toy as a prop, children may create a spontaneous story. This helps them organize their thoughts into a sequence and will lead to the time when they will be writing a story with a plot.

*5. Dictating.*    As was said earlier, dictating is the beginning of the reading-writing process. The child tells the teacher what he has said in the picture. We all know that some five year olds can chatter on indefinitely, so the teacher helps him summarize in his own words; that is, to choose from all that might be said, the most important part for the teacher to write.

It is important that the child observe as the teacher prepares the finished copy. Through observation the child discovers many things: he sees how letters are formed, he begins to see that every time he says a certain word the teacher uses the same symbols, he observes spacing between words, he discovers that the things he said today have been recorded and will be there in the future for others to read and enjoy.

A very exciting way to take dictation is with a typewriter. The child discovers that the words he says appear on the paper in the same form as in a printed book.

*6. Summarizing.*    The skill of summarizing, begun during the dictation process, is pursued more seriously with older students. In research projects students gather a great deal of information. Then it is necessary to summarize, to decide on the most important points to include in the written report.

*7. Making and Reading Books.*    When children feel that their stories have value and are worth recording, they enjoy writing. Discouragement comes when they feel they are just writing for the sake of writing. Therefore, it is important for them to feel that what they have written will have future use.

To bridge the span between dictation and independent writing, model sentences are utilized. Illustrations also assist in the writing-reading process. A child may create a story to go with a picture or may illustrate a story someone else has written.

To be given the status of an author provides tremendous motivation. Older students may contribute a book a month to the classroom library. In many cases students prefer to read each other's books rather than published materials.

Reading is done in different situations with a variety of materials. Since it is impossible to write without reading, considerable reading takes place as a child writes a book. Printed books are vital to a complete, balanced program. Students read individually with the teacher and to each other in groups. In a well rounded reading program there must be adequate provision for pleasure reading.

*8. Writing Independently.*    When children feel good about themselves and feel that their ideas are worth recording, they move quickly toward becoming independent writers.

Students may prepare their stories in chart form. To enable students to become more independent, some schools have prepared a dictionary consisting of the words children use most often.

Of course, there are times when they need the teacher's assistance in spelling words they just can't find anywhere else; but they have the feeling of independence. The teacher becomes a resource, not a person who tells her what to do and say.

## Studying Words Themselves

*9. Developing Word Recognition Skills.* Word recognition skills are learned initially through the dictation process. A child recognizes that every time he says a word that starts with a certain sound, the teacher uses the same symbol. This is a natural and logical way to introduce the sound-symbol relationship. After the child has said the word and formed the sounds that constitute that word, the teacher and later he, chooses the symbol that best represents that sound.

The numerous word recognition skills may be presented to children in a variety of ways through teacher made and student made materials. Since the most effective learning takes place when the children are actively involved, most materials should be student made. Commercially prepared games are perhaps most helpful as testing and reinforcing devices.

*10. Developing Basic Sight Vocabulary.* To assist students in becoming independent writers and readers, the words of high frequence should become an automatic part of their reading and spelling vocabulary. Lists of high frequency words are used in charts, games, dictionaries, and repeated in writing so that students become well acquainted with them.

*11. Expanding Vocabulary.* Our language has some wonderful, expressive words which children should feel free to use. They should never be reluctant to use a word simply because they aren't sure how to spell it; that can be learned later. After all, if the thing we have to say is important, then the writer has the privilege and responsibility of choosing the words which best express his ideas. Students may prepare lists of words from social studies, science, holidays and seasons.

There is no finer way to expand children's vocabularies than through reading to them. Carefully chosen materials expose children to a variety of words and ideas.

*12. Studying Words.* Games are a pleasant way of studying words. Students may check each other to see how much they know about words. Under the guidance of the teacher, and with the assistance of the dictionary, older students can study the structure of words in more detail.

## Recognizing Words and Relating Them to Experiences

*13. Improving Style and Form.* Style and form improve as children become aware of correctness. The teacher is responsible for raising this level of awareness through a variety of means. Teacher and students worked together preparing a chart listing items which they will be conscious of as they write or re-write their stories.

Seminars are a beneficial means of getting children actively involved in analyzing style and form. Children evaluate a classmate's writing, making suggestions for improvement and pointing out correct usage and ways of making the story more interesting. When the evaluation comes from the students, there is more active participation than if the teacher does it herself.

In any seminar it is crucial for students to approach the evaluation of their work with the attitude of helping. A child's self confidence can be destroyed if the proper climate is not maintained. A writer should feel free to use any word to express a desirable idea, knowing that during the seminar someone will help him reach the point of correctness. It is obvious that as students help each other, they become more aware of correctness themselves.

Older students contribute on a more mature level during a seminar. They may meet in small groups or as a class. With older students a seminar is devoted to a specific topic. The teacher will review student writings, determine a common error, and call a seminar to discuss that topic. During the discussion, rules for correct usage are debated, determined, and listed on the chalkboard. If a difference of opinion occurs, the language text is consulted. Following the seminar, a chapter on the subject discussed is added to the student's writing handbook. The handbook then becomes a reference for use as students write and edit their work.

Another very effective means of raising levels of awareness is by using student editors. The teacher may assign partners or children may choose their own editor.

Students cannot be expected to improve style unless they are exposed to, and made aware of, different styles. The most effective means of accomplishing this is by reading to students. The teacher has the responsibility of selecting books that represent a variety of styles: an adventure story by Mark Twain, a biography by Carl Sandberg, a poem by Robert Louis Stevenson. The teacher must do more than just read—she must read with excitement and drama, drawing attention to the style of each author.

*14. Using a Variety of Resources.* It is important for students to understand and appreciate the fact that information is found in many places.

Objects on the science table make it possible for students to get information by first hand observation. It is up to them to decide what to say or write about these objects. Other sources of information include: listening center, encyclopedia and other reference books, film and film strips. Students should be encouraged to get information from many sources and then compare and draw their own conclusions.

*15. Reading a Variety of Symbols.* Perhaps we should start by asking, what is reading? When does a child begin to read? If reading is interpreting, or gaining meaning from something, then a baby starts reading shortly after he opens his eyes for the first time. He reads the expression on his mother's face, he reads the difference between night and day. Later he reads pictures. In reality, reading involves the total environment—calendar, clock, thermometer, map, etc.

*16. Reading Whole Books.*    Reacting with an author does not just take place under the supervision of the teacher. A child discovers that a book is a wonderful friend—always available to entertain and inform—one with whom you can agree or disagree.

*17. Improving Comprehension.*    One way of checking students' comprehension is through the individual reading conference. As the teacher works with each child individually, she checks his comprehension of the content and his knowledge and application of the skills necessary for success in reading.

*18. Outlining.*    Students use various methods to briefly restate ideas in the order in which they were written or spoken.

*19. Integrating and Assimilating Ideas.*    Students use reading and listening for specific purposes of a personal nature.

*20. Reading Critically.*    What is a mature reader? One who can repeat back what the author said? Or is he one who can evaluate, or be critical of what is read?

Maturity in reading calls for the ability to react in an extended way to what has been read. First, of course, one must comprehend or understand what the author said. Then he should see the author as another person with whom he can discuss the topic.

During the individual reading conference, the teacher is helping the student reach the point of critical reading by asking questions such as, "Why did the author say that?" "What experiences may he have had before writing that?" "Do you agree with him?"

If, through the writing portion of the language program the child has gained the feeling that he is an author who has ideas worth recording, then he will progress naturally to the point of reacting to what other authors have said.

# On
# the
# Teaching
# of
# Literature

**Frank G. Jennings**

# Time Machines, Space Ships and Frog Ponds

If you are book people, and I am perhaps rashly assuming that all of you are, your earliest memories of the printed leaves will have familial associations. This surely is so with me.

I remember it was shortly after the First World War, or before the coming of Prohibition, or perhaps it preceded the Vote for Women—all three disruptions of our way of life serve as historical markers—; it was my fifth year.

I remember a plethora of aunts hovering about me while I sat at one of those remarkable round oak tables, the kind that could be pulled out into a gridiron shape for Thanksgiving or Christmas dinners, or wakes. There was a Tiffany lamp shade over its center with two glowing Wellsbach mantels over the jets through which the gas hissed softly while tiny blue flames darted in and out of the incandescence. The lamp was fringed with a glass-bead frill that caught an occasional aunt's hairpin as she leaned across to show me the exact place of the word she was so very carefully pronouncing. I was being inducted into the "wonderful world of books," and she was a librarian and therefore an expert on child growth and development. I liked books better than I wanted her to know. I desperately wanted her to go far away, for another aunt, who sang sweet and terrifying songs of Irish death, had given me a tin carrousel, and I wanted to wind it up and run it through all the mysterious colors of the lamp. In the determined anguish known only to puppies and little boys, I did what the library aunt wanted. I read the words, biting my lower lip and pointing to them as I did so. Then they all went away, and I was left at last alone under the lamp, with my private magic.

I played earnestly for a long time, watching the tin horses and hippo-griffs move up and down and around to the sound of the music-box calliope,

283

when suddenly one of my own movements flipped the offending book to another page, and there across a center spread was a colored picture of the grandest carrousel with knights in armor and ladies in distress and dragons and pennants floating on some permanent breeze. I sat, caught in the wonder between the tin reality and the marvelous shadow and suddenly made an imaginative leap to the merry-go-round in Prospect Park by the shores of the swan-boat lake. Why was *that* a merry-go-round; why was the toy a carrousel; what was the picture of? Into my perplexity and out of the dark quiet where the adults talked, the aunt who sang sweet songs of Irish death came to my side and poked her bent, nail-less forefinger at the picture and said, "That's a grand old battle there—that's what they used to call a carrousel—a fine word for a great fight—and later the poor dear word was worn down to mean just fun and drinking—and then it was used to name a merry-go-round—I think the French did that; bad cess to them!" And she disappeared into the pantry, where the bottles were kept, futilely out of her reach, while I was left wondering of words and swords.

Since that evening so many years ago, I have had many occasions to wonder about words and swords. I have learned that words are slippery things and that swords stay put, marking graves and footnotes. I have learned that swords are generally irrelevant to the affairs of this world and that words can wound more deeply and shine more brightly than the finest damascene blade. I learned too that my Irish aunt was an incompetent etymologist, but she was a great story-teller.

There was this tale of a frog who left his pond somewhere in County Connemara, planning to go to Spiddal on Galway Bay, when a great voice out of the clouds demanded to know his destination. The little creature said out of the corner of his ample mouth, "I'm off to Spiddal on Galway Bay."

"No, you don't mean that at all, at all, 'tis to Spiddal on Galway Bay, ye're goin',—God Willin'!" said the voice, sounding like a mixture of Mother and Dad.

The little frog cocked his head and scanned the sky and said, "I am off to Spiddal on Galway Bay." With that there was a trembling in the air and little puffs of dust came down the road, tangled the feet of the frog, and before you knew it, he was back in the frog pond.

This little charade was repeated on successive Sundays, with the voice from the clouds becoming ever more intemperate and the return to the pond ever more peremptory, until, on Whitsunday, when the frog was asked his destination, he replied, "I am off to Spiddal on Galway Bay—or back to the frog-pond."

The tale must be told with great elaboration, larded with metaphor and cosmological commentary, but when I first heard it, as a five-year-old realist, I was sure that it was unfinished. It was not until I saw my first opera, *Don Giovanni,* that I discovered that in some stories you never ask the end. Later, Christopher Marlowe taught me more about its meaning in *Doctor Faustus,* and the legend of Prometheus traced out for me the dimensions of human valor in an uncertain universe.

This, of course, is what Virginia Woolf meant when she wrote, "To continue reading without the book before you, to hold one shadow shape against another, to have read widely enough and with enough under-standing to make such comparisons alive and illuminating—that is difficult. . . ." (1)

I am saying, of course, that the tale of the frog pond was part of my "reading readiness" program for Faust and Prometheus, and for philoso-phy, too. But this "reading after the book is closed" is another matter, for the book is a time machine in several senses. Biography and history let us live elsewhere and through other minds. Fiction of any sort can lift us beyond the possible where the ordinary is strange and the awful is tolerable. For with the printed page you can test yesterday and try tomorrow, if, and only if, you have met Virginia Woolf's requirement of having read so much and so widely that you can get at the meanings behind the manner of the writing. More than that, you must be able to sense the presence of the past in a piece of flint, a broken shard of pottery, or a faded paisley shawl. The connections are always important.

The space ships in my title represent all voyages and travels, long and short, across deserts and through the pages of ancient books. But they also represent the present reality that was once a childhood fantasy for most of us here. Our planet was our first space ship, could we but realize it. But how I came upon H. G. Wells, Edgar Rice Burroughs, Jules Verne, and the others, I will report on shortly, and, forgive me, only indirectly. For the present, I want to return to those "rites of passage" by which I was given membership in the "wonderful world of books."

One of my earliest memories of classroom reading is a painful one. My knuckles were smarting from a whack of a ruler administered by a lady-ogre who stood above me, grey-haired, her grey eyes glinting behind square-cut rimless pince-nez spectacles. "Jennings, how many times have I told you not to come to a book with filthy hands?" I remember that book with distaste to this day. It was all about a boy called Dickey Dare who met a cow on the way to school—by the way, I lived in Brooklyn and did not see a live cow for another seven years. It was a silly book, which I had to read and which I read, according to the lady-ogre, very badly.

I had already at that tender age, in the first grade, become schizoid about reading. I could read quite easily before I ever came to school. I read silently, and as swiftly as the matter and the manner required, never moving the lips, never sub-vocalizing, always letting the sentence pieces flow from the page through my eyes and across the scanning areas of my brain, getting the senses ordered as to taste, color, sound and texture, knowing and experiencing the scenery of the book, listening to the rustle of life that I lifted from the printed page.

In school I was quickly taught (trained is the more appropriate word) to pronounce the words loud and haltingly. If I tried to read aloud as quickly as I took in the information from the page, my voice would drop too low and the words would run into each other, bringing a warning from the teacher that I was fudging the job, pretending to know what I was about.

So for me, very early in my academic career, I learned that there were two kinds of activity that went by the name READING. One I did alone and at home—a wonderful, magical affair every bit as compelling as television must be today to young children—devouring books by the hour, tirelessly, efficiently. The other I did in school, awkwardly, with embarrassment, mouthing silly little words, a few at a time, before and after other children in the classroom, or chanting the words with the other children according to a ritual not very different from the prayers I was learning in Sunday school, and no more meaningful. Reading in school was a SUBJECT. Reading at home, or anywhere other than school, was a special kind of living that had none of the dangers of the real world of soap and water, alarm clocks, and spinach. I made my peace with these differences and learned early how to tolerate ambiguity.

I do not know when or how I learned to read. My parents say that I just started doing it one day when I got tired waiting for someone to do it for me. I imagine, however, that it must have been rather the way Bryher reports it happened to her. Bryher* is that wonderful historical novelist, author of *The Roman Wall, The Fourteenth of October, Gate to the Sea,* etc., who in the first volume of her autobiography, *The Heart to Artemis,* records the occasion on which she "learned" to read.

> I was just five when I was given a new and exciting picture book. Unfortunately I then had a disagreement with Ruth [her nurse] that ended again in my kicking her. Retribution was swift. "After being so naughty, nobody will read to you." I decided not to howl but took my present with me to a favorite hassock in the shelter of the drawing room sofa. I opened the book at the picture of two girls and a small boy sitting around a tea table in a garden. There were a dog and cat in front of them and verses about them on the opposite page. I had some alphabet blocks with the symbols of "A is for Apple" and "Z is for Zebra" but I had never learned to put the syllables together. Full of fury, I sat and struggled. Dog and tea were easy, but there were some longer words that were very baffling and difficult. "What can she be up to?" I heard, "She is so very quiet." It was such a wet afternoon that for a wonder I had not been dragged out for a

*Winifred Ellerman.

walk. Teatime came, I wasn't even hungry, "Come along, darling, what-ever are you doing?"

"I am reading my book," I replied proudly.

There were the usual incredulous smiles so I read a poem out to them, slowly, stammering a little over one or two long words but without making any mistakes. I can still hear my mother's astonished words, "She has taught herself to read!"

Alas, we are so concerned with morals when it comes to children that we fail to recognize how much motive power there is behind anger and stubbornness. Few remember that to learn to read and write is one of the greatest victories in life. I would never allow anyone to read to me again but I devoured every scrap of print that I could find from my father's novels to the timetable (2).

Of course, these are the words of a novelist looking back through the mists of sixty-five years and are therefore doubly suspect. But she does describe the power of creative fury with which we all attack problems that must be solved to ease a hurt and give us personal control of some part of the universe that is close at hand.

I would like now to turn to the report of another novelist who, unlike Bryher, came from what we now call a "disadvantaged home." (There is, in fact, a newer locution now gaining currency; it is "children from a harsh environment.") Whatever it is called, there is a special magic, a powerful energy field that is set up between a child and a book that must be exploited if we are to achieve any success in this disorderly enterprise of education.

My second exhibit is drawn from that section of Maxim Gorky's autobiography called *In the World.* He was, at the time of which he writes, a young adolescent, hard-working peasant boy among a gang of laborers. He had been introduced to books by the lady of the estate and through those books he discovered a new world:

With something to read [he says] I felt fit and strong; I did my work briskly and well, and had something to anticipate. The quicker I got done, the more time I had for reading. Without my books I became apathetic and forgetful, which I had never been before.

These books bathed my soul, carrying off the dregs of sterile and sour realities. I appreciated the quality of these books which had become indis-pensable to me. One gain to me from their reading was the realization that I was not all alone on this earth; a sense of not being lost in this life took hold within me . . . for a book was magic for me too. It held the writer's soul, which spoke to me personally, when I opened the book and set it free (3).

Gorky's testimony is not unique. You can match it with those of Dickens, London, Mike Gold, Jim Tully and with scores of the so-called proletarian writers of the 'Thirties, as well as the members of the earlier realist's school both in this country and Europe.

The point I wish to emphasize here is that we have for a long long time tended to celebrate this special quality of the consequences of the act of reading. One of my favorite quotations of this kind of celebration I found in an old volume called *The Best Reading* by Frederic Beecher Perkins, published by Putnam in 1877 and offered as a combination annotated bibliography and course in "effective reading for young gentlemen and ladies." The style is pure Victorian:

> Now, reading is the best means of nourishing Thought. Oratory, on the other hand, is the worst, since it depends on moving the feelings, which disturb the reason ... compared with books, public speaking is a war-dance, conversation a beating bushes for wild fruit; well enough for savages and strays, but having small place or power in the discipline of a cultured mind.

Although it is not relevant at all to the present discussion, I cannot resist adding this other gem from the wisdom of F. B. Perkins:

> For those who read much a green shade over the eyes is a great economy of sight. Gas-light is of a very harsh quality, and very hot. Besides, it is better not to deal with an irresponsible monopoly when you can help it. A far better light to read and study by is the still, white light of the German Student Lamp. This lamp can be had for either kerosene or the finer vegetable oils.

How far we have traveled since those days of horse-hair sofas, velour drapes and the fumed-oak whatnot standing in the corner opposite the Baltimore Heater. Now we have Tensor lamps and prismatic reading glasses, air-conditioners and conversation pits. I am not yearning for the snows of yesteryear or the Golden Days that never were, but there is a little of the antiquarian bookman in me that is roused by such prose. I want to tell you how I came to be this way and perhaps in so doing display more clearly what I think reading is all about and what this means for those who would dare to teach.

The most effective reading teacher I have ever known was Frank Summerbell, a burly little white-haired Lancashireman. He had a glass eye which could hypnotize any browser in his dusty and disorderly bookshop. By trade and training he was a bricklayer. By political persuasion he was an articulate and loud Fabian Socialist. This is the way I met him: I was a very indifferent freshman at Brooklyn Technical High School, not at all sure how or why I had come to "Tech," which was, in those forgettable pre-Depression days, housed in a former shoe factory close by the Brooklyn entrance to the Manhattan Bridge. Since I lived in the far reaches of East Flatbush, I had to walk each day several very long blocks to the trolley car, and so I would pass this bookshop whose outdoor stands were cluttered with five-cent literary treasures, such as *Lavender and Old Lace, The Keys to the Kingdom, The Royal Road to Romance, Under Two Flags,* some of the Waverly novels, Bulwer-Lyntan, *The Rover Boys,* etc. These did not attract me. But there was one corner of these stands that did. It held a stack of Hugo Guernsback's *Amazing Stories* magazines, which were the ancestors of that now numerous genre, science fiction. When I first discovered this true treasure trove, I shot my weekly allowance of 25¢ on the complete serial of *The Skylark of Space* by Edward E. Smith, Ph.D. A prim little lady took my quarter, and I went home with my enrichment program. I could hardly wait until the following Monday for my allowance to be replenished. When I again entered the store, this time with all of A. Hyatt Verrill's *The Moon Pool,* I was confronted, not by the little old lady, but by this white-haired gnome, hunched behind a waist-high mound of books, whose strangely glinting left eye frightened me. He took my intended purchase, dropped it upon his hidden desk, rose to his towering five feet, two inches, and said to me softly, "Mister, you fooled me. I thought you were intelligent."

I was not then, nor am I now, loathe to dispute such an implied evaluation. I had looked for a kind old lady and had been met by a dilapidated bulldog. I pointed out to him that science fiction was, I think I said something like, "the wave of the future." He retorted that there were practitioners of this art superior to the hacks I was encountering. He cited H. G. Wells, Jules Verne, Arthur Conan Doyle, and Joseph Conrad (*The Inheritors*). I had heard of Verne, and I knew Sir Arthur as the inventor of a detective. He barked ungraciously and said, "Then it's about time you discovered *Marricot Deep,* Sir Arthur's best." Since I had not yet become a bibliomaniac and knew nothing of the ways of booksellers, who are closely akin to the vendors in oriental bazaars, I muttered something about wanting my magazines so that I could catch the trolley and go home. He looked at me as he almost absentmindedly wrapped a string around the package and handed it to me. He had made a mistake. It included a hardbound book. "Mister," he said, "take that along with your randy-dancing nonsense. If you don't like it, bring it back. If you do like it, keep it."

I got out of that shop quickly. And it wasn't until the trolley was passing between Prospect Park and the Botanical Gardens that I set aside the exciting magazines to look into the plum-colored volume. It was by someone called Christopher Morley. It had a ridiculous title, *The Romany Stain.* I probably was thinking appropriately adolescent thoughts about the behavior of arrogant adults. I started to read something about a sea shell in Normandy. The next thing I knew, the conductor was walking past me to lower the trolley pole. "Hey, kid, this is Bergen Beach. It's the last stop." I had ridden twenty blocks past my destination, the victim, as my reading of *Amazing Stories* had taught me, of a time warp. I had been in another dimension in some wondrous land beyond use and wont where strange things were important and familiar things didn't count, where people became excited over the disputed virtues of a forgotten poet, and where the only mysteries of any consequence were those that hid the true identity of a first edition. And I had made a discovery. I didn't know it at the time by its proper name, but it was "style." This Christopher Morley wrote like an angel. I walked home through the dusk not quite sure what had happened. I ate quickly and did not do my homework, which had to do with a summary of S. Wier Mitchell's house-broken little masterpiece, *Hugh Wynn, Free Quaker.* I read the music of Christopher Morley's prose into the night, and the next morning in my English class had to confess that I had wrongfully employed the preceding evening. When I told Miss Herstein what I had read, her face grew strangely soft and, miracle of miracles, she simply said, "That's all right, Jennings, you can do the assignment when you're finished with your Mr. Christopher Morley."

That was the beginning of a twenty-year association with Mr. Summerbell. I tried to return *Romany Stain* that day, but he said that he meant it to be a gift, or rather that the only payment he wanted was to know what I thought about the book. I rebelled at first, but I sensed that he was NOT demanding a book report. I talked in a way I had never talked before about a book or anything. And when I went home the second night I had another gift, another Christopher Morley which was called *Where the Blue Begins.* You know—it's the story about a dog named Gissing (an author!).* Now, I had read dog stories before. I knew all about Albert Payson Terhune's dogs. They were forever collies. I had read *White Fang* and *The Call of the Wild* by my earliest idol, Jack London. Summerbell suggested *The Iron Heel* and *The Mutiny of the Elsenore.* But Gissing was a different dog. He talked and he thought and he was kindly disposed towards the foibles of human nature.

Visits to Frank Summerbell's shop became a ritual. I learned quickly that I didn't have to buy anything, and that whenever I did want a book, it somehow never cost more than I had to spare. Mr. Summerbell would say to me one day, "Mister," (I don't know why, but this "Mister" always flattered me) "have you ever heard of Thomas Hardy?" I was fourteen, and I hadn't. "Let me tell you about Tess," he would say. And he did, and I found another part of the universe—the universe of books, books that teamed with humanity, with ordinary people who suffered in ways not very different from what I could observe around me, who spoke in accents that

---

*George Gissing, 19th Century English author of working-class novels: *New Grub Street, Workers of the Dawn, The Private Papers of Henry Ryecroft,* etc.

were almost common speech, but somehow transfigured so that there was an insistent song in the syllables.

During the first year of my rather specialized reading program under the tutelage of Mr. Summerbell, I rediscovered poetry; I found my Irish literary heritage in the person of John Synge, James Stevens, the poetry of William Butler Yeats. You see, Frank Summerbell knew nothing about the scope and sequence of the English syllabus for the New York City schools, and although it seemed to me that he had an incredibly effective instinct for knowing what I ought next to read, yet somehow I even then knew that there wasn't any magic in it, but that he and I were engaged in something that has since been reduced to the name of a textbook series; we were in fact engaged in an adventure in reading.

Because I was going to Brooklyn Technical High School and presumably not illiterate in matters of science and mathematics, Mr. Summerbell thought that I should know the words of Sir James Jeans and Arthur Eddington. "You're not going to understand all of it, but, Mister, that's what learning is all about. If you understand all of anything, you'll never learn anything about it." I discovered that my apprenticeship in the stews of the science fiction magazines stood me in good stead with Eddington and Jeans. I knew about the Michelson-Morley experiments in the measurement of the speed of light. I had heard about the Lorentz-Fitzgerald contraction and knew that it had something to do with Einstein's theory of relativity. I had heard about Clark Maxwell's little demon and could even recite the second law of thermodynamics. (Sir Charles Percy Snow would have been proud of me.)

But, although I was a student at Brooklyn Technical High School, I was, so far as science and technology were concerned, foresworn. For my discovery of style in Christopher Morley led me into a life-long enchantment with the miracle of language and the ineffable wonders of the printed page. And I, who had been a less than indifferent student in the English classroom, now developed a high tolerance for everything that had to do with that language, written, spoken, or printed. I even participated without complaint in the dissection of poor sentences on the diagrammatic wracks the teachers drew upon the blackboard. I wanted to write, and somewhere between the bookstore and the classroom I learned how to write and even found my way into the offices of the student newspaper. But that is another kind of a story, related, but not directly pertinent, to Mr. Summerbell's reading program.

He read, it seemed, omnivorously. But this was wrong. He always read with a high purpose. Each day he read all of the daily New York newspapers and there were eight of them then. He read the *London Times* and the *Manchester Guardian*. He read the *Christian Science Monitor* and occasionally what he called the other great American newspapers. He read the

*Saturday Review,* which then still was "of literature." He read *Harper's,* the *Atlantic,* the *Scientific American,* the *New Masses,* and *The New Republic.*

He read all of them and could talk, and would talk, about whatever he read. He was a challenging talker who elicited response in kind and with him I discovered the delights of what could be easily misunderstood as namedropping, but was really a form of embryonic scholarship. I discovered I could remember things I had read. And it was exciting to me to be able to say, "I like the way G. D. H. Coles said it when he talked about the Luddites." (I like these Englishmen with their triple initials. C. E. M. Joad, the philosopher, was another one. Mr. Summerbell gave me his intellectual autobiography, *Under the Fifth Rib.*)

But, mainly, I liked to talk at that time about the novels. I came upon them in a hodge-podge way, and Mr. Summerbell never took a methods course in his life and knew nothing at all about developmental reading. So he would have me jump from Thomas Hardy to J. B. Priestley to Richard Aldington to Henry Fielding to Aldous Huxley and on quite illogically to the prose works of Milton. We would talk about Gibbon and *The Decline and Fall of the Roman Empire,* and it would occur to him that the story of Nell Gwynn, her fall and rise, was absolutely apposite. He was never parochial in his interests, and I learned not to be. He found Hemingway exciting, T. S. Eliot exasperating. "But that expatriate stinker writes like an angel," he would say, "Better than that West Coast yammerer, Robinson Jeffers." And, of course, I ran to read Robinson Jeffers, and was deliciously terrified by the brocaded verse of his *Tamar.* He was high on Thomas Wolfe. He reluctantly admired James Branch Cabell, whom I worshiped. He thought that Francis Scott Fitzgerald was a lot better than he appeared to be. He was angry with Floyd Dell for being an amateur bohemian. He thought that Mike Gold's novel *Jews Without Money* was better than anything that Sholem Ascher would ever write; and then came James Joyce, the *Dubliners,* the *Portrait,* the *Pomes.* And all the while he talked, I would listen to the familiar and the unfamiliar names, and when there were neither business nor browsers in the store, we would wander together along the stacks straightening out the volumes, sharing annotating comments, remarking about the virtues of one edition and the vices of another.

But ever and again we would come back to the realities of the world around us, because there were breadlines in the streets of New York and apples were being sold by people who had higher skills and training. And there was confusion in the land because our engineer president seemed to have been caught, at least according to Mr. Summerbell, in that web of economic and social contradictions that covers any capitalistic society. We read Karl Marx and his prophets on *The Daily Worker* and the liturgical literature from the *Communist Manifesto* to *Anti-Duhring,* and Mr. Summerbell, being a good Fabian Socialist, looked upon these works with proper Protestant contempt, pointing out that, as a sociologist, Marx did make a modest, if useful, contribution toward understanding of the housing plight of working-class Londoners, but that the poor German was innocent of economics, and, being a German, had no real sense of the role and nature of philosophical discourse. He would say that a paragraph of old Jeremy Bentham and a page and a half of John Stewart Mill would go a lot farther than either *Das Kapital* or *Value, Price and Profit.* But then he would advert to things as they were around us and say, "God forbid, I never thought I'd live to see the day when there would be a dole for the citizens of these United States, but it's coming, Mister, and it better come quickly."

The world was bigger than the bookstore and more troubled than our city, and so we were aware of the clank of steel in Germany and the cries of terror from China. And yet, there were other and more immediate discoveries to be made. "Mister," he would say, "have you never seen a play —the actors speaking their lines on a stage?" And he took me to see *The Playboy of the Western World* in a dingy little church basement somewhere in the depths of Queens. At that time there was a legitimate theater in Brooklyn—the Majestic was across the street—and occasionally a Broadway show would be imported. And there I saw, at his insistence, Eugene O'Neill's *The Emperor Jones.*

And, somehow, from that Mr. Summerbell led me to a hidden resource of his bookstore. Just as covered with dust as his books were stacks of records on the floor. I knew nothing of opera, and, for that matter, probably because of classes in music appreciation, I knew nothing at all of the world of music. So we began to talk about singers and composers. And, since at Brooklyn Technical High School I had been developing a few of the skills which James Byrant Conant declares to be marketable, I was able to assemble an audio-amplifier, and out of the remnants of an old wind-up Gramophone I made a semi-electric phonograph. And so, now, parallel to my reading, there was Wagner, and Debussy, and Sibelius, and Bach, and mostly Schubert—the leider. I am to this day illiterate in reading the musical score, but whatever sophistication I have in music I trace back to the bookshop.

Although it is tempting to continue this biography and autobiography, and I am, as I recount these happenings, conscious of a more formal celebration that I owe to the memory of a strange and wonderful little man, I think it is more appropriate that I indicate some inferences which I hope are obvious to you.

I was fortunate in having discovered the bookstore. I was doubly fortunate in having been discovered by the bookseller. The English program at Brooklyn Technical High School was an appendage to a curriculum heavily committed to producing engineers and mechanics. It provided no amenities and was concerned, as one of its formal testing programs indicated, with "minimum essentials of the English language." Its students were expected to achieve a high order of literacy, but if the English teacher wanted to open the doors of our literary storehouse, she would have to do it on her own time—and one such teacher did, and I will pay homage to her on some other occasion. The point that is to be stressed here is that one man, filled with his subject, which one might call "Books in Life," could light a fire in another's mind.

This man, with a capacity for understanding and tolerating an adolescent boy, was able to do what a school ideally ought to do, but, given the nature of our society, is rarely likely to do. Summerbell was not a specialist in anything but bricklaying. In England he had served his apprenticeship and won his journeyman's status in that trade. In this country he followed his heart and mind into the world of books and developed some wonderful, if imprecise, skills. But all of these were subsidiary to something far more important. And this was, to use an existential term, his engagement with life as it must inescapably be lived. Although he recognized that books and their reading can be noble ends, these ends must always be provisional. For knowledge of any kind to be of any value, it must be put to use. To put knowledge of any value to use, it must be directed with definite purpose, and purpose leads round about and back to books, because to have a purpose one must know what is of value and what is of value is what makes life tolerable, endurable, and exciting, and we record this, of course, in books.

Perhaps I should have displayed one of my more important credentials earlier. I am a card-carrying English teacher. Once, not too many years ago, I was employed in the school system of Bloomfield, New Jersey as a reading specialist. I am not sure whether that employment was a result of or in spite of my protests that I was not then and had no intention of ever becoming whatever it was that a reading specialist was supposed to be. Now, it is easy to interpret that behavior of mine as a form of gamesmanship. The evidence is clear. I got the job. I did work with children and with teachers seeking ways to enhance the quality of reading experiences. I was not concerned with *remediation,* which is a most unlovely and very fuzzy piece of jargon. I have taught children to read. I know the psychological and physiological mechanisms which are associated with the more trivial aspects of the reading act. I have for many years been a close student of language. I confess that I read with a kind of addictive horror the ever-increasing reports of quasi-, crypto-, and proto-research that issues from the laboratories and scholarly lairs of those who seek manageable truth.

I want, please, not to be misunderstood. I am not opposed to research. I do not denigrate scholarship. But I am much more concerned with what goes on in the classroom in the form of significant learning. (Please note that there is no "s" on the word "learning." Forgive this aside, but we in education are more prone to retreat behind a shield of jargon than anyone in any other profession. I do not intend to expand upon this; I point to it merely as a sure sign that wherever you see a tortured or distorted word you can safely assume that someone is disguising ignorance or confusion, or both.)

If there is any justification for my being here, I infer that it is to talk with you about professional matters which concern us all. What does concern us is the mandate that is implicit in the act of accrediting a teacher. That is: "Go forth and make a literate society." At the risk of sounding tiresomely pompous, let me speak to the teacher's credo, which should be implicit in such a mandate.

1. If you do not read, don't you dare try to teach. By this I mean that any teacher of any subject at any level who is not first of all a literate person does not belong in the classroom. Let me specify: Although I recognize the shortcomings of Sir Charles Percy Snow's arguments on the two-culture problem, there is merit in his insistence that, whatever your specialty, you'd better know that there is more to the world than your microscope or your monographs or your criticism or your "insight into the nature of human nature." I do not insist that the teacher of English be able to pronounce the second law of thermodynamics, but I do insist that that teacher must know that the law was not established by legislative fiat. I do not insist that the teacher of mathematics be able to distinguish among the competing critical canon in exigesis of the more obscure works of John Donne. But I do insist that such a teacher who might have learned to look upon beauty as Euclid saw her should also be able to comprehend the nature of a poet's terror when he sees a butterfly trapped in a spider's web. I do not intend to course through the curriculum scoring such cheap points as these. I am certain that you understand the burden of my message. But, let me repeat, if you do not read, don't dare teach.

Let me offer you another element in this credo:

2. If you do dare to teach English (and by English I mean all that our language is and has been, all that has been done with it and through it, and what it can become). . . . If—I repeat—if you dare to teach English, and you are graceless in your speech, you are clumsy in managing the written word, yourself, and the forms of literature are inaccessible to you, then get into another line of work; leave students alone; they have enough to contend with.

I offer a third element in this credo, by taking as my text the formulation of a man wiser than any of us, Alfred North Whitehead, who, on the first page of his wonderful book which every teacher should know by heart, his *Aims of Education,* declares:

(3) "Do not teach too many subjects and what you teach, teach thor-

oughly." Taken in one sense, this is a defense of and a license for specialization. In another sense, it is an injunction against the false and philandering proliferation of subject matter.

There is a lesser Englishman whose observations have some pertinence here. I refer to the law as enunciated by Northcote C. Parkinson having to do with work expanding to fit the time and the multiplication of idle hands to handle idle work. There *is* need for the specialist in the school, in the hospital, in the halls of justice, in the political arena, and in sewage disposal plants. But specialists are dangerous. They organize into fraternal societies. They create professional pressure groups. They must justify themselves by procrustean efforts, and by their acts, in spite of what good they may do, they often leave behind them the fag ends of the disciplines they were created to enrich.

The credo I have displayed before you is not to be considered either as revealed truth or the product of an N.E.A. Commission on the Professionalization of Education. It is a credo to be pronounced differently by each of us as we confront our task, and that task is to teach a subject thoroughly to students whom we get to know well, in order that they may gain and understand and use their language and the thought processes it represents, that they may come to understand the nature of the world they live in and the human nature they acquire in that life. To this end is the teacher's responsibility, out of his own experience, to lead students on voyages of discovery and self-discovery, in order that they by the very process of growing into adulthood acquire values that will hold the society together while they reach for new goals by which to make the world of man more humane.

I do not offer this as idle preaching. I offer it rather as a test by which to measure what you do in the classroom, to children and for children. Do you, as you induct the child into the world of letters, as you provide him with the keys to the kingdom of books—do you play the game of the artful dodger? Do you seduce him into believing that the vapid pastel illustrations in his basal reader have any referent in the world he already knows? Do you offer him the nostrum of the never-never land of sun-drenched Sunday afternoon on tree-bowered streets and on velvet-carpeted parks where blonde and blue-eyed children play out charades and there is no death?

Do you in the later years hide behind the bulwark of a reading series that offers the treasures heaped up for us by Chaucer and Shakespeare . . . and Kerouac and Ginsberg. (The last two, not having been sanctified, have not yet been sterilized onto the pages acceptable to the textbook selection committee.) I mean by this to ask you whether you have been, and will continue to be, party to a conspiracy which under the name of Christianity and "child growth and development" reduces the songs of our poets to the level of a singing commercial. I do not intend here to expand on this theme;

I have said it before, and others have been more loud than I in denouncing the pap that we offer in the place of literary protein.

Things do change, however. The Department of Education in the State of New Jersey has been doing something about this desert. I refer to the experiment currently under way in the schools throughout the state in the use of paperback books in the classroom. They are, as I understand it, not being used because they are paperbacks, or because they are cheap, or because they stand up surprisingly well under rough handling, all of which is true, but rather because there exists, no further away than a phone call or a letter, a library of over 26,000 titles currently in print, a library which includes a fair representation of the wit, the wisdom, and the folly of our race, a library which, for simple economic reasons, consists in the main of books that are as yet unsullied by the trembling hands of a textbook editor buying insurance against attacks from anyone anywhere.

A great deal has been said and written about the paperback revolution. It is not really a revolution; it is something at once simpler and more glorious than that. It's one of the few genuine and defensible reasons for the existence of what we think we know as free enterprise. In short, the publication of paperback books today makes it possible for any teacher of any subject at any level with any child (to paraphrase Dr. Jerome S. Bruner) at any stage of his development to provide that child or student with books that are appropriate to his needs, his interests, his hopes, and his fears.

There is no magic in books, or in reading programs of any kind, or in gadgets, or gimmicks, or specialists. The only magic is the act of teaching by a person deeply committed to providing the best opportunities for students to discover themselves and to establish skills and working habits which will secure to them the available fruits of life in an open society.

## References

1. "How Should One Read a Book?" reprinted in *The Great English and American Essays,* edited by Edmund Fuller (New York: Avon Books, 1964), p. 333.
2. Winifred Bryher, *The Heart to Artemis* (New York: Harcourt, Brace, and World, 1962), p. 14.
3. Maxim Gorky, *In the World,* Isidor Schneider, trans. (Bombay: Jaico Publishing House, 1949), pp. 136, 186 passim.

**Norman M. Goble**

# The Day the Anarchists Were Hanged—Some Thoughts on Literature As an Educative Instrument

In one of the first literary references to the act of reading, Homer (Iliad VI) tells us that, when the hero Bellerophon was falsely accused by the wife of his royal master of attempted rape, his patron shrank from the blood-guilt of taking his life and sent him instead to his father-in-law, carrying his own death warrant in sealed tablets—"baneful symbols . . . to work his destruction."

The father of the alleged victim read the tablets only after the ritual nine days of welcome, and found himself in a quandary. He had read the character of Bellerophon (and, no doubt, of his own daughter); reading the message, he read also the elements of his own self-interest, read the social obligations of rank and convention and the moral injunctions of custom and religion. Observing a nice balance between the claims of self and society, he evaded decision by sending the young man off to pursue the monstrous, murderous Chimera.

Bellerophon, perverse young man, killed the beast and came back to prolong the embarrassment of his host. Eventually, of course, propriety triumphed: Bellerophon was judged insane. Pindar says he was struck down by the thunderbolt of divine Authority when he sought to invade the precincts of Olympus; in Homer's version the gods of the Establishment were content to doom him to wander in dreadful loneliness, shunned by his less wayward fellow men.

Note the irony: the written word first appears as an instrument of orthodoxy in putting down vexatious probity. (Note too, if you like, that a century later all the kings of the Asiatic Greeks were claiming Bellerophon as an ancestor. Today's pariah risks becoming tomorrow's paragon: but that is a theme that has been over-worked, out of all proportion, and it is time we learnt discernment in our admiration of the outcast. It takes more than disparagement to make a Gauguin, more than crucifixion to make a Christ.)

What I see in the story is the dilemma of the teacher. The young Bellerophons come to us bearing the damnation of their origins and their inheritance. But we are too busy reading the signs of our own environment, achieving our own balance in society, to help them much. It is easier to entertain them for the ritual time, and then send them off to the long, fatal pursuit of chimeras.

They don't go so readily any more. They don't believe in our chimeras. They want to do what we should always have taught them to do: read their own dossier of "baneful signs," and learn how to go back and right the wrongs. And it is high time we learned how to help them.

The essential objective of the teacher is, I think, implied in Marc Belth's definition of the educational goal of schooling: "a more highly developed creative intelligence by means of which the world is encountered, organized, understood and used" (1).

Consider the first stage—the encounter. Meaning begins with identification of self; but the dimensions of self can only be established by the encounter with environment: the borders of self are determined by interaction with society. Similarly, the nature of society, its pressures and demands, are discovered by observation of their interaction with one's self. By observing, we learn to predict, and when we can predict we are in a position to *select* desired effects—that is to say, to "organize and use."

All this depends on *encounter*—conscious encounter, a communicated awareness of environment. The teacher's task is to contrive a continuing and controlled encounter, and the key instrument is the written word.

This needs emphasis in a time when the picture is said to be the dominant mode of communication. The picture is at best a blunt instrument: it is the *word* that transmits specific thought under the control, and at the will, of the thinker: it is the word that formulates the essential interests and desires of the other "we" that we must learn to see in society. The picture shows us the way things *look,* but only the word can tell us how it *is* with others, how it feels (which in the human world is the important part of the way it is). The picture evokes response, but it is the word that hones response to discriminative sharpness.

Neither the individual nor society can maintain health in the absence of encounter. We are our real selves only in relation to the real, outer world (human behavior in disaster shows us how much we depend on relationship to our environment for maintenance of our identity), and we must constantly be probing to know where we stand. Society, too, needs the continuing probe, to keep it trimmed and tuned as an efficient time-vehicle for human culture. If the vehicle stalls, if it settles into a static structure instead of a dynamic machine, its foundation will be eroded by the flow of time until it collapses.

Besides, the distinction between our individual selves and the collective self of society is really a false one: the two are aspects of one identity, and failure to maintain the encounter is an amputation that leaves us incomplete, our consciousness abbreviated and our vitality lost.

Life is never static: it is a constant effort of organization—the creation of order in a world which the laws of physics tell us is in a constant state of flow towards chaos. It is this effort to create order that is the defiant assertion of life against the doom of mortality: but it must be a constantly renewed effort, and a constantly reborn order. Order ossified is the anticipation of death. Order animate is order constantly re-ordered by an impulse of change—the shock that reforms the kaleidoscope pattern.

The precarious equilibrium of dynamic order is the only condition of life. The saving graces of man are the product of sustained effort to maintain an ordered society, through discriminative perception of what is expedient for the welfare of each individual self. A concept such as love, for example, is not the spontaneous outgrowth of nature, but a highly complex and sophisticated and painfully acquired state involving an ordered suspense of self-indulgence, and restraint upon "natural" impulse.

But order is not, and must not be, inert quiescence—rather the stability of the gyroscope, which stays in balance only as long as it is free to precess. It is this kind of dynamic disequilibrium that we need in society and in the individual, to maintain the evolving flow of life. And to set the mind precessing we need the disturbance of encounter—a thrust to trip the mechanism.

The thrust to the mind must come by the word—the caustic word to etch meaning on the blank mind, the resonant word to shiver the silence of the smug spirit, the disturber of our peace.

This is the essential value of the word—to be the instrument of change; and it can be this only by being a mark of *difference.*

What we especially need is repeated reminders of how it feels to be someone else. Contained in our own mould, we cool and set, and lose our power of motion—our ability to be a moving, formative force in the society around us. We need the irritant of a different viewpoint to keep alive our awareness of our own being. It may be, for instance, a discovery of a new facet of the familiar, like Harry Golden's superb little essay on Shylock (2) which should be required reading in literature courses; it may be a deliberate challenge to our assumptions—a book like *Lord of the Flies,* or any of the more mature Graham Greene novels; it may only be the engaging unorthodoxy of the historian who reminds us that thirteenth century Europe, which gave us the sonnet, may have enriched our lives more by the invention of the button (3); but it must jar us into a consideration of unfamilar perspectives.

We need to be constantly reminded that society is not just an impersonal surrounding mass in which we hew our own space, but a composite living organism, a composite of individuals, interdependent, with whom we seek accommodation so that we and they, human beings all, may become what each best may be.

And, I repeat: the way to achieve this is not to cultivate recognition of sameness, which is deadening and destructive of values, but to cultivate recognition of difference. "In this toboggan ride into total, perfectly adjusted mediocrity," says John D. MacDonald, "the great conundrum is what is worth living for and what is worth dying for." We shall never know, unless we cultivate the faculty of discrimination.

The teaching of discernment, then, is a vital part of schooling, and the word is the key instrument. It follows that in the teacher's own education the development of discriminative judgment through disciplined, directed and purposefully selected reading is a vital element.

I stress selection because difference in itself is not always significant; the thrust is not always forward; disturbance can be fruitful change or sterile deviance. The inspired flip of the mind can trip the mechanism of kaleidoscopic readjustment; but the spent flopping of the empty spirit is not a valid substitute.

And of this we have too much around us: too much of philosophies which MacDonald calls "simplifications which indignant people seize upon to make understandable a world too complex for their comprehension," of those "which small dreary people adopt in the hope of thereby finding the Answer, because the very concept that maybe there is no answer, never has been, never will be, terrifies them."

There is no fruitfulness in the response which, instead of tripping the mechanisms of constructive thought, entraps the passenger mind in the mechanism of helpless trips that are circular tours back to vapidity. There is no discrimination in the petulant complaint of the individual who has lost the lines of contact with society, and so lost his own definition, and is crying because he has nothing left but his dismay. There is no merit in deviance for its own destructive sake.

The difficulty is in learning to discriminate between the necessary thrust and the random blow; and between dynamic equilibrium and static stability. "Thought," said Bertrand Russell, "is subversive and revolutionary, destructive and terrible . . . anarchic and lawless." Sometimes it is. But it need not always be—not unless it is suffering the intolerable constraint of a dead institution, the shrinking cocoon from which the reborn life must break out.

And when the impetuous sage goes on to say that thought is "indifferent to authority, careless of the well-tried wisdom of the ages," he is letting rhetoric outrun reason. For the word, which is the necessary instrument of thought, sharpens its meaning on the whetstone of time. And from its meaning it draws a proper authority that we are foolish to reject. The *word* is a gathering-up of a history of pain and pleasure, fear, comfort, disappointment—a *human* history, a multiplicity of lives flowing into our own. The ever shifting vocabulary of the young betrays the absence of meaning, of this kind of truth that is the only real truth—the sum of human experience; and their rejection of the authority of the word is a denial of their own professed aspiration to discover "real" values.

Yet opposite Scylla is Charybdis; opposite the danger of sterile deviance is the danger of rigid persistence; and the word has its own risks. Because it is meaning and feeling crystallized, it can be an instrument of crystallizing what should be fluid. It may confirm and establish what it should only be defining or calling attention to, so that the reward of learning becomes only "base authority from others' books." The printed word is less clamorous than sound or pictorial image, but it is abiding, and is always in danger of creating an orthodoxy. How many of the elements, for example, of the curious orthodoxies of our present society—the generation war, the cult of self-indulgence, the compulsion in the young to choose among uniformities and crush eccentricity—have been codified by the opportunist accord of the popular commercial press, in which a felicitous phrase discovered by one writer will bring the whole flock of weeklies and monthlies seagull-swooping down to snatch at the profits of mass reader appeal?

My argument is, then, that the discriminative faculty develops through identification of self by interaction with society, and must then be applied to predict and select the desired effects of that interaction; and that it may be helped to develop through reading because the written word has the unique quality of formulating and transmitting, under the close control of the author, his essential interests and perceptions. I have asserted that this faculty is a necessary one because it alone, by detection of *difference,* can save self and society from stagnation, and also, by discernment of *significance,* save us from unfruitful and random response to irrelevant stimuli.

The discriminative response distinguishes fruitful difference from sterile deviance. The day the anarchists were hanged, society perhaps stifled the stimulus that would have reactivated its living impulse; or perhaps it only stifled a noise. The distinction is one we have to make daily: when we make it we are readers; to the degree that we are widely and wisely read we shall be more or less fit to make it, and to teach others to make it.

Our point of view on literature, as part of the educational process, has tended to move uncertainly among three positions: it is an instrument of moral and socio-philosophical orthodoxy, or it is a means of displaying the aesthetic achievements of our culture, or it is a kind of bath of undifferentiated and unstructured "experience" in which young people are dipped, as in a mineral spring, in the hope that the immersion will somehow be good for their system.

I am no believer in the special virtue of accidental, as opposed to deliberate, effects of the educational process. If we set up a planned and systematic process of schooling, we should be doing so in the expectation of certain definable outcomes, and we should try to use, in the process, the instrument that we judge likely to produce those outcomes.

I propose that we concede that reading, at all ages, is a necessary and powerful educative instrument; that we set ourselves the objective of developing criteria of selection to shape the instrument more closely to the defined purposes of the general system—purposes derived from our concept of the goals of self and society; and that experience in the development and application of such criteria is a necessary part of the education of the teacher.

## References

1. Belth, M., *Education as a Discipline,* (Boston: Allyn and Bacon Inc., 1965), 44.
2. Golden, H., *Only in America,* Permabooks Edition (New York: Pocket Books Inc., 1959), 158.
3. Trueman, J. G., *Unlearning History,* O.S.S.T.F. Bulletin, O.S.S.T.F., Toronto 47, 6 (December 1967).

# Northrop Frye

## *Sign and Significance*

I begin with a very simple distinction, and one which I have used elsewhere. Whenever we read anything, we find our attention moving in two directions at once. One direction is centripetal, trying to form a context out of what we are reading. The other direction is centrifugal, where we keep going outside what we are reading to our memory of the conventional meaning of the words used. We become aware of the continuity of this latter movement when we read something in a language we imperfectly know, and have to keep consulting a dictionary. In my *Anatomy of Criticism* I suggested that this distinction might serve as a rough but workable basis for dividing literary structures into the literary and the non-literary. If the verbal structure has been made primarily for the sake of a body of facts or concepts which it reproduces, it is discursive and non-literary; if it exists for its own sake as an interesting verbal pattern, it is literary, and can no longer be judged by the accuracy with which its represents phenomena outside itself. This difference is usually in the intentionality of the work itself, but sometimes social acceptance has a power of veto over it; thus a work originally intended to be historical, or even medical, like Gibbon's *Decline and Fall* or Burton's *Anatomy of Melancholy,* may come to survive as literature.

Let us now apply this distinction to criticism. When we read a work of literature we are always subconsciously trying to answer the question "What does this mean?" It is clear from what we have said that there are two answers. The centrifugal answer, when we are reading a poem particularly, usually involves giving a prose paraphrase of the poem and saying "This is what it means." If we insert an adverb of value into that remark, we reveal a good deal about our critical attitude. If we say, "This is roughly, or more or less, what it means," we are conceding the autonomy of the form of the poem. If we say, "This is literally what it means," we are reflecting the assumptions of a writing culture, in which the norms of verbal meaning are established by non-literary writers, and the poet is a licensed liar. If we say, "This is essentially what it means," we have committed ourselves to taking a position about where the essence of a poem is which is very common but ultimately indefensible.

Nevertheless, giving a prose paraphrase of a poem's meaning is not only defensible but necessary as a basis for certain types of criticism. These forms of criticism are centrifugal, in the sense that they take the poem to be a document illustrating some context established outside the poem. The simplest way of doing this is to regard the poem as a statement by the poet of his own views or attitudes to life. Here the context is biographical, and the critical attention is focused on the manifest content of the poem as a communication from poet to reader.

No one can doubt the relevance of biography to criticism as a whole, but of course the biographical context is a limited one. It depends on our possession of a fully documented body of material about a poet's life, and we normally need some explicit statements from the poet himself. Where the poet's life is imperfectly known, the limitations in this form of understanding show up very clearly. Thus in the nineteenth century, the heyday of biographical criticism, a critic would simply have to invent a poet's biography if he did not possess it. Hence we get editors of Horace explaining that we know from Horace's poems that he was violently in love with a series of damsels named Lydia, Delia, and Phaedria, and students of Shakespeare would tell us that the key to understanding Shakespeare's sonnets consists in identifying the Mr. W. H. of the publisher's blurb with the appropriate pansy, hopefully a noble one.

In any case, in the twentieth century at least, a biographical context tends to expand into a psychological one. Here we are moving from the manifest content to the latent content as our area of study. The approach is still documentary, and therefore allegorical: that is, the poem is treated as an allegory illustrating the poet's own attitude to life. The manifest content is usually rendered by some kind of conceptual allegory: the poem illustrates a certain aspect of the poet's view of life, and this aspect is normally some theme such as love, death, ecstasy or fatality. Here the poem is being assimilated to conceptual and discursive structures which are produced voluntarily and with a conscious mind. Since we recognize a latent content as well as a manifest one, we concede the importance of unconscious and involuntary factors in the creative process. The poem thus records, perhaps unconsciously, various tensions and conflicts in the poet's mind, and hence it becomes an allegory of certain typical and recurring psychological situations, such as the contest of ego and id in Freud or the individuation process in Jung. In this area a certain determinism is apt to make its appearance. The psychological conflicts are often regarded as the origin of the poem, and as essentially accounting for the poem's structure as well as its content.

Another aspect of unconscious meaning is that every poet addresses his own time, and yet may be able to communicate to future generations through qualities that would not be fully known to him. Thus when Tillyard writes about the unconscious meaning of *Paradise Lost,* he is really writing about that aspect of the poem which makes it relevant to the twentieth century, and not merely to the seventeenth. At this point we begin to wonder whether in fact we can accept the poet as being the sole source of his poem. Perhaps, after all, the poem does not come so much from the poet as through the poet from somewhere else. That somewhere else is, most obviously, the society to which he belongs and of which he is a spokesman. At this point centrifugal criticism becomes historical criticism, including the history of ideas, and the poem is studied as a social, historical and cultural document.

This aspect of criticism is too familiar to need further explanation. It is not only essential to criticism but one of its most liberalizing aspects. To concentrate solely upon a poet's relevance to our own time is to translate him into our own conventions and modes of thought, which both distorts him and increases our own complacent provincialism. To anchor a poet solidly in his own age is also to become acquainted with alien cultures and habits of thought, and so to enlarge our own experience. Thus historical criticism becomes a means of liberalizing our study of the humanities, and is part of the general sense of responsibility and respect for subject matter that impels us to read everything we can in its original language, or at least to demand the most literal possible translation if we do not know the language.

But here, as with the individual poet, the critical interest is likely to extend from manifest content to latent content, from what a historical period explicitly tells us to what it unconsciously reveals of its class tensions, its sense of its own context in time and space and history. This means the development of a historical criticism content within a unified view of history. There have been several of these. The earliest one, which flourished from the Renaissance to the eighteenth century, saw Western culture as reaching a golden age in the time of Augustus, as declining through silver and brass to iron with what Gibbon called "the triumph of barbarism and religion," and then going through the "dark" age to a new light with the revival of Classical learning. This was succeeded by the Romantic view, which exactly reversed this and saw culture as reaching its height in the medieval period. This survived into the last generation with a conservative, and usually Catholic, view of history which placed the summit of cultural integration in the age of St. Thomas. The Classical view modulated into the

Hegelian one, which saw a gradual actualizing of the idea of liberty in history. And this, metamorphosed into the revolutionary view of Marx, still occupies a good deal of critical thought today. Here again we find determinism, and a tendency to explain form as well as content by the controlling view of history.

All these centrifugal types of criticism are, I repeat, essential to the entire critical process. It is only when we refuse to concede the validity of other types of criticism that we begin to go wrong. Every form of documentary criticism is in the long run analytic: it takes the poem apart in order to put it together again in a non-literary context. Thus it does not account for the fact that the poem was in the first place written as a poem. We need to develop a complementary type of criticism which accepts the poetic form of utterance as its basis or literal meaning. The types of criticism we have been dealing with have as their great strength a sense of context, a place to put the poem. But, in themselves, they can only give us an education through literature, not an education in literature.

It was inevitable, therefore, that there should have been a reaction against historical criticism in favour of a type of criticism which preserved the poetic form of the poem as its basis of operations. Such a reaction took place with the explicatory school of critics which were called the "new critics" in America a quarter of a century ago. In some respects this movement resembled the "formalism" in Russian literature which has been attacked by the Marxists as a form of bourgeois idealism. The Marxists were shrewd enough to see that once we begin to concede the formal autonomy of the poem, the whole structure of Marxist determinism and "social realism" would begin to crumble, and Marxist bureaucracies would be compelled to give novelists and poets the same kind of freedom that they had reluctantly been compelled to grant to scientists.

As with all reactions, there were excesses on both sides: some new critics went to simplistic extremes in ruling out every kind of "background" from the critical operation, and some historical critics assumed that explication was nothing but a kind of solitaire-playing, with no rules in history or culture. And in fact, explication did run into one difficulty: the absence of the sense of context which had been the great strength of historical criticism. Hence most of the more responsible new critics, as they developed, tended to accept one of the contexts that were already provided. In most cases this was ordinary historical criticism: a few, because of the anti-Marxist historical setting of the movement, adopted the conservative and Catholic type of determinism; one or two were even Marxists. In Marshall McLuhan, who was trained essentially in this school as a critic, an extreme and somewhat paradoxical formalism, which identifies medium and message, has been placed in a neo-Marxist context of determinism in which communications media play the role that "means of production" do in more orthodox Marxism. A good many traces of an older religious determinism can be found in *The Gutenberg Galaxy.*

Another difficulty with explication takes a little more space to describe. In addition to the two directions of attention we speak of, which go on simultaneously, there are also two actions which succeed one another in time. While we are reading a poem or listening to a play on the stage, we are participating in a linear narrative: this linear participation is essentially pre-critical. Once finished, the poem or play tends to freeze into a single simultaneous unity. This sense of simultaneous unity is what is symbolized by "recognition," which may be a crucial point in the play towards the end or some crucial emblematic image, like a scarlet letter or a golden bowl, and which is usually indicated in the title. It is in this sense of total comprehension of structure, or "verbal icon," that the critic can begin. The process of explication is consequently easiest to follow, and best organized, when it starts with a sense of the poem's unity and works deductively from there. Explication sometimes gets so involved in retracing the process of reading, and with mapping out the intricacies of ambiguity and the like encountered on the way, that it tends to lead one away from the sense of unity. McLuhan, again, reflects this difficulty, which he makes the basis of a distinction between print and electronic media. This is of course a technical difficulty only, but explicators who have been most successful in overcoming it, such as Spitzer and Auerbach, raise implicitly other questions of theory.

Explication, in any case, has established itself as the centripetal counterpart to biographical criticism. It studies the poem rather than the poet, but it approaches every work of literature without much regard to its genre, and without building up any connecting links between one explication and the next. The next step in centripetal criticism is clearly to try to create a context which binds together our different efforts in critical reading. Such a context can only be sought for within literature itself.

The most obvious context within a literature for an individual poem is, of course, the entire output of its author. This is best studied through the consideration of the poet's structure of imagery, as every poet puts images together in his own way, and in a way that does not and cannot essentially change throughout his productive life. This is a "psychological" criticism based on the principle that what a poet succeeds in communicating to others is at least as important as what he fails to resolve for himself. The more important the poet, the more obvious it is that to read any poem of his without also reading the whole of his work is simply reading out of context, and leads to all the fallacies of isolated reading.

As soon as one thinks seriously about this, one begins to understand something of the immense importance of such features as convention, genre, and the recurring images of literature, which I call archetypes. To read a comedy of Shakespeare is not a very serious critical activity in itself until one has read all the comedies of Shakespeare. But as soon as one has done this, one becomes aware of certain conventional laws underlying the comic structure, which apply to all other writers of comedy. One begins, not merely to note the fact that the heroine often disguises herself as a boy, but to understand the reason for such conventions and their place in comedy as a whole. Such a study begins to clarify the outlines of a history of literature that operates within literature itself, and is not simply an external historical and non-literary "background" to literature.

At this point one begins to suspect that a poet's relation to poetry is very like a scientist's relation to his science or a scholar's to his scholarship. The scientist cannot think as a scientist until he has immersed himself in the structure of his science, and until whatever he thinks becomes an organic extension and development of the science, so that in a sense the science itself is thinking through him. Similarly, a poet immerses himself in the conventions of his time, writing in the same way that all his contemporaries are writing. As he matures, he takes on more individuality. But this individuality does not break away from the conventions of literature: it sinks more deeply into them. This is not the way in which criticism usually thinks of poets. Under the influence of the documentary or centrifugal conception of poetic meaning, they think rather of the poet as an ordinary man with a special knack of writing up an imaginative experience. But it is certainly the way in which poets have invariably talked about themselves. From Homer invoking a Muse to dictate his poem to him down to Rimbaud saying that for the poet the statement "je pense" ought to be "on me pense," poets have always insisted that they were simply places where something new, and yet something recognizably poetic, took place in poetry.

From here it is clear that one must take a final step, corresponding to the more unified historical perspectives of the Marxists and other social determinists. One has to see literature as a unified, coherent and autonomous body of imaginative experience historically conditioned but not historically determined. Conventions of literature are, within literature, stronger forces than social change; and poets in the London of Charles II, using the Courtly Love conventions, differ far less from their predecessors in the London of Richard II, using the same conventions, than the difference in the two ages would suggest.

From here one would have to proceed historically, and show how poetry arose in oral and preliterate cultures, and how, after writing and continuous prose developed, poetry became assimilated to the habits of a writing culture. The dead end of this assimilation is the present educational attitude to the teaching of literature. One normally studies a subject by starting at the center and working outwards to the periphery. A literary education which started a child off by teaching him the simpler rhythmical movements of poetry and by telling him stories, along with encouraging him to tell stories on his own, would be both following the child's mental education and recapitulating the history of human culture. As such education developed, it could become more conceptual and abstract, moving outwards to prose and finally to utilitarian prose. The more usual practice today is to present literature in reverse, starting with it as a technique of communication, and moving cautiously from utilitarian to literary speech, finally approaching the mystery of poetry, as cautiously as though it were boiling oil. This approach is founded on an absurd identification of prose with the language of ordinary speech. Actually prose is a very difficult and sophisticated way of conventionalizing ordinary speech, far more difficult than verse, and for younger children, at least, prose is a dead language with no direct relation to the way they actually speak.

The results of this educational muddle are clear to every teacher of literature. They are especially clear to me, teaching at the university level, when I see how many of my students regard poetry as a perverse and hopelessly obscure way of distorting ordinary prose statements. But two things have happened in the last decade or so. In the first place, oral culture has made a very strong resurgence, and we are once again in the age of the balladeer and the folk singer, whose poetry is directly addressed to a listening audience. In the second place, a habit of thinking in symbols and images has been fostered not only by this change in literature, but by the development of movies and television, which show extraordinary power of communicating through symbols. The result is that, while educators appear to be as ignorant and confused as ever, their victims are less helpless, and have been teaching themselves to a point at which poets who a generation ago were regarded as fantastically difficult are now regarded with much less panic. It only remains for educational theory to catch up with contemporary practice.

**John Owen Regan**

# Drug Outcomes and Language Programs: A Problem of Communication

The reading and writing curriculum serves the diety of communication with open devotion. For the sin of lack of communication between the teacher and student in this aspect of the school, the atonement might expectedly be high. However, this last year has revealed a widening gap between the secondary student and the school. This is part and parcel of a consolidating feeling of separateness that is developing among various students, drug using youths and bright articulate young agitators. A strange indication of this feeling of separateness on the part of the student was suggested to me in some work in an education drug-use project.

Confidential interviews of students were found to include students' statements of claimed drug outcomes which sounded remarkably like the aims of the poet and the language curriculum. My argument here will be that our secondary language classrooms are the scene of an unnoticed example of non-communication. One startling fact is that the situation has developed around high level aims of the language program in particular. Some results that youth claim are experiences of drug use are very similar to the results the language arts curriculum in the abstract is considered to be seeking.

I recently heard of a teacher who made an unusual lesson preparation. She took LSD before she inspected the nature trail along which her class was later to hike. She claimed this preparation enabled her to notice what others pass perhaps a hundred times nor care to see, as the poet might say. She claimed she was able to be aware, as are poets and artists, of each detail of sense as though for the first time. And she claimed the pupils reported the hike as the best they had experienced. The success of the lesson the teacher attributed to the "expanded awareness" of the drugs which she said stimulated her own observations and which she passed on to her pupils.

Henry Thoreau lived at Walden 'deliberately,' as he said, with nature that he might experience its 'essence.' He studied ways to expand his perceptive capacities so that he would notice and appreciate the texture of the environment; as he watched a detail, time passed as though he were himself a ripening element of nature. Thoreau's Walden activities sound very similar to what many school drug users declare are theirs while watching a leaf or a rock, a tree or wave.

Notice the similarity of the following lists of results claimed by school drug users and English curriculum. This list is extracted from some fifty California drug users from an upper middle class school district.

"It makes you aware"
"My mind is broadened"
"It does something to my perception"
"It expands the mind"
"It makes you appreciate the world"
"I am totally involved in the environment"
"I notice difference more"
"It makes me involved and appreciate people"
"It increases my potential"
"The world is more interesting"
"Grass teaches you how to find and notice"
"It's an intense total experience"
"It gives you a sense of awe of nature"
"It's something happening all around you, it's a total thing"
"I don't understand why people find boredom in living, every minute is different"
"You can appreciate your senses better"
"It put me in a world by myself. I was out in a field and it was early morning and I just sat there and watched every dew drop evaporate"
"I know that I have to accept the ugliness in me, and when I take the drug I can do it"

This second list includes education aims culled from curriculum outlines and education literature:

*Free Inquiry, Exploration, Spontaneity, Creativity, Imagination, Maximization of potential, Expanded awareness, Extended understanding, Broadened horizons, Appreciation of life or literature or world or nature, Development of perceptual skills, Stimulation of sensory perception, Involvement in the total environment, Respect for fellow man, Development of divergent thinking, Critical thinking, Sensitivity to beauty, differences,*

*shades of meaning, Self awareness, fulfillment, Creative expres-*
*sion, communication, Original thinking, Reading for maximum*
*meaning.*

Other drug using students with whom I have talked declare statements of the first list are their own independently created aims. Or they say the difference is that they live theirs whereas educators only say them like meaningless prayers. There are arguments to be made on the other side, of course. Certainly the educators' terms are more abstract, the students' more personal and intense. The teacher uses these terms often against his will in curriculum meetings: but they are there in the background of his professed rationale as they are in the spoken foreground of this growing drug experimenting and experienced student body.

In their interests in capacities to communicate and to be aware, the language teacher and school drug user unite. Both claim an array of communication-meaning-awareness skills as outcomes of their media. For the drug user marijuana and LSD are claimed as means of increasing a capacity to communicate and to be aware.

The language teacher wants to enhance a student's capacity to notice. We desire this development so that he will become aware of the detail and totality of his experience, so that he might live life abundantly. The language program uses reading, noticing and observing skills so that the student can become aware of himself and his environment. The teacher desires to provide the student with means of communicating and expressing himself—desires specifically the making and gathering of literary meaning, the expressing and communicating through literacy.

Yet even our most abstract stated objectives recognize that reading and writing are only one means of obtaining and transmitting meaning. Like the psychedelic happening, an English program today seeks to integrate the oral, visual, and tactile to provide a total experience. Literacy skills are part of larger awareness and communication media. The recruitment of the senses to assist efforts of producing an aware and communicating individual indicate the concern with 'the whole child' and his 'whole' awareness.

Curriculum guides and frameworks demonstrate the commitment to the specific and general skills of communication and awareness; the perception of beauty, of difference, of detail; the appreciation of life and literature; the ability to discriminate; reading for meaning; the creative reorganization of experience; the understanding of life and literature.

The pivotal position of 'meaning' in the school language program has been joined in our rhetoric by the word 'creativity,' another term that is shared by education and the underground network. But creativity is an illusive goal for us to praise in the schools, as indeed are each of the aims in the second list. At some point creativity in fact becomes such a rearrangement of the established perceptions and expectations that is most difficult to evaluate. The new meaning and communication media generated out of the psychedelic movement are based on a free movement of senses. The happenings and light shows, the pulsating overlying colors, forms and rhythms are part of the new means of expressing a communication, and of being aware. In the romantic period of literature when there were experiments in media and feeling, the basis was always words and sentences. The signs and symbols being read by our students are quite new. Each sense is recruited in what Ferlinghetti calls a 'Coney Island of the mind.'

The new media and methods appear very much like a derangement of the senses which might be experienced in the fantasy non-sequitor world of a Coney Island fun palace. But can we deny the creativity of the use of new media for communication of meaning? Sounds deceive; mirrors distort; colors, lights intermingle and fade into each other. Ask one of the students you know is taking drugs to describe these experiences. The description of the more articulate ones will remind you of Thoreau or Browning of Coney Island 'creative perceptions.' And these statements center around the popular language arts terms of 'meaning,' 'awareness,' and 'communication.'

One grade 11 girl I listened to talked of watching apparently for hours, with great delight the unaccustomed shapes that people and objects took on as LSD exerted its influence. A boy told of the novel elongation of time he experienced just as Thoreau reported the contraction and expansion of time as he lived 'deliberately' with nature. The word 'creativity' has also become an accepted value of some student world but they scorn our alternative while we are not aware of theirs. But, surely, the substance of our teaching's concern has the potential for being an alternative to the 'mind expanding,' 'communicating' drug experience. If the curriculum has the possibility of providing students with the tools of creating and communicating meaning, of appreciating and being aware, it can compete with the new forms some students are claiming to be effective.

What, after all, makes the reading of literature a more substantial clue to the inner expressive awareness than a mechanical, chemical, drug device? I have discussed this question with individuals from the drug world. While they will question the likelihood of success of non-drug means, they acknowledged that some men of literature, some artists have apparently achieved these states without drugs. They will acknowledge too that if a person could be the total master of his awareness he would be more of a human being than if he had to rely on outside aids like drugs. If we are convinced that the language arts program is a means of making meanings by which awareness can be developed and sensitivity to the details of the life achieved, let us prove our beliefs by our tangible works.

Let us directly discuss the question with those articulate, bright, students who are experimenting in mind expanding experience. If we have a medium that has strength we must use our skill to prove our product. We will not escape from the dilemma by denying the students' claims. We need not get into the jurisdiction of the legal, medical, psychological professions by arguing the vices or incapacitating aspects of drug use. Be those as they may, the educator has the responsibility to prove the power of his medium.

The new psychedelic songs are not the simple love-dove, moon-spoon ditties of the past. The images and words are complex and overlapping. They move and pulsate like the experience that the drug user is praising. The meanings are interlaid, they have levels, the metaphors and allusions are subtle and intricate. The rhythms, forms and words are products of new drives to communicate about new awarenesses. The adolescents read the multi-media message well as the creativity named song groups suggest. The Byrds, The Beatles, The Mother's of Invention, Canned Heat, Yard Birds, Blue Cheer, The Cream, The Association, Doors, Sopwith Camel, Jefferson Airplane, The Animals, Fraternity of Man, The Small Faces.

In the lyrics are seen many of the characteristics praised by language teachers—economical use of words; creative use of words, order, form, images, allusions; old and new metaphors, symbols. These and "Yellow Submarine," "2001," or "Hard Day's Night" comprise media and messages that can be considered versions of what the language program is all about.

The intent of the new literacy communication patterns and the musical, visual environment in which they are embedded is to provide a total involvement, an overlapping, intermoving, many faceted totality. Keats attempted the same; Faust aimed as high. The colors are those bright, brilliant, ultra type that the advertising world predictably adapted. The images fade and the psychedelic pictures we see in the underground press are suggested by the words, "a girl with kaleidoscope eyes." Whether our successful teaching has produced the new audience is a matter not open to precise judgment; however, all this can legitimately be regarded as an unexpected outgrowth of the work we have advocated for the writing and reading classes.

We have extolled experimentation: in knowing, in skilled use and understanding of words, symbols, metaphor, multi-media meaning, in expanded awareness, expression and communication of inner feelings. We have taught students to respond to the vivid expressions of others.

But of course the considerable use of words to explain the values of drug use does not tell us the actual meaning these words carry for the individual student. Then too, the educational use of the coinciding terms are more impersonal, other directed, future oriented; they are not taken from the immediate subjective level of the individual educator. They are drawn from a professional store of terms relating to the future becoming of others. What has been reported here may not be so much a question of non-communication as one, to use a statement by Charles Enos, of bivalent communication in which both groups are mutually misreading, in different ways, a previously internalized message.

Nevertheless, there is something instructive for me in the surprise I have encountered in drug using students when I have confronted them with the coincidence of terms. They are incredulous or annoyed to find their sensitive, almost religious creed is the substance of schooling's ethics.

When we talk to students about the claimed qualities of the drug experience or when we read the underground papers, we will at least become aware of terminology that may assist communication. We will also gain a perspective on the extent to which our aims may be reinterpreted by the new generation. But our greatest energy should be directed toward ensuring that this alternative available through the curriculum can be as efficient and effective as that being claimed for other sources. At least let us use what we see around us for some benefit. Or else we will never know what we might have done because we did not recognize the challenge many students are presenting to us.

# Views
# from
# the
# Margin

# John Farrell

# *Fun Among the Phonemes*

> A talk's a talk; it drops down dead
> After the bloody thing is said.
> A talk becomes mere fossilization
> When stripped of flesh for publication,
> A thing of leftover woofs and warps,
> Like making out with a day-old corpse.
> Vanished the mild and magnificent eyes,
> The scintillant wit, the mellifluous cry,
> The well-timed gesture, the anecdote,
> The slotted pause and the comical quote.
> Once a talk's ended, its body is slain.
> Only the cold bakemeats remain.

At Claremont, I talked about humor in the life of the teacher of English. I enjoyed my talk. At least I enjoyed the hearing myself talk. Certainly I enjoyed my first visit to California where tufted palmtrees featherdusted the seven a.m. sky. Most certainly, I enjoyed the hospitality of the campus, and the strangely eponymous names of Pitzer, Pomona; Harvey Mudd, Claremont and Scripps.

The title, *Fun among the Phonemes,* sanctified a marathonsworth of irresponsibility. It allowed the telling of tales, not merely with impunity, but even with the compulsion of a duty.


## Student Humor

Once, legend has it, a play-proud young dramatist brought the manuscript of his comedy to David Garrick. Garrick skimmed it perfunctorily and said, "I'm afraid your genius doesn't lie in comedy." The playwright went home and wrote a tragedy. Garrick liked it even less and said, "I'm afraid your genius doesn't lie in tragedy." "Damn, Mr. Garrick!" cried the writer. "Will you please be so kind as to tell me where in the devil my genius does lie?"

I would guess that the genius of your writing students lies much closer to humor than to tragedy. When young students attempt tragedy, they usually end up mired in bathos, with a sort of parody of *East Lynne.* They write of love and death without the artistic detachment necessary to render these no doubt overwhelming emotions palatable.

But exaggeration, the unstuffing of stuffed shirts, the puncturing of the balloons of adult pomposities—at this they excel. Restraint is not their thing. But hyperbole comes easily to a generation for whom all movies are epic, all groups larger than the Smothers Brothers are hordes of people, and all people of the opposite sex are living dolls.

Young people resonate to the groundswell of black humor, sick humor, and the theatre of the absurd. And it begins early. Ionesco might have looked with admiring eye on the insouciant irrelevancy of this seven-year-old:

> A noise walked into our house. It was all mouth and when it clump-clump-clumped, it flopped down its six front teeth and walked like a spider.
>
> "What have you got to eat?" the noise said. It was always hungry because when it ate, it ate all over.
>
> "Just pork and beans with pineapple," said my sister who had just come back from exercising the rhinoceros on the farm.
>
> So Mr. Noise ate all the pork and beans, and left the pineapple because the hole in the middle gives them a tummy-ache.

The cathartic effect of fictional death and tragedy are as remote to the young as Arcturus. The young are too obsessed by their narcissism for much genuine self-probing. When self-probing does penetrate, it is likely to come through the pores of mirth.

Take the case of Debra. Debra is intelligent, piquant, wonderful to the eyes. She is also spoiled, a born leader who is followed warily by reluctant apostles. Debra wrote:

> I've got this problem. I lose friends. I just can't understand it. I mean, really, I'm a knockout with long golden hair, naturally gold, too, and silky; you know the kind that all the ads say that girls have fun with. And great eyes with just fantastic batty lashes. My figure is bikini-good.
>
> I'm not actually intellectual, but I do get good marks; I mean, I sit right in the front row of all the classes, you know, and smile a lot. It doesn't hurt to let a teacher feel he's appreciated.

I've got scads of hobbies: I collect clothes and cosmetics and poodles, and, of course, men. When I sit back and take a look at myself, kind of overall, I'm a fairly fantastic person.

But I lose friends. I just don't understand it.

There is hope for the wry Debras of the world, and it often lies in the acidity of their pens.

I must omit almost entirely the rabbit-like fecundity of students in giving birth to unconscious humor. The unwitted laugh is one of the fringe benefits of the teacher of English. Margrit tells me that Gloucester in *King Lear* "had his eyes disembowelled." Randy informs me, man to man, that the Reverend Mr. Davidson in Maugham's "Rain" "sort of let loose with his ibid and adulterated." My mind drifts to Melina Mercouri who "loved Oedipus. He was so nice to his mother." Even *The Times,* with monocled aloofness, gets into the act: "The body of the girl was found decapitated and dismembered but not interfered with."

## No Time for Comedy

Like Queen Victoria and her nose-atilt virtue, Americans have recently carried self-pity to the point of self-indulgence. We need to hug to our breasts the corrosive but healing laughter of such medicine men as Mark Twain, James Thurber, Joseph Heller, Dorothy Parker, John Barth.

The genius of the English-speaking world lies in comedy. But somehow we think of comedy as a minor art form. Gilbert and Sullivan suffered a lifetime because they were writing musical satires when they thought they should have been writing *Revenger's Tragedies* and the *Missa Solemnis.* This carpet-bickering pair, plus Lewis Carroll, plus Canada's Stephen Leacock, felt compelled to look upon *Iolanthe* and *Alice in Wonderland* and the Mariposa County tales as mere divertissements in a world dedicated to symphonies, mathematics, and political economy.

Americans did not invent humor, but they ruthlessly hewed out the tough irreverent humor that seems so strongly and healthily American. American drama to me is Judy Holliday trying to make a junk tycoon couth rather than Blanche Dubois pathetically nymphomaniatising. If I wanted to take a play from the Twenties as representative of America, I would choose the sardonic *What Price Glory* rather than *The Hairy Ape.*

It is humor that pricks the bladder of our pretensions. A sense of humor is a sense of balance, a sense of proportion. It is more than a belly laugh. It is a comment on life. It is concerned with human imperfection. It tells us that bishops have to go to the bathroom. It tells us that, for most of us, it is more important to appear important than to be important. It tells us that, looked at dispassionately, sex is a somewhat ludicrous way of perpetuating the species a sort of cosmic guffaw. Comedy smiles at our godlike ambitions, but in the long run it slowly and impudently helps us to become more godlike.

Humor deals with the specific. You cannot be very funny about an abstraction. In life, one doesn't fall in love; one falls in love with Dorothy. For instance, it is difficult to be funny about poetasters as a group. But Mark Twain is funny when he becomes specific about an individual poetaster, the ineffable Emmeline Grangerford. Paul Hiebert, a Canadian professor (of Chemistry, no less), does the same thing with Sarah Binks, sweet songstress of Saskatchewan and winner of the Wheat Pool medal for poetry.

## The Jargonocracy

Surely some of our academics are letting their funny bones atrophy when they solemnly write their verbiage. I mean nonsense like this:

> The teacher in an educational institution must find a viable methodology for dealing with the disadvantaged child. This involves an exploration in depth of the rationale of the socioeconomic continuum in which the child finds his entity. It also involves an evaluation of the psycho-physical complex of the child plus the instructional elicitation of the subconscious traumata of his psyche.

Anyone who must call a school "an educational institution" and an environment "the socio-economic continuum in which the child finds his entity" lacks both a feeling for English and a sense of humor. I'm reminded of the philosophy professor of whom it was said, "He sounded as though he had fallen into an automatic washer with Immanuel Kant." Too many educators seem to have fallen into a mixmaster with John Dewey.

When I told one of my colleagues that I was going to speak on the topic, *Fun among the Phonemes,* he professed to be aghast. "No one will ever treat you seriously with that topic," he said. "They'll refuse to pay your expenses. Better change it to *The Risibility Phenomenon in the Educational Continuum.*"

Some self-styled experts in language know all about baking powder and flour, but nothing about cakes. They are no gourmets of language. They seem unaware of the kind of disciplined improvisation that produces fresh writing. Too often their students ask for mirth and are given morphemes, satire and are given syllabics, fun and are given phonemes. Sometimes we become so busy with the nitpicking that we forget how to laugh. We forget that more things are wrought by comedy and more evils headed off by ribaldry than this world dreams of. Humor destroys in order to build, hurts in order to heal.


## Educational Myths

Comedy allows one to play with ideas. I don't mean promulgate ideas, issue edicts, make pronouncements as though they were tablets from the mountain tops. I mean—*play* with ideas. This playing with ideas is the trickle of water that feeds the rivers of conversation. Conversation today has become either a cocktail-party jackrabbitting from topic to topic, or a series of monologues by specialists. What we need are men with fertile minds and gifted tongues, ready to theorize tentatively rather than decree definitively.

Perhaps this is what President Nixon meant when he said in his Inaugural Address, "We cannot learn from one another until we stop shouting at one another—until we can speak quietly enough so that the words can be heard as well as the voices." When McLuhan says that the medium is the message, he seems to be saying that it is the voice that matters, not the words; it doesn't matter overmuch what you say as long as you yell loud and in living color. This absense of humor, this willynilly commitment to commitment, can well be the road to destruction, anarchy, nihilism, to be replaced, if history be any guide, by an ultimate tyranny.

What I am saying, I suppose, is that when passion has made change possible, a sort of humorous detachment is necessary to make the change workable. Life, for me, is bearable only through employing a fair measure of good-natured cynicism. I would hope to steer a middle course between what James Billington has called "the passionless mind" of the academic and "the mindless passion" of the student.

When I begin playing with ideas, I often find myself on the picket line with the student. I become skeptical about many of the grand myths of education. There is, for instance, the Course Complex. In Canada, when anything goes wrong, we try one of two solutions: either a Royal Commission or a new school course. Someone makes sin conveniently surreptitious by inventing a contraceptive pill? O.K. Course in family living. Bloody weekend on the speedways? O.K. Driver training courses. Growing frequency of Reno divorces? O.K. More household science courses. Canadians have difficulty doing anything from playing a bridge game to procreating children without taking a course.

I wonder how long we can keep on proliferating courses all over the educational maternity ward. Why, some mothers will not even venture to change a diaper without resorting to the Gospel according to St. Spock. Universities are the worst breeding grounds of all for these calendar malignancies. Surely the basis of a worthwhile education is simple: sound knowledge, clear thinking about the knowledge, and the ability to get the knowledge and the thinking together in clear speech and clear writing.

Closely linked to the Course Complex is the Diploma Dilemma. Nowdays you need a degree in chefmanship to make a bowl of clam chowder. Soon every caretaker in the country is going to be fired unless he holds a sheepskin in Sanitary Engineering, specializing in dustbane or writing a 200-page dissertation on plugged sinks and elbow joints. The trouble is that the diploma, the degree, the piece of paper, the label, have become more important than the education they are supposed to represent. Once received, the diploma all too often leads to the exultant cry, "Thank God my education is finished for life!"

A third myth is called the Knowledge Explosion. It goes like this: the fund of human knowledge has increased more the past thirty years than in all the previous thirty centuries. If your generation had a thousand things to learn in school, your children have five thousand. Therefore teachers must keep stuffing harder and harder, and children must keep swallowing faster and faster and longer and longer in order to keep pace. Education becomes a sort of desperate race between human knowledge multiplying like rabbits fed with aphrodisiacs and human capacity for digesting rabbit stew.

Of the knowledge explosion there is no doubt. The myth arises out of the panic philosophy that has gone with it. The myth is based on the theory that schools are places where you stuff children like Thanksgiving turkeys and give them a certificate (for life) as soon as they are stuffed enough. But education should not be a stuffing of the mind. It should be a training of the mind so that it can stuff itself later if the occasion arises.

I've a firm notion that, if Isaac Newton could meet a modern physicist like Einstein, he would with his razor-sharp mind bring himself up-to-date on modern physics within a week or so. He would bridge the knowledge chasm of the centuries easily because he would bring to the task a trained mind and not a stuffed mind.

The fourth myth might be called the Mechanical Mentor myth. It embraces the view that as long as you have a whole lot of stuff in a school that plugs in and lights up and costs a lot of money and has chrome trimmings you can replace teachers and books in the future education of students. This can be the most dangerous myth of all. I have little faith in the transistorized teacher.

No teacher in his right mind would reject the hardware if it were suited to what he is doing. However, I find the truce between me and the machine becoming an increasingly uneasy one. Why, I can remember when a hectograph was exciting. Nowadays teachers are like the Beatles and the Vanilla Fudge—they don't get anywhere unless they are electrified. Often, though, it seems that as teaching becomes more electrical, it also becomes less electrifying.

A machine is efficient, accurate, fast. The trouble is that it just doesn't give a damn about children. It is aloof, impersonal. It has no sense of values. It is part of the dehumanisation of our society. It does not laugh, it does not cry, it does not care. Teaching by machinery is like conceiving children by artificial insemination. It may be efficient, but it isn't much fun on a cold Canadian night. It lacks human warmth, human dignity, human understanding, human love. Robot education can too easily lead to robot products. As one student wrote, "At university, I am becoming increasingly a cipher, taught a pilfer knowledge, to pretend on examinations it's my own, and be prepared to have a mechanical monster assess the state of my mind and my feelings. It's a dismal business."

## Wit and Humor

When humor puts on white tie and tails, we call it wit. Wit is verbal, rather than physical, sophisticated rather than earth-bound. It is more likely to result in a private chuckle than in a public guffaw.

A marriage counsellor might take hours to say what Stephen Leacok said in seconds: "Many a man in love with a dimple makes the mistake of marrying the whole girl." Each of us has considered certain people unpleasant, but it took Walter Prescott Webb to say, "He's the kind of man that makes you wish birth control could be retroactive." Oscar Wilde impaled the female psyche on a specimen board when he said, "Women begin by resisting a man's advances and end by blocking his retreat." "If triangles had a god," said Voltaire, "he would have three sides," and thus he capsulized entire theological tomes.

These epigrams are not nonsense. They contain a basic attempt to explore ideas and to find truth. Wit is the distillation of wisdom by means of the ingenious and the irreverent.

## The Truths of Literature

The crowning value of humor is to provide man with a working philosophy of life. Humor enables a man to meet the minor troubles of life with the anodyne of laughter, and the major tragedies with a certain dignified equanimity.

Our lives should be floodlighted by two kinds of truth: the truth of science and the truth of literature. The truth of science has been dominant over the last century. Yet, while science provides the picture tube, it isn't much help in deciding what pictures to show. Science enables us to talk with three men encircling the moon, but does not tell us how to talk with our own wife, or our own children, or our own students. A scientific historian tells us what Napoleon's Russian campaign was like in a strategic sense, but only a Tolstoy can tell us what the icy trek and the spilled blood and the naked terror were like to the individual soldier.

And each of us remains an individual despite the injunctions against bending or stapling or mutilating. I resist being categorized. I refuse to be a consumer, a middle-income type, a good credit risk, a WASP, a Democrat, a Republican, an average voter. I refuse to become Auden's unknown citizen. I want to withdraw into my uniqueness. I feel that Shakespeare and Dostoevsky and Goethe knew this, but I never really feel that the new-day scientists of the western world, the economists, the psychologists, the sociologists, see me as any more than a nondescript ant on a statistical antheap.

Science and computers want to place me in one of two categories. That's the way they work, the only way they can work. It's called the binary system. It's the either-or syndrome. It's also a big part of our modern malaise. I'm negro or I'm white. I'm high I.Q. or low I.Q. I'm conservative or radical. I'm square or hip. I'm student or establishment. I'm communist or capitalist. I'm scientist or humanist. Or, at its most elemental, I'm man or I'm woman. And we feel easy in this simplistic world of all or nothing. We have a name for it: committed, involved. "Get involved, man," I'm told. But I notice that when someone wants me to jump off the fence, he always wants me to jump off on his side.

Once I'm placed in a category, I'm stereotyped: I'm the hot-tempered Irishman, the thrifty Scot, the lazy Indian, the lascivious Turk, the inscrutable Oriental. Someone has said that if people can really be divided into two categories, they are: those who think people can be divided into two categories; those who do not.

Surely one of the chief functions of literature, especially humorous literature, is to make us aware of the big gray area in the middle that allows me to be proudly me. Through humor we discover that we cannot line up the sinners on one side of the football field and the saints on the other side. There are lively sinners and there are dull saints. Between the hells of sin and the heavens of purity lies a region that most of us inhabit, a land of rather drab peccadilloes and somewhat offcolor virtues. A sense of humor is the surest safeguard against the sheep-goats division. Even the best of us do sneaky things in bathrooms and bedrooms, and pimps and prostitutes gather sentimentally around the bawdy-house Christmas tree.

Clearly in the twentieth century one cannot be against science. I've not the slightest desire to chop up my television set, throw my automobile on the nearest junkpile, or huddle, during a prairie blizzard, outdoors in a privy with crescentmoon ventilation, as I once did. There is a place, an important place, for science in education and teaching.

The trouble comes when you begin *to equate* science with education, when you try to make human relations and love and teaching and values the slaves of standard deviations, coefficients of correlation, and all the other abracadabra. Half the riots in universities have come about because the students feel frustrated by the increasing mechanization of higher education and machine-like teaching. Sometimes the student in desperation has cried, "Hold! Enough!" He feels that no one up there likes him. He finds that he can't be friendly or reasonable with a machine. In fact, it is difficult to be much of anything with a machine. In education as in sex, it's impossible to replace the personal factor. Robert Frost said, "There's a whole half of our lives that cannot be made a science of." And it is the key part of our lives if our concern be with human happiness and individual fulfillment.

As you must have guessed by now, I have no profound research discoveries to report. I simply wish to reaffirm my faith in the teacher as the sentient and warm person without whom effective schools cannot exist. The teacher of English is no mere transmittor of knowledge. She is a human being. She is one of our last hopes. The problems of the world all the way from Watts to Winnipeg, from Bangkok to Biafra, are human problems more than they are technological problems.

It is the teacher who can read your poems, laugh at your jokes, understand your uniqueness as a person even though you may have a slight difficulty in the use of "who" and "whom," who can share your growing up. To put it simply, the teacher cares. In a world where more and more of us are caring less and less, this is not unimportant.

Edward Moreno

# The View from the Margin

## What Is the Margin?

Let us begin by reaffirming the reality that the Anglo-American is the majority in the land, but that this picture changes very radically in some communities. Perhaps because most Anglo-Americans are conscious of the first part of this reality, and chose to ignore the second equally important part, they tend to consider other cultures unintelligible or alien, with no proper place in American life, even when such cultures are truly native to American soil, or were there before the Anglo culture pushed them to the side. Thus, while a few very perceptive social scientists recognize the existence of the Mexican American and his culture as part of the present day reality of America, for the rest, our lot is called "culturally deprived," our adjustment to, and functioning in the general culture is a question of assimilation, or non-assimilation, or marginalism. Or to put it into the general cliche, what the melting pot cannot melt is "hard core," maladjusted, peripheral. America is the "unum," the "pluribus" must be erased. There must be one culture, one way of thinking, one single language. Even the indivisibility of our political nation must be expressed as physical and intellectual monochromism, a perfect theory, but a reality incompatible with the way America truly is. In this land of ours, almost all the languages of the Earth are spoken daily; as a people, we can claim ascendants or relatives in almost all corners of the world, and no racial stock, no cultural strain can claim monopoly to being a true, loyal, good American.

## Wide and Narrow Margins

We pride ourselves in our ability to tolerate dissent, to criticize ourselves, and to search for better ways of mutual understanding. With the physical and economic means at our disposal, we travel to foreign lands for pleasure or business of all kinds. We fall in love with señoritas and geishas, get excited with toros and pagodas, learn quaint or exotic customs, come to appreciate foods and fads. We drink gallons of imported alcohols, drive a Volkswagen if we are commoners, a Mercedes or Jaguar if sophisticates or professors of education, dress our women in Chinese silks, photograph our kids with Japanese cameras. We dance to the Liverpool sound, and embellish our gaming nights with dancers imported from Montmartre or from Baia. We feed a famished India, ally our progress with our neighbors' poverty, and fill with our gold the coffers of the most covetous Frenchman we have ever known. We make our presence felt in Saigon, Canberra, Moscow or Peking. And, despite all our external internationalism, our all embracing ecumenism, we are provincial and parochial to the point of almost total intolerance of the expression of cultural manifestations dissimilar to ours, in our midst.

## To the Other Side

From my Anglo teachers, I have learned an important thought, that to study any subject in depth, to really understand it, I must pay attention not only to the main text, but to all references and marginal notes. Let me give you back your own recommendation; in studying the ways to improve the education and opportunities for my people, the Mexican American people and their children, *read beyond the printed page.*

Let us discuss what the orthodox reference does not do, and examine, even if partially, the reverse of the question. Few, if any, references available are written by Mexican Americans, and even those that are cannot avoid circularity, that is quoting and requoting the Anglo point of view. There are works of Mexican and Latin American writers available, but even when somewhat applicable to the people of those origins in our midst, most of those works are unknown to you, or are written in the "alien" tongue.

So come with me to the very edge of the eight-point Roman bold, give a broad spiritual jump, and take a trip with me to that you call "the margin." This is the AGE OF THE TRIP, and the trip with me will be less dangerous and costly than the psychedelic, but perhaps more effective in amplifying perception and expanding consciousness.

## Who Is Marginal

Despite what James B. Conant, Martin Mayer, and vice-admiral Rickover may say to the contrary, we know we have one of the best systems of education in the world. We educate teachers better and longer than most other nations to keep it that way. We teach them objectivity and methods of research. We try to make them expert in the art of never jumping to conclusions; well, at least not much ahead of the principal. We force upon them volumes of social science, and psychology, so that they can meet the needs of the child. For some fortunate ones we even have invented the "Sabbatical leave," to let them go abroad, see the world, and return with a more liberal perception.

Then, one day, we give them an assignment in Boyle Heights, La Puente, or Pacoima, among children of Mexican descent, who are bilingual, have parents who, for their communication, prefer that tongue-twisting Spanish . . . and all our objectivity, preparation, internationalism, and liberal perception go out the window with that simple assignment. Our very nature claims that such a situation is intolerable . . . How those parents are doing a disservice to their own kids . . . and "If they like Spanish so much, why don't they leave the country, and go to where only Spanish is spoken . . ." With a mixture of chauvinism and evangelistic hypocrisy, and thundering against inconsiderate aliens, we set ourselves to change their reality to our own image and semblance. Quaintness then loses all its exotic attraction, and "one nation" means no cultural pluralities. Their "other-ness" is to our "we-ness" a pain in the neck . . . The margin, man, the unadapted, hard-core, resistant, unmelting, culturally deprived margin. Anathema!

Perhaps it is a question of perception. The Mexican and Latin American in our country are today a reality of some seven million people. A dynamic, measurable, tangible reality, bigger than the ideal ratio per class we face at Lincoln High, or Riggin Elementary in East Los Angeles. Seven million people; more people than in any of the Central American Republics, or some of the South American countries, or several of the new African states put together. Seven million people with a real live language, real live desires and aspirations, real presence in the life of the nation; as American as the rest of us; not separatist as the French Canadien, not oriented towards White Power, or Black Power, or Mexican chili powder, . . . power, I mean, but loyal, good Americans, as the ratio of Medals of Honor per capita, and the number of fallen in battle show with largesse.

True; we have our differences of opinion from conceiving Paradise as a boarding house for American tourists in Puerto Vallarta, to believing that total acceptance of, and total submission to the Anglo culture is going to bring the individual total acceptance by, and total admission to the Anglo culture. But this great mass, whose cultural tenets were already a reality in

America at the time the tide of Manifest Destiny swept towards the West, has a right to remain as another one of our life influences. Not subordinate, not unequal, inferior or destructible, but side by side with the Anglo culture, in full harmony with it, in perfect adjustment and adaptation, interwoven, yet apparent. That was the covenant, and that is the righted guarantee. And it is consonant with our insistent clamor for individual freedoms and rights, and the main text of the book of our national existence.

## Margin or Cultural Thread

We admit that there are various orders, or genre of us Mexican Americans, Hispanos, Latins, what-have-you. But almost all of us are in agreement that, despite our differences of thought, the ability to master the English language is a demand from reality we cannot ignore, and that although one is not a necessary consequence of the other, a better mastery may better our chances of success. There is no conflict with the feeling of many Latin parents that, at present, they can teach better Spanish to their children than our schools can; nor is there any quarrel with the belief that some of our children may never need to speak Spanish in their lives. Our main contentions are, as I see them: 1) with the orthodox methods used in teaching children from bilingual, bicultural families; 2) with the emphasis on imposing myths and orthodoxies on the curricula, at the expense of the real needs of the child; 3) with the concept that the bicultural person is marginal, unhappy, incompletely adjusted, and maladapted; 4) with the idea that the educator, being the only expert, has little or nothing to learn from the Mexican American parent and his culture; and, 5) with the concept that the Americanization process is the formal, academic process that ends with the last bell of the last period of the day in the case of the child, or with the granting of the High School diploma in the case of the adult.

## Teaching the Marginal Child

Undoubtedly, one of the greatest needs of the child in some of our barrios is to communicate better in English. But when for 18 years or more, I have observed that the schools have advanced very little in this field of teaching the child to communicate, I must conclude that there must be something wrong in the system. Even including some of the compensatory programs, the same methods have produced failure after failure, year after year. Isn't it time to take a good look at the system, and stop blaming the child alone?

Out of 1019 pupils in the Harrison Street School, at least 957 are of Spanish surname. In a class of 25 to 32 pupils of this type, and with one

Anglo American teacher, where do you place the margin? Who must begin making allowances? With what experiences must you begin building that proficiency you consider desirable? Have we ever stopped to consider that in such a situation, the annoying reality is that the real marginal person, the true minority is the teacher, and not the pupils?

Specialized programs such as the Tenaya School project in Merced, the NES program of Belmont High in Los Angeles, and the hush-hush Malabar Reading Project in East Los Angeles, have confirmed my suspicions that more daring and nonorthodox methods are needed to teach English to our children. These are methods in which the communication resources a child brings to school, even if these resources are that confusing mixture of Spanish and English we irreverently call "Chicanglish," are fully considered and used. These are methods in which origin, cultural background, language and parental influences are totally accepted as "necessary," and are even recognized and encouraged. These are methods in which the conversion to English is effected gradually, without drastic demands of total abjuration of loyalty to one's own culture, nor the adoption of a false role, nor the suffering of undue anxiety and opprobrious confusion.

And, before anyone mentions the "Hawthorne effect," that defense many of us use when we try to cover our own indolence, jealousies, or impotence to formulate and carry to success new experiments, let us learn all we can about the project mentioned, and let us see them in operation. With pleasant surprise we will notice the change in affect, perception and participation attained, for instance in the Spanish-for-Spanish-speaking group at Belmont High; or the community pride developed by Malabar and its Reading Project; or the degree of cohesiveness and enthusiasm noted at the Tenaya School; or how similar methods can operate in another dissimilar culture, such as the Japanese, as proven by the success of the Maryknoll Mission School. Then, those accustomed to the mutism, reticence, shyness and withdrawal of the bilingual school boy, will perceive a dynamic, vocal, aggressive, articulate, participating and accomplishing student, who has acquired a new pride in playing the role of what he really is. The difference might lead us to speculate that perhaps a little more of that which produces the "Hawthorne effect," is what is needed to teach the bilingual, bicultural child.

## When We Impose Our Orthodoxies

When someone tries to impose his orthodoxy upon children of another cultural orientation, scenes like this develop. Margarita, a child of Mexican American extraction, on her first day in second grade is asked to introduce herself to the class. Already under undue anxiety, for, in her culture, modesty is a prime virtue, she blurts: "I am Margarita ..." The rhythmic cadenzas of Darío's poem still dance in her ears,

> "Este era uney que tenía
> un palacio de diamantes ...
> ... un quiosco de malaquita,
> un gran manto de tissú,
> y una gentil princesita,
> tan bonita, Margarita,
> tan bonita como tú."

Then, the cold lash of reality across the face. In precise, and perfectly rounded syllables, the teacher retorts, "Yes, but you know now that we are in an A-mér-i-can school. So your name is *really* Margaret. ... Right, children?"

American has now all the exclusivist connotations of the zealot's gospel. But the stoning of the sinner cannot be yet fully enjoyed, nor justified by her conscience without the full assent of the captive audience. So, Margarita, who for all the seven years of her life has been Margarita, must now be a different child, or herself, but under false pretenses. For Mrs. All-Understanding-and-Accepting, requires, for total acceptance, that one become ashamed of what one really is, and that after public abjuration, one pretend to be what one really is not. An isolated incident? Oh, no! This is a daily occurrence in many of our schools.

Can you now imagine the case of a child from very traditional parents, who was named in honor of the saint of the day, Petronila, or Pancracia. Can you imagine the day of the rechristening ... the teasing thereafter in the play yard ... the unbearable psychic pain ... Would you believe "Peternelle," or "Punkcraze" ...?

Dealing with the psychiatric patient, and from the lips of master therapists, I learned the meaning of the concept "depersonalization," the state in which a person loses the feeling of his own reality, which is characteristic, I was told, of a serious personality deterioration. So the price of adjustment we are exacting from the child in our classes, is the very symptom the psychiatrist is trying to cure in his patient in the clinic. We are asking our children to escape from their own identity, culture, and reality, and adopt a false role. No wonder the healthy personality rebels against blind compliance. No wonder those who submit sometimes show such a shallow affect and disloyalty to Anglo and Latin cultures alike, and so tenaciously cling to that strange world of their own fabrication, that of being a nonbeing.

## Unhappy Who ... ?

Someone in the literature began the rumor that what is generally called the "marginal man" is an unhappy being, not full Anglo, nor fully Latin; with problems of one side and from the other. I do not think of George Santayana as marginal par excellence, or of Salvador de Madariaga, or the hundred others who attained intellectual, economic, and social success, as unhappy or maladapted despite maintaining their own identity. On the contrary. With the tendency our abundant civilization has to satiate, and cause ennui, isn't it fortunate he who can ascend, as well as rise, fall as well as descend, who can add depth and profoundness to his expression: who can titillate his palate, tired of roast beef and hamburgers, with paella, and who tired of roast turkey can sink in the ardent sea of mole oaxaqueno, "black as sin and hot as hell, and as both so tempting . . ." who can delight his full senses with the velvety emerald of the guacamole, and can find some new pleasures with the pungent tastes of the guava and the quince compote . . .?

Leave the manacles of the Liverpool sound and the Nashville twang for the intolerant monocultural who prefers his state of grace. I have, in addition to that, the mariachis that Herb Alpert appropriated for his un-rivalled success, the amorous tempo of my beloved bolero that fascinated George Gershwin, and the picturesque impressionism of Granados and Albeniz which so impressed Leonard Bernstein. Why should I live in an impenetrable one-room castle? I want for my expression the primitive beauty of the Walt Whitman verse, or the refined elegance of Ruben Dario. For my conceptions of Democracy I want the expressions of Lincoln and the maxims of Juarez. I wish to drink, taste and enjoy the same fountains that delighted Washington Irving, John Steinbeck, and Ernest Hemingway, among many . . . Look, ma . . . no chains!

## Reading the Marginal Notes

The emphasis on the total abandonment of the maternal language and culture that many educators express as necessary to succeed in school, leaves me baffled for its inconsistency. In order to be able to pick it up again at High School, I must at the elementary level, forget my language. What will later be a requirement, I am now required to forget. To better under-stand a world in which my country has an undeniable pre-eminence, and in order to understand my country and its formation, I must abandon my present participation in, and understanding of, one of the cultures of my own country. To free myself from provincialism, I must adopt parochialism. We, who believe that we must give our children the richest, amplest, most complete, and varied and expensive, and practical education, must place our children from so called minorities in an emotional concentration camp where we must feed them the monocultural inflexible line. This, when we learned as V. G. Childe said that "Human minds are not . . . mass produced machines into which uniform experience has only to be fed for them to turn out uniform thought"?*

## But We Are the Experts

But we are the experts. The teacher is supposed to know all the liturgy and incantations which produce "good Americans." And these unsophisticated parents, what can they really offer?

These parents which many educators consider so poor, unreliable, culturally disadvantaged, dull and unsophisticated, are a very interesting lot, if we take at least the trouble to know a little bit more about them.

Poor? Despite the lack of education, their average income is over $5700 per year. Unreliable? Their credit rating is excellent, in general; their savings amount to quite a lot at Panamerican Bank, their own bank, and at Eastland, Atlantic, Home, Monarch and other savings associations. Illiterate? They support two local dailies, seven other daily editions of Mexican papers, more than one hundred weekly and monthly magazines of all topics, and from one of their specialized bookstores alone, they buy more than 1200 volumes per month, ranging from 89 cent paperbacks to 59 dollar deluxe editions. At La Casa del Mexicano, they have for their perusal too, more than five thousand volumes of all topics.

Disinterested? They listen to two full-time radio stations and a variety of other programs, watch two television stations, have more than seventy-two clubs, and support a movie house showing Spanish language films in almost everyone of their neighborhoods.

Culturally disadvantaged? These dull nonsophisticates prodded the Mexican government into exhibiting in Los Angeles the Masterworks of Mexican Arts, the most fabulous exposition the local museum has ever seen. They also persisted, until the Native Arts and Crafts Exposition of Mexico came here, where it was a tremendous success despite the miserable locale where it was presented; and their support of the Ballet Folklorico de Mexico has allowed the troupe to visit this city three times already.

Why then, do the same teachers who rave and rant about cold cultural artifacts, or marvel at the dazzling dances, consider as dull the individuals to whom such rich manifestations of culture really belong?

When we blame the Mexican American for being uncommunicative and rustic, couldn't we just search a little within ourselves to see if perhaps

---

*V. G. Childe, *Social Words of Knowledge.* Hobhouse Memorial Lectures 1941–50 (London: Oxford Univ. Press, 1952).

our superior attitude has helped alienate them? With this question in mind one of our local schools decided to be revolutionary. When the parents did not come to the school, the teachers went to the parents' homes; when the program for the school year was planned, the school asked the parents to help it set curricula, and to make to the original plan the necessary changes, and then they began implementing them. And it went beyond the cold formalities of the "Open School Day," and established the "Open School Year." Harmony and communication improved to such a point that last Christmas, in the supposedly wild and dangerous neighborhood, the teachers, on their own time went Christmas-caroling, receiving only the warmest and friendliest welcome ever. Ask Malabar who has taught what to whom in this unique experiment. The answer is worth at least six additional credits in Human Relations.

### Understanding the CF's

Americanization should not be the process that ends with the last bell of the last period of the day, and the granting of the high school diploma. Forced by the realities observed in some of our barrios, some of us have tried to develop the concept of "schools that work." This is a school which never closes, but acts as a real community center, teaching and learning; where, when the children have gone home, the other aspect of total service to the community can begin. This school not only teaches formal curricula, but it is also the place where all the community needs are traded for services. It is the school that has become a repository for the cultural manifestations of the locale, that helps develop local talent in all orders of life; that operates cultural fairs, and even acts as town forum. With such a school, with such a penetration into the community, can you imagine the savings just in the reduction of vandalism against it? Can you imagine parents giving you a hand as volunteers with your groups, your clerical details, your beautification projects? Can you imagine the school helping the individual in consumer programs, better understanding of the American system of government, serving as clinic, acting as a museum, theatre, and so forth, a true part of the community?

### Let Us Erase the Margin

I am encouraged by the results we are beginning to observe even in a scanty way, and by the interest of the governments at all levels, by State Teachers Associations, the NEA, and other professional associations in compensatory programs. But there is much yet to be accomplished, especially in the revision of textbooks and programs, which have failed to give the Mexican American the feeling that he and his culture are a real part of America past and present. And although change is difficult to come by, it is already occurring. We need only to speed it. The Malabar Reading Project, with its first objective investigation and new methodologies, is a great hope for the elementary level. So is the Tenaya Intermediate School project for the junior level.

For High School, let's now experiment, for instance, with an ungraded plan of 23-minute units instead of the sacrosanct 48-minute unit, a program in which there is regrouping according to the ability of the student, and the result of his entrance tests. In this program, and wherever possible, all academic requirements are conducted in Spanish. Spanish-for-Spanish-speaking is conducted as in the experimental plan of Belmont High, but with at least one daily period devoted to comparative language structure. We now have a large block for English as a second language. Let's also include now the traditional "buddy system" of the Army, and allow those with greater proficiency in English help teach the less proficient student. It is an idea.

We have all kinds of clubs. How about beginning a new one, right at the elementary level? At first we are the Cabrillos interested in California as it has really been; then we move to the intermediate level, a Columbus Club, for a comparative study of cultures, and finally we expand to the Panamerican Club in High School, for deeper studies in all areas about Latin America. In all three levels we will require participation in cultural manifestations of folkloric, interpretive, pictorial or musical art. It's another idea.

We want quality education, and inventiveness, creativeness, resourcefulness, and community involvement are the only ways to get it. Texts, materials, aids and resources we do not now possess can be obtained or created. We are creating some of them right now.

Business and Industry have discovered the necessity of handling our people as another one of their vertical markets. But with them, it is perhaps imperative for survival. Well, in their case the success and rewards have been plentiful. How long does education have to wait for its success?

The problem is not so big. Bring yourselves to full acceptance and understanding of us, we will bring ourselves and our children to full development and complete accomplishment as you define it. Give us your instant of positive recognition, we'll give you our lifetime of total involvement.

## Epilogue

We are celebrating this year the Centennial of Ruben Darío, the prince of poets of Spanish Literature. I'd like to close with one of his most famous epigrams. If you cannot translate it yourselves, have it translated. It is full of insight. It reads:

> Ve un zorzal a un pavo real
> que se espanta y gallardea;
> le mira la pata fea
> y exclama: "¡Horrible Animal!"
> sin ver la pluma oriental
> el pájaro papanatas.
> Gentes que llaman sensatas
> son otros tantos zorzales
> que si encuentran pavos reales
> sólo les miran las patas.*

Happy insight, ladies and gentlemen.

*Darío, Rubén, *Poesías completas,* Aguilar, S.A. de ediciones (Madrid, 1954).

# Y. Arturo Cabrera

## *Schizophrenia in the Southwest**

Mexican-Americans and Anglos live in different worlds with reference to each other. Contrary to a complacent belief, Anglos really do not know the Mexican-Americans even though the two frequently interact with each other in occupational and other distant roles. Mexican-Americans do not always function effectively in the United States for the simple reason that their individual and group roles in society are uncertain and full of ambiguities. Now, other Spanish-speaking people in the United States may share with Mexican-Americans, in part but not totally, the effects of belonging to minority ethnic, language, and culture groups in a society which essentially values the Puritan ethic and much that it implies and tends to relegate culturally different groups to subordinate roles.

### Premise

The life of Mexican-Americans is complicated by certain fictions in the worlds in which they live. One of these worlds has historical foundations in Europe, another is Indo-Mexican with its folk-culture characteristics, and a third is Anglo-American(1). Because an individual's role in each world is fluid, or on a continuum from one polarity to another, none of these worlds becomes a full reality for Mexican-Americans. These worlds are mixtures of fact and fancy, and individuals of Mexican ancestry continually attempt to maintain an equilibrium but they are not always successful. The Anglo tendency to place people and groups into stereotypic roles exacerbates the existing error.

*Revised November, 1971, University of Colorado.

The dilemma of Anglos is compounded by the fragments of Hispanic tradition and history they have learned. Obviously, the past political and economic episodes between the United States and Mexico in a distorted sense occupy a prominent role in the Southwest. A vital distinction exists, however, between the conflicts and split worlds within which Anglos and Mexican-Americans must operate. The impact and consequences of inadequate perceptions for the Anglos in these relationships are peripheral and often inconsequential. Mexican-Americans are continually faced with crises, and they must select those elements from their worlds that will best contribute to an adequate adjustment in a society controlled by Anglos. Tragically, some Mexican-Americans are unable to transcend the conflicts they are forced to face. In a final sense the situation for both groups is similar to the idea of the split personality, and a condition akin to schizophrenia can be said to exist in the Southwest. This situation faces both Anglos and Mexican-Americans. For the Anglos at worst it can be an irritant, but for many Mexican-Americans it is a matter of survival.

## Studies and Research

Upset by social and civil rights confrontations, agency people in the United States are making efforts to learn more about disadvantaged minorities. As this information relates to the Spanish-speaking, much has been unearthed in dusty library archives that was published as long ago as thirty and forty years.

Considerable review of these older studies has been undertaken, and credit *must* be given to some of the older classic references. But time is a factor, and though many of these studies have historical value they lack much contemporary relevance. Scholarly commitment has simply not kept pace with developments and alterations which have taken place in the status of this ethnic group. Recent publications, though providing an historical orientation and helping to initiate an awareness of the plight of the group, do not make substantial contributions to our knowledge of what is happening to Mexican-Americans today. Some Mexican-Americans are caught in the vortex of accelerated alienation while others have managed to slip into the mainstream without so much as a ripple. These older sources do not provide sound bases for projection and planning of programs for this ethnically-different minority group.

## Romanticized Hispanic History

The romanticism cranked into the usual treatment of the historical role of the early Spanish-speaking in America is an example of unreality facing Americans of Mexican descent.

Legends about the early California mission days and of the resolute Spanish *Conquistadores* who explored the American Southwest in search for the Seven Cities of Cíbola are part of the unreality for Mexican-Americans. As traditionally emphasized, these events clash with the Mexicanism in their personal orientation. Out of this created fiction Anglos have established, in their formal and informal learning structures, value hierarchies between European and Indo-Mexican relationships of a superordinate and subordinate quality (2).

The historical and folk culture descriptions in America's history books and popular media which serve as bases for most reports about Mexicans and Mexican-Americans evoke two types of images. One of them includes dark-eyed *señoritas* with roses in their hair, dark men on spirited horses, excitement at three in the afternoon with the running of the bulls, of sprawling haciendas which were managed in a manorial style—leisurely, abundantly, inefficiently, but always grandly and graciously.

The other side of the coin reflects a folk culture base which conjures images of the *indio* and of the *peon* who were victims of a feudal system which was part of the heritage from Europe. Out of this folk-culture concept a way of life emerges. A style of living allegedly dominated by present-time orientation, of respect for and docility to authoritarian institutions, of low deferred gratification, of fatalistic attitudes toward life, of obeisance to a highly structured church, of low expectations for personal social mobility, and consequently, of little need for formal education (3). This and more is the legacy of a folk-culture the descendants of Mexicans are believed to share.

Anglos have accepted these fictions of history with little question, even though today there is growing evidence of their limited relevance to contemporary life (4). The truth is that Mexican-Americans feel little attachment to most of this portrayed past. Transcending the psychological distinction between that which is glorified in the European tradition and the concrete reality of the Indo-Mexican ancestry and its implications to Anglo culture is the dilemma facing many.

## Base Line Data

By most available base line data many Mexican-Americans in the United States are socioeconomically disadvantaged. Estimates suggest a population of 9.2 million Spanish-surname individuals in the United States (5). California, for example, has a 12 percent Spanish-surname population and is the state with the greatest ethnic population. Eighty-five percent of this population in the Southwest is native-born, it is young, and it has a high proportion of large families. Mixed marriages are more noticeable. Averages for levels of formal education are low. Approximately two percent of this group is reported attending institutions of higher education.

Occupationally, Spanish-surname individuals are found in manufacturing, trade, and agricultural industries, and while some achieve some success most are typically in limited-income and low-skill jobs. Their median income, consequently, is much lower than for total population averages. Unemployment rates, in turn, are substantially higher than for the population at large.

Part of the difficulty in understanding and appreciating the potential as well as true achievement of the total Spanish-surname group is that individuals engaged in professional, white-collar, business, and skilled occupations are not adequately reflected by the use of group norms. So, the popular Anglo stereotype remains unchanged.

## Acculturated Mexican-Americans

Individuals of Mexican descent in the United States are on the full continuum of Anglo acculturation (6). At the high end of the continuum are those who fit the classic description of the successful middle-class Anglo, but this prototype of the middle-class Mexican-American does not exist in the minds of many and this itself is part of the problem of understanding.

One of the worlds Mexican-Americans live in retains some of the folk-culture tradition of Mexico with a language and culture at variance with that of the Anglos. Studies today are only partially beginning to explore the degree of culture retention as well as the effects of interaction with the dominant society.

The most common complaint of grass-root Mexican-Americans is that acculturated middle-class Mexican-Americans abdicate their "public" Mexicanism in their relationships with the ethnic group as well as with Anglo communities. The leadership potential of these individuals for the good of the ethnic group is consequently weakened. These persons are frequently selected by the community power structure as official representatives of Spanish-speaking groups, but because they have lost direct ties with the Mexican-American community they are plainly not the grass-roots spokesmen.

The tragedy of culturally marginal Mexican-Americans is that they attempt to reject without success the Mexicanism of their heritage. They are asked frequently to interpret what they do not well understand—what it means to live and function consciously as Americans of Mexican descent.

## Anglos

Anglos are a product of a culture and history that predisposes them to certain views and feelings about Mexican-Americans. In the United

States the tendency continues to place Mexicans and their descendants in subordinate roles. Neither does the dominant group understand successful Mexican-Americans well, and somehow the best explanation for this achievement is that they are exceptions to the rule. The majority community continues in unchanged views and expectations toward Mexican-Americans. In turn Mexican-Americans tend to live with some hostilities and suspicions about Anglos.

## Implications

A major implication of this writing is that instructional and civic objectives in our schools and communities will continue to fall short of their marks unless and until educators and communities operationally recognize the imperative of understanding culture and language differences as well as ethnic and racial diversity in schools and communities.

## References

1. Cabrera, Y. Arturo, "A Study of American and Mexican-American Culture Values and Their Significance in Education," unpublished Ed.D. thesis, University of Colorado, 1963.
2. Rubel, Arthur J. *Across the Tracks: Mexican-Americans in a Texas City* (Austin: University of Texas Press, 1966).
3. Saunders, Lyle. *Cultural Difference and Medical Care* (New York: Russell Sage Foundation, 1954).
4. Guerra, Manuel and Y. Arturo Cabrera, *An Evaluation and Critique of the Mexican-American Studies Project:* (A Ford Foundation Grant Extended to the University of California at Los Angeles) (Los Angeles: The Education Council of the Mexican American Political Association, 1966).
5. "Persons of Spanish Origin in the United States." November, 1969: Current Population Reports, United States Department of Commerce/Bureau of the Census, Series P-20, No. 213 (February 1971), 1.
6. de Hoyos, Arturo. "Occupational and Educational Levels of Aspiration of Mexican-American Youth," unpublished Ph.D. thesis, Michigan State University, 1961; Fernando Peñalosa. "Class Consciousness and Social Mobility in a Mexican-American Community," unpublished Ph.D. thesis, University of Southern California, 1963; and Richard G. Thurston, "Urbanization and Sociocultural Change in a Mexican-American Enclave," unpublished Ph.D. thesis, University of California at Los Angeles, 1957.

# Charles H. Herbert, Jr.

# English as a Second Language: The Fringe of Meaning

I recently witnessed an English-as-a-second-language lesson between a sixth grade teacher and a Mexican boy who had recently arrived in an American school. The exchange went something like this:

TEACHER: This story's about a mayor. Do you know what a mayor is?
STUDENT: (No response)
TEACHER: (rising intonation) Would he be someone of importance?
STUDENT: (Nods "yes")
TEACHER: (rising intonation) In a city's government?
STUDENT: (Nods "yes")
TEACHER: Yes, that's right, the mayor of a city is an important person.

The teacher turned to another student.

I was sitting next to the boy and asked him if he would tell me in his own words what a mayor is.

He nodded quickly and replied, "Yes, eets a horse!"

The lesson illustrates but one of the fringe areas of understanding for a child learning English as a second language. The speech of this child bears many resemblances to that of a disadvantaged child in that it is characterized by a less varied vocabulary, short, simple sentences, lack of connectives, errors in forms of plurals, verb agreement and the like, and pronunciation difficulties resulting from immature speech habits or from conflicts in the sound system of his native language and English. It is therefore possible to define such a child's language restrictions and categorize them under the headings of vocabulary, structure, morphology and phonology.

## Vocabulary

The vocabulary of the ESL child is often limited or less varied than the language of the native speaker of English. The choice of words, particularly synonyms and antonyms, is not as broad, leading to a tendency to mass concepts into more gross categories. Bernstein(1) has shown this same restriction in the language of certain socio-economic groups. Since one of the ways that concepts are brought down from their global potentiality to manageable units is through vocabulary, the more gross and vague the category system, the more the child finds himself on the fringe of meaning. This involves the use of important concepts such as those of identity and similarity, cause and effect, size and weight, etc.

One example of concept confusion is that which young children experience when they work with size and length. Native English-speaking children show a tendency to group the two until they gain some intellectual maturity, at which time the differentiation becomes distinct.

Of course, paucity of rich language does not mean a small vocabulary; rather, that the ESL child's vocabulary is of considerable size but that it is not of dictionary status. Fries long ago pointed out this lack of richness of expression evident in fluent speech of non-native speakers of English(2).

## Structure

Vocabulary by itself is of little use. It must be organized and presented in thought groups, in phrases and sentences. For this reason, the ESL child needs a competence in syntax or structure. If he does have this type of competence an important hurdle has been scaled. But it may well be that another remains—that of inter-language structural conflict. Structure, or word order, differs in major ways from language to language as Stockwell and Bowen have pointed out in their comparison of the structures of English and Spanish(3). Other inter-language structural comparisons are also available. Simple sentences such as *The dog bit the boy* or *The boy bit the dog* demand a knowledge of structural placement of actor and acted upon. Without such knowledge, the student remains on the fringe of understanding important details or for that matter from basic comprehension. Word order is but one of the problem areas of syntax. Use of reflexives, the requirement of subject, pronoun or noun, and meaning and use of the passive are among the others that Stockwell and Bowen describe.

## Morphology

Morphology—word forms—presents difficulties that are similar to those of syntax. The ESL child must first learn the word forms and then the systematic way in which these forms occur in the language. Plural forms, verb agreement, word derivation and adverb formation are a few. Sometimes these are glossed over by the teacher and briefly explained. Some that cause particular difficulty, such as internal plurals (foot, feet) are often passed off as exceptions. What must be shown with such forms, as with all forms, is the pattern and regularity of form that helps the child learn them more efficiently.

## Phonology

Just as morphology is allied to structure, when morphological changes involve phonemic contrasts (ship: sheep; racer: razor) the ESL child is faced with a difficulty that blocks comprehension. The confusion in this case results from the phonological system of his native language in contrast with that of the new language, English. When a Spanish-speaking child hears the two words *ladder* and *lather,* he must be trained to hear the contrast of the medial consonants which in English is phonemic, since that is what makes the difference in meaning. Although the sounds exist in his native language, they never appear in phonemic contrast.

Other phonological combinations occur in English that cause difficulty. Some initial consonant clusters (*sp, st*) are new sounds in that position and for that reason difficult if not impossible to pronounce as a native speaker would. Since the *sp* combination never occurs in initial position in Spanish, the ESL Spanish-speaking child must learn an entirely new articulatory habit. A further complication results because such clusters in Spanish are always preceded by a vowel when they occur in initial position. The student must then learn a new pronunciation habit and, in addition, overcome a learned behavior at the same time. Add to this the learning of meaning, structure and learning the intricacies of a whole new language and culture and the hurdles seemed insurmountable.

Of course, they are not, and children become operative in a new language with amazing ease and rapidity. This fact leads to a deception, the deception that the ESL child's performance in English indicates a level of competence comparable to that of the average monolingual English-speaking school child. Yet, from the previous discussion, we know that interlanguage conflicts exist and that these can block meaning or at least distort it. In addition, we have not yet mentioned cultural dissonance. Language differences in cultural groups have been studied extensively and some generalizations appear, although we must be cautioned against blanket generalities with a large group. Low socio-economic children are at a disadvantage in articulation, verbalization, sound discrimination and vocabulary. Bilingualism presents other problems although these have not been studied as closely or in such depth. Several studies show that the bilingual child may be further disadvantaged if he also happens to be a member of the low socio-economic group.

As is the case with most groups, there are sub-groups within the bilinguals. Some operate with abundant, expressive language, although the language may be "uneducated" and not the standard variety needed for an individual who reads and writes with proficiency. Others, bright children, mask their brightness by their lack of words in English. They experience frustration each time they try to express ideas for which they do not yet have the words. A third group still thinks in Spanish and speaks only broken English. A fourth is the silent minority, the ones who do not speak in English or Spanish, those who have turned inward as a result of their frustration. Many of these youngsters can associate letters on a printed page with sounds. In other words, from a mechanistic point of view, they are literate; they can release the oral counterpart from the printed symbols on a page.

But this is only a first step. The next, that of understanding the ideas represented on the page, is reading. The two processes are separable, a fact which can be readily proven by the fact that we can read technical material printed in English without understanding it. Many ESL children are decoding, releasing the oral counterpart, rather than reading. Although the decoding process is the first and basic problem, we must give great attention to the second, that of concept development, building comprehension and understanding. I would therefore make the following suggestions in considering language and reading programs for ESL children:

1. That vocabulary be taught in context and that the context be interesting and pertinent to children. Isolated word lists will not be remembered.

2. That grammatical structure be patterned and presented in systematic fashion. The child must learn to read structures if he is to gain real understanding.

3. That children be presented materials in print that they already control in the listening comprehension and speaking skills.

4. That visual materials be utilized to help develop concepts that are included in the reading materials. Too often visuals are not included at all; if present, they are more decorative than useful.

5. That lessons be single focused—that is, beginning reading materials should develop the skill of grapheme-phoneme transfer. And this sound symbol drill should present patterns of spelling rather than focus on single letter-single sound.

6. That materials be so sequenced that understanding can aid learning to master the skill of reading. In other words—material

should be first presented for the oral skills of listening and speaking before the reading of these materials is attempted.

7. That numerous contexts and associations be provided including sensory-motor activities to further develop perceptions.

Many see teaching the bilingual the skills of literacy and reading as a challenge. I prefer to see it as an opportunity, an opportunity for exciting and valuable research and experimentation. But more than that, it is the opportunity to open a bit further the door to those bilingual children who stand on the threshold of understanding.

## References

1. Bernstein, Basil F. "Aspects of Language and Language Learning in the Genesis of the Social Process," *Language in Culture and Society,* edited by Del Hymes (New York: Harper and Row, 1964).
2. Fries, Charles. *American English Grammar.* (New York: Appleton-Century-Croft, 1940).
3. Stockwell, Robert P., and J. Donald Bowen. *The Sounds of English and Spanish* (Chicago: University of Chicago Press, 1965).

Kenneth R. Johnson

# Raising the Self Concept of Black Students

Many black students have a negative self-concept. One of the obvious tasks of the schools is to help these black students realize that they are "as good as everyone else." Stated another way, one of the purposes of education is to help black students develop a positive self-concept. The reading program must be a necessary part in this effort.

## Formation of the Self-Concept—The Special Case of the Black

The self-concept is learned. Each person's self-concept is unique, yet it has a social origin. It is impossible to conceive of a self-concept arising outside of a social experience because the self-concept is formulated in relation to others—that is, the individual uses the collective image of society as a reference point to evaluate himself. The individual makes a qualitative judgment as to *who* he is and *what* he is. The situation is like society's popularity contest in which everyone is entered, and each is his own judge.

In making a judgment, the individual get his cues from those who are unlike him as well as those who are like him, especially his family.

The black population is disproportionately disadvantaged, and many disadvantaged black students come from families that are disintegrating. The Moynihan Report revealed the frightening and disgraceful extent of family breakdown in the black subculture. Even though the disadvantaged family label does not have the luster or prestige of the middle-class family label, the disadvantaged black student must still wear it—and he doesn't have to make a careful comparison of his family to the middle-class family to realize that there is something pathologically wrong with his family. The disadvantaged black student also knows that what his family is, that is what he is.

349

That actual status of blacks in our society tends to give only one cue to blacks: black people are "no good." The stigma of black skin is a symbol for all the social troubles of blacks. Blacks have grown to believe that black skin, in itself, is bad.

Individuals who are stigmatized attempt to hide, or "correct" what society sees as their failing. Blacks have attempted to correct their black skin by lightening it, and their kinky hair (another stigma) by straightening it. Significantly, more advertising space in black publications is given to products that attempt to correct the stigma of black skin and kinky hair than to any other products. These ads continue to reinforce the negative attitude toward black skin and kinky hair by telling blacks that these are "bad."

The color black in our culture is always associated with things that are "bad." In other words, the color black carries a negative value judgment. Thus, blacks are taught by a kind of stimulus generalization that their skin color is bad. Their status in society reinforces this. It is difficult for many black students to develop a positive self-concept in this kind of situation.

The Negroes' attitude toward black skin and, also, kinky hair is changing, however—not because of greater acceptance or improved treatment of blacks by society, but because of actions by the blacks, themselves. The civil rights struggle has given blacks a new dignity and pride in being black. Because of their increased pride in being black, more and more blacks are developing a prideful acceptance of their black skin and kinky hair. This acceptance is reflected in the label blacks have adopted for themselves—black people; and, their new hair style that accentuates kinkiness—the "natural." This is ironical, because blacks are increasingly accentuating the identifying physical qualities—skin color and hair texture—that have prevented their assimilation.

The schools have also contributed to the reinforcement of a negative self-concept in black students. Often, teachers inadvertently and unconsciously communicate attitudes of superiority and rejection, even contempt in some cases, toward black students and their way of life. Unfortunately, these teachers tragically teach black students that they are inferior persons, and this kind of teaching can erode the self-concept.

Textbooks can also provide a basis for self-assessment. Many reading textbooks, which present a romanticized middle-class culture and its people in language that implies rejection of anyone who deviates from the description, help form a negative self-concept in black students whose subcultural experience is unlike the middle-class cultural experience depicted in many reading textbooks. Teachers, of course, give secondary reinforcement to these textbooks. Also, there are examples in literature, such as "The Gold Bug," "Old Black Joe," *Robinson Crusoe,* "Black Sambo," and *Huckleberry Finn,* where black characters are portrayed negatively or the black race is referred to in negative terms. In addition, the omission or slight attention given to blacks in reading and history textbooks is a kind of negative "silent comment."

The schools are achievement-oriented—the cultural background of many black students, however, inhibits their achievement. Too many black students get caught up in a cycle of failure, and repeated failure is damaging to the self-concept of these students.

Finally, the whole problem of a negative self-concept can be covered by one word: segregation. The Supreme Court school desegregation decision of 1954 recognized the effects of segregation on the self-concept of black students. The Court stated that to separate black students ". . . from others of similar age and qualifications solely because of their race generates a feeling of inferiority as to their status in the community that may affect their hearts and minds in a way unlikely to be undone."

Can the schools, however, really raise the self-concept of black students who live in a society that continually treats blacks as if they are inferior?

## Raising the Self-Concept of Black Students

Numerous studies have revealed that many black students have a low self-concept. Because there is such a wealth of evidence on this problem, one would expect to find an equal number of studies on how to raise the self-concept of black students. This is not the case, however. The number of studies on how to raise the self-concept of black students is pitifully small, and this is remarkable in relation to the magnitude of the problem. Further, most of the studies reported concentrate on the relationship between self-concept and school variables (i.e., teacher attitude, teacher training, student achievement, student aspiration, etc.). Programs to raise the self-concept of black students can only be inferred from these kinds of studies. What many of these studies reveal is that non-achievement and poor self-concept have a positive relationship—a not surprising revelation. The immediate inference for program planning to raise the self-concept of black students is to raise their achievement, and their self-concept will rise accordingly. This points out one obvious limitation of these studies: they don't give any direction in *how* to raise the achievement of black students. Furthermore, the same social and cultural factors that cause non-achievement also cause students to develop a negative self-concept. Since these same social and cultural factors are at the root of the black problem, the inference that should be drawn from these studies is to go after the destruction of these roots rather than construct a curriculum in spite of these roots.

The scant research on testing ways to raise self-concept of black students has been pointed out; suggestions (or speculations) on ways to raise the self-concept of Negro students are many. All of the suggestions need to be thoroughly tested by research, however, to determine whether they can raise the self-concept of black students. Thus, the question of whether the school can raise the self-concept of black students can't really be answered authoritatively until more research is conducted. Even without empirical confirmation, however, many of the suggestions to raise the self-concept of black students appear to be valid on the basis of educated judgment.

One of the suggestions that has been made is that Negro students—especially secondary black students—should be helped to acquire insight about their status and some of the factors that influence their status. This insight, perhaps, will help them relieve some of their frustrations, point out "escapes," and cope with their problems in a positive manner. The product of this greater insight will contribute to the formation of a positive self-concept.

Obviously, the reading program must play a significant role in helping blacks develop greater insight. There is an abundant source of reading material that can be used in the reading program for this purpose—the problem is to get the people who are in decision-making positions to approve the use of these reading materials. So far, approval is not usually granted because these reading materials often deal with unpleasant, controversial, but never-the-less real topics. Reading supervisors, curriculum supervisors, administrators and others who are in decision-making roles need to develop more courage to use these reading materials, or step aside to permit more courageous persons who are interested in change (which can subsequently lead to improved self-concept) make the decisions.

The suggestion to help black students improve their self-concept that is given most often and loudest is to teach "black history." The advocates of black history have not clearly defined what black history is, or adequately explained how it would be included in the curriculum. Black history has been vaguely defined as the part blacks have played in the development of our society. Blacks have made many great contributions, and these contributions should be included in the curriculum fully and accurately, without sentimentality or condescension. But the contributions of blacks were not made in a vacuum: they are an integral part of the total development of the society. Therefore, it is inconceivable that the contributions of blacks should be treated as something distinct and separate from the total effort to build a society—to do so would be to establish a kind of "curriculum Jim Crow." The role of reading in teaching the history of our society is obvious; also obvious is that blacks must be included in the textbooks. This will contribute to the effort of the school in helping black students develop a positive self-concept.

The civil rights struggle should be the focus in teaching United States history to black students, because black self-concept is dependent on the outcome of the civil rights struggle. If this is the case, then the school should also concentrate on helping black students win the civil rights struggle—then, the school is directly involved in the formation of a positive self-concept in black students.

The self-concept arises out of a social situation, and the self-concept is inexorably determined by the "group-concept" of the group to which the individual belongs. Thus, if the status of blacks can be improved, a rise in the group-concept and, subsequently, a rise in the self-concept of many of the individuals in the group will occur. The status of blacks has been improved through the civil rights struggle. When this struggle is completely won, black students *as a group,* will no longer disproportionately have a negative self-concept. This doesn't mean, however, that the civil rights struggle will have to be completely won before any improvement in self-concept occurs. The self-concept of black students is improved even in the *process* of carrying on the struggle. That is, blacks derive a sense of pride and dignity in the process of confronting "Jim Crow" barriers and directly dealing with the causes of deprivation and caste status. Black self-concept is given a boost each time the causes of their negative self-concept are engaged in struggle, whether or not a particular engagement is successful or unsuccessful in eliminating a cause. The process to attain total victory is almost as significant as will be the victory itself in raising the self-concept of blacks.

But what does this mean to the school? What are the implications for program planning (particularly, the reading program) that can be derived from a recognition of the relationship between the civil rights struggle and black self-concept?

First, the school should actively help blacks achieve the goals of the civil rights struggle. This means that the school must make a philosophical commitment to social reconstruction.

Second, the civil rights struggle should become as much a part of the school curriculum as mathematics, science or English. Through a study of the civil rights struggle, the self-concept of black students can be raised. This struggle has resulted in the most dramatic and profound increase in black self-concept and a study of it will be effective in raising the self-concept of black students.

Black history as it is usually described is not what is meant here in referring to a study of the civil rights struggle. Black history as it is usually described, means the study of outstanding "safe" blacks, such as Booker T. Washington, Ralph Bunche, and Mary McLeod Bethune. Of course, reading about the progress of black accomplishment and "safe" blacks should be included in the kind of study of the civil rights struggle meant here—

but also included would be reading about major civil rights confrontations to determine effective techniques of protest and pressure (legal, of course) that can be put to practical use on current problems. In addition, a study of "dangerous" blacks would be included—that is, blacks who have battled bigotry and said things white folks don't put into school books. Yet, these kinds of blacks are esteemed by other blacks for their acts: for example, Malcolm X, W. E. B. DuBois, Cassius Clay, Adam Clayton Powell. These men, and other blacks like them, are esteemed by blacks because they took aggressive action to counter oppression instead of waiting for handouts from white society or asking politely and apologetically for civil rights *that are already theirs.* If reading about people with whom one can identify has value in raising the self-concept, then these are the blacks ("dangerous" blacks) black students should be reading about instead of the "safe" blacks —who may even be considered "Uncle Toms" by contemporary black students (Booker T. Washington is an example).

## Conclusion

The school should not attempt to formulate a piecemeal program to attempt to raise the self-concept of black students. This is a limited approach and, possibly, an ineffective one. Instead, the school should strike at the very roots of the black students' negative self-concept: social injustice. The school can do this by helping black students win the civil rights struggle. The reading program must be an important part of this effort. If the school can help blacks win the civil rights struggle, it will have helped blacks remove the main cause of not only a negative self-concept, but many other marks of second-class citizenship. Further, the school will help enrich our democracy and make our ideals realities. The school cannot be committed to a more noble cause.

## References

1. Butts, Hugh F. "Skin Color and Self-Esteem." *Journal of Negro Education* 32 (Spring, 1963).
2. Clark, Kenneth B. *Dark Getto* (New York: Harper and Row, Publishers, 1965).
3. Davidson, Helen H. and Gerhard Sang. "Children's Perceptions of Their Teachers' Feelings Toward Them Related to Self-Perception, School Achievement and School Behavior." In Roberts, Joan I. (ed.) *School Children in the Urban Slum* (New York: The Free Press, 1967).
4. Erickson, Erik H. "The Concept of Identity in Race Relations: Notes and Queries," *Daedalus: The American Negro* 95 1, (Winter 1965).
5. Fishman, Joshua A. "Childhood Indoctrination for Minority Group Membership," *Daedalus* 90, 2 (Spring 1961).

6. Goff, R. M. "Some Educational Implications of the Influence of Rejection on Aspirational Levels of Minority Group Children," *Journal of Experimental Education* 23 (1954).

7. Goodman, Mary Ellen, *Race Awareness in Young Children* (Cambridge: Addison-Wesley Press, 1952).

8. Kvaraceus, William C., *et al. Negro Self-Concept: Implications for School and Citizenship* (New York: McGraw-Hill, 1965).

9. Levy, Lidney L. "This Way to Self-Improvement," *Personnel Journal.*

10. Perkins, H. V. "Factors Influencing Change in Children's Self-Concepts," *Child Development* 29 (1958).

11. Radke, Marion and Helen Trager, "Children's Perceptions of the Social Roles of Negroes and Whites," *Journal of Psychology* 29 (1950).

# About
# Reading
# Disorders

Alice C. Thompson

# Reading Deficit and Its Relation
# to Social Maturity

The dilemma surrounding the plight of thousands of children who have been unable to learn to read print well has to do with two major conceptions of human success: first, success in school, where reading bears the brunt of acquisition of academic information; and second, in adult life where reading is expected to contribute to vocational, cultural, and recreational effectiveness.

If we were to divorce the acquisition of information in academic pursuits from *the acquisition of such information by means of reading,* much of the force of the argument that children *must* learn to read well in school would be lost. Unfortunately, the machinery for this separation is still embryonic. It is frequently observed that many children who read poorly nevertheless possess adequate funds of information which they have acquired through experiential contacts. This circumstance suggests that auditory learning channels are operative, and that there may be considerable visual-perceptual processing of some nature not routinely exploited in learning to read print. If a child can gain information by auditory means, then the incorporation of regular auditory training in the school program as an adjunct to reading is mandatory.

When we examine the statistics concerning the use of reading by adults, either vocationally or recreationally, we find much to discourage faith in the excellence of reading skills as a necessity. Alternate means of communication have dulled the perspective of the adult with limited reading ability as to its urgency.

The thesis here is that reading skill above the third grade level is less important in itself than it is as part of the constellation of limitations which usually attends poor reading. For millions of people in the lower third of the normal distribution of general mental ability, limited reading development constitutes no major obstacle either to job performance or recreational and informational opportunities. Thus, our consideration is limited to those individuals in the average or above average range of ability whose reading development seems not to match or support other evidences of ability. It is this dislocation or contradiction to which attention is called, together with its effects upon human life.

First, however, it seems imperative to make note of some kinds of reading problems. We may ignore for present purposes this one-third of the general population whose below-average composite mental ability places upper limits on their acquisition of so complex an intellectual ability as reading. Such individuals will not often learn to read easily nor miss the art in daily adult life any more than they will miss excellence in arithmetic, spelling, writing, and other school achievement. A society alert to its citizens' needs in terms of information about culture, history, and the world around will eventually reinforce these areas in school life by means of other modalities than reading print, as it has ably though not sufficiently done for adults through radio and television.

Numerous hypotheses have been offered to explain why otherwise apparently intelligent individuals have not learned to read. These usually divide themselves roughly between "emotional" and constitutional etiologies, or imponderable combinations of these. Commonly, the emotional causes are thought of as either primary or secondary. Primary emotional causes are supposed to derive from circumstances (usually familial) in early life which induce the child to reject learning to read as a part of his resistance to parents, against whom it has become psychologically imperative to offer challenge. The child subconsciously is saying that the expectations of authority are menacing in some way to his well-being. To read is to surrender individuality, or to suffer diminution of qualities deemed essential to self, or to face extinction. If maturation demands a renunciation of childish dependencies and protections which are considered indispensable, and if reading is equated with such maturation, then clear recourse against the threat of loss is not to learn to read.

Secondary emotional causation refers to conditions in which early exposure to reading has brought no success or only partial success, and the child becomes convinced that he cannot learn to read print. Therefore, he steadfastly resists all efforts to aid him. There is more honor left through not trying than by trying and failing. The school system must accept most of the responsibility for this sad state. To the child, school experience has often been synonymous with failure, unpleasantness, reproach, pressures, conferences, and appeals to the home which extend and intensify the unhappy situation. He finds nothing in school to look to with joy or hope, little to motivate him beyond the negative factor of getting out from under some of the cloud.

The human spirit does not thrive in a negative atmosphere. We all possess a readiness for flight from unsatisfactory conditions—a natural protective mechanism which should be cherished and nurtured rather than punished. Yet the temper of school practice has been to increase the pressure for investment (and with it the yearning for escape) without doing much to make the situation tolerable or productive. It is difficult to imagine how children can be expected to go on and on investing in activity whose dreariness is unrelieved.

What warping effect these failure years have on human personality cannot be accurately assessed, but in the total picture of reading and living its influence cannot be discounted.

Hypotheses concerning constitutional factors include the possibility that genetically determined obstruction or lack occurs in brain centers crucial to the acquisition of communication skills. Another is that the neural mechanisms involved in visual perception (i.e., the interpretation into meaning of intricate visual symbols) are weak, or damaged by physiological misadventure (disease, injury), or operate in insufficient effectiveness as a learning modality. Another suggestion is that dyslexia may be less a "learning" problem than a retention problem—the mnemonic deficiency being brought about by neural turbulence which disturbs the deployment and/or stabilizing of the molecular patterns which constitute memory. Still another theory is that in some slow-developing children the neural maturation necessary to learning to read may not be achieved before the age of ten or eleven.

Whatever the causes, or complex of causes, involved in reading retardations among apparently able children, the immediate urgency is that all major remedial approaches should be tried with each child who exhibits reading problems in case one should prove to be more effective than another. The hope remains of major breakthrough in reading training in the foreseeable future.

But it is with the syndrome or syndromes rather than the symptoms of reading deficiency that this discussion concerns itself. Reading problems seldom exist in isolation. And among the most serious of the accompanying manifestations are factors which greatly impair living adjustment. Although the research is limited, it is beginning to be suggestive that different types of reading problems are associated with differing attendant behaviors, all with some implications for social integration.

A relatively rare complex has been identified in recent years. The reading problem is so severe in most cases as to warrant the term dyslexia. The affected individual, in contrast to a majority of poor readers, exhibits little, if any, of the kind of visual-perceptual impairment which is so clearly seen in distortions of the Bender Gestalt test. The question naturally arises as to why the victim can discriminate and interpret intricate geometric forms and still not be able to cope with the intricacies of print.

Behaviorially, such persons also depart from the common pattern of hyperactivity, short attention span, distractibility, and social unattractiveness found in many poor readers. In contrast, too, is the pervading earnestness and application. Whereas the disorganized child incurs the displeasure of his associates and of most adults, this individual is appealing and cooperative. Instead of giving up the unremitting struggle to read, he persists doggedly and earns the unqualified respect of his mentors. He can make and keep peer friends. Nevertheless, he has social problems. He may be shy and sensitive to the point of full flight from what he perceives as an aggressively tainted approach. His thinking processes, which may be generally good, appear to slow down in crises so that judgment is adversely affected, and decisions may be made which are disadvantageous. This characteristic may be lifelong, and although the person grows up to be fully self-sustaining, and impeccable as a citizen, his potential seems never to be realized.

Another discernible "type" of poor reading syndrome is the late blossomer. Occasionally some dedicated remedial reading teacher "teaches" a ten or eleven-year-old to read. Great joy is understandably felt by both teacher and child. Here we have the possibility that he had just reached a level of cerebral maturation which enables him to learn to read print.

In any case, this delayed achievement occurs in a child who is already scarred by the oppressive effects of years of failure. How much this personality scarring impairs his living successes, and how much contribution to the adjustment problem derives from the developmental lag which engendered the retardation are imponderable at the moment. But the limited social effectiveness appears to forecast problems throughout the individual's life. Behavior problems do tend to ameliorate once the reading skill is reliably in progress, but complete habilitation of social facility is dubious. In these cases there is more resemblance to intellectual limitation than in the type earlier discussed. Instead of being disparate in operative behaviors, his adjustive pattern suggests dullness.

Another mode of behavior maladjustment associated with reading deficits is observed in the frequency with which delinquent and anti-social tendencies are accompanied by poor reading. The glib assumption is made that the academic retardation is the result of negligence and resistance. Because a child can exercise ingenious learning resources to avoid confrontation and investment in another learning skill (reading), it is easy to assume that no genuine learning disability is operative in reading. The child appears not so much to refuse to learn to read as merely to desist. His mind seems to be elsewhere. A related confusion is the supposition that because the individual is articulate and informed with respect to social expectations, he is therefore culpable when he does not apply the rules to his own conduct. Learning to recite a catechism of social graces is not synonymous with the learned judgment necessary for wise self-direction. Learning is no unitary process—not even the learning necessary to reading or to socially safe conduct. There will be less confusion when professional people themselves learn to distinguish between the abundant implications of delinquency and psychopathy for public morality and the non-moral nature of a gestalt of learning disability.

Some individuals with character disorders do learn to read competently but it is noteworthy that such competence appears to be seldom employed consistently in either personally or socially useful ways. The position taken here is that reading retardations found in delinquents and pre-delinquents are usually intimate portions of a broad spectrum of learning inefficiency which affects many of life situations and which has its roots in cerebral malfunctioning. In cybernetic conception, the computer-brain possesses mechanical flaws of operation which distort the processing of input data.

By far the most common constellation of manifestations concurrent with reading disability is the great group of apparently intelligent children who are motor-driven, inattentive, distractible, and whose Bender test performance looks like blobs and slashes which score from two to five years below chronological developmental norms. Not to be able to decipher the complexities of print seems reasonable in view of the difficulties encountered with simple geometric forms. Teachers have been assuming that if attention could be held, and visual-perceptual training applied, the reading difficulty should begin to dissolve. Unfortunately, the formula is over-simplified in a majority of cases. Overcoming of inattention and distractibility serves to uncover the full magnitude of the learning problems, and improvement in the usual forms of visual-perceptual training are not always paced by reading improvement.

This group of children do improve very gradually in reading, particularly if phonetic methods are included in their teaching, but a majority of them do not close the grade placement gap. Whether we can devise a broader variety of visual-perceptual training methods which will transfer to reading or facilitate reading to a greater extent than heretofore is uncertain but promising. How unyielding the basic group of learning dysfunctions is remains largely unknown at present. The trend to regard these children less as wayward and undisciplined, and more as impaired has modified management procedures in many settings in ways which forestall or diminish the demoralizing influence of failure and ostracism.

Of all the manifested effects of this syndrome which includes reading deficits, the most threatening to lifelong effectiveness is the social environment which the children's conditions generate. They are social misfits to begin with—impulse-ridden, hot tempered, tactless, unsympathetic. In return they experience friendlessness, disapprobation, and diminished self-esteem.

The vicious cycle characteristically gains momentum with the passing years. By adolescence the pattern has often become crystallized and irreversible. Some modification of the apparent severity occurs with conclusion of school attendance, because at this juncture the individual ceases to be plagued by school requirements upon his weakest functions and can capitalize instead on what he can best do. The vast majority become self-sustaining, but the vulnerabilities of poor judgment, impulsivity, inadequate self-direction, job instability, poor social relations, all remain in various guises to hamper their effectiveness.

The frequency with which reading deficit is to be found among people who lack adequate self-direction and sound judgment lifts the study of reading from an academic capsule to the arena of life adjustment. It seems certain that the most rewarding approach to resolution of reading problems will be one which considers the broader social problem of which it is so often an integral part. No social dilemma is presently more pressing than the influence of multitudes of youth and adults who lack judgment, self-esteem, and self-direction. The life histories of these troublesome individuals reveal adjustment problems and reading problems with monotonous frequency. We are now equipped to identify potential reading failure at the school-entering period, and this observation process includes the first manifestations of social problems. To regard reading problems as one manifestation of a complex of handicaps, and to begin at the beginning with a remedial thrust which includes all exhibited aspects of disability will accomplish incomparably more toward the total welfare of the child and the adult whom he is to become than any amount of capsulated reading training.

Elena Boder

# Developmental Dyslexia: A Diagnostic Screening Procedure Based on Three Characteristic Patterns of Reading and Spelling

## Introduction

The behavioral and learning disorders of school children play an increasingly important role in today's pediatric practice. Specific learning disabilities, notably developmental dyslexia,* are seen to be far more frequent among underachieving children than heretofore recognized. As one of the most common and least recognized causes of school failure, specific developmental dyslexia is a significant factor underlying school behavioral problems, dropouts, and the drift to juvenile delinquency (1, 1*).

Early diagnosis of developmental dyslexia is of central importance, both for successful remediation and to prevent school failure with its concomitant emotional overlay and loss of self-esteem. Nevertheless, many professionals in the field are reluctant to make the diagnosis. One reason is that the characteristic emotional disorder of the dyslexic child tends to be interpreted as the primary fundamental cause of his inability to read, rather than as secondary and reactive to it. More importantly, no definitive diagnostic criteria for developmental dyslexia have been established.

Developmental dyslexia is clearly a multidisciplinary problem. A *team approach,* which may be termed "neuropsychoeducational," is essential to its diagnosis and management. There is a widely recognized need for a practical, *objective* diagnostic screening procedure that can be utilized by a variety of multidisciplinary personnel—by teachers, who are usually the

---

* *Terminology:* "dyslexia," "specific dyslexia," and "developmental dyslexia" are used here interchangeably with "specific developmental dyslexia." Other synonyms are "specific reading disability," "strephosymbolia,"(2) "developmental alexia,"(3) "primary reading retardation,"(4) "Gestalt-blindness"(5, 6) and "specific language disability,"(7) The older term "congenital word blindness" is still widely used.

first to observe a child's learning difficulties, as well as by psychologists and physicians.

The purpose of this preliminary paper is twofold: 1) to describe a *diagnostic screening procedure* for developmental dyslexia that has evolved out of the writer's experience in the School Neurology Clinics at the Parent-Teacher Health Centers of the Los Angeles City Schools and at Cedars of Lebanon Hospital, and 2) to describe *three distinctive patterns* of reading and spelling revealed by our diagnostic screening procedure which provide a basis for classification of dyslexic children into three main groups. These distinctive patterns represent the child's *total* performance in the reading and spelling tasks—and not merely his characteristic errors.

These atypical reading-spelling patterns are found consistently among children who fulfill standard diagnostic criteria for developmental dyslexia. It appears, therefore, that these patterns are *specific* and can be viewed as diagnostic in themselves of developmental dyslexia. In addition, they have the advantage of reflecting the child's functional assets as well as his functional deficits, and thereby have implications for prognosis and remedial education.

The diagnostic screening procedure described in this paper represents an effort to approach the diagnosis of developmental dyslexia directly through *objective* patterns of reading and spelling. It is based on familiar school tasks which are readily adaptable to use by a variety of professional personnel—in schools, clinics, or private pediatric practice. In the writer's opinion this approach greatly expedites diagnosis and suggests means for dealing with developmental dyslexia on a broader scale within the realistic limitations of current shortages in skilled personnel and facilities.

As an empirically evolved procedure, it calls for further study, refinement, and validation on larger groups of dyslexic and non-dyslexic children. Like any screening procedure, it has recognized limitations and does not supplant more formal, standardized diagnostic tests of psychological and psycholinguistic functions when more precise evaluation of reading ability and achievement is indicated.

## Diagnostic Screening Procedure

This screening procedure for developmental dyslexia has been used as an integral part of the neuropediatric evaluation of every child referred to the School Neurology Clinics for school behavioral or learning problems. The overall approach to the diagnosis and management of these children has been described in a previous report (1).

The purpose of this screening procedure is not merely to do a quantitative evaluation of the child's reading ability, but a *qualitative* one. It is the analysis of *how* he reads and writes, rather than *at what level* he reads and writes, that enables the examiner to make a diagnosis of specific dyslexia and to give a prognostic evaluation and guidelines for remedial teaching.

Briefly, the screening for dyslexia in the School Neurology Clinics is begun with the *Informal Word Recognition Inventory,* used widely in the Los Angeles City Schools as a test for reading achievement. This test consists of groups of 20 words graded from the pre-primer to the senior high school level. The words are based on word frequency counts of books commonly used in grades 1 through 10.*

The presentation of the word list at each level has two parts: the "flash" section, which determines the child's *sight vocabulary,* and the "untimed" section, which calls upon the child's ability to employ *word-attack skills.* When taking the test, the child first looks at each word for about one second. If he identifies it correctly, he continues down the list. If he misreads the word or cannot read it at all, he is asked to study the word for as long as he wishes and then make another attempt to read the word. Misreadings are immediately recorded for later evaluation of his characteristic errors. The untimed exposure reveals his ability to analyze and synthesize words phonetically—his word-attack skills. Words that the child cannot read either "flash" or "untimed" are termed his "unknown" vocabulary.

Following the administration of the word recognition test, the child is screened for atypical spelling patterns. He is first asked to write (or, some-times, to spell orally) eight or more words selected from his "known" or "sight," vocabulary and then the same number from his "unknown" vocabulary. Analysis of his list of "known" words reveals the child's ability to "revisualize," while analysis of his list of "unknown" words reveals his ability to spell phonetically. The sequence of tasks is designed not only to disclose the number and kinds of perceptual dyslexic errors the child makes, but to enable the examiner to ascertain his *pattern of reading and spelling* and the group into which he falls (Table I).

Finally, the reading of a paragraph from a textbook at the child's grade level or below may be included among the tasks to determine if his ability to read is improved in context, and to assess his reading comprehension.

## Diagnostic Reading-Spelling Patterns Among Children With Developmental Dyslexia

We recognize that a variety of complex psychoneurologic functions, perceptual and integrative, are being tapped by the reading and spelling

---

*The Informal Word Recognition Inventory for the pre-primer through sixth grade levels was developed by Millard H. Black, Elementary Reading Supervisor, Los Angeles City Schools. The word lists used for junior and senior high school levels are those developed by Gilbert B. Schiffman of the Baltimore County Department of Education(1, 8).

tasks in our diagnostic screening procedure. *Reading* requires visual perception and discrimination, visual memory and recall, and directional orientation. It also requires *visual-auditory* integration—that is, the translation of visual symbols into meaningful auditory equivalents, which includes the synthesis of lettersounds into syllables and syllables into words. The still higher level of integration required for reading comprehension is not drawn upon by our screening procedure (9, 13). *Spelling,* in contrast, requires the translation of speech sounds into their visual symbol equivalents. In addition to the visual functions prerequisite to reading, this *auditory-visual* integration requires auditory perception and discrimination, and auditory memory (9, 12, 14). Writing, further calls upon the fine motor and visuomotor coordination (13).

Our diagnostic screening procedure has gradually revealed *three distinctive patterns of reading and spelling* among dyslexic children. The correlation between a child's pattern of reading and his pattern of spelling has been found to be so consistent that one is predictive of the other. From the way the child reads, it becomes possible to predict how he spells, and vice versa. It would appear that the same functional assets and deficits underlie both the reading and the spelling of dyslexic children. Thus, the reading-spelling patterns the writer has observed have diagnostic, prognostic, and therapeutic implications.

On the basis of these three correlated patterns, three groups of dyslexic children have been delineated (Table I). The description of these diagnostic reading-spelling patterns is purely clinical. No attempt is being made at this point to relate the patterns and the deficit functions they reflect to neurophysiological mechanisms.

### TABLE I

*Classification of Children with Developmental Dyslexia—Based on Diagnostic Reading-Spelling Patterns.*

**Group I:** Children Whose Reading-Spelling Patterns Reflect Deficit in Symbol-Sound Integration and in the Ability to Develop Phonetic Skills, i.e., Deficit in Ability to "Auditorize." (They have no gross deficit in ability to "visualize.")

**Group II:** Children Whose Reading-Spelling Patterns Reflect Deficit in Ability to Establish Visual Gestalts of Letters and Words, i.e., Deficit in Ability to "Visualize." (They have no gross deficit in ability to "auditorize.")

**Group III:** Children Whose Reading-Spelling Patterns Reflect Gross Deficit in Both Ability to "Auditorize" and Ability to "Visualize."

*Group I.*    The child in Group I typically has a limited "sight vocabulary" of whole words that he recognizes on presentation and reads fluently. Even in high school he rarely achieves a sight vocabulary beyond the 4th or 5th grade level. He reads through *whole-word visual Gestalts,* the component letters of which he may not yet be able to identify. When he confronts a word, however common, that is not yet in his sight vocabulary he is unable to decipher it. Lacking phonetic concepts, he has no word-attack skills and is unable to "sound out" or blend the component letters and syllables of a word. He is unable to auditorize (1).

He tends to read words better in context than separately, since he may guess a word from minimal clues; for example, from the first and last letters. However, he may substitute a word similar in meaning though quite different phonetically.

This child may be said to read "by sight" and not "by ear," since he has difficulty learning what the letters sound like. Unable to read by ear, he cannot spell by ear. He spells correctly to dictation only those few words in his sight vocabulary that he can *revisualize.* His correctly written words are islands in a hodge-podge of misspellings in which the original words can seldom be identified even by himself.

In the writer's experience, the most striking dyslexic errors typical of this group of children are semantic substitutions of words that are closely related conceptually but not phonetically. This may occur in spelling as well as in reading. *Examples:* "funny" for "laugh," "human" for "person," "answer" for "ask," "quack" for "duck," "airplane" for "train," "Los Angeles" for "city."

*Illustration of Group I.*

*Vincent — Age 10 — Grade 5*

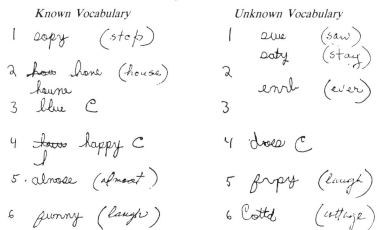

Known Vocabulary     Unknown Vocabulary

*Group II.* This child reads laboriously, as if he is seeing each word for the first time. Just as the children in Group I have difficulty learning what the letters sound like, the child in Group II has difficulty learning what they look like. The term "letterblind" can be aptly applied to him. Although he often can recite the letters of the alphabet fluently, without error, he may not be able to recognize or write the letters until the 4th or 5th grade. Even then, he may still be said to be "wordblind" or "Gestalt-blind," for he has little or no visual memory for words. He reads "by ear," by a laborious process of phonetic analysis, sounding out familiar as well as unfamiliar combinations of letters—rather than by visual whole-word Gestalts.

The Group II child also spells poorly, though not bizarrely as a rule. He spells as he reads—phonetically, "by ear." In contrast to Group I, the original word can usually be readily identified in his spelling list by himself and others. *Examples:* "sed" for "said," "letl" for "little," "lisn" for "listen," "sos" for "sauce," "rit" for "right," "bisnis" for "business," "onkl" or "uncal" for "uncle."

A striking finding is that *nonphonetic* words in this child's limited sight vocabulary are often written incorrectly, whereas a perfectly *phonetic* word, even when it is totally unfamiliar, may be written correctly. In fact, he can often spell better than he can read.

*Illustration of Group II.*
*(Shows phonetic spelling.)*

*Danny — Age 9½ — Grade 3*

| Known Vocabulary | Unknown Vocabulary |
|---|---|
| 1  aWaK  (awake) | 1  ф Chahs (chase) |
| 2  OLMoSt (almost) | 2  Frint (print) |
| 3  Fot tner (father) | 3  BeleV (believe) |
| 4  Grut (great) | 4  Wohpefol (wonderful) |
| 5  Other | 5  traFiK (traffic) |
| 6  rorsmes (promise) | 6  BiSnis (business) |

*Group III.*    Group III comprises the "hard core" dyslexic children, who tend to be the most severely handicapped educationally. The child in Group III, combining the deficits of both Group I and Group II, cannot read either "by sight" or "by ear." Even in high school he remains a virtual "nonreader." The occasional word that he recognizes on sight or can write is typically on the primer or pre-primer level. Characteristically, his response to remedial teaching is painfully slow.

As would be expected, since he cannot read, he certainly cannot spell. Like children in Group II, he has difficulty in learning what the letters of the alphabet look like, and like children in Group I, he has difficulty in

*Illustration of Group III.*

*Gordon — Age 10 — Grade 4*

*Known Vocabulary*                    *Unknown Vocabulary*

1 aḥᴊ    (and)          1 Ẍɸᴜfr     (farm)

2 Ɓll    (ball)         2 Ca'n      (saw)

3 Oh      c             3 Paʋr      (play)

4         (yes)         4 nay       (not)

5 funḷ   (funny)        5 CaD       (sat)

6 Toy     c             6           (with)

learning what the letters sound like. He usually has marked visuo-spatial difficulties and tends more than children in Groups I and II to confuse the reversible letters b-d-p-q, m-w, and n-u and letters with subtle graphic differences, such as h-n, g-q, v-y, etc. His spelling pattern is nonphonetic, like that of Group I, but his misspellings appear even more bizarre: sometimes a single inappropriate initial letter; sometimes a formless scribble, as if imitating rapid writing; usually an unintelligible jumble.

This child's sense of defeat and his phobic withdrawl from reading and writing tasks are often striking.

## Comments on Other Dyslexic Errors

Confusion of reversible letters (b-d-p-q, m-w, n-u), the so-called *static reversals,* have been observed in all three of our groups, particularly among the younger children. So have mirror-reading and -writing, the so-called *kinetic reversals.* This is consistent with observations by others on young dyslexic children (8, 15), and underlies the fact that such visuo-spatial reversals are ubiquitous among normal, young, beginning readers.

*Letter-order errors,* described by Kinsbourne and Warrington (16) as characteristic of dyslexic children with the developmental Gerstmann Syndrome, have also been observed in all three of our groups.

As noted earlier, visuo-spatial reversals appear to occur more frequently in our Group III and to persist for a longer time. However, the distribution of reversals and letter-order errors in Groups I, II, and III has not yet been statistically evaluated, and we are not prepared to state that any of these errors and the functional deficits they reflect are definitely more characteristic of one of our groups than another.

## Implications for Remediation

The three delineated reading-spelling patterns reflect the child's functional assets as well as his functional deficits, and suggest the sensory modality upon which the *initial* remedial techniques should be based. This permits the reading therapist to teach to the child's assets, not to his deficits —i.e., to his abilities rather than to his disabilities, and thus insure the initial successes that will help to motivate the dyslexic child and lead to a positive attitude toward learning.

Ultimately, of course, a multisensory approach to remediation will be used for all three groups of dyslexic children, but the techniques used *initially* will vary with each group.

*The child in Group I* can be called "visile" rather than "audile," and since he is primarily unable to auditorize letters and words his dyslexia would be called "auditory dyslexia" by Myklebust (13). The initial remedial approach for these children—contrary to general practice and belief— might well be through *whole-word techniques.* Only after he has developed sufficient sight vocabulary (reinforced by tactile-kinesthetic clues) should the teaching of *remedial phonetics* be initiated. It is important, of course, for the teacher to be aware from the outset that phonetic concepts will not come easily to such a child, because this is precisely the area of his primary deficit.

This type of child, like the Group III child, will always tend to be a nonphonetic speller, whose spelling is typically unintelligible except for those words in his sight vocabulary which he is able to revisualize. The *initial* remedial efforts, therefore, should realistically be directed toward converting him from a *nonphonetic* speller to a *phonetic* speller so that everyone, including himself, can at least interpret what he has written.

*The child in Group II* can be called "audile" rather than "visile," and since primarily he is unable to visualize letters and words, his dyslexia would be called "visual dyslexia" by Myklebust (13). The implications for remedial teaching would be to start with tactile-kinesthetic techniques (17) if the child has not yet learned the letters of the alphabet visually. Remedial phonics, e.g., the Orton-Gillingham (2) technique, would be the indicated initial method if he has already acquired visual recognition of the letters.

In contrast to Group I, the child in Group II will learn through phonics readily because he has no primary difficulty in auditorizing letters and words. To develop a sight vocabulary, i.e., visual Gestalts of the whole words, the use of tactile-kinesthetic techniques would also be ultimately required.

*The child in Group III* is neither "visile" nor "audile" but has the combined deficits of both the Group I and Group II children. The initial remedial technique of choice for this child would appear to be the tactile-kinesthetic method for learning letters and whole words, until there is some sight vocabulary as a basis for subsequent remedial phonics and multisensory techniques. The remedial approach to this child's spelling disability would be the same as for the child in Group I.

### Distribution of the Three Reading-Spelling Patterns Among Dyslexic Children

In a preliminary survey, the distribution of the three reading-spelling patterns among dyslexic children seen during the first three months of 1968 in the School Neurology Clinics was determined. Of the total group of children who fulfilled the diagnostic standards of developmental dyslexia, 61 were selected according to the following criteria: 1) All children are of normal intelligence. They generally attained I.Q. scores of 90 or more on the Stanford-Binet, or on either the Verbal Scale or the Performance Scale of the Wechsler Intelligence Scale for Children. The few exceptions, who have I.Q. scores between 80 and 90, showed wide scatter in their test results reaching well into the normal range. 2) All are in the third grade or beyond. 3) All are two or more years retarded in reading according to the Jastak Wide Range Achievement Test and our Informal Word Recognition Inventory.

In the total sample of 61 children, 57 were boys and 4 were girls. These children represent essentially a random sample of dyslexic children in the regular clinic population, although a special effort was made to include the dyslexic siblings of our patients. Of the 61 in the sample, 37 (61 percent) fell into Group I; 9 (15 percent) into Group II; 10 (16 percent) into Group III. Of the total sample, only 15 patients (8 percent) had to be placed in an "undetermined" group, to be studied further.

Most of the classifications into the three groups were clearcut, as evidenced from the small number in the "undetermined" group. Some of the children in the sample have been followed for as long as five years, and their patterns on the whole have remained consistent.

It has become apparent, however, from a comparative study of the records that differentiating certain Group II children from Group III children may present difficulties. Their reading-spelling patterns may be indistinguishable, particularly if Group II children are seen before they have had the benefit of remedial phonetics. Thus, some of the children in the sample now classified in Group II showed earlier reading-spelling patterns that would have placed them in Group III.

Long-term observation and trial of remedial phonetics may be required to distinguish such Group II children from Group III children. The Group III in our sample may therefore contain some Group II children who are still "letter-blind" or who have not yet been taught phonetics.

It is of interest that Group I is the largest of the three groups, and it is the one to which the terms "word-blindness" or "Gestalt-blindness" are not really applicable, although these terms *can* be aptly applied to Groups II and III. The higher incidence of Group I pattern corroborates the observations of Ingram (12) and others (14) that difficulties in auditory perception and discrimination or in symbol-sound integration and word synthesis are more important causes of developmental dyslexia than visuo-spatial perceptual difficulties.

## Discussion

The diagnostic screening procedure described in this preliminary paper represents an effort to approach the diagnosis of developmental dyslexia directly, through three *objective* patterns of reading and spelling. These three distinctive patterns reflect the dyslexic child's functional assets as well as his functional deficits, and thus have diagnostic, prognostic, and therapeutic implications.

Children with developmental dyslexia are commonly referred to as if they were a *homogeneous* group. Their characteristic errors in reading and spelling, and the functional deficits these errors reflect, tend to be discussed as if all of them were applicable to the whole category of dyslexic children and occurred at random.

The three reading-spelling patterns delineated here provide a basis for classifying dyslexic children into three main clinical groups. This is consistent with observations by several other investigators (13, 16) that children with developmental dyslexia are to some extent a *heterogeneous* group, not only etiologically but clinically.

It has been standard practice to refer to the so-called dyslexic errors as bizarre, and even to say that the very bizarreness of the errors is diagnostic of developmental dyslexia. Understood as *patterns of errors* in reading and spelling, the errors cease to be bizarre; they become direct reflections of specific functional deficits in the dyslexic child.

Another advantage of diagnosis by patterns of reading and spelling is that it provides a rational basis for *grouping dyslexic children for effective remedial teaching* according to their functional assets and deficits, i.e., their abilities and disabilities. This may make it possible to meet individual remedial needs on a group basis and prove more effective than the teaching of heterogeneous groups of dyslexic children in the usual remedial classes.

These readily demonstrable reading-spelling patterns can be effectively used in helping parents to gain better understanding of the child's dyslexic problem and the specific goals toward which his remedial reading instruction will have to be directed. *Parent and children counseling* is of paramount importance in dealing with the dyslexic child, and has been discussed in some detail in a previous publication (1). The reading and spelling patterns are also effective in interpreting the child's dyslexic problems to school personnel.

It is not within the scope of this paper to discuss the prevailing diagnostic criteria of developmental dyslexia, which usually vary with the professional discipline involved. The reader is referred for discussions elsewhere (11, 12, 13, 16, 18, 19, 20). How the writer's concept of direct diagnosis of developmental dyslexia by patterns of reading and spelling fits into the context of prevailing diagnostic criteria will be discussed in a subsequent report.

It is the writer's belief, along with other clinicians in the field, that specific developmental dyslexia always has a neurologic basis, due either to a familial genetic trait or, less frequently, to brain damage. In its milder and transient forms developmental dyslexia may represent a normal variation in psychoneurological maturation, i.e., a maturational lag in "reading-readiness."

On the other hand, nonspecific reading disorders, or so-called "secondary reading retardation" (4) may have a variety of nonspecific causes—physical, mental, emotional, cultural and educational—and interactions between them.

The concept that specific developmental dyslexia is by definition always of neurologic origin greatly simplifies differential diagnosis of reading disorders. The diagnostic objective becomes, in essence to differentiate between specific dyslexia and nonspecific reading retardation. The differentiation has a direct practical bearing since specific dyslexia calls for certain remedial reading techniques that are not essential in the management of nonspecific reading disorders (1).

A child with a *nonspecific reading disorder,* or secondary reading retardation, reads poorly but has a normal reading potential. In the writer's experience the reading and spelling performance of such a child is quantitatively different from that of a normal reader, but not qualitatively, whereas a dyslexic child reads differently both *quantitatively* and *qualitatively.*

The child of normal intelligence whose reading retardation is non-specific reads and spells normally at whatever grade level he has achieved, his performance being indistinguishable from that of an average younger reader at the same grade level. There are none of the dyslexic children and no persisting dyslexic errors, such as static and kinetic reversals, beyond the age of eight.

Unlike the reading disability of dyslexic children, which is often selective and in sharp contrast with their other abilities and achievement, nonspecific reading retardation is usually part of a global underachievement. Nor, in the writer's experience, is it ever as severe in relation to grade level and mental age as the reading retardation of dyslexic children—one or two years at most.

The reading retardation secondary to *mental retardation* is also part of a global underachievement, but one that is commensurate with the child's mental age. It should be noted, however, that specific developmental dyslexia and mental retardation may coexist. The diagnosis should be suspected if the retarded child's reading level is two or more years below his mental age and if he presents the abnormal patterns of reading and spelling found in dyslexic children of normal intelligence.

The *familial incidence* of dyslexia is impressive. In the writer's experience a positive family history has usually been elicited for children with any of the three delineated reading-spelling patterns.

It is also typical for developmental dyslexia to be associated with a variety of minimal, or "soft," neurologic signs pointing to a parieto-occipital dysfunction and neurophysiological immaturity. Among these associated signs are crossed and confused dominance, nonspecific motor clumsiness, finger agnosia, hyperkinesis, and developmental speech and language disorders.

It should be emphasized that specific developmental dyslexia is viewed as *a multidisciplinary problem,* and a team approach that may be termed "neuropsychoeducational" is essential to its diagnosis and management. The screening procedure for developmental dyslexia described in this preliminary paper has been systematically used as an integral part of the neurological examination of every child referred to the School Neurology Clinics for behavioral or learning problems.

As a screening procedure, it has recognized limitations and should, when feasible, be used in conjunction with more refined and standardized psychological testing instruments.

It is hoped that this preliminary report on a diagnostic screening procedure for developmental dyslexia and the distinctive reading-spelling patterns it has revealed will stimulate further study and validation on larger groups of dyslexic and nondyslexic children.

## Acknowledgment

The author wishes to express appreciation to Sylvia Jarrico, M.A., for invaluable editorial assistance in the preparation of the manuscript.

## Addendum

Since this preliminary report was originally published, more definitive discussions have appeared in two chapters:

Boder, E. "Developmental Dyslexia: A Diagnostic Screening Procedure Based on Three Characteristic Patterns of Reading and Spelling," in *Learning Disorders, Vol. IV,* edited by B. Bateman (Seattle, Special Child Publications, 1971), 298–342.

Boder, E., "Developmental Dyslexia: Prevailing Diagnostic Concepts and a New Diagnostic Approach," in *Progress in Learning Disabilities, Vol. II,* edited by H. Myklebust (New York, Grune & Stratton, 1971), 293–321.

The diagnostic screening procedure is described in detail in the first chapter. In the second, the diagnostic approach to developmental dyslexia through the identification of three subtypes is discussed in the context of prevailing diagnostic criteria in the fields of medicine, psychology and education.

It has proved useful to describe the deficits in the basic reading process that underlie the three atypical reading-spelling patterns as deficits in the Gestalt and analytic functions rather than as deficits in what Myklebust refers to as the abilities to auditorize and visualize.

The terms *dysphonetic dyslexia* and *dyseidetic dyslexia* have been introduced as descriptive clinical terms having remedial implications. The coinage *dyseidetic* specifically denotes impairment in the perception or recognition of the visual Gestalts of whole words (from *eidos* meaning form or shape in Greek, as *Gestalt* does in German). Group I children are described as dysphonetic, Group II as dyseidetic, and Group III as mixed dysphonetic-dyseidetic.

## References

1. Boder, E. "A Neuropediatric Approach to School Behavioral and Learning Disorders: Diagnosis and Management." *Learning Disorders, Vol. II,* edited by Jerome Hellmuth (Seattle: Special Child Publications, Seattle, 1966).

1* Boder, E., and Foncerrada, M.: "Disfunction Cerebral Minima." *Manual de Pediatria,* R. H. Valenzuela, 7th Edicion, Mexico City: Interamerican, 1967, 589–597.

2. Orton, S. *Reading, Writing, and Speech Problems in Children* (New York: W. W. Norton and Co., 1937).

3. Jackson, E.: cited by Heller (20).

4. Rabinovitch, R. D. "Dyslexia—Psychiatric Considerations," in J. Money, *op. cit.* (15).

5. Bender, L. *Psychopathology of Children with Organic Brain Disorders.* (Springfield: Chas. C. Thomas, 1959).

6. de Hirsch, K. "Specific Dyslexia or Strephosymbolia," *Folia Phoniatrica* 5 (1952): 231.

7. Gallagher, J. "Specific Language Disability: Dyslexia," *Bulletin Orton Society* 10 (1960): 5.

8. Schiffman, G. B. "Dyslexia as an Educational Phenomenon: Its Recognition and Treatment," in J. Money, *op. cit.* (15), 45–60.

9. Bauza, C. A., M. A. C. de Grompone, E. Ecuder, M. E. Drets, *La Dislexia de Evolucion* (Montevideo: Garcia Morales-Mercant, Graficos Unidos S.A., 1962).

10. Benton, A. L. "Dyslexia in Relation to Form Perception and Directional Sense," in J. Money, *op. cit.* (15).

11. Critchley, M. *Developmental Dyslexia* (Springfield, Ill.: Chas. C. Thomas, 1964).

12. Ingram, T. T. S. "Delayed Development of Speech with Special Reference to Dsylexia," *Proc. Roy. Soc. Med.* 56 (March 1963): 199.

13. Myklebust, H. R. *Development and Disorders of Written Language* (New York: Grune and Stratton, Inc., 1965).

14. Wepman, J. M. "Dyslexia: Its Relationship to Language Acquisition and Concept Formation," in J. Money, *op. cit.* (15), 179–186.

15. Money, J. *Reading Disability, Progress and Research Needs in Dyslexia* (Baltimore: The Johns Hopkins Press, 1962).

16. Kinsbourne, M., and Warrington, E. K. "Developmental Factors in Reading and Writing Backwardness," in *The Disabled Reader,* edited by J. Money (Baltimore: The Johns Hopkins Press, 1966), 59–71.

17. Fernald, G., cited in Money (15).

18. Clements, S. D., and J. E. Peters, "Minimal Brain Dysfunctions in the School-age Child," *Arch. Gen. Psychiat.* 6 (1962): 187.

19. Eisenberg, L. "Reading Retardation: 1. Psychiatric and Sociologic Aspects," *Pediatrics* 37 (February 1966): 352.

20. Heller, T. M. "Word-Blindness—A Survey of the Literature and a Report of Twenty-eight Cases," *Pediatrics* 31 (April 1963): 669.

Robert E. Carrel

*Neurophysiological Aspects of Learning*

The fields of reading and learning are not only exciting but quite obviously timely as shown by the great interest in these conferences. Although much is being learned regarding them, our concepts are in a continual state of flux and our overall ignorance is all too clear. As teachers in the 1960's, you hear much about the "neurological examination" and "EEG." In fact, it often appears as though a complete understanding of these two terms alone would provide a cure for your many children with reading problems, just as your predecessors in previous decades were impressed by psychiatry and depth psychology. This is hardly true, but hopefully, a better understanding of the functioning of the central nervous system might give you some insight into reading and learning problems and the massive literature regarding this subject.

From an historical point of view, the concept of learning is comfortably explained by the classic linear theory. A subject is perceived through an intact peripheral sensory organ (the eye, the ear, etc.), and then through sensory paths this information is conducted to the brain and there registered for either immediate use or "stored" for future use. When the "stored" information is needed, it is called upon, and through the various motor paths (nerve pathways leading the way from the brain), a suitable motor action ensues. These motor actions consist of verbalization, the use of arms and legs, etc. The linear concept is simple, rigid and comfortably explains problems in learning caused by gross damage to the nervous system. (With damage to the eye, certain light sensations cannot be registered, and with damage to certain areas of the brain, vocalization cannot be accomplished.) It soon becomes obvious, however, that numerous subtle problems cannot be explained by these concepts and that the problem of learning is indeed much more complex than the adherents of the classic linear theory would lead us to believe.

To illustrate this point I would like to mention briefly some recent studies done in the field of neurophysiology, show some of their associations with learning, and then finally, demonstrate how an awareness of these studies might help in understanding reading and learning problems.

## Some Chemical and Physical Components in Learning

Dr. Mark R. Rosenweig (1), Professor of Psychology at the University of California at Berkeley, has done much work with descendents of Tryon's maze-bright and maze-dull rats. He has demonstrated that only a few generations of selective breeding are necessary to produce strains of rats which differ significantly in maze learning ability. The superior strains differ inasmuch as they seem to have brains which are more excitable, both electrically and chemically as demonstrated by seizure thresholds. In addition, they seem to be better endowed with acetylcholine, a substance which appears to be important in the transmission of the impulses from nerve to nerve, as well as acetylcholine esterase which destroys acetylcholine, thus allowing further transmissions. He has demonstrated that when either the so-called maze-dull or maze-bright animals were given enriched experiences, they differed from their counterparts kept in an impoverished environment by having thicker and heavier cortices (the outer layer of the brain), greater total acetylcholine as well as acetylcholine esterase. In other words, one might infer that the greater the learning experience, the greater is brain growth as measured by certain chemical and physical determinations. Dr. Rosenweig suggests that a larger brain is not necessarily created, but a more intricate one in terms of nerve branches. Although the exact mechanism of storage of information in the brain is not understood, this work by Dr. Rosenweig suggests some explanation of "storage."

## Current Concepts of Nervous System Functioning

Initially in my discussion, reference was made to the classic linear theory of learning. It was noted that the linear theory could not adequately explain many of the subtle problems of learning. Adherents to this theory assigned a rather rigid role to various parts of the nervous system. In contrast, at the present time it is felt that the nervous system is quite plastic. Dr. Robert Livingston (2) of the National Institute of Health, has demonstrated this plasticity in working with animals without central anesthesia. What were once considered sensory pathways because they conducted impulses in a centripetal (toward the brain) direction, turn out to be more variable in their transmissions during the waking state. This variability appears to be related to an active interference by centrifugal transmission (away from the brain). The widespread distribution of sensory-evoked impulses allows an intermingling of sensory with other impulses throughout these various parts of the nervous system. Thus, the nervous system seems to be made up less of independent linear pathways than of mutually interdependent loop circuits which connect the various parts of the brain into a whole. Along ascending as well as descending paths, various parts of the brain such as the brain stem reticular formation, cerebral and cerebellar systems, are linked closely together to modulate impulse activity. For example the intactness and plasticity of your nervous system are essential for your ability to register what I am saying here today. Your brains, acting under the influence of prior experiences, attention and emotional states, feed back into the input circuits to amplify some sensations, modify others, and even extinguish some. Your interest in the subject as teachers, along with prior experiences, amplify some of the information I am discussing. Also, the sensations created by shoes which might be too tight, hard chairs, and hunger prompted by the lateness of the hour, as well as the sunlight filtering through the window, are either modified or extinguished so that you may concentrate on the words that I am saying.

## Some Effects of Prior Experience on Learning

Dr. Ronald Melzak (3), Associate Professor of Psychology at McGill, has shown that behavioral data obtained with restricted beagles lends support to these current concepts of information selection by the central nervous system. His studies showed that dogs raised in experimental cages for nine months were extremely active when placed in the new environment, exhibited abnormal behavior to visual, auditory, etc., stimuli, and had great difficulty in inhibiting irrelevant responses in training situations. He felt, that the neural correlates of experience in the environment acted, in the beginning stages of information selection, to prevent massive sensory imports from overwhelming the animal. In other words, you can concentrate on the subject being presented here because past experiences with tight shoes, hard chairs, gnawing stomachs, and flickering lights, prevent the sensory stimuli from overwhelming you.

It has been observed that children from a restricted environment need a period of "toning down" before they can make good use of new experiences. A young student entering the classroom for the first time is faced with rows of desks, windows, etc. The situation is generally quite unfamiliar and it is not surprising that under these conditions, the student may at first fail to learn many of the simplest things that the teacher is attempting to teach.

Because of his lack of experience with the situation, he is unable properly to amplify some sensations, modify and extinguish others. It takes some time before the environment becomes sufficiently familiar so that the student can focus attention on the relevant inputs and ignore or modify irrelevant stimulation. As Dr. Melzak stated, "the education process thereby promotes the acquisition of significances and meanings of stimuli and provides the student with the basis for the selection and filtering processes that appear to be so important for all later learning."

### Understanding the Neurophysiological Correlates of Learning Problems

I have touched on but a few of the complexities of the central nervous system functions. It is obvious that learning is an extremely complex problem and much more knowledge has to be gained to fully understand it. But an awareness of both these complexities and the need for an intact nervous system to learn in the manner previously outlined, should help you suspect that a student might have a learning problem based on some impairment of the nervous system. In the past, it was the custom of teachers, physicians, and parents to attribute learning and behavioral deviations in students almost exclusively to the child's interpersonal relationships and emotional well-being. Certainly the neural correlates of these emotional problems could act to modify the input of a particular learning experience preventing a satisfactory registration of it. However, today it is felt that we must search among the myriad of organic causations as well as the emotional in attempting to understand each child's learning problem.

It is easy for us to understand the particular school problems of the blind or the deaf who have been sensory deprived, but not so with the child who has not been so obviously stigmatized. Also, I believe we can comfortably understand and accept the abnormal behavior of the restricted beagles or the environmentally impoverished children. But it is much more difficult to accept the hyperactive, impulsive, emotionally labile, awkward activity of some of our children with learning problems as being related to some subtle organic impairment. It was previously mentioned that the intactness of your nervous system allowed you to concentrate upon this subject matter despite other massive sensory inputs (tight shoes, hunger pains, etc.), you are receiving. Certainly it is conceivable that the inability of your nervous system to amplify, modify, and extinguish these inputs would prevent this material from registering. Certainly then, it does not seem improper to attribute some learning problem to an impaired nervous system. A child with poor "circuitry" has difficulty in functioning in the normal teaching situation. Because of his impairment, it may be inferred that he has been unable to acquire significances and attribute meanings to stimuli. Because of the poor circuitry as well as the apparent inability to acquire significances and attribute meanings to stimuli, the child does not have the filtering processes apparently so important for additional learning. He is unable to handle adequately the massive sensory stimuli present in a classroom. It does not seem inconceivable that this problem, coupled with the child's own awareness of his inability to achieve, results in the observed abnormal behavior.

## Summary

An attempt has been made to discuss a few current basic concepts of neurophysiology. It is hoped that this information will be used to heighten your index of suspicion in regard to learning problems. Hopefully, you will see in a number of cases that it is not that "he seems to be bright enough, but he just isn't applying himself. He seems to be bright enough, but he has an emotional block." Although reading and learning problems are oft discussed, an understanding of them seems to be in the toddler stage of development. If there is a suspicion that a neurophysiological problem exists, then proper diagnostic studies should be performed. The problem of diagnosis itself is indeed complex, and to be done properly should be performed by professionals from a number of different disciplines. (See the excellent work by Clements and Peters (4) regarding this multi-discipline approach.) If a diagnosis is made, and a cause for failure to achieve is established, it is to be hoped that the child will be able to avail himself of one of the many special programs now developing. Unfortunately, there is no panacea for managing children with learning problems but by developing a greater awareness of these problems, additional learning and behavior complications may be prevented. Placement in a special education program will not be adequate unless a careful educational diagnostic workup is performed and an appropriate therapeutic educational program is prescribed.

## References

1. Rosenzweig, M. R. Effects of Heredity and Environment on Brain Chemistry, Brain Anatomy and Learning Ability in the Rat. Kansas Studies in Education 14 (1964): 3.
2. Livingston, R. Handbook of Physiology, Section 1, John Field, editor, 1959.
3. Melzak, R. Influence of Early Experience on the Cue-Arousal Effects of Stimulation. Kansas Studies in Education 14 (1964): 79.
4. Clements, S. D. and J. E. Peters, Minimal Brain Dysfunctions in the School-Age Child. Archives of General Psychiatry 6 (1962): 185.

John B. Isom

# Some Neuropsychological Findings in Children With Reading Problems

The data in this presentation and the conclusions drawn therefrom are based upon observations of several hundred children during the last four years. The majority of these children were in attendance in school systems in the greater Portland area at the time they were seen at the University of Oregon Medical School. The immediate source of the referral was the child's teacher or parent, in the majority of cases, and various third parties originated the referral in the remaining cases.

### Reason for Medical Evaluation

The children were referred directly to the essayist for neurological evaluation or they were referred because of his locally known interest in reading disabilities in children. This is a selected population and the findings are not to be construed as necessarily characteristic of poor readers detected in a randomly selected group of school children.

### Selective Features of Children Influencing Referral

That the children referred to a medical facility for evaluation of reading disability represent a selected group is further attested to by examining the ratio of the boys to the girls in several school settings. The ratio of boys to girls in the present series is approximately 6 to 1. Ratios equal to or higher than this have been noted in other diagnostic referral clinics, whether the clinic is in a medical or pedagogic setting. Ratios of boys to girls from 2.0 – 2.4 to 1 have been noted in remedial reading classes in public schools in Portland, Oregon; Boston, Mass. (1); and Stoke-on-Trent, England (2), extending over a 35 year period. The ratio of boys to girls in regular classrooms in the larger public school system is approximately 1 to 1. The degree of reading retardation, whether or not "corrected" for I.Q. is not the only factor that determines whether a child will be referred from his regular classroom to a remedial reading class or from the latter to a diagnostic or evaluation clinic in a medical or educational setting. Doubtless there are many factors which, in general, reflect subjective evaluation of the child by the child's teacher, either in the regular classroom or in the remedial reading class. These factors have not been precisely defined but to the author it appears that they may be grouped under the heading of *pupil-teacher interaction.* In effect, this is a measure of the teacher's acceptance or rejection of the child's reading and non-reading behavior. It is not implied that this is the only factor operating, nor necessarily, the most important one, in all instances. However, it is almost certainly important in a significant number of cases and is probably responsible for the ratio of boys to girls in the referral populations.

The children ranged from 7 to 16 years of age; all but a few were between 9 and 14 years of age. The I.Q., as measured by the WISC or Stanford-Binet, was between 80 and 90 in a small percentage of cases and between 90 and 120 in the bulk of the remainder, a very small number of children had I.Q. scores in the range from 120 to 130 and only one or two above 130. They had no obvious neurological deficit, their vision and hearing were intact. The children showed varying degrees of skill and ease of accomplishment in performing such tasks as tandem walking, standing on one foot, standing with feet together and eyes closed, and execution of rapid, repetitive or sequential movements. These operations are commonly employed to assess the degree of "awkwardness" or "incoordination" that a child demonstrates. These concepts are difficult to define and almost impossible to quantitate. Suffice it to say that the majority of children performed these tasks well and were considered by their parents to be reasonably well, and in some cases, exceptionally well coordinated. Some of the children had been considered ill-coordinated in early childhood and this had persisted but did not prevent the children's dressing themselves completely, including tying shoe laces, or engaging in such activities as riding a bicycle, skating, etc.

We can distinguish two general groups of children by the history given by the parents. In the first group, much the larger, the age of onset of intelligible speech and subsequent oral language development was within expected limits and was not different from that of the child's siblings who do not have reading problems. In the other group, the onset of speech and/or the age of intelligible speech was delayed. In almost all instances the speech subsequently became normal, with or without speech therapy. A few individuals have a persistent lisp or other speech impediment that does not interfere with understanding of the individual's speech.

## Laterality in Poor and Average Readers

We determined the eye which the children preferentially used for monocular sighting and the hand which they preferentially used for unilateral tasks. "Eyedness" is defined by the eye which the child uses to look through a kaleidoscope when it is presented to him in the mid-line and he grasps it with both hands before putting it to his eye. "Handedness" is determined by the hand the child uses when writing, holding a fork, and throwing a ball. If the individual uses the same hand for all three of these tasks, he is considered "handed" for that side. If the hand used for these three tasks is on the same side as the eye used for monocular sighting, he is said to have consistent laterality. If "handedness" and "eyedness" are on opposite sides of the body, then he is said to have crossed laterality. If he does not use the same hand for all three tasks, he has mixed "handedness" and mixed laterality. Obviously, by this operational definition, an individual can be only left- or right-eyed. The frequency of left handedness is approximately 10% in the poor readers and in the average readers. Left-eyedness occurs twice as often in the poor readers as in the average. Consistant hand-eye laterality is noted in 50% of the poor readers as compared to 75% of normals; crossed hand-eye laterality in 47% of the poor readers and 15% of the normals; mixed hand-eye laterality in 3% of the poor readers and 10% of normals. These figures suggest that mixed or consistent hand-eye laterality, but not crossed, right-eyedness, or right handedness, are associated with better reading ability. The group of poor readers and normals were equated for intelligence.

## Laterality in Superior Readers

To further test these conclusions, it was decided to examine a group of superior readers of the same age. We were unable to equate the groups for I.Q. since the superior readers were all in the I.Q. range of 125 to 170, considerably above average-normal or high-average levels. However, the findings are of interest and cast considerable doubt on the suggestion that right-eyedness or consistent hand-eye laterality are causally related to reading ability. Of the 50 advanced readers examined, 6% were left-handed and 33% were left-eyed. The superior group demonstrated consistent hand-eye laterality in a larger percentage of cases than the dyslexic, but in a smaller percentage than the average readers. Superior readers demonstrated crossed hand-eye laterality in a larger percentage than the average readers but in a lesser percentage than the poor readers. They showed mixed hand-eye laterality in a percentage equal to that found in average readers.

In summary, comparisons of these three groups indicated that left-handedness occurred with approximately equal frequency in all three; left eyedness was seen with approximately equal frequency in the advanced and normal groups and yet the difference in reading ability between these two groups was enormous. The advanced readers were five to six years ahead of their grade placement level in reading ability. Consistent hand-eye laterality was found in the advanced readers in a higher percentage than the poor readers, but in a lesser percentage than in the normals. Crossed hand-eye laterality was noted less often in the advanced than in the poor readers but more often in the advanced than in the average readers. Mixed hand-eye laterality was seen more often in the advanced and in the normal groups than in the poor readers.

A recent report by the English Ministry of Education (3) compares the hand-eye correspondence in 11 year olds as it relates to their reading ability which is qualitatively judged to be poor, fair, or good. The ratio of the number of children with crossed hand-eye laterality and consistent hand-eye laterality at each of the three reading levels is approximately unity. This indicates that no advantage in reading is conferred upon the individual with consistent hand-eye laterality at 11 years of age.

## Laterality in First Graders

We examined the reading achievement as it relates to hand-eye correspondence in several hundred children who were in the eighth month of the first grade. The children were divided into three groups, those reading at or below a grade level of 1.7, those reading at a level from grade 1.7 to 1.9, and those reading above grade 1.9. The ratio of the percentage of children with consistent laterality to those with crossed laterality was approximately unity in each of the three reading levels. This indicated no advantage in reading achievement, measured late in the first grade, conferred by consistent vs. crossed laterality.

## Changing Laterality in Childhood

We have had opportunity to perform serial examinations over several years on the same children, currently numbering several hundred. One of the findings of this systematic observation on a single population is that handedness and eyedness are not constant in all children in the late pre-school and early school grades. Approximately two hundred and fifty children were seen at age four, again prior to entering kindergarden, and then prior to entering the first grade. It is of interest that approximately 20% of the children changed "eyedness" and a little less than 10% changed "handedness" during the period of observation. The definitions of eyedness and handedness that have been previously applied are the ones operable here. These findings clearly indicate that one cannot speak of "handedness" and "eyedness" in children unless operational definitions are presented and the age of the children examined is clearly stated.

## Extension Test

Silver and Hagin (4) have employed the so-called extension test of Paul Schilder as a presumed manifestation of cerebral dominance. The test is a relatively simple one in that the subject is asked to fully extend his arms parallel to the floor, with his eyes closed. After the passage of several seconds, sometimes a minute or a minute and a half may be required to gain an end-point, one may see one arm elevated with respect to the other or both arms may remain at the same level. The normal response consists of relative elevation of the hand and arm which are used for writing. If neither arm is elevated, with respect to the other, or if the arm other than the one used for writing is elevated, the response is abnormal. The test is based upon the presumption that the relatively higher arm will reflect greater muscle tone because the "dominant" cerebral hemisphere will deliver more impulses to the peripheral musculature than will the "non-dominant" hemisphere. Silver and Hagin (4) have found this a useful tool in a relatively limited number of individuals, in that more than 90% of individuals with reading disability will have an abnormal extension test or more than 90% of individuals with the abnormal extension test will be found to have reading difficulty. We have not found such a high incidence of abnormal responses in the children with reading disability and it is of interest that 27 out of 50 superior readers had an abnormal response to Schilder's extension test.

The significance of preferential use of an eye and/or a hand on one side of the body for certain tasks and the significance of so-called "crossed" or "consistent" laterality or dominance is obscure. It is evident from this study, as well as several others published in recent years, that observations on various aspects of laterality or so-called cerebral dominance do not serve to distinguish the individual poor reader from the good reader nor do they shed any light on the etiology of reading disability or indicate a consistently successful remedial program.

## Right-Left Concept Development

In contrast to the preferential use of eye or hand, an individual's awareness of the concept of right and left on his own body, on that of a second person and of the right and left relationships of objects in extracor-poreal space does seem to be significantly related to reading achievement.

Our findings in this area parallel those of Belmont and Birch (5), as well as others, although the precise meaning of the association is unclear at this time. We have found that practically all children, whether average or poor readers, are able to identify right and left upon their own person by eight or nine years of age.

The ability to identify right and left on another person lags behind that of identifying right and left on one's own person. There is a distinction between the poor and average readers in the age at which right-left identifi-cation on another person can be made. The majority of normal readers are able to identify right and left on another person by age 7 and in another year or two they can do this on a second person. Poor readers lag markedly in this skill. Less than half are able to identify right and left on a second person at age 9 and it is not until 13–14 years of age that virtually all poor readers can perform this task.

The recognition of the right and left relationships of two or three objects in extra-corporeal space is the most difficult of these identification-tasks and the test with two objects is easier than the test with three objects. Normal children are able to identify the relationship of two objects two or three years before they can that of three. Almost all children can order correctly two objects by the end of the first decade of life. It is not until 11–12 years of age that the majority of children can orient correctly three objects. In contrast, the poor readers are markedly delayed in the acquisi-tion of this facility. By age 14 years, only 84% of our sample could order correctly two objects and only 66% could order correctly three objects. These findings indicate that in the normal and the poor reader, the acquisi-tion of this facility is coincident with the maturation of an underlying process(es) which is completed by the end of the first decade, or early in the second decade, of life in the normal but is not complete in poor readers several years later. However, there is a cumulative increase in the percent-age of poor readers who can perform these tasks as they grow older.

In general, strongly right-handed individuals tend to develop facility in right-left identification at an earlier age than do those who are left-handed. Strongly right- or left-handed individuals are more advanced than those who do not have well-defined handedness. However, this association is not absolute.

## A Basic Process in Poor Readers

Our observations on poor readers suggest a basic difficulty in poor readers. These observations focus on the child's ability to process sequentially presented information, particularly via the auditory channel. The assessment of this function obviously requires a minimal level of auditory-perceptual and visual-perceptual function. In none of our children were we able to detect aberrant auditory or visual perception. The tasks set to the children are, in part, a measure of short term or mnemonic memory and the ability to learn and remember common information, whether formally taught or not. Poor readers have particular difficulty acquiring this kind of information.

The tasks are oral and written. The child is asked to state his complete birthdate, the days of the week, the months of the year, in order, and to write his name, address, phone number and the letters of the alphabet, in order. These tasks apparently reflect maturation of an underlying process(es) of the central nervous system, as well as learned behavior.

Children who are poor readers show a cumulative increase in the percentage who can perform these tasks at successive age levels. They are decidedly retarded in development of this function compared to normals and strikingly retarded when compared to superior readers. The three groups are of comparable chronological age. Excluding recitation of the months of the year and production of the written alphabet, almost all poor readers can perform these tasks by age 16. Only 50% of the group can state the months of the year in order and only 50% can write the alphabet. The distribution of poor readers is such that only 25% of all poor readers who are 16 years of age or more* are able to accomplish both of these tasks.

Comparison of the advanced, the average and the poor readers in the 10-12 year age range indicates that all of the superior readers could perform all of the tasks with the exception of stating the months of the year. Eleven percent of the superior readers were unable to recite the months of the year. Almost all of the average readers could perform all of the tasks except recitation of the months of the year. Approximately 50% of the average normal were unable to state the months of the year in correct order. None of the tasks were accomplished by 100% of the poor readers and, in general, they were decidedly retarded in the rate of development of their ability to perform these tasks. Only 15% of the poor readers knew the months of the year and only 37% could write the alphabet.

These tasks reflect an auditory or auditory-visual skill and in an attempt to distinguish the more important channel, the auditory digit span retention of each of these three groups of individuals was determined. The results were rather similar, in pattern, for all three groups. Each of the three groups showed progressive increase, with age, in the number of digits they could repeat. The advanced readers were superior to the average and they, in turn, were strikingly advanced with respect to the poor readers.

---

*We have examined 18 poor readers who range from 18-44 years of age.

Observations made by Rosenberger (6) would suggest that "sequencing" is also at fault in poor readers as contrasted to good readers. In their study, a three by three matrix was visually presented and the child was required to match letters in the central cell with combinations of the same letters in the surrounding cells. The word "the" was in the central cell in two matrices. In one matrix the surrounding cells were blank or contained various combinations of the three letters in "the." In the other matrix, cells were blank or contained combinations of the three letters in the word "the" or substitution of an "l" for a "t" in "the" or the "o" for an "e" in "the." Another matrix contained the letters "laj," meaningless in English, in the central cell and blanks or various combinations of these three letters in the surrounding cells. The fourth matrix presented a circle, a square, and a triangle in that order in the central cell and blanks or various combinations of these geometric figures in the surrounding cells. It is of interest that there was no differentiation of the poor readers versus the good readers on the task employing geometric figures. However, there was a striking difference between the poor readers and the good readers when the center cell contained "laj," or "the," and the comparison was with combinations of "t," "h," "e," or "l," "a," and "j," respectively. There was a lesser degree of distinction between poor and good readers when the central cell contained "the" and some of the possible comparisons include substitution of "l" and "o."

Lecours (7) and Lecours and Twitchell (8) have indicated that poor readers make sequential errors in written language. We have noted similar errors and have also found that poor readers make sequential errors in spoken language when the material is unfamiliar or difficult. The children are asked to repeat motorically complex speech units such as "persistence," "essential," and "success" and the sentence, "Persistence is essential to success" (9). Poor readers perform much less well than the average readers.

In summary, it appears that the poor readers differ significantly from average or superior readers in the facility with which they may process sequentially presented information. Depending upon the complexity and the familiarity of the material to be processed, they appear to have more difficulty with the auditory than the visual aspects of this process. Conversely, those who perform well on tests designed to assess the ability to process auditorily and visually presented, sequential information, in general, are good or superior readers.

The poor readers we examined have average-normal intelligence and are able to use spoken language adequately. They may have less facility with language than the more accomplished readers, particularly those with superior ability. The poor reader does not have language disability in the sense of an individual with *aphasia.*

Our observations suggest that poor readers may be distinguished from good readers by deficiency of short-term memory, or in the rote processing of nonsense or non-meaningful material—so called automatic or mnemonic memory. This is in contrast to the extraction of meaning from printed words.

To the beginning reader, all printed words are nonsense and he appears to process them in rote fashion. Initially, he processes them word-by-word, later by groupings of words or phrases or sentences. Once the reader is able to speak or name the printed word, he learns the meaning of that word. Learning the meaning of the word is made easier if the reader can associate the spoken word with some object, person or situation in his own experience. When these serial processes have been accomplished, the word may be considered part of the reader's active, oral vocabulary. The individual cannot read skillfully or create meaning from what he reads until he has reached this stage of development in the art of learning to read.

We need not dwell upon those factors influencing the deriving of meaning from printed material except to emphasize that it *must* follow the process of associating spoken word with written word.

Most children accomplish these two tasks, association of auditory and visual symbol and learning the meaning of either or both easily and simultaneously (10). Individuals who have difficulty with reading have difficulty with the first stage of learning to read. This is reflected in difficulty with other kinds of mnemonic or rote tasks which we ask them to perform. This study is, in a sense, a retrospective one and we cannot conclude that individuals who have difficulty with these tasks at the time they enter school will necessarily show subsequent difficulty with reading although it is our impression and tentative opinion that such would be the case.

Theoretically, if reading is composed of two discrete processes, and one must preceed the other, then we should find, in clinical practice, two different kinds of reading disability. All of us are only too familiar with individuals who have difficulty with the rote processing of written material and also have difficulty understanding printed material. Only rarely do we encounter individuals who are very skillful in the rote processing of printed material and have great difficulty with or are unable to appreciate the meaning of the material. Why one kind of disability should be so frequently encountered and the other so rarely encountered is obscure.

## References

1. Durrell, Donald D., *Improvement of Basic Reading Disabilities* (Yonkers-on-Hudson, N.Y.: World Book Co., 1940).

2. *The Health of the School Child.* Report of the Chief Medical Officer of the Ministry of Education for the year 1960 and 1961. London: Her Majesty's Stationary Office, 1962 (Reprinted 1963), 22.

3. *Ibid.,* 23.

4. Silver, Archie and Rosa Hagin, "Specific Reading Disability: Delineation of the Syndrome and Relationship to Cerebral Dominance," *Comprehensive Psychiatry* I (April 1960): 126–133.

5. Belmont, Lillian and Herbert G. Birch, "Lateral Dominance and Right-Left Awareness in Normal Children," *Child Development* XXXIV (1963): 257–270.

6. Rosenberger, Peter, "Visual Recognition and Other Neurologic Findings in Good and Poor Readers," *Neurology* XVII (1967): 332 (abstract).

7. Lecours, Andre-Roch, "Serial Order in Writing—A Study of Misspelled Words in 'Developmental Dysgraphia,'" *Neurophsychologia* IV (1966): 221–241.

8. Lecours, Andre-Roch and Thomas E. Twitchell, "Sequential Errors in Written Language: Their Form, Occurrence and Nature," *Neurology* XVI (1966): 313 (abstract).

9. Blakely, Robert, "Oral Sequencing Ability: Norms for Ages 5-12 Years," ASHA 7 (September 1965): 321. Paper presented at the 41st Annual Convention of the American Speech and Hearing Association, October 30, 1965. To be reprinted in *The Practice of Speech Pathology: A Clinical Diary* (Springfield, Ill.: Charles C. Thomas, *in press*).

10. Bateman, Barbara, "Reading: A Controversial View, Research and Rationale," Curriculum Bulletin XXIII, 278 (Eugene, Oregon: School of Education, University of Oregon, 1967), 14 (Mimeographed).

# C. Keith Conners

## *Neuro-Physiological Studies of Learning Disorders*

Many of the behavioral features of children with reading disorders, such as poor sequencing ability, right-left confusion, poor auditory or visual discrimination, figure-ground impairments, have led some investigators to ascribe the reading disorder to minimal brain dysfunction syndromes (MBD). Some authors, like Critchley, maintain that there is a very specific dyslexic syndrome that is largely genetic or constitutional in origin, and which is separable on clinical grounds from those disorders arising from insults to the brain or delayed maturation.

The difficulty with the MBD, maturational, and genetic hypotheses, is that, *a priori,* from what we know of human behavior and development, all are likely to be true in some instances; but the available diagnostic tools are seldom adequate to rule one or the other hypotheses in or out for a specific case. Moreover, it seems reasonable to suppose that some, if not all, reading disorders arise from the interaction or joint influence of several kinds of variables acting together. In a particular case it may be difficult to know whether to place greater weight on the biological or social-environmental factors. Even the pediatric neurological examination is largely behavioral in nature, and inferences regarding defects in the nervous system are necessarily indirect. Instruments like the EEG are seldom specific enough to provide clear information regarding brain dysfunction, even though statistically there is a significant association between reading disorders and abnormalities of the EEG.

In this paper I will briefly describe recent studies aimed at discovery of specific brain dysfunction associated with reading failure, and the development of a taxonomic classification system of the learning disorders. In our studies we have had the use of two powerful physiological tools: cortical evoked responses and pharmacologic intervention.

Electrical activity is always present in the brain and can be observed through the use of the amplification techniques known as the EEG. However, the electrical rhythms measured in this way give only gross measures of cortical background activity and do not show the specific electrical changes which occur when specific stimuli, such as flashes of light or clicks are used. These "evoked responses" (ER) are very small in magnitude when compared with the background noise of the larger EEG rhythms. However, the ER can be measured by using computers to average the EEG following stimulation, gradually building up a waveform which becomes distinct when the responses to many stimuli are averaged (this is possible because the random background voltages, consisting of both positive and negative values will average out to zero, while the non-random responses will tend to summate). These ERs are sensitive to changes of state in the brain, such as the attentiveness of the subject, his level of arousal, the magnitude or energy of the physical stimuli, and so forth.

The value of this technique can be illustrated by one of our patients, a boy of 11½ years, referred with a severe reading disorder. He had great difficulty in word recognition, comprehension and silent reading, despite above-average intelligence. He reversed many letters in spelling and writing, and had difficulty concentrating in all subjects. Though he was said to be easily distracted he was not noticeably hyperactive at home, school or in the clinic, and was not in any way a behavior problem. His motor coordination and development were above average, but his age equivalent for spatial orientation tasks was at a seven-year level, and he had considerable difficulty with figure-ground problems (both auditory and visual), and with form constancy. He had a marked left-right confusion, but generally performed best with the right hand.

The neurological examination was normal, and a psychiatric examination revealed him to be cooperative, serious and somewhat subdued and with a poor self-concept. His peer relationships were generally good and he had normal interests for a boy of his age. Copying of designs and drawing of a person were poor for his age.

Two features of his history were important: delivery was difficult and labor had to be induced, and there was respiratory congestion requiring oxygen for one week. Secondly, the father and three siblings all had severe reading problems. The paternal grandfather and paternal uncle also were said to have had reading problems.

The first figure shows the cortical ER taken from the left and right occipital and parietal areas of the scalp. It can be seen that the left parietal response to visual stimulation (the third of the four tracings) is markedly attenuated. The father and three siblings were also examined with the visual evoked response method, and all showed a similar asymmetric response, with the left parietal area showing definite abnormality. The mother, who was a normal reader, did not show this abnormality of the ER.

Since normal children, and indeed most of our patients, do not show this profound loss of responsiveness of the ER we have some suggestive evidence to support the hypothesis of altered brain function in this family of poor readers. The picture is complicated by the fact that all of the siblings also had a difficult labor and delivery, raising the possibility that some genetic influence on maternal reproductivity may be operative and producing cerebral trauma of a very specific, limited type which then affects the growth of symbol-processing abilities. Other children, however, with several affected family members, have also shown this specific abnormality of the ER in the absence of birth difficulties. In any case, the evidence would suggest that for *some types* of reading disorder there may be direct involvement of neural structures in the reading failure which is detectable by the ER method.

Further evidence that the reading disorder has a physiological basis is given by the fact that this patient, when treated with a stimulant drug

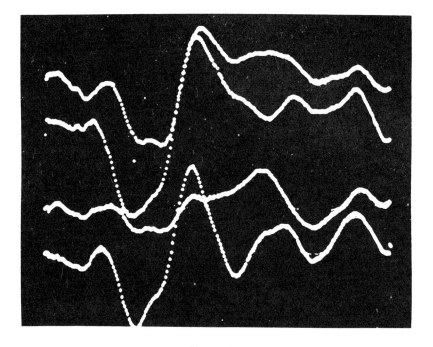

**Figure 1**

*Visual evoked response from four scalp locations: left occipital, right occipital, left parietal, right parietal.*

showed an immediate and dramatic improvement in reading and spelling ability. During the first month of treatment the boy gained 9 months in reading and arithmetic, and 7 months in spelling on the Wide Range Achievement Test (WRAT), with accompanying improvements in figure-ground ability, auditory blending, and Performance IQ (the latter went from 99 to 117, which is considerably more than expected from practice effects). The teachers also noted a general improvement in concentration and school work, and parents were impressed with the much greater degree of integration and organization in the boy's homework.

Our first larger study of the ER was done with 27 children attending a summer remedial reading program. All of the children were examined with the ER and the WRAT, with the latter given both at the beginning and end of the summer. The results were rather astonishing to us: the large component of the visual ER correlated .61 with reading and .64 with spelling, a result significant at less than the .01 level. This finding only occurred for the left parietal measure.

This study was replicated on 20 children from a private school for children with learning disorders, with the correlation of the reading quotient and left parietal visual ER being almost identical to the first study, .63. This study utilized the "learning quotient" of Myklebust which adjusts the reading score on the basis of expected level of performance as predicted from chronological age, grade placement and IQ.

In a third study we selected two groups of 13 children from our clinic files, carefully matched on age, sex, Full Scale IQ and social class. One group was average in Verbal IQ but low in Performance IQ, and the other group was average in Performance IQ and low in Verbal IQ. Once again, significant differences, largely in the parietal region, were found between these groups in the amplitudes of the ER, with the low verbal children having smaller amplitudes in the parietal region (though this time the effects were almost as strong on the right as on the left side). The low Performance children had significantly slower ER responses in the occipital region and were also rated as more neurologically impaired by a pediatric neurologist.

In a recent study we examined the effect of the stimulant drugs (methylphenidate and dextroamphetamine) on both the behavior and the evoked responses of children with a variety of learning disorders. The next figure shows some of the effects of the two drugs as compared with a placebo on the psychological test measures. The results show, as have several of our previous studies, that a number of cognitive and perceptual changes occur for the drug-treated children. The drugs also significantly reduce the latencies of the ER, but the effects on the amplitudes are minimal for the group as a whole.

What is most interesting is the correlation between the behavioral changes produced by the drugs and changes produced on the evoked re-

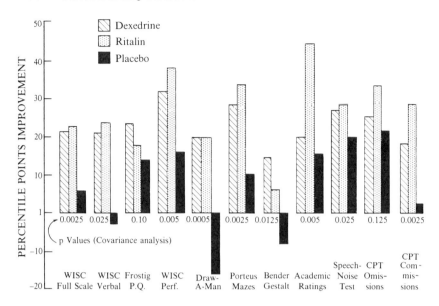

**Figure 2**

*Psychological test changes for Dexedrine, Ritalin, and placebo (N=25 per group). Change scores based on percentile improvement of the normal curve.*

sponse. For example, highly significant concomitant changes in ER and reading and spelling occurred. As reading and spelling improved, there was a significant change in the amplitudes of the ER. These correlations range from about .30 to about .50, all significant at less than the .05 level, with several of them significant at less than the .01 level (that is, less than one time in a hundred would such correlations have occurred by chance alone). Changes in latency were not correlated with the verbal changes, but highly significant correlations with improvement in arithmetic were found: those children who improved in arithmetic tended to have faster latencies in response to drug treatment.

Finally, a further step in our research has been to attempt to further refine our diagnostic classifications by grouping children together on the basis of their psychological test profile (1). One approach to this problem is to sample a wide range of functions, and place children into groups on the basis of their profile similarity. This is essentially what clinicians do in arriving at clinical syndromes or types. Boder (2) for example, has described three types of poor readers based on the type of reading errors the children make. We have taken a number of commonly used psychological tests and sorted children into groups using some 35 test scores. These scores are first factor analyzed to reduce them to a smaller number which gives a set of measures independent of one another.

We had a sample of 178 children with learning and behavior disorders who all received the same 35 tests before and after drug or placebo treatment. A computer was used to arrive at the smallest number of distinct groups. The next figure shows the pretreatment profiles which resulted from this procedure.

Several important findings emerged once we had classified the children into these homogeneous clusters. First, we noted that several tests showed drug-placebo differences that had not previously emerged for the group as a whole. For our purposes here, one of the most interesting of these is spelling. Only group I and group VII showed significant drug effects on spelling. Group IV showed only one drug effect, improvement in the Bender Gestalt Test. Group V showed virtually no drug effects.

Secondly, when we examined the ER we found highly significant differences between the groups in the amount of change in ER amplitudes.

Thirdly, we found that if one takes a ratio of the left hemispheric activity to the right, the groups differ quite markedly in these left-right ratios. Specifically, groups I and VII are highly "right-dominant"; that is, the right amplitudes are almost twice as large as the left; and group IV is highly "left-dominant," with a ratio of 3.9. It would thus seem to be no accident that groups I and VII show improvement in spelling, and group IV shows an improvement in the Bender drawings.

You will recall that much evidence points to the fact that after birth the left hemisphere becomes increasingly specialized for language functions and symbolic processing, while the right appears to become specialized for spatial and temporal processing. Thus, it should not be surprising to find that many people, starting with Hinshelwood and Samuel Orton, have noted some relationship between "dominance" and reading disorders. Unfortunately, this fact has been obscured by the relation of cerebral dominance with handedness, which is only a rough guide to cerebral dominance, especially in left-handers.

But if the normal course of development consists of increasingly specialized use of the left hemisphere for language, then, as Orton suggested, incomplete cerebral dominance could result in the lack of the ability to decode symbols. Similarly, delayed development or injury to the right hemisphere could produce reading disorders whose basic cause is the inability to analyze spatial or temporal sequences. Obviously good reading requires both functions at different stages of the information processing sequence. The eye must recognize the shapes which convention uses as letters or graphemes, and certain sequences of such shapes must be assigned meaning on the basis of previously learned correspondences between graphemes and phonemes. Presumably while one function is operative the other

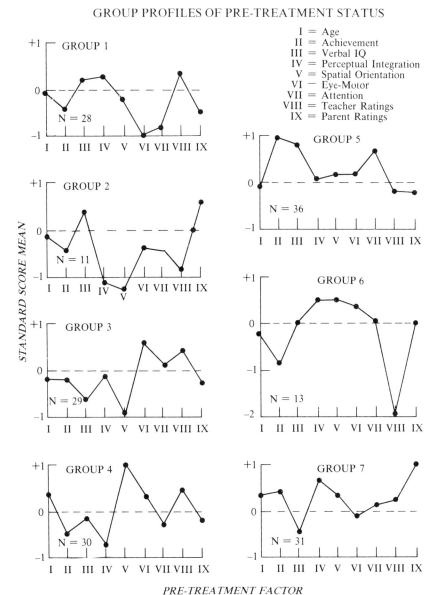

GROUP PROFILES OF PRE-TREATMENT STATUS

I   = Age
II  = Achievement
III = Verbal IQ
IV  = Perceptual Integration
V   = Spatial Orientation
VI  = Eye-Motor
VII = Attention
VIII = Teacher Ratings
IX  = Parent Ratings

GROUP 1    N = 28

GROUP 2    N = 11

GROUP 3    N = 29

GROUP 4    N = 30

GROUP 5    N = 36

GROUP 6    N = 13

GROUP 7    N = 31

*STANDARD SCORE MEAN*

*PRE-TREATMENT FACTOR*

**Figure 3**

*Profiles of 7 groups identified by cluster analysis.*

must be inhibited, and we know from neurophysiological studies that there is provision for very rapid exchange of information between the hemispheres via the corpus callosum and other commissural structures. Moreover, for any of these activities to be functional, the brain stem, via the reticular formation must provide tonic activation and stimulation to the cortex and regulate the threshold sensitivities of the cortical areas involved in a given behavior.

With these ideas in mind, we may speculate as follows regarding our findings: in certain children either cerebral trauma or genetic factors lead either to left hemisphere, right hemisphere, or diffuse impairment. The latter could be subdivided into impairment involving the diffuse reticular activating system, diffuse cortical damage, or delayed development of both cortices. We might expect that the stimulant drugs would improve reading, spelling or other language behavior either when the cause is a generalized impairment of attentional functions (probably due to reticulocortico problems), or when the impairment to either hemisphere is such that by increasing stimulation to those areas some threshold is achieved which allows the system to function consistently.

It should be possible to construct an adequate taxonomy for reading disorders by grouping children in terms of the kinds of errors they make in reading. Thus, a general attentional deficit might show up as errors randomly distributed throughout the reading performance, with no characteristic semantic, phonic, visuo-spatial or other kinds of errors predominating. Errors due to impairment of right hemispheric function should show up as perceptual confusions, in dysgraphia as well as dyslexia, while left hemispheric abnormalities might be expressed by syntactic and semantic errors. Our own work has shown, as a beginning, that cortical evoked responses may provide some direct tests of selected areas of the brain's responsivity; and it has shown that stimulant drugs can alter reading and spelling performance in some children. We are currently constructing a comprehensive spelling and reading error analysis which we hope will give us a further basis for such a taxonomy. Once the types of reading failure are classified, then measures of brain function may tell us which types have a significant biologic component, and then hopefully we will have rational diagnostic procedures to assist us in deciding which treatment or combinations of treatments are indicated.

In summary, the following conclusions seem warranted from our studies of learning disorders to this date:

1) Learning disorders are a heterogeneous set of disorders, probably arising from various forms of environmental, maturational, and genetic influences on the central nervous system;

2) these disorders can probably be classified into a limited number of "types" on the basis of psychological and/or physiological procedures;

3) some of these types respond quite dramatically to treatment with stimulant drugs, and show concomitant changes in brain function which can be measured directly;

4) there is no one response to drug treatment, but rather, different children respond to treatment in different ways, depending on prior physiological and psychological state;

5) cortical evoked responses may provide important direct evidence regarding central nervous system dysfunction where other clinical evidence does not do so.

Needless to say, the results and conclusions stated here require much further work before they can be effectively translated into practical diagnostic and treatment plans for the clinician. Perhaps their most important role is to alert us to the significant biological factors which underly, and in some cases, become critical for satisfactory learning in the child. Judicious pharmacologic treatment is clearly useful in certain carefully diagnosed children whose underlying problems are of central nervous system origin, but should never be used without clear indications.

## References

1. Conners, C. K. Stimulant drugs and cortical evoked responses in learning and behavior disorders in children. Paper presented at the 2nd Annual Cerebral Function Symposium at the Brown Palace, Denver, 1970.
2. Boder, E. A. Neuropediatric Approach to the Diagnosis and Management of School Behavioral and Learning Disorders. In J. Hellmuth (Ed.) *Learning Disorders, Volume II* (Special Child Publications, 1966), 15–44.

## Acknowledgements

The work presented was supported by grant No. MH-14432 from the Psychopharmacology Section of the National Institute of Mental Health and Research Scientist Development Award No. K2-MII-7839 of the National Institute of Mental Health.

This paper is a condensed version of the paper read at the 38th Annual Claremont Reading Conference, February 5–6, 1971, Claremont, California.

Clara Lee Edgar

# Perceptual Motor Training as an Aid to Development of Reading Abilities

Recent trends in psychological inquiry emphasize relationships between the development of intelligence and experience. J. McV Hunt's book, *Intelligence and Experience,* is one of the better known recent books dealing with some of these notions. In it he points out, for example, that we once thought of intelligence as being "fixed"; the child came with a certain degree of intelligence. We could measure his I.Q. and be reasonably certain that his score would not vary too much during the years of his development. We now know that this is false and that experience has much to do with how the child develops. A number of recent experimental studies illumine this point. For example, Dr. Austin Riesen, now at the University of California at Riverside, did some remarkable work with apes. The animals were reared in the dark, and not only were they unable to recognize visually such common objects as their nursing bottles after a number of months of dark rearing, but actually the optic nerves were under-developed. Not only was the behavior, the intelligence if you will, retarded, but the actual physical development of the animal was retarded, primarily because of the lack of visual experience.

Of equal interest to us are the Wayne Dennis studies with children in the orphanages in Teheran. Children from state orphanages, which had a great number of children, too many for the number of personnel to care for, were contrasted with a private orphanage where the children got more attention. In the state orphanages the children lay on their backs most of the time; they were propped up somewhat for feeding and their bottle propped beside them. They were not placed on their tummies nor on a hard surface, like the floor, often enough to develop any creeping pattern. These children didn't walk until they were three and a half to four years old. The lack of practice retarded their motor development. The children were later shown to have normal intellectual potential.

Mention might also be made of an interesting experiment by Richard Held, at M.I.T. Held has conducted experiments which have to do with perceptual development and perceptual change through experience, using both human beings and animals. One of the interesting things that he did was to dark-rear some kittens. These kittens were reared without visual experience; they had no opportunity to learn to perceive visually. Subsequently the kittens were then given experience in a little carousel apparatus in an enclosure which had a visual pattern on its walls. The carousel held two kittens, one on either side, and when the carriers revolved around the center post they exposed both kittens to the same patterned visual experience. However, in one carrier the kitten propelled the carousel by walking on his own feet. In the other carrier, the kitten stood on a platform, and was pulled by the walking kitten. The walking kitten therefore received the sensory feedback from his own motor activity—the "re-efferent" stimulation from his walking—while receiving the visual experience. The kittens were later subjected to some elementary visual tests; for example, they would be gradually lowered toward a flat surface to see whether or not they would extend their feet in anticipation at seeing the surface below them. Only the kittens who walked on his own feet while viewing the environment had sufficient perceptual development to pass the visual tests.

Now we know, from the many studies like these, that sensory motor experiences do aid in the development of perception. *The question is, however, not only what sensory-motor integration has to do with perception, but what it has to do with something which develops at the same time and which becomes much more complex, and that is cognition.* Reading specialists are well aware that there are many aspects to this problem of reading. Some of them are purely, or more nearly purely perceptual, but many of them are primarily cognitive, dealing with manipulation of verbal symbols, with language. Today we are talking about sensory-motor development which begins in an infant at birth, or as we now know, before birth, and we are wondering what its possible relationship is to something as complex as printed-word reading, which begins to develop rapidly for most children after they are six years of age. I think we need to consider the tremendous developmental gap between the sensory-motor beginnings of development and something involving as many cognitive functions as reading, so that when we ask why Johnny doesn't read we will realize that there are many subtleties of perceptual and cognitive development, many changes which evolve in the interim period between birth and the age of six or seven or eight, and consequently many chances for something to go wrong. There are many kinds of experiences which the child needs to integrate before he is ready to read print. If we place perception and conception at opposite ends of a single dimension as Wohlwill does—if we believe that the difference between a purely *perceptual* and a purely *inferential* task is one of greatly increased opportunity to supplement or replace sensory data with information or knowledge *not* contained in the immediate perceptual situation, then we can see that the child needs to integrate an enormous number of experiences before he is ready to read print.

In order to explore how something like sensory-motor training might possibly relate to the complex problem of reading, we need to examine the nature of the child's thinking processes between birth and age seven, his cognitive development during these years. For this purpose I have chosen to review Piaget's Cognitive Theory. You may wonder, why Piaget? Why not Gesell's, or someone else's theory of development? This is because we need a theory which tries to show not only *what* the child does at a given age, say two or three, or four, but *why* he does it and *how* he does it. In other words, we are interested in looking at *qualitative* changes in his development; he may solve the same problems at four that he does at seven, but he goes about it differently at seven.

Piaget calls the period between birth and two years the Sensory-Motor Period of development. Much goes on during this period, and in some cases when we do something like Kephart's training exercises we may in some cases be going all the way back to this level to eliminate some gaps in the child's development. From ages two to four, Piaget talks about a period of "Pre-Conceptual Thought;" and from four to seven he calls the period "Intuitive Thought."

Piaget believes that an organism develops because of constant exchange or contact with its environment. He says that the organism acts on the environment, and that there are slight changes every time the baby acts, slight changes in the *conditions* under which he acts, and consequently slight *modification* of the action itself. The baby, therefore, adjusts to these changes by *accommodation,* that is by slightly modifying his acts to the conditions of the environment. When he accommodates to changes, he *assimilates* the sensory feedback from his motor acts in his central nervous system. So, there is something like a spiral of assimilation and accommodation between the organism and the environment. At the bottom of the spiral, for example, are only reflexes; between birth and two months the infant refines the reflexes that he brought into the world. For example, if you stroke his cheek downward, he turns his head in the direction of the cheek which is stroked. If you touch his palm he will grasp your finger. Now, during these early months he refines his reflexes in response to the environment; he becomes more efficient at nursing—at finding the breast, grasping, sucking and finally learning to focus his eyes at the same time on the mother's face. Between two and four months he becomes very efficient at integrating various reflexes together; he becomes an efficient nurser, and if you hold a bell to the side of his visual field at three months, he will turn his head and grasp with his eyes what he is already grasping with his ears. Later, he will grasp the bell with hand and mouth as well.

Between four and eight months he begins to do something very interesting. All this time he has been acting on the environment, primarily with his eyes, and the environment has contacted him through the skin, through touch, temperature, and muscles and joints. He has been perceiving the world through the *near* receptors; that is he is interested in motion, touch, lights, taste, smell, warmth, and so forth. But now he becomes able to go a little beyond himself, he develops his distance receptors, the eyes and the ears. He becomes interested in objects outside of himself; he can reach for them, examine them with his eyes, try out his various propensities for shaking, banging, patting and otherwise exploiting objects. He now becomes interested, Piaget says, in trying to reproduce sights and sound which originally occurred by chance alone. This is the period of "making interesting sights last." For example, one of Piaget's own children happened to notice a mobile hanging on one end of his baby carriage, and the baby happened to be kicking its legs when he noticed the mobile moving. Now, to us, this seems like a direct cause and effect relationship. But Piaget says, not at all; the baby doesn't have any realization that it makes motion, and the motion jiggles the carriage which causes the mobile to bounce. It only happened that, magically, he happened to be doing the one thing when he noticed the other. The same thing occurs when the mother goes out of the room; if the baby is waving its arms when her face appears in the doorway, the baby will wave its arms and look in anticipation for the face to reappear. There is a connection between the sensory awareness of the motor act and the visual experience. This is the rather "magic" *motor* precursor of true means-end behavior, the sensory-motor analogue of means-end behavior. Later, at eight to twelve months, there is also the beginning of a sort of sensory-motor analogue of forming classes and relations. There is a class of shaking, of banging, plucking and so on. "To shake and hear noise" is one of the classes he employs. So, in this period, one can see that in a physical sense, in a sensory-motor sense, the baby is beginning his cognitive development. Classifying things is something the child will do verbally when he is about five years old. So that here we have sensory motor development and cognitive development as parts of the same process.

At eight to twelve months, the baby no longer picks up an object just to employ as an aliment—a "nutritional element"—to satisfy one of his sensory motor behaviors; Piaget calls them schemata. In other words, a cup, a ball, a box are no longer exploited in order to satisfy the child's need to bang. Thus far he has employed all objects to exercise his need for scratching or banging or grasping and mouthing. Between the ages of eight and twelve months, the baby begins to see what the object is good for; he explores the character of the object. He tries out all of his schemata to find out what can be done with the object. Heretofore, all objects have been a part of an "action-object" sequence, in which objects have not possessed a character separate from the action in which they are embedded. Now, there is some separation between person and object; sensory-motor patterns are employed as a means to an end concerning the object and not as an object in themselves.

Between twelve and eighteen months the baby pursues novelty for its own sake. He wants to find out what can be done with things; he wants to find out what can be done with himself, his body, in space. He explores the environment, and objects in the environment achieve true separation from his actions and assume a character of their own. Verbal symbols begin to be attached. Following 18 months, there is increasing internal, symbolic representation of sensory motor problems. Increasingly, after age two, objects can be manipulated in the mind, and have names; actions are carried out in space, but increasingly they can be carried out in the mind. He can now see, for example, a cup, and it reminds him of the action of grasping the handle, lifting, and drinking. The cup now has true object character of its own. Now the word "cup" may be attached to the object, and the action carried out internally. A pillow may symbolize the action of putting one's head on it. Until this is achieved through sensory-motor experience with objects, meaningful language cannot develop.

Between two and four years, although the child has some meaningful language there are certain characteristics—limitations, in his thinking which are important because the problems they impose may not be entirely worked through until he is six or seven years old. One, he is *ego-centric*. He is unable to view any situation from any stand-point except his own. For example, one of Piaget's experiments consists of a mock-up of several mountain peaks. The child is asked to indicate which of several views a doll would see if the doll were standing on various sides of the mock-up. A child of this age is unable to conceive that the situation would appear differently from the way he sees it at a given moment or position in space.

Another characteristic is *centration*. This means that the child is unable to consider more than one characteristic or element of the problem situation at once. For example, if you take a beaker of water, tall and thin, and pour the water into a beaker like this, low, flat, and wide, and then ask which contains the most water, the child may say the low one does, because it is "big," or because it is "wide," or that the tall one did because *it* is "big," or because it is "high." He is dominated by the perceptual qualities of the object, and cannot think his way past them.

A third problem with which he is faced is a lack of "reversibility"; the inability to trace back through his mind the steps by which he got to where he is in a given problem situation. If you pour the water from this tall beaker into these two shorter ones, and then ask him what set has more water, he may say the two small beakers do, because there are more of them. He hasn't achieved what Piaget calls, "conservation," in this case, conservation of volume—the ability to trace back and remember how things were at the beginning. In Wohlwill's terms, he cannot yet contribute much additional knowledge and bits of information which are not contained in the physical scene before his eyes. He is still dominated by what he perceives. He may be seven years old before he overcomes this limitation to his thinking; but between four and seven years he gradually works through these problems. Now, his ability to deal with meaningful language can only advance to the extent that he understands, that is, comprehends because of increasing practice with them, some of these problems of *time, space, causality,* the *permanent character of objects and so forth.*

In what way does sensory-motor training contribute to his readiness for reading? How do exercises which may pertain to the earliest level of development have any direct relationship to the processes of reading and writing? It is easier to see that establishing laterality and directionality in Kephart's sense will aid in the perception of form, including the forms of letters, and in the child's ability to remember these forms and to translate what he perceives into a motor response, as in drawing or lettering. Beyond this, it is possible that sensory-motor training contributes to thinking, problem solving and the like. This process is more readily observed with the retarded child than with the normal first or second grader, who may hide his deficiences better. When a retarded young child is placed on a walking board, or on its substitute, a mattress, and not allowed to step off, he is faced with an immediate and physically demanding situation which captures his attention. This problem has elements of awareness of time, space, causality and object permanence at a very primitive level. As he is forced to negotiate the walking board he develops a body-sense of the time, in effort expended, from one end to the other. At the motor level, he carries out a temporal sequence; he begins, carries through, and terminates a physical task. He notices his feet and has to determine where to place them; his attention returns many times to his own body, alternating with attention to the adult, the end of the board, the section of the board where he stands, and so forth. His awareness of all of these is forced, and possibly object permanence, including self awareness, is enhanced. He develops a working sense of space and means-end behavior, causality.

At a more advanced level, gross sensory-motor apparatus such as the mattress, walking board and balance board is supplemented by such exercises as "angels in the snow," alternating the arms with bongos or tamborines, connecting points in space on the chalk board, and so forth. While undoubtedly helping the child to integrate the sides of his body and developing his perception, the games may well also facilitate cognitive development more directly. It is possible that any situation which demands attention to more than one aspect of what is happening, be it integration of left arm and right leg as in the angels game, alternating attention to the parts of a rhythm pattern, or keeping a series of several points in space in mind at once, will aid the child in overcoming the centration effect. In these games the child must overcome by mental effort the tendency to lose himself in the part of the activity that his eyes and his momentary attention are riveted on. While watching his right arm beat a tamborine held on his right he must remember to switch to his left. Although these activities may represent quite a primitive, sensory-motor analogue to such cognitive achievements, they do represent a mental tracing through the action sequence in both forward and backward direction, a mental process necessary for what Piaget calls "operational thought." The same process is necessary to overcome "ego-centrism" and to develop "conservation." All of these processes demand that attention be switched from the *end product* of the action, say the beating of the tamborines themselves, to the *process* by which the action was accomplished, in this case the remembering of the sequence of the rhythmic pattern. The roots of operational thought, as well as pre-operational thought, must therefore lie in sensory-motor development; the meaningful use of language thus is closely tied to developing thought patterns.

If tests of gains from sensory-motor training are to be made, they must be made at the level of development which the child has reached. Laterality integration, such as "angels in the snow" might produce, if given to a kindergarten child, could be measured in some immediate, non-verbal test of right-left discrimination. To give such a child a reading test a year or two later would probably fail to measure the *type* of generalization which probably occurred, *at the level of development* at which it occurred. Recently two such tests of generalization were made at Pacific State Hospital. The question being explored was whether generalized gains, intellectual gains, if you like, result from sensory-motor training. Does the child who is trained on the walking board merely become an accomplished gymnast, or does some more general gain occur?

In the first of these studies, a group of kindergarten children was trained for four months. A control group was given individual attention in the classroom. At the end of the training period, Head's "Hand, Eye and Ear" Test in a non-verbal form was repeated with both groups. This is a test in which the child imitates pointing to one or another eye or ear with the hand on either the same or the opposite side of the body. In the case of the group which had received sensory-motor training, the children crossed the midline of the body, in other words used the hand on the opposite side to cross to the opposite eye or ear, significantly more times than their controls. This is one form of a test of generalization—the neural integration of the sides of body, or body-image development, if you will, is reflected in Head's "Hand, Eye and Ear" Test. It is interesting that this integration occurred apart from any progress the child may or may not have made in labeling his parts as "right" or "left."

The second of these studies concerned generalization at the level of the sensory-motor period of life, that is, during the first two years of development. The Gesell Scales of Motor, Adaptive, Personal-Social and Language Behavior were given before and after an eight-month training period to mentally retarded toddlers. These children averaged 15 months in mental age. While it would be expected that motor development would improve significantly due to sensory-motor training, it is especially interesting that the other three behavior scales, the Adaptive, Language and Personal-Social Scales, also improved significantly. The experimental groups averaged 7.7 months mental age gain in 8 months compared to 1.9 months for the controls, who were given individual attention but not sensory-motor training.

These two studies are good evidence that there is generalization, that is, general intellectual gain, from increased sensory-motor integration. It must be emphasized that tests of generalization in both cases were made at the level of development expected to be attained by the child as a result of the training. With more advanced perceptual training, tests more nearly related to academic work might be made. The answer to the question of whether and how sensory-motor and perceptual training is related to reading development, must therefore be answered by showing experimentally that such training promotes gains in specific areas of development, or at given general developmental levels for which the training was aimed. And, of course, such training must be consistent with the child's general level of development.

*    *    *

I have attempted to show, first, that gains in development are related to experience with the environment; that sensory-motor experience itself is related to adaptive behavior, to general cognitive development. Second, Piaget's developmental theory of the first seven years was reviewed in order to suggest how these aspects of development are related. Third, I have presented several studies which indicate that there is generalization or, gain in general cognitive development, resulting from sensory-motor training. Finally, I have cautioned that tests of generalization must be suitable to the level of development, perceptual or cognitive, which the child has attained during the training.

# Leon Oettinger, Jr.

# *Physical Concomitants Of Reading*

Reading disorders are organic and not psychogenic; genetic and not situational in origin, according to MacDonald Critchley (1). This basic concept, while not shared by many investigators in the field of learning, is the point of departure for this presentation. Too often in the past generation there has been noted the simultaneous occurrence of reading disorders with emotional instability, and the easy assumption made that the reading abnormality was due to the emotional problem without real research into the origin of either.

Physical attributes or deficiences have definite impact on the learning process and particularly involve speech and reading. In part this is situational since the English language, because of its richness and complexity, is one of the most difficult to learn and use properly; hence any minimal or mild disturbances of the cogitative and reproductive function of language becomes quickly and glaringly obvious. It is not true, however, that only the English speaking races and particularly Americans suffer from reading problems as such eminent educationalists as Admiral Rickover would have us believe. The universality of this problem is testified to in the research papers being published throughout Europe, particularly in Switzerland, Germany, and the Scandinavian group. Some physical concomitants of learning are outlined in Table One.

## TABLE I

For ease of discussion the physical aspects of learning defects may be divided into two groups, genetic and acquired. In the interests of clarity however, it should be stated that it is often difficult to identify accurately the origin of a specific defect and that frequently two or more physical changes may be present in the same individual.

411

An outline of Physical factors affecting learning follows:

A.  *Genetic:*
   1.  Inherited low intelligence, hypomentia
   2.  Inherited dysrhythmias
   3.  Inherited metabolic defects:
      a.  Thyroid
      b.  Pituitary
      c.  Diabetes
      d.  Galactosemia
      e.  Phenylpyruvic oligophrenia
      f.  Porphyrinuria
      g.  Other
   4.  Inherited reading defects (other than visual)
   5.  Inherited visual defects
   6.  Inherited speech defects
      a.  Stuttering
      b.  Delayed Speech
      c.  Immature Speech
   7.  Inherited dominance variations
      a.  Eye
      b.  Hand
   8.  Slow Maturation
   9.  Epilepsy

B.  *Acquired:*
   1.  Hypomentia (decrease in intelligence)
      a.  Anoxic
         Traumatic
      c.  Infections
      d.  Toxic
   2.  Brain injuries with behavioral disturbances as in 1
   3.  Visual defects
   4.  Auditory defects
   5.  Mixed dominance
   6.  Epilepsy
   7.  Other

The polemic to follow will use the outline as a guide.

## Genetic Factors

*1. Hypomentia.*    Although it has become increasingly popular in recent years to credit everything that a child is or is not to environment, genetics still play an important part in the ultimate outcome. It is well known that in some families there is an inborn hereditary lack of intelligence (2), just as in other families there is an inborn, hereditary hypermentia or increased intelligence. Genetic hypomentia is usually of moderate degree with intelli-

gence quotients lower than fifty rarely being found (2). The effect of hypomentia on learning is so obvious that no expansion on the subject seems to
be needed, but in the classroom it must always be borne in mind that there
is a relation between intelligence and learning.

*2. Inherited Dysrhythmias.*    This is one of the more controversial points
in the understanding of reading difficulties, and perhaps should be discussed
under heading four, Inherited Reading Defects. However since this is a
subject of particular interest to the author, it is treated separately. Cohn (3)
in his excellent article on delayed acquisition of reading and writing found
that the incidence of cerebral dysrhythmia, or abnormal electroencephalograms, was five times as great in children with learning problems as in a
normal control series. In some individuals these dysrhythmias are so severe
that actual reading epilepsy, that is convulsions triggered by reading, have
been described by Bickford (4) and Stevens (5). The actual manner in which
abnormalities of the brain, manifested by cerebral dysrhythmias, but not by
hypomentia, influence reading is not known but it would seem from pathological and experimental studies that abnormalities of reception or transmission in the visual or associative areas of the brain can lead to such
disturbances. It is of great interest that most children with inborn errors
which lead to delayed or poor reading usually have accompanying neurological and physical signs (3, 6). Kinnard (7) has shown that cerebral
dysrhythmias can be inherited in behavior disorders and Lennox (8) has
shown the same to be true of the abnormal electroencephalograms accompanying epilepsy. If it is true that cerebral dysrhythmias can be inherited
in two disorders which are frequently associated with reading disability,
then it seems probable that the dysrhythmia associated with reading can be
inherited, particularly in view of the other findings relating to inheritance
which will be discussed under inherited reading disorders.

*3. Inherited Metabolic Diseases.*    The metabolic disorders listed are only
a part of those which are known to be related to disordered mentation. In
no one of them is decreased reading ability a specific loss with the possible
exception of hypothyroidism, but in all there are changes in mental ability.
Diabetes, when uncontrolled or poorly controlled, pituitary disease, and in
particular phenylpyruvic oligophrenia (PKU Disease) may all be associated
with a decrease in intelligence and a decrease in learning ability. Dr. Mateer
of Claremont years ago felt that subclinical hypothyroidism, i.e. hypothyroidism at a level where classic obesity, lethargy and dullness did not
occur, was frequently associated with reading difficulties. However the tests
available at the time could not demonstrate this, and in general her ideas
were scorned by the medical practitioners. With the advent of the protein
bound iodine (PBI) test and the butanol extractable iodine (BEI) test sensitivity was increased and Starr (10), Tobias (11), and others showed that

individuals where the PBI was less than 5.0 micrograms/100 cc of blood there would be a decrease in ability relative to measured intelligence and that reading seemed the function most disturbed.

To try to discuss all of endocrinology which would affect learning would require a large tome so we will restrict our remarks to pointing out that now we have a specific enzymatic metabolic disturbance, phenylketonuria, which untreated leads to hypomentia, convulsions and institutionalization, while if it is recognized and treated early results in full recovery. It seems probable that other such diseases will be recognized and that with our increasing knowledge of enzymology we may be able to isolate other causes of learning disorders and hypomentia and successfully treat them.

*4. Inherited Reading Defects.*    As indicated by the opening paragraph, the author feels that many, if not most reading disorders are genetic in origin. Critchley's article (1) is an interesting one that should be read by everyone in the educational field. His views that reading covers a broad range or spectrum which extends from the person who can read fifteen hundred to two thousand words a minute or engulf a whole page at a glance, and extending through the normal to the individual who is word blind and can no more learn to use symbols meaningfully than a color blind male can be taught to recognize colors. The juxtaposition of congenital dyslexia to color blindness is not accidental. No one suggests that color vision is psychological in origin, yet it also involves primarily males and extends through a whole spectrum of recognition. The Scandinavians have studied the genetics of reading intensively and Hallgren (9) in a study of 278 individuals flatly stated that congenital word blindness, or severe reading disorder was genetic in origin and was an autosomal dominant. This view is also held by Norrie (13) who studied twins and found that congenital dyslexia was concordant in all monozgotic twins, while twenty of thirty dizygotic twins were similarly afflicted. A similar study was done by Hallgren with much the same conclusions.

In our own experiences it is felt that reading disability is present as a familial trait in at least sixty percent of the children whom we see. Usually such histories are not obtained because there is no questioning as to incidence in maternal and paternal uncles, cousins and grandparents. When such histories are taken the incidence is revealing and almost overwhelming.

*5. Inherited Visual Defects.*    Any severe ocular defect acquired or inherited can obviously interfere with the process of reading. It is of interest, however, that often visual defects of moderate magnitude may be present with little effect on reading. It would seem that the simple finding of a visual acuity of 20/40 or 20/50 is unlikely to explain severe reading problems. On the other hand the literature if filled with references to the effect of myopia, hyperopia, astigmatism and aniseikonia. Myopia or shortsightedness is more likely to cause problems in reading material on the blackboard than in reading from books. Increased incidence of myopia in reading disorders has been reported however by Bartlett (14) and Eames (15).

Hyperopia is said to be incompatible with good reading (16) but a farsightedness of one or two diopters is commonly found in immature children. Eames (15), Farris (17) and Hirsch (18) all stated that hyperopia was significantly present in association with reading defects, but did not correlate the degree of hyperopia with the reading difficulty, though Eames stated that moderate and low degrees were more common than were high degrees. Hyperopia certainly influences the ability to converge and thus produces tiredness and blurring of the visual image.

Astigmatism, that is irregularity of the lens, can cause blurring and thus might induce reading difficulties. However, there are no papers to show that it is significant.

Romaine (19) has observed that when the visual images produced by the two sides are of different sizes, reading problems result and that treatment by glasses improves this condition. Anderson and Dearborn (20) felt that aniseikonia was present in about fifty percent of children with severe reading disorders, even though they felt that dyslexia was seldom due to a single factor.

Muscular imbalance has been cited to be of importance by Park and many other workers. The degree of imbalance is hard to evaluate however and its influence correspondingly hard to evaluate. Delacato (6) also has emphasized eye imbalance and has felt that retraining and correction are of prime importance.

At present it would seem that we can best summarize the situation by stating that undoubtedly all of the various diseases of the eyes and their related muscles can impair reading, but the degree to which this occurs and the mode of affectation is not completely clear.

*6. Inherited Speech and Hearing Defects.*    Visual aphasia is usually associated with some degree of auditory aphasia (1) and this points up the problems of "method" teaching. The child who has problems with "sight" or Gestalten reading is also likely to have problems with phonic methods of teaching. About one fifth of speech disorders have an organic cause (2) while in others there is either an inherited or emotional cause. It is the opinion of the author that most of these are genetic or maturational in origin. This is in contradiction to most authors who feel that it is emotional in origin and cite the absence of stuttering in primitive tribes, such as the Indians. Cobb and Cole (21), however, divided stuttering into three groups of etiology. Disturbances of the speech mechanism, psychologic origin and a disturbance of the entire language function including reading, writing, as well as the production and understanding of speech.

Orton (22) feels that in most instances there is evidence of disturbed laterality although it can appear in pure dextrads.

The child, in the first few grades of school, has a marked handicap if he has a speech defect, even if it does not directly affect other language function. Poor speech holds the child up to the contempt and jibes of his peers and also gives the teacher a perverted view of his reading ability. Unfortunately no one has found a means for the communication of silent reading hence it must be used. Greater use of comprehension evaluation would seem to be in order, and a child's reading grade should not depend to a large degree, as it does, on verbal facility.

*7. Inherited Dominance Defects.*    No field in education, psychology and medicine is more confused than the field of mixed dominance. We have views that range from those of Blau (23) who felt that all left handedness and mixed dominance were neurotic in origin to those who feel that only inheritance is causative. Part of this confusion arises from the methods of evaluation since in general the testing has been for handedness and not eyedness. Thus Gesell and Ames (24) found that the tonic neck reflex usually predicted handedness. They unfortunately did not report eyedness. In studies done in my office we have predicted eyedness and found that only in rare exceptions does eyedness differ from the directions taken by the tonic neck reflex, though in many left-eyed individuals there is a learned, I believe, righthandedness. If this concept is allowed, that is, there is a predisposition to handedness which can be modified by environment, all of the data make better sense.

How mixed dominance affects reading and learning is not known, but in our own studies sixty-five percent of poor readers have mixed laterality and this is in agreement with the findings of many other authors. The group at Claremont, however, in their studies did not feel that there was any relation between dominance and reading ability.

Wile (25) listed a group of symptoms which he felt were associated with mixed dominance. These included:

1.  Defects in writing, including slowness, illegibility, mirror writing and reversals.
2.  Speech defects including slowness, unclear speech, stuttering, cluttering and late development.

3. Physical defects, including incoordination, instability, motor restlessness and increased fatigability.
4. Emotional unrest, inadequacy feeling and inferiority complexes.

It would seem then that mixed dominance is an unresolved physiological-psychological problem and worthy of further well controlled, well documented studies.

*8. Slow Maturation.*   Delay in development is one of the common causes of reading difficulties in the lower grades, and is of particular interest because the prognosis is extremely good. In these individuals there is seldom a true visual-perceptual defect (2) and once maturation approaches normal, the child usually catches up with the peer group and continues in a normal fashion.

In our practice we have many families where there is a history of reading problems that exist in the first three or four grades and then disappear. For this reason it is most important to take adequate family histories.

Since boys develop somewhat more slowly than girls at an early age, this may be one of the contributing factors to the observed difference in reading abilities between the two groups. A secondary emotional problem may also result from these sex differences since the girls develop more quickly, do well in the first two or three grades where most of the grading is based on reading, and then may have their grades drop from A's and B's to B's and C's with resultant child and familial trauma. If schools were run on a sensible basis two reading standards would be available, one for boys and one for girls, and the two would not go to school together until after the fourth to sixth grades.

*9. Epilepsies.*   Epilepsy is but another form of dysrhythmia in which there are somewhat more obvious symptoms than usually found in the neurologically handicapped child. The intelligence is usually stated to be lower than average (26), but these figures vary greatly according to the type of patient studied. Lennox (27) found that in idiopathic epilepsy where there were no overt signs of brain damage the intelligence was normal. This lowered intelligence found in a statistically significant portion of epileptics would account for some reading problems. Additionally there are other characteristics which have been described by Bradley (28), consisting of variability of mood and behavior, hyperactivity, hyperirritability, poor attention span and a significant difficulty in mathematics in both sexes, and reading in boys. Treatment may aid or hinder scholastic treatment. If the patient is given anticonvulsants, particularly phenobarbital and other barbiturate derivatives to the point where seizures are controlled but the patient is markedly sedated, little is gained and much is lost. As epileptologists, our first consideration is to reintegrate the individual into his environment in the most satisfactory way possible. An occasional seizure is not nearly as great a hazard as is social and scholastic failure.

## Acquired Physical Factors Affecting Reading

Basically all of the abnormalities which have been described under the heading of genetics are also found under acquired abnormalities. The only major problem is the relative incidence of each. Kawi and Pasamanick (29) found that exposure to two maternal complications was ten times as frequent in children with reading problems as in normal children. Gesell and Amatruda (30) also found that there was a surprisingly frequent association of reading disabilities with minimal brain damage. These observations on a clinical level have been verified by electroencephalographic studies where it is usual to find that seventy-five percent of children with reading difficulties have abnormal electroencephalograms. Cohn's study (3) is probably the best of these dealing with reading and electroencephalography and is well worth reviewing.

## Summary and Conclusion

Reading difficulties are often rooted in physical abnormalities but the basic etiology cannot always be determined. Before a child is said to have reading disorders on an emotional basis, it is necessary to have a complete history, including that of the family, a neurological examination with particular emphasis on the so-called "soft" signs and an electroencephalogram and a thyroid check. Only if these are negative and there is no evidence of maturational lag, can emotional disturbances be considered as the sole etiological agent.

Many or most of children with reading problems have emotional problems but these may well be due to the reading difficulty and not the cause of it.

Treatment should consist of special education, geared to the child's need and not to some theory or method. It should also include remedial reading, medical care and psychiatric or psychologic care, along with explanation to and supportive treatment of the family.

## References

1. Critchley, MacDonald, Inborn Reading Disorders of Central Origin. *Tran. Ophthalm. Soc.* United Kingdom 81 (1961): 459.

2. Bakwin, H. and R. M. Bakwin, *Clin. Management of Behavior Disorders in Children.* 2nd Ed., (New York: W. B. Saunders & Co. 1960), 287.
3. Cohn, R. Delayed Acquisition of Reading and Writing Abilities in Children. *Arch. Neurol.* 4 (1961):153.
4. Bickford, R. G., J. L. Whelan, D. W. Klass, and K. B. Corbin, Reading Epilepsy. Tr. Am. Neurol. Assn. (1954), 100.
5. Stevens, H. Reading Epilepsy. *NE J. Med.* 257 (1957): 165.
6. Delacato, C. The Treatment and Prevention of Reading Disorders. (Springfield, Ill.: C. C. Thomas 1959).
7. Kennard, M. A. Inheritance of Electroencephalogram Patterns in Families of Children with Behavior Problems. *Tr. Am. Neurol. Assn.* (1947): 177.
8. Lennox, Wm.: *Epilepsy and Related Disorders* (Boston: Little Brown & Co., 1960).
9. Hallgren, B. Specific Dyslexia. *Act. Psychat. of Neurol. Supp.* 65 (Stockholm 1950).
10. Starr, Paul Subclinical Hypothroid; Recognition and Treatment. *Calif. Med.* 97 (1962): 263.
11. Tobias, M. Personal Communication.
12. Posner, C. Slow Thyroid can slow Child's Reading Ability. *Sci. News Letter.* 68 (1955): 8.
13. Norrie, E. Ord blind hedens (dyslexins) arveganz. Laese Paedagogen. Juxis 1954. Quoted in *Expanding Goals of Genetics in Psychiatry.* (New York: Grune and Stratton 1962).
14. Bartlett, L. M. The Relation of Visual Defects to Reading Ability. Doctors Dissertation, U. of Mich., 1954.
15. Eames, T. H. Comparison of Eye Conditions among 1000 Reading Failures, 500 Ophthalmic Patients and 15 Unselected Children. *Am. J. Ophthalm.* 31 (1948):717.
16. Schubert, P. E. The Doctor Eyes the Poor Reader. (Springfield, Ill.: C. C. Thomas), 10.
17. Farris, L. P. Visual Defects or Factors Influencing Achievements in Reading. *Calif. J. Secondary Educat.* 10 (1934): 51.
18. Hirsch, M. J. The Relationship of School Achievements and Visual Anomalies. *Am. J. Optometry.* 32 (1955): 262.
19. Romaine, H. H. Ocular Blocks in Reading Disabilities. Proceed. Spring Conf. on the Exceptional Child. Child Research Clinic of the Woods School. (May 1946), 29.
20. Dearborn, W. F. and I. H. Anderson, Aniseikonia as related to Disability in Reading. *J. Exp. Psychol.* 23 (1938): 559.
21. Cobb, S. and E. M. Cole, Stuttering. *Physiol Review* 19 (1939):49.
22. Orton, S. T. Some Studies in the Language Function. *Assn. Research Nervous and Mental Dis.* 13 (1932): 614.
23. Blau, A. The Master Hand-Research Monographs #5 (N.Y. Am. Orthopsychiat. Assn. 1946).
24. Gesell, A. L. and L. B. Ames, Development of Handedness. *J. Genet. Psychol.* 70 (1947):155.
25. Wile, I. S. Handedness Right and Left (Boston Lothrop, Lee and Shepard Co. 1934), 352.

26. Sullivan, E. B. and L. Gahagan, On Intelligence of Epileptic Children. *Genet. Psychol. Monog.* 17 (1935): 309. Deutsch, L. and L. L. Wiener, Children with Epilepsy Emotional Problems and Treatment. *Am. J. Orthopsychiat.* 18 (1948).

27. Lennox, Wm. Psychiatry, Psychology and Seizures. *Am. J. Orthopsychiat.* 19 (1949): 432.

28. Bradley, C. Behavior Disturbances in Epileptic Children. *JAMA* 146 (1951): 436.

29. Kawi, A. and B. Pasamanick, Association of Factors of Pregnancy with Reading Disorders in Children. *JAMA* 166 (1958): 1470.

30. Gesell, A. and C. S. Amatruda, Developmental Diagnosis, Normal and Abnormal Child Development (New York: Hoeber 1947), 248.

# Authors
# Look
# at
# Reading

# Maurice Sendak

## *On the Importance of Imagination*

On preparing this talk I encountered a number of unforeseen problems. The first was my awareness that an artist should not talk about his own work. He is, in my opinion, the last to have any clear, concise or objective point of view about his work. He is not very often endowed with this gift. And on the whole he is hostile to anything and everything that doesn't conform to his point of view. I speak for myself, of course, and now having said that I can forget it and talk my fool head off.

My second problem was trying to prepare this talk on the flight from New York City. It was absolutely hopeless. I was competing with Astrovision which is nothing anyone should attempt competing with and the most alarmingly stereoized music I have ever heard, and a very smug seventeen year old who confided in me the fact that he bet he and his dad made a lot more dough in a half year than I made in ten. I think he said he sold automobile tires. This kind youth also ventured to guess my age—needless to say—without my having asked him to. He took me to be near forty-five, and with all my warmth and compassion for children, I easily could have slammed him. My third problem was more peculiar. I had difficulty with the title of my talk, "On the Importance of Imagination." I simply couldn't tackle the subject with any proper solemnity. Rather, I thought very foolish thoughts. This was due, I discovered, to an unconscious association to the title of Oscar Wilde's, *The Importance of Being Earnest.* And actually both are very excellent titles for the subject and I think Wilde's humor is really far more appropriate to a discussion of imagination in children's books. One has to keep one's humor in the face of the dreadful lack of imagination in most books for children. An air of solemnity has always pervaded the subject of children and books for children; an air I find particularly irksome, tiresome, and having little to do with the subject, and really another example to me of the adult inability to see through the eyes of the child. Perhaps this is too much to ask of all adults but I think it's not too much to ask of the creative writer and illustrator of children's books. This discussion of my varied problems is by way of forewarning you that this talk will be sort of a grab bag of thoughts on the importance of imagination. Some will be earnest and I hope not too solemn; and my own work, those books I consider my best attempts, are based on these thoughts.

There is nothing so difficult as to define the word "imagination." I'd like simply to free associate the word. Imagination as related to the child in my mind is synonymous with the word "fantasy." And childhood, contrary to most of the propaganda in books for the young, is only partly a time of innocence. It is, in my opinion, a time of seriousness, bewilderment and a good deal of suffering. It is too, perhaps, the best time. Imagination for the child is the delightful and freewheeling device through which he courses his way through the problems of each and every day. It is on one level the cathartic means by which children grapple with a confusing, painful and often ambiguous reality. It is a normal, healthy outlet for corrosive emotions such as rage and impotent frustration—the positive and appropriate channeling of overwhelming, and to the child, very inappropriate feelings. Ordinary street games become the creative and imaginative ordering of a frightening and disordered reality. Children devise these games to combat one very awful fact of childhood—their vulnerability—vulnerability to emotions which they perceive as ungovernable and dangerous. Emotions such as fear, anger, hate are to a large degree controlled in the imagined world of fantasy. And this world becomes the battlefield of disturbing emotions where the child hopefully emerges the victor. His prize is the attainment of a measure of tranquility and self-assurance. It is through fantasy, the creative use of the imagination, that children achieve this catharsis. Now this is a solemn aspect of childhood imagination and happily children are totally aware of its therapeutic value.

Obviously, fantasy is not always an attempt to exorcise fear. The child is simply having fun, and after all games are for fun and the "I'll shoot you dead" is for fun. I recently read a book called *The Plague and the Fire* by James Leasor and I was both chilled and terribly moved by the image of children playing in the streets of London amid filth, stench and the terrifyingly common face of death, but being children they devised a song to suit the occasion. We all know it: "Ring around the rosy, pocket full of posies, ah-choo, ah-choo, all fall down." Everybody knows some variation of that —in Brooklyn, we never said "ah-choo, ah-choo." But how many of us know the meaning of that seemingly innocent rhyme? According to the author, the rosy refers to the rosy rash of plague, ringed around with inflammation. The posies were herbs and spices to sweeten the air. Sneezing was a common symptom of approaching death. All fall down is self-explanatory. Thus, death and the grim reality of death, too terrible to comprehend was compacted into a four line rhyme, a song they could dance to, clap their hands, make a game of, and how much fun to all fall down: a classic example as far as I'm concerned of the imagination at work, preserving sanity and maintaining hope in the face of seeming hopelessness. Thus the beauty of the imagination.

What happens to this flexible and beautiful device as we grow older? It is sad, but common knowledge, that the attainment of adulthood is often synonymous with loss of creative imagination. We have learned to cope in more practical if duller ways. It is called adjustment to reality, whatever that is. Adulthood is a calamitous loss of contact with the child self. I use the word calamitous because for me it signifies loss of creativity and I flatter myself perhaps by believing that I maintain an essential link with my own childhood. By that I mean only that imagination hasn't lost any of its impetus. It operates for me now as potently as it did for me when I was a child. This suggests that I am not properly adjusted to grown up life and in fact I'm not. My closest friends have confirmed this fact. But I honestly believe no artist can be, certainly no writer and illustrator of children's books. Maintaining a strong link with his childhood is crucial to his art. The still live, unbruised imagination is that link. He gives up being the sober, grown up and solid citizen and in my opinion that is a small sacrifice. The artist like the child still believes in a flexible world of fantasy and reality, a world in which he can skip from one to the other and back again, firmly believing in the existence of both. It is a vital and fresh world, unspoiled and unsparingly true to the child's life and it does not allow for half truths. The artist's vision must be honest and expressed so convincingly that children recognize it as true to their own lives.

Truthfulness to life, both fantasy life and factual life, is the basis of all great art. And in my opinion there are very few books for children that one can call great works of the imagination. Certainly in our time we are inundated with books filled with half true notions, sugar caned and tacky concoctions that bear no resemblance to anybody's life. It is an expurgated vision that has no relation to the way real children live. And by shying away from those aspects of child life that as adults we consider too grim or distasteful we lend support to this large body of ersatz books for children. The common rationalization is that we musn't frighten children. It is not the artist's purpose to frighten children by exposing them to experiences beyond their intellectual and emotional capabilities. But as I have suggested, children live in daily conflict with disturbing emotions and to ignore that fact is to misjudge the child's strength and his enormous need. In general, our books do not treat them justly and they know it and resent it.

In my own experience, the child has vindicated me often and allayed my doubts as to my purpose. When I have reached them they tell me so and seem overjoyed with the discovery of a new friend disguised as an adult. When I fail they tell me too. Then I am merely another hostile adult who has sinned by coyly condescending to their needs and rightly they despise such hypocrisy.

My goal is to reach myself and thus hopefully some children. Writing and illustrating for children is an excursion into the self and the reward is the child's approval. Essentially it is to please myself, and to be dishonest, whatever the critical acclaim and so-called success, is to have miserably failed. To falsify or consciously eliminate truths for fear they will meet with disapproval or hostility is to be no artist at all. The risk of disapproval and miscomprehension is common to all artists. It is necessary to the artist. The goal is not to please indiscriminately. Not too long ago I was accused in an article of cashing in on the monster fad in America, of scaring children to death merely for the sake of earning a quick buck. I was shocked, not at my work being so blatantly misunderstood but rather that a monster fad existed, and what had it to do with me! What the reviewer could not know was that my "wild things, wild imaginings" are the still palpable recollections of my still living childhood and have nothing to do with current fads, fashions or anything else.

How does one analyze a work of the imagination? For me it is the exquisitely subtle balance between fantasy and reality. It is the stories or pictures that operate on both levels, adding dimensions of light and dark. It is the telling of one story and the suggesting or insinuating of quite another on a deeper level. It is the flexible moving back and forth between two worlds, something going on below the surface that is eagerly absorbed by the unconscious, that exists and rings true. And there are great writers of the imagination. Some of my favorites are George Macdonald, Hans Andersen, the Brothers Grimm, Beatrix Potter, Randolph Caldecott, Wanda Gag, Else Holmelund Minarik, and William Nicholson. I think perhaps my favorite of them all is George Macdonald. His stories conform beautifully to my ideal of superb imaginative writing. The tale of The Princess and The Goblin, which you all know, is completely fascinating just as a story. But as in all Macdonald's stories there is a deeper, more primitive fantasy or myth that exists under and inside the elaborate trappings of the plot—a mysterious underworld of childhood imaginings and dreams, of strange distortions and dangers. This double layer of story telling makes the princess and the goblins for me a rare masterpiece. This ultrasensitive and acute awareness of the private life of children is a special gift few artists are endowed with. As an illustrator, it is this specific quality that draws me to Macdonald's work. It is this aspect of the book I most want to illustrate —that allows my re-experiencing something of my own childhood and thus hopefully contributing something further to the illustrating of the book. To illustrate Macdonald's *Princess and the Goblins* and to suggest through pictures as Macdonald does with words some further dimension, some deeper insight that is pertinent to me, to the book, and to the children reading and looking at the book,—that is the joy of creating books for children.

In a recent film on children's books I was asked the question, "Why do you do books for children?" The answer I gave was somewhat unsatisfactory to me. I used expressions like "obsessed," "I must"—all rather indefinite and peculiarly grim sounding. I think it's truthful to say that as far back as I can remember I've wanted to illustrate and write books for children. To anyone outside the profession this devotion to childlife does not always seem altogether reasonable. I remember a cousin shocking me with the question, "When will they give you a grown-up book to do?" Obviously, so far as he was concerned I must certainly now have proved that I can do a children's book and about time I was taken off the kid stuff and given a man's job. It would never have occurred to him that this was my choice, that I had no desire to communicate my thoughts and feelings to the adult world, and in every sense of the word, I was obsessed with childhood, my own childhood, and that my work was an endless endeavor to rediscover, explore, understand, relive and not lose a minute of that remembered childhood.

Writing for children is not at all remembering childhood, it is reliving it again with children. Ideas, stories or pictures are for me the modes or forms necessary to communicate a personal moment of one's own childhood that is perhaps typical of all childhoods. And as far as I'm concerned it is easy to distinguish between the purely idea kind of story book, an ersatz expression of what seems typically childhood, and the kind of story that uses the technique of story telling almost as a disguise for the real thing, —the real thing being the necessary exploration of some aspects of the author's own childhood. I suppose "obsessed" is not such a bad word.

Why do I do books for children? The answer can really be put only as a question: Is there anything more satisfying, more completely imaginative, more in tune with the best of life? I personally don't think so and I'm rather grateful for my obsessions. If I don't do grown-up books it's because the adult world in comparison to the child's seems in many respects rather gray and lifeless and quite simply, I like being where the action is.

**Richard Armour**

# The Significance of Satire: A Satirist
# Looks at Books

Most readers, I suppose, feel a little apologetic about reading anything that is funny. This is true of American readers, anyhow, because that old Puritan strain in us makes us feel we are wasting our time unless we are improving ourselves. And just as self-improvement supposedly comes from non-fiction rather than fiction, so also it comes from the tragic rather than the comic. We are cured, like so many olives, in the brine of tears.

Matthew Arnold, a Victorian (and an English Victorian is a little like an American Puritan), thought Dante was a greater writer than Chaucer because Dante had "higher seriousness." As one who taught Chaucer for more than thirty years and named his first-born son Geoffrey, I doubt that Matthew Arnold knew his Chaucer any too well. But not only Arnold but the great majority of readers believe that tragedy is what we learn from, while comedy has a secondary function. It relaxes us, like the comic relief in Shakespeare's plays, making us ready to face what is really important: more tragedy. Put into educational terms tragedy is the classroom, comedy is the playground.

All this, I think, is untrue, or only partially true. As a writer, I know it is as hard to make people laugh as it is to make them cry, and I think it is every bit as important. One thing students know, but many teachers and parents don't, is that comedy is fully as useful as tragedy in learning about life, or making life worth living. In fact comedy and tragedy go together to make the completeness of life; the one requires the other, as do day and night, life and death, man and woman.

As Horace Walpole wisely said two hundred years ago, "The world is a comedy to those who think, a tragedy to those who feel." We need both thinking and feeling, especially when the feeling takes the form not of passion but of compassion. But I rather like the idea that the kind of writing

I am involved in is the kind that is related to *thinking.* And of all the forms of comedy, satire is the one that calls the most for cerebration and rationality.

But before I come specifically to satire—what it is, how it is written, and how the reader should approach it—I want to amplify my remark about students and how they seem to appreciate and understand the comic better than some persons who are older.

Recently I received a very revealing letter from a student. It helps make my point, and I should like to share it with you. This is the way it goes:

Dear Richard Armour:

There is nothing more frustrating to a high school English student than a term paper assignment, especially when the task is limited to American authors.

The average high school student's library must include James Bond, Peanuts, and a few old classics. You can imagine my surprise, therefore, to find that all other American authors are either dead or dull. Then I found you. Thanks for not being in either category.

Since you aren't dead or dull, it is hard to find any references on your own personal life. I need, according to my teacher, something more about your own life written by other authors. In other words, I need to "pad" my bibliography.

I have really enjoyed reading your humorous adaptations of "high brow" books and have learned from them.

Would you please send me a list of books or reviews about you, personally, and your writings. I would appreciate it very much, and my teacher, Mrs. B - - -, may even "pad" my grade.

Sincerely,

Granted, this student's primary interest was in getting a good grade. But I like to think that he gets honest enjoyment from what he calls my "humorous adaptations of high brow books" and that he has learned something from the literary criticism inherent in them. Also he had to read those more serious books before he could get much out of my parodies of them.

This student, you will say, has a sense of humor. Well, I think everyone has a sense of humor. The sense of humor—the ability to detect and enjoy incongruity and absurdity—is something with which every human being (and only a human being) is born. To be born completely without a sense of humor is as rare as to be born without one of the physical senses. It happens, but not often. Moreover, the sense of humor is like a muscle. It can atrophy without use, and it can be developed with exercise. One way to develop the sense of humor is to read humorous works, of all kinds.

In this connection let me say that I think the sense of humor is at its height—and its breadth—in the adolescent. Teen-agers can enjoy humor that ranges from James Thurber to *Mad* magazine. Adults tend to specialize in everything else, and they sometimes get to the point, the pinpoint, of reading only one author, whether it be Peter DeVries or (in the case of a few enlightened readers of exquisite taste) Richard Armour. I know one professional man, very much of a specialist, who limits himself to Walt Kelly's Pogo. This is like developing only your triceps, muscles which they tell me are of use mainly in throwing the discus. And this man, alas, is not a discus thrower. I wish he would read a little more widely. He might, for instance, try Art Buchwald or Ogden Nash or S. J. Perelman or Leonard Wibberley. Or he might drop back a bit in time, but not in quality, and read Robert Benchley and Stephen Leacock, or, still further back, the greatest of American humorists, Mark Twain.

Humor and satire (and Mark Twain wrote both) are closely related. Humor can get along without satire, but satire cannot get along without humor. Humor has been defined as "the sudden recognition of incongruity." This is also involved in satire, but satire is different from humor in that it has a purpose, perhaps a social or political target. It sets out to deflate, debunk, or ridicule something that, in the opinion of the satirist, needs this treatment.

But satire is like acid. It cannot be used full strength on the reader. It needs to be laced with the alkaline of humor. Straight satire becomes preachy or mean. The objective is too evident. Indeed, straight satire is perhaps not satire at all. It is sermon or diatribe.

I learned my lesson about this when I wrote *It All Started with Marx,* a book that is still, I believe, the only full-length satire on Russian history and Communism—a book that keeps me from visiting the Soviet Union. The first pages I sent to my editor came back with the comment: "You are deadly serious, and I do mean deadly. It's obvious you don't like Communism. Be less obvious and be funnier. Your reader will get the message just as well, maybe better. The main thing is, he will keep reading."

So I brought some humor into the satire, where it belonged. And I let the Communists satirize themselves. This I did, for instance, by picking out a passage of *Das Kapital* that is sheer gobbledygook. I'll admit that I chose it with care and with a certain degree of malice. Then I praised its lucidity and the greatness of the concept. The contrast between the passage and my comments provided the incongruity that is one of the ingredients of humor. At the same time it pointed up, or let Marx point it up himself, the muddiness of this German philosopher's explanation of economic principles. On another occasion in this same book I told of how Marx, the spokesman of the worker, had himself rarely held a job, and how he was supported, during much of his writing against capitalism, by his friend Engels, who had inherited a factory and was therefore himself a capitalist. Sometimes, when writing on such a subject as this, it is necessary only to state the facts to achieve absurdity.

At the outset I said that satire is the most intellectual and rational of the forms of comedy. Satire requires more of both the writer and the reader than, let us say, straight humor. This is part of the significance of satire. It contains information, however purposely exaggerated or distorted. It has intent, and the reader must be alert to catch what that intent is. Whether in a book or a poem or a political cartoon, satire may call attention to some fault that has been missed or has been unthinkingly accepted as no fault at all. More than that, it may stir to corrective action.

My own master and model in the field of satire is Jonathan Swift. His *Gulliver's Travels* is the master's masterpiece. The adventure story and the humor of absurdity carry the reader along. In addition, if he knows enough (perhaps if he has had some good courses in eighteenth-century history and literature), he will learn a good deal about Swift's targets, from war to government boondoggling—universal, timeless subjects that are very much with us today and will probably be with us tomorrow.

One of the remarkable things about *Gulliver's Travels* is Swift's use of a different satirical technique in each of the four books. In the first, about the Lilliputians, everything is reduced in size until the stupid and inhumane things man does become trivial and ridiculous. In the second book, about the Brobdingnagians, everything is magnified until defects, not previously noted, become apparent. Even the creamy skin of a beautiful woman's cheeks becomes far from lovely when magnified six times. In the third book, the foolishness of the Royal Society (translate into today's use of tax-free or tax-payer's money for dubious projects) are exaggerated just enough to make the ridiculousness clear. In the fourth book, about the Houhnhnms and the Yahoos, there is a reversal in which horses are dominant over men, morally and intellectually as well as governmentally. I know of no other work of satire that has such variety of technique and such a nice blend of those elements that keep a reader reading and those that keep a reader thinking.

One of the subtlest and, if successful, most effective of the techniques of satire is irony: saying one thing and meaning another. This is the technique Swift uses in another of his works, *A Modest Proposal.* His proposal, you will recall, is to prevent the children of the poor people of Ireland from becoming a burden to their parents by fattening them until they are one year old and then selling them for meat. "I have been assured by a very knowing American of my acquaintance in London," Swift writes, "that a young healthy child well nursed is at a year old a most delicious, nourishing, and wholesome food, whether stewed, roasted, baked, or boiled; and I make no doubt that it will equally serve in a fricassee or a ragout." While others may get rich raising and selling year-old children to meat markets, Swift disclaims any hope of profit for himself. "I have no children by which I can propose to get a single penny," he says, "the youngest being nine years old (and presumably too tough), and my wife past child-bearing." But he generously passes along his excellent idea to those who can use it.

And thus Swift used satire, in the specific form of irony, to jolt his readers into a realization of the dire poverty in Ireland.

Some, in Swift's day, who had not attended a Claremont Reading Conference, probably took him seriously. The writer of irony needs to keep a precarious balance, else it is not irony, but he should give the reader a few clues to the correct interpretation. The reader, for his part, has to be alert. I have known readers of my own things to take them straight and to castigate me bitterly. Or could their letters have been irony too? Before the reader looks for the *significance* of satire, he had better be sure it *is* satire.

Dryden, by the way, defines irony as "A sharp, well-mannered way of laugh a folly out of countenance." I like that "well-mannered" part. As I have indicated earlier, satire need not be, indeed should not be, mean or uncouth. In fact it is a highly civilized kind of writing for highly civilized readers.

I have mentioned my admiration for Swift and for his use of irony in *A Modest Proposal.* I myself have used irony many times in magazines pieces, for instance in "The Depopulation Explosion," on man's efforts to do away with himself through air pollution, water pollution, and the like, in a recent issue of *Playboy.* I also used it once in a chapter of a book. This was "How to Burn a Book," the last chapter of *Going Around in Academic Circles.* Only once, however, have I managed to sustain irony for book length. I refer to *It All Started with Stones and Clubs,* a Swiftian satire on the history of war and weaponry. Let me quote a few sentences from the opening pages, to illustrate the technique of irony—the saying one thing and meaning another, the apparently being serious, the deadpan attitude:

> Back in the Stone Age, man was too uncivilized to wage war. All he did was eat and sleep and try to keep warm. Not only was man too uncivilized to wage war, but he had no reason to do so.
>
> He had no desire to take territory away from other men, since he had more territory (and more stones) than he could possibly use.
>
> He had no desire to take *anything* away from anybody else, because every man had roughly the same things: a rough, cold cave, a rough, cold wife, and an empty stomach.
>
> He did not declare war when someone came bounding over his boundary, because there were no boundaries. There were not even any walls or barbed wire or border guards or customs officials.
>
> He did not declare war out of dislike for someone else's ideology, because everyone had the same ideology, which was: Try To Stay Alive If You Can.

He did not wage war to save national honor, because there were no nations and there was no honor. Nor did he wage war to save face, face at that time being only the front part of the head and in no danger of being lost unless the whole head was. . . .

Had man remained in this unhappy condition, there would have been no fortunes made through the manufacture of munitions, no memoirs ghostwritten for generals, no heroes, no medals, no war orphans, no national cemeteries. There would be no veterans' benefits, no veterans' hospitals. There would be no victory monuments, and pigeons would have to find some other place.

The situation was intolerable.

Fortunately, man took things into his own hands.

The first thing he took into his own hands was either a club or a stone. He may even have had a club in one hand and a stone in the other, an early instance of overkill. . . .

Enough about irony, my favorite satirical technique. My favorite technique, that is, except for the use of verse rather than prose. Verse has the advantage of compression. It enables the writer to make his point in as little as two lines, a couplet, and he usually keeps within the limits of around sixteen lines. Moreover, it forces the reader to fasten his attention on the individual word or phrase. The reader cannot skip or skim. He must catch and savor the nuance of each word. In verse more than prose, the writer and reader work together.

Let me close with two examples of light verse that are a blend of humor and satire. If they have any significance, along with their playfulness, so much the better. The first has to do with a subject that, like Chaucer, I have taught for many years and have written serious books about, the Romantic Poets. It is an instance of my writing satirically and irreverently about what I know best and love most:

### The Rheumatic Poets

Much have I traveled in the realms of cold
And drizzly damp round Grasmere, Windermere,
Where Nature's gifts the Lakers once extolled
In lines that if not great are very near.
And though of course I've not seen Southey plain
(I came a hundred years too late), I've walked
Where Coleridge and Wordsworth in the rain
Once talked and talked and talked and talked and talked.
Yes, I have felt the pre-pneumonia chills
And clambered from the sticky lakeside ooze,
And thought of Wordsworth hymning daffodils
While water stood two inches in his shoes.

In addition to the main theme, this contains several twisted literary allusions and half quotations. It is the sort of thing I would bring into the classroom *after* the students know and love the Lake Poets.

The second piece of light verse is a quiet, understated comment, more effective I hope than overemotionalism, that I hardly need to explain:

### Born Too Soon

When I was a student,
I was quiet,
I didn't protest,
I didn't riot.
I wasn't unwashed,
I wasn't obscene,
I made no demands
On prexy or dean.
I sat in no sit-in,
I heckled no speaker,
I broke not a window,
Few students were meeker.
I'm forced to admit,
With some hesitation,
All I got out of school
Was an education.

Though I admit to being partial, I think satire has significance. That is, it has meaning and purpose. Satire does not flourish, in fact it is not permitted, in a totalitarian state, whether Fascist or Communist. The reason for this is that a totalitarian government fears above all else ridicule. It knows it can be laughed out of existence.

Happily, democratic governments permit satire, let the satirist ply his trade. They are strong enough, healthy enough to take criticism. They are flexible enough to profit from this criticism and make changes.

I am glad to say that in our country today, whatever its faults and in part because of its faults, satire flourishes. It is even on the upsurge, in both quantity and quality, in recent years. I urge you readers to read it and enjoy it and understand it and maybe even act upon it.

**Mary Stolz**

# Children's Books, According to an Ex-Child Who Not Only Remembers But Writes Them

As childhood is a self-limiting condition, merely to be an ex-child does not entitle me to lay claim to having something of value to say upon the subject of literature for children. I am able, luckily, to add two other qualifications. One, that having spent my minority reading books, I appear likely to spend my majority writing them. Two, because I write for children they in turn write to me and they tell me what they think about books.

A friend of mine once said to me, "I don't understand about people who don't read Smollett. I mean, what are they *doing* with their lives?"

A bit extreme, possibly. I didn't tell her that I've never read a word by Smollett. But there is validity to her question. What are people who don't read at all doing with their lives? What holds them up in the crises? What reference points, what measuring rods do they have for the thousand ills and alarms that flesh is heir to? How do they range from the narrowness of their individual lives? The broadest, most adventurous, most far-ranging life must after all be lived in one finite body. How do they learn to know themselves?

Socrates said that the unexamined life, the life of a man who knows nothing of his own real needs and desire, is not worthy to be lived by a human being.

Socrates felt, and I'm happy to agree with him, that one way to know yourself is to know others. To some extent we can learn to know others by human contact, but few of us have many such contacts that are deep, complete. We devise our masks early and wear them throughout life, taking them off sometimes, for some people, for brief periods. But the peoples in books—I am speaking of good books and of fiction—are utterly revealed. We know Rochester as few are privileged to know a living man. Madame

Bovary wears a mask for her husband, her lover, her neighbors. She doesn't wear one for us.

And we who are so fortunate as to read from early childhood learn through those magnificent anthropomorphized animals great lessons about life, about ourselves. They are lessons we don't forget.

Once having met those two high-handed, opinionated, overbearing creatures, Rabbit and Toad, we know them the rest of our lives. Against their pretensions, the modesty and good sense of Pooh and Piglet, of Ratty and Mole, are revealed in their beautiful worth, and no child could miss it. I feel the same emotion toward the blusterers and braggarts I encounter, or those in public life we all know and sometimes have to rely on, that I felt for Toad and Rabbit. I am alternately exasperated, bewildered, angry, but mostly inclined toward sympathy. And I first learned to feel so not because somebody told me that boastfulness and bravado are symptoms of insecurity. I learned it because I knew Rabbit and Toad as well as I knew my friends. In fact, better.

The emperor Hadrian, toward the end of his memoirs as presented to us in a great book of fiction by Marguerite Yourcenar, said, "As a traveler approaching an unknown land begins to discern the outline of the shore, so I begin to discern the profile of my death."

It seems to me that we can apply that thought, in an altered fashion, to what a child feels on first looking into Beatrix Potter. He begins to discern the profile of Life when he encounters the poor old Tailor of Gloucester, who was very ill with a fever, tossing and turning in his four-post bed, dreaming of the Mayor's embroidered waistcoat, to be lined with yellow taffeta, and crying out in his dreams, "Alack, I am undone, for I have NO MORE TWIST!"

Reading of Simpkin, cold and hungry in the snowy midnight streets as he looks in at the mice, so cozy and safe in the candlelight, a child learns something of the disparity not of the animal, but of the human condition.

And when bad-humored, frustrated, starving Simpkin recognizes the goodness of those stitching mice and relinquishes the hidden twist of cherry-colored silk, the reading child recognizes what Mr. Hemingway called "grace under pressure." The child wouldn't call it that, but he knows what it is.

And so with Peter, that rabbit with the rage to live, and Benjamin Bunny, his feckless cousin, and those conformists, Flopsy, Mopsy and Cotton-tail. A reader is going to go on meeting these characters all the rest of his life. There is a good chance that because he knew and understood them early, he will know and understand them late, and therefore, inevitably, better know and understand himself.

Children read, as we do, for entertainment, for knowledge, for inspiration. They read to escape, to pass the time, to find reference points and measuring rods for their own experience. They read for help. They discover early that there are books in which you lose yourself and books in which you find yourself and the real reader will gather them all in losing himself or finding himself according to the hour's need.

To this day I like escapist books. History books, mystery books, cookbooks. The child with a ranging, curious mind will certainly not spurn Thornton W. Burgess, though chances are he'll feel less for that Peter Rabbit than for Mr. McGregor's Peter.

Later on, he'll read the Hardy Boys. She will read Nancy Drew and the Hardy Boys. There seems to be some law, scrupulously observed by boys, that for a certain period of their lives they will not read anything a girl might read. Among early and mature readers, no such distinction is made. A boy's love of P. L. Travers or Laura Ingalls Wilder is in no way less than a girl's, and among the most devoted Jane Austen buffs are many very masculine men.

So children read for amusement and escape, and that's good. They also read to find themselves. That's better, even if it hurts. They must also, of course, be entertained, otherwise they won't read the book at all. But that's the business of the writer. From my observation of one son, seven nephews and a niece, from exchanges of view with my friends and relations, from my own experience, I know the extent of the influence of books on children. And I have to concede that it is not always beautiful.

My two sisters and I are close, chronologically and in most other ways, but the variation of our response to books could be taken almost as a *Middletown* of childhood reading. In our house we had, always, the Brothers Grimm, Anderson, the Andrew Lang books, Oscar Wilde's fairy tales. Recently—actually for the purpose of writing this paper—I asked them to recall their feelings about these books, if they could. To my astonishment I found that one sister had merely glanced at them, and decided they weren't for her. The other had loathed nearly all of them. I asked why she'd read them at all, in that case, and she replied that she hadn't, I had read them to her. She's the youngest and apparently had no defense.

Particularly, she hated *Hansel and Gretel.* Now, to me, *Hansel and Gretel* was a marvelous experience. I had a mystical and, I've concluded, not very imaginative, certainly not empathetic, response to those two children. I remember chiefly the excitement of the walk in the woods, the mysteriousness of the gathering dark, the marvel of the birds covering the children with leaves when they slept. The gingerbread house seemed to me perfection, and the ultimate punishment of the witch a just and excellent retribution.

My sister felt the anguish of two children, lost, hungry, without any grown-up to protect them. She was afraid of the dark, and sickened by the witch's awful habits, and also by her horrible end. To this day my sister is a little afraid of the dark and thinks it may well be because of those evenings when I would read aloud the *Fisherman and His Soul,* the *Little Mermaid,* or the *Singing Bones* and then go to sleep, leaving her awake to face the night and the nightmares.

I am drawing on personal recollections, because these are the most reliable I have, but please understand that I was in no way singular as a reader, granting that I speak of children who read enormously, who literally need to have books. Even in our television-oriented time, there are many such children left.

I was, then, a child who suffered, like millions of others, from a fear of death—my own and that of the people I loved. In some very substantial way, *Little Women* helped me through that period. Reading how the March family faced what seemed an unsuperable loss, that of Beth, and somehow survived it, and lived again, and lived happily, never forgetting what they once had had in this youngest sister, almost convinced me that that sort of loss could be endured.

The end of the *Biography of a Grizzly* taught me in a way I have never forgotten that death can have majesty and bring peace. I experience the emotion now that I felt then when I remember . . . "—and he lay down as softly as he had in his mother's arms in the Greybull long ago." I may not be quoting precisely, because I haven't read Ernest Thompson Seton in years, but the feeling remains—poignant, painful, rather sublime.

Again, and still using myself as an example only, I was one of those children who are always in trouble. I did a good deal of what was then termed lying, but which I have now decided was symptomatic of my wish to be a writer. I was reckless and irresponsible and someone in authority was forever crooking a finger at me and using that grimmest of phrases, "May I see you for a moment, please?" In the midst of this turbulent time, I read a verse by Edna Millay(1). It went:

> One thing there's no getting by—
> I've been a wicked girl, said I;
> But if I can't be sorry, why,
> I might as well be glad!

Miss Millay, when she wrote this was in her twenties and doubtless had something quite different in mind than I, who was twelve and always in trouble, took her to mean. But oh, the wonder of how it helped me. I went right on getting into trouble, of course, but it never bothered me in the same way again. I'm not saying this is good or bad, I'm simply saying it was so.

Perhaps I should say that I did not, as a child, read to the exclusion of everything else. It's just that in looking back it always seems to me that the reading was more important than anything else. Perhaps it was inevitable that I should go on to become a children's book writer.

The children's book writer is in a unique and splendid position. He can tell an audience that actually listens how many opportunities we have to be rich. In mind, in spirit, in our relations with others. Every writer has his message. Not singular, of course, since there aren't that many messages, but still his own. Mine is a simple one, and an old one. I think we should love one another. I can say it in a hundred different ways, and if I am entertaining, which I try to be, the children listen, and they respond. I know that, because they write to me. So even in a book about mice and cats and chihuahuas I talk of coexistence and say that is not only a possible way for the world to go, it's the only possible way, if we are to keep our world. Without, I trust, moralizing, I say to children that the color of a person's skin is a matter of no matter. It's unimportant, save that we make it so. Trying always to tell a story, to keep them turning the pages, which is, after all, the only hope of success a writer has, I say to the children that beneath our black or white or saffron skins we are just people trying to have fun, to learn something, to live together in respect and amity.

I hope that the pen is mightier than the sword. I hope that I, and the many writers who feel as I do, will persuade these people too young yet for swords that fighting and hating have no place in the world, and that, unchecked, they'll destroy it.

Perhaps I assume too much for us, the children's book writers. Perhaps my reliance on our persuasion is inflated. But on this hope I stand, and work . . . that we have at least a chance to reach the children who will be the adults who direct the world tomorrow—providing it's still here—and that they may remember something of our message.

After all, reverting to my own experience, Ernest Thompson Seton and Beatrix Potter and Kenneth Grahame taught me to love animals. Alice taught me to smile at pretensions. Hans Christian Anderson taught me that laughter and weeping are strangely the same emotion. And Cinderella gave me a conviction I have never recovered from, which is that clothes make the woman. Granted, I was impressionable. But the truth is, all children are.

People often ask me why I write for children, or, anyway, so rarely write for adults. Well, last February I received a Valentine. It was a red paper cut-out heart, and stapled to it was a white paper cut-out heart, and on the white paper heart was written: To a dear good Book Writer.

That's one of the reasons I write for them.

Another is that I think I serve a purpose, which is to lead the children on to other books that will lead them on to others, and so on and on through a lifetime. I think that if one does not start reading, loving to read, needing to read, as a child, he very likely never will read at all. Then all that meaning, all that help and joy and even sadness will be lost to him. I guess

I write, very selfishly, because I want to be part of the meaning of books to children.

## Reference

1.From "The Penitent" by Edna St. Vincent Millay. *Collected Poems,* Harper & Row. Copyright 1922, 1950 by Edna St. Vincent Millay. By permission of Norma Millay Ellis.

# Elaine L. Konigsburg

## *Language: The Perimeter of the Suburbs*

A couple of months ago, a certain distant relative of mine told me that I ought to buy an electric typewriter. She said, "Just think how much better you could write if you had an electric typewriter. In your line of work, darling, you ought to have the best tools." She then suggested that even a reconditioned electric typewriter would be better than what I'm using.

With some relatives you just can't explain anything that isn't tax deductible. But *you* understand. What I use in my line of work, darling, is not a machine at all. I use what you use—language, sometimes fresh and sometimes electric and sometimes reconditioned. Language is my tool. It is also a weapon, a set of symbols, a key. And it is a perimeter. It is a perimeter because it does what perimeters do: it shows the shape of and defines the limits of something. In this case, culture.

Language shows the shape of culture by reflection. When one is grown up, he finds that the language plunges deep and comes up with a double image; it not only reflects the culture of now but also the culture of then. A grown-up's *now* is made up of a lot of *then,* a lot of past, his own special past and an accumulation of the past of his culture.

Let me show you what I mean about language as a perimeter showing the shape of culture present as well as culture past. Listen with me. Listen to language reflect a double image in the tattersall of suburbs that I have lived in. A tattersall that spreads across a horizontal of time and a north to south vertical of geography.

Listen first to the talk that bounces out of my first suburb, a neighborhood of three bedroom, ranch-type homes in a new subdivision of medium priced houses three miles from the city bus stop in Jacksonville, Florida. The time is early marriage, early family-hood, and time itself is limited, for there are so many imperatives in this language, and they must all be obeyed.

*Imperative One:* Recognize your child's needs.
*Imperative Two:* Respect your child's individuality.

Listen to a young mother obey One and Two as she explains the laws of physics to a two and a half year old who is runny-nosed from crying:

> I'm sorry, Gregory, but you cannot take your wagon *through* the tree. You see, don't you, Gregory, that the tree will not move. Daddy always takes his wagons around trees. To the right or to the left. But *around.* Around the tree, Gregory. Why don't you try that? . . . No, Mother cannot move the tree right now. She has to feed your baby sister.

Only a demand greater than Gregory's, *demand feeding,* keeps her from axing down the tree.

Or listen to this conversation between a young husband and wife, and see if it, too, doesn't show the shape of a culture.

> Ronald, why don't you call the Harrises and tell them that we'll be late. About an hour late. I still have to bathe Stevie and put a load of his things in the washer. You know that if he doesn't get his bath just before bed, he'll be restless all night. And we both know what that will mean.

That will mean that they have failed Imperative Number Three: Adjust to your child's schedule.

There are other imperatives in this Spockled suburb. Discover your child's creativity. Provide your child with the companionship of others his age. Adjust to him.

And there, in that three mile outer limit from the city bus stop, you can observe all the nice young middle class ladies and all the nice young middle class men adjusting. The conversation of an afternoon among the young mothers or the conversation of the evening among the mixed couples changes little. Sitting in any living room in the whole of that suburban subdivision, and listening to the talk, one becomes overwhelmed with a feeling of *deja vu,* a feeling that you've heard it all before. That the language is reflecting not only life in this culture, perhaps, but in some other life once upon a time.

Once upon a time.
That phrase is the clue.
Listen to James Thurber tell it:

> Once upon a time, in a kingdom by the sea, there lived a Little Princess named Lenore. . . . One day Lenore fell ill of a surfeit of raspberry tarts and took to her bed.

The Royal Physician ... sent for the King, Lenore's father, and the king came to see her.

"I will get you anything your heart desires," the King said. "Is there anything your heart desires?"

"Yes," said the Princes. "I want the moon. If I can have the moon, I will be well again."

Now, the King had a great many wise men who always got for him anything he wanted, so he told his daughter she could have the moon (1).

Or listen to George MacDonald's King as he asks his daughter, the Light Princess:

"Is there nothing you wish for?"
"Oh, you dear Papa! Yes," answered she. "I have been longing for it—Oh such a time! Ever since last night."
"Tell me what it is."
"Will you promise to let me have it?"
"Tell me what it is first," said he.
"No, no. Promise first."
"I dare not. ... What is it?"
"Mind, I hold you to your promise. It is—to be tied to the end of a string —a very long string indeed, and be flown like a kite.
Oh, such fun!" (2)

Oh, such fun!
Oh, such fun for whom?
I had dreamed about such a fun land when I was THE CHILD, but it existed only in fairy tales then. The fairy tale land of Sleeping Beauty where the environment adjusts to the princess. A land where I, the princess, wouldn't have to learn to recognize spinning wheels or even have to take my red wagon *around* trees. A land where the spinning wheels would all be removed so that I would never prick my finger. At last I was living in that land. But *I* was the one moving the spinning wheels. Isn't that ridiculous? To at last be living in a fairy tale land but at the wrong end of it? To be moving spinning wheels out of the way of perfectly normal, middle-class children—without all the king's men or even one fairy godmother to help with demand feeding?

We left the sounds of those suburbs a half dozen years ago, but before we left, we had added another sound to them. Laughter. Laughter at ourselves.

We moved to new suburbs, and the language of our new neighborhood sounded strange until I located it in Ruth Benedict's book, *Patterns of Culture.* Listen to this chant of a Kwakiutl Indian chief from Vancouver

Island. The chief was host at a great potlatch feast, and as he sang, his song reflected his culture as well as my new one. Listen:

> I am the only one of the tribes.
> The chiefs of the tribes are only
>     local chiefs.
> I am the only one among the tribes.
> I search among all the invited chiefs
>     for greatness like mine.
> I cannot find one chief among the guests. (4)

That was his chant at a potlatch feast; the purpose of the feast was simple: to outdo all the other chiefs by showing how much property he could afford to burn up. And if they didn't believe his greatness, his chant kept reminding them of it as they watched. Blankets and oil and even canoes were added to his bonfire. Conspicuous consumption is the name of that game, and the song of the chief as he watches the great bonfire is a clear reflection of what was important in his culture. Uncomfortably clear. Here was a culture that was built upon an ample supply of goods, inexhaustible, and obtained without excessive expenditure of labor. A culture that could only happen in a land where the living was easy. A land where life's necessities were provided without a huge investment of energy, so all the left-over ambition went into accumulating property and showing it off. Such a culture existed years ago on the Northwest coast of the United States.

Such a culture exists now on the North*east* coast of the United States. The affluent suburbs of New York. That was our new neighborhood. Here is a culture that is also built upon an ample supply of goods, inexhaustible, and obtained without excessive expenditure of labor—a thirty-five hour work week, maybe. A culture where left-over energy goes into accumulating property.

For the Kwakiutl there was only one thing better than collecting property, and that was to show how much of it could be given away or destroyed. It was important to always give away more or destroy more than the other chiefs. Thus, the great potlatch feasts which could use up a year's savings. Sort of like a wedding in the bedroom suburbs. Vancouver Island could be Long Island. Listen:

> I don't know what to get Edna and Bill. They gave us a twenty-five dollar bond. That's eighteen seventy-five. I figure that if we get them a twenty-five dollar gift certificate from Saks, we'll be safe.

The Kwakiutl's language was only a little more direct; *I search among all the invited chiefs for greatness like mine.*

The Kwakiutl were always pursuing those experiences which they most dreaded. Dancing with glowing coals held in their hands, self-inflicted torture, starving in isolation to bring on frenzy, always striving for an experience outside of the day to day, something at an acute angle from the middle road.

Pursuit of the dreadful is reflected in the language of the affluent suburbs, too. Here it is an attenuated pursuit. It is often talk of experience instead of experience. Talk of meaningful experiences, exciting experiences, enriching experiences, *an* experience, *quite an* experience. Listen to this conversating bouncing back from the walls of a chic room in which a dinner party is going on:

> Johnathan dreads going to camp, but we feel that it is something he really needs. We think that he must be made to try it. At least for one session.
>
> Do you think, Jane, that four weeks is a fair trial? You really should send him for the full eight weeks. Otherwise, I'm afraid, it will be nothing but an aborted experience.

Thus, parents in this civilization often plan safe, dreadful experiences for their children. They also plan group play experiences, and making Jello becomes a science experience. Here is a passage from an article in the *New York Times Magazine.* See what culture this language reflects:

> A nursery school administrator feels most earnestly that mothers cannot begin to provide as valuable an experience as nursery schools can. Nursery education is so extremely important and so complicated that it requires all the training and experience a teacher can acquire (3).

He was talking about middle class children, ages three to five, children from homes having refrigerators and stoves and books and mothers with bachelor degrees. Does his statement not sing, does it not chant of the Kwakiutl need to experience that which is outside the home? Outside of the mother's range? Outside of the norm?

In his pursuit of the exotic experience, the Kwakiutl would eat human flesh. Cannibalism was regarded with horror by them, and yet the most highly honored society among the Kwakiutl was the Cannibal Society; an initiate would take bites out of the arms of bystanders while a chorus of onlookers would count the mouthfuls of skin he had taken. The Kwakiutl was not an epicurean cannibal; he took emetics immediately afterwards and tried not to swallow the bits of skin at all.

Listen to Ruth Benedict describe how it was done on the Northwest Coast before that civilization died:

. . . the final thing they strove for was ecstacy. The chief dancer at least at the high point of his performance, should lose normal control of himself and be rapt into another state of existence. He should froth at the mouth, tremble violently and abnormally, do deeds which would be terrible in a normal state (4).

Now hear *Life* magazine describe how it is done in a newer civilization:

She had taken LSD twice before. . . . This time she "went up" slowly at first, wandering about the room, savoring her heightened perception. Then she began to turn nervous and furtive, and started rubbing her face with her fingers. Sucking her thumb, she rolled out of her chair and onto the floor, then bit down on her whole hand. For a while she lay silent, but soon began to sob, pushing herself about the floor as if trying to escape something that was biting her from within (5).

That was written in March of 1966; it reflects a culture that reincarnates the Kwakiutl.

Language shows the shape of my newest suburb, too. A city on the southeast coast of the United States, a city remote from others, bound by the sea on the east, a wasteland on the north, and country all around. A city that is a speck of downtown, a little urb, completely surrounded by suburbs. Jacksonville again. But the time is different. The time is now upper middle class, and the suburb fits the time. Four bedrooms, two and a half baths, a family room and a formal dining room. Living is easy. Warm. The isolation of the people has bred a certain closeness to each other. A refined closeness, where manners are more minuet than rock and roll. The lack of availability of high culture has left the land as one of the few remaining places where conversation is a principal form of entertainment. The usual place of entertainment is the home, and the ready availability of household help makes partying much easier than in northern suburbs. There is a lot of language to reflect culture when conversation is a form of entertainment.

One evening in a traditionally furnished brand new living room, one of a guest couple said to one of a host couple that she longed for some good French food, and she went on to complain about the lack of good French restaurants in town. The hostess wife mentioned that her maid was from New Orleans and made a terrific onion soup, and that she, herself, had a recipe for chocolate mousse, somewhere. As a matter of fact, having the first and the last of a great meal, all it would take would be someone who could fix the in-betweens, and she knew that Sally Jo Hazen had a wonderful recipe for beef burgundy. A thought was born, and the hostess wife continued:

"We can have a regular Gourmet Club. Take turns having a different menu every month. The hostess decides the menu. No fussing though. No extra work for the hostess. The food will be the thing."

"I think," said the guest wife, "that when it is my turn, I'll serve Mexican food. World Bazaar up at the shopping center has the cutest Mexican tin plates and place mats."

"When you serve Mexican style," added the hostess, "I'll make the tacos. I happen to have a package of taco mix that I bought when we were down there. And I'll wear my poncho."

One of the husbands suggested, "Why don't we all just fly down to Mexico. It sounds simpler."

And his wife answered, "C'mon now, George, don't be a party poop."

You've heard that before. Doesn't that sound echoes from another suburban culture? Another gentle, remote culture? Another culture where if we can't go to the restaurant, we'll bring the restaurant to us. Or would you believe, theater? Hear Jane Austen tell about it in *Mansfield Park,* somewhere outside London at the beginning of the 19th century.

Tom Bertram says, "Yates, I think we must raise a little theatre at Mansfield, and ask you to be our manager.
This, though the thought of the moment, did not end with the moment; for the inclination to act was awakened. . . .
Henry Crawford said, "I really believe . . . I could . . . undertake any character that ever was written. . . . Let us be doing something. Be it only half a play—an act—a scene; what should prevent us? . . . and for a theatre. . . . Any room in this house might suffice."
"We must have a curtain," said Tom Bertram, "a few yards of green baize for a curtain, and perhaps that may be enough."
"Oh, quite enough!" cried Mr. Yates, "with only just a side wing or two run up, doors in flat, and three or four scenes to be let down; nothing more would be necessary. . . . For mere amusement among ourselves we should want nothing more."
"I believe we must be satisfied with *less,*" said Maria.
"Nay," said Edmund. . . . "Let us do nothing by halves. If we are to act, let it be in a theatre completely fitted up with pit, box, and gallery. . . . let it be a play . . . with good tricking, shifting afterpiece, and a figure-dance, and hornpipe, and a song between the acts . . ."
"Now, Edmund, do not be disagreeable. . . ." (6)

In this soft, Southern land of friendly persuasion, hear this telephone conversation:

"It started out being a get-together for a few of our friends after the Florida-Georgia football game, but I decided that it would also be a wonderful opportunity to pay back some of our social obligations, too. Now, it turns out that we're expecting thirty-five couples."

Here is Jane Austen's *Persuasion:*

> It was but a card party, it was but a mixture of those who had never met before, and those who met too often—a commonplace business, too numerous for intimacy, too small for variety.

Thus, language is a reflection of my specific cultural present, my now, and it is also a link to a broader cultural past, my then. Everyman's then. As an adult, writing for the future, and all writing for children is for the future, I must use my tool, language, honestly so that it will reflect a culture. So that kids reading my books know my neighborhood, a suburban one where fathers commute and mothers sometimes have to take over the management of Little League. They must know about my neighborhood, *About the B'Nai Bagels,* just as I know the neighborhood of Jane Austen or Ruth Benedict's Kwakiutl or the fairy land of George MacDonald. I owe that to myself, and I owe it to the children that I write for. For my now is their tomorrow. Just as my now is Jane Austen's or the Kwakiutl's yesterday. And if language in my books is to mean anything, it should reflect a culture and by that reflection show the shape of it.

Showing the shape of something is only one function of a perimeter; the other function is to define the limits of something. Sometimes those limits are a hard edge and are very visible. Like the time several years ago when my daughter was listening to a song being sung in French; she didn't understand a word of French, and she turned to me with a glowing smile and said, "I love to listen to songs in a foreign language; it's like a design." There she sat totally outside that design, the whole of which was abstract to her, and because she was so far out of it, she saw its hard edge, the perimeter of which I speak.

If one understands French, he has moved inside that perimeter, and the elements of the design are no longer abstract but are representational. Any stranger to a language must be told what the designs mean, what the symbols mean, what the words mean, if they are to mean what society wants them to. For language is our guide to social reality.

A child is, in a sense, a stranger to even his own language. When an adult writes for children, he is writing as one who is living somewhere within the language pattern of culture, and he is writing for one who is standing on its perimeter, on its edge. I keep thinking about my daughter hearing the sounds of that French song and finding it an abstract design. And I realize that I want my words to do something else besides reflect a culture. I want the language in my books to be the tool that pokes holes in that perimeter. To let my daughter in. To let my readers in a little bit deeper into the pattern of culture. I want the pattern to be familiar, to be representational, to be reflecting a neighborhood, but not all of it. I also want to push out the limits of that edge a little.

Kids have to bump into something unfamiliar. Let them meet the unfamiliar in words. Let them have language patterns of a social reality that they have not met yet. Let them use that language as a tool to poke holes with. Let them find enough familiar symbols so that they will feel at home, so that they can gather the words of an adult's now, an adult's social reality to use as a template for broader patterns of their own. Let them read about having a secret interior as the children in *From the Mixed-Up Files of Mrs. Basil E. Frankweiler* did, or let them read about how it is to be an outsider named Elizabeth who makes friends with another outsider named Jennifer. Those are the holes that I hope I poke in that perimeter, and that I hope all my readers see through.

Our way of using language actually influences our views of both the physical and social worlds. Perhaps, if I give you an example where a lack of language served a positive purpose, I can make more clear this idea about language being a guide to social reality.

> There once was a boy who could not begin a sentence without repeating the initial sound or syllable in it. This boy had a wise father who told everyone in the household to listen to the child as if he spoke as normally as they did. Friends were asked to cooperate, and when the youngster started kindergarten, the father went to the teacher and asked that she do the same. The teacher replied that the school had a speech therapy program that would help a stutterer.
> And the father said, "No thank you. I don't want him put in therapy; I don't want him called a stutterer. If he has no word for it, he can't think of himself as one."
> And the teacher cooperated, and so did friends. Even relatives did. And the little boy is nine years old now, and he said to me the other day, "You know, Mom, I used to have trouble saying some sounds. Like at the beginning of a sentence, I would go l-l-l-l-l. That was a funny kind of baby talk."

That dumb kid still doesn't know that he was a stutterer. He never learned to fear being one. He could never adjust to the reality of being a stutterer because he didn't have the language tool to tell him so.

But what about some positive words? Try to keep some out-of-sight problem in mind without thinking of it in terms of language. Try to think about buying groceries or finishing some assignment without language. Now try to think about privacy or loyalty or conformity without language. Try to think at all without language.

I bring all of my adulthood to my writing for children. I make an effort to help them hear the language of my culture, a culture that reaches into the past and spreads over the present. And I also make an effort to expand the perimeter of their language, to set a wider limit to it, to give them a vocabulary for alternatives, perhaps. Because language not only tells you the shape of a culture; it helps shape it.

> Humpty Dumpty said to Alice, "When *I* use a word, it means just what I choose it to mean—neither more nor less."
> "The question is," said Alice, "whether you *can* make words mean so many different things?"
> "The question is," said Humpty Dumpty, "which is to be master, that's all." (7)

Which is to be master, indeed!

Only a Humpty Dumpty can be master by proclamation. The rest of us are at the mercy of the particular language which has become the medium of expression for our society. Most kids are in the position of Alice listening to *Jabberwocky* or my daughter listening to the French song. That is, until Humpty Dumpty comes along to explain it.

Or until we help them learn to do it themselves.

## References

1. James Thurber, *Many Moons* (New York: Harcourt, Brace and World, 1943).
2. George MacDonald, *The Light Princess* (New York: Ariel Books, Farrar, Straus, & Giroux, Inc., 1969).
3. Marie Winn, "The 'Do-it-yourself' Nursery School," *The New York Times Magazine* (February 18, 1968).
4. Ruth Benedict, *Patterns of Culture* (New York: Houghton, Mifflin & Co., 1959), p. 191.
5. *Life* 60, no. 12 (March 25, 1966), p. 30.
6. Jane Austin, *Mansfield Park* (New York: Macmillan and Co., 1903), pp. 109–10.
7. Lewis Carroll, *Alice in Wonderland*.

# Leonard Wibberley

## *History For Those Who Couldn't Care Less*

The title of my talk is History For Those Who Couldn't Care Less, and I am encouraged to see that there are so many of you. I don't know whether when I am through with what I am saying you are going to care any more, but I am going to try to put history into a broad frame and show it to you as the bright story of the living rather than, as we are inclined to think of it, as the dull annals of the dead.

You will notice that I wear glasses. A few years ago I did not need them. Anything put before me I could clearly see. But changes took place in my eyes, the printed page became a blur, individual letters lost their outline, and I had to go to a man who supplied, with two lenses of glass, the deficiency of my eyes. With these lenses I can read again and because of two pieces of glass I can go on with my continuing education, and I am not cut off from the words and thoughts and actions of millions of writers of all kinds—dead some of them two thousand years before I was born—but who still live in the words they wrote.

It is a little humbling to realize how much the quality of a man, the exercising of his mind and its development, depends on two pieces of glass ground to a particular formula. You could look at these glasses of mine and say that but for them there would go a moron, or at least an oaf; a creature whose mental development had ceased because he was isolated from the centuries and the thoughts and actions of those who had lived before him. Without my glasses I would be lonely indeed, imprisoned in the present; my explorations cut down to the few years of life granted to me upon earth.

We need glasses of another sort to approach history—to bring its record into focus, and not only bring it into focus, but to breathe life into it and get away from the fallacy that what happened to Rome, to Tarshish and to Rory O'Connor the last King of Ireland, has no interest for us whatever. The glasses we need are imagination. Not great quantities of imagination. Just enough imagination to hear the silence in the Third Continental Congress when a rider from Boston flung into Philadelphia and handed to John Hancock a letter stating that the Continental militia had withstood two charges of the King's forces at Breeds Hill and the war with the Mother Country had started. Just imagine the silence which followed that message. That is not a great deal of imagination.

Let us for a moment take a look at man—Homo Sapiens as he calls himself without a blush, while he continues with a great deal of foolishness —and see if we can find one aspect of him in which he differs markedly from his fellows upon earth. Many aspects spring immediately to mind and not all complimentary. But the one that profoundly impresses me is that Man is the only creature who is actively and insatiably curious about the past of his specia. Study as we will, we can find no indication that a Holstein bull is at all concerned to find out something about the short black wild cattle from Northern Europe who were his forefathers. The wretch doesn't even care what happened to his immediate father. If he did, he might be a little worried. The same is true of the most advanced of the apes in so far as we can discover. The Orangutang despite his comparatively high intelligence doesn't care about the story of previous Orangutangs—of the troop battles they fought to gain certain territories, of the evolvement of their species from ground to tree dwellers. All he cares about is the banana you put in his hands or the cigarette you give him to smoke. Orangutangs have not heard of lung cancer.

But man does care. And curiously, primitive, uneducated man cares quite as much, if not more, than western, educated man. However, obscure the race, the Hottentot or the Bushman of Australia, he cares so much about the story of his people, that he transmits that story from generation to generation, through hundreds of years, determined that it should not die.

What is this urge to know about the past? Why is it there? What hunger does it satisfy? I think some part of the answer lies in man's continuing speculation about his purpose on earth because even the most backward of people seem to be aware that man has a purpose, and it is important to discover what that purpose is. The history of their peoples gives these primitives perhaps a sense of the direction in which they have traveled in the past and the way the road should lead ahead. Another part of the answer lies in man's hunger not to be alone. By alone I do not mean the individual by himself (yourself in a room). I mean the need of an individual, a race, a nation and a culture to feel that all are connected with what went before, that all are part of a vast continuum emerging out of obscurity and heading —we don't know where . . . a magnificent pilgrimage through twilight that we sense at some time will glow to a full and splended noon.

This then is history in its proper perspective—not a classroom subject for which grades are given and parents are left to argue the subtle difference between B plus and A minus (which to my mind is the same difference as exists between B flat and A sharp). Not a mere memorizing of events with a number stuck before them or behind them to signify the year. Not that at all. No. History properly seen is the story of man on earth, and the Declaration of Independence in this context is related to the laws of the Medes and the Persians and both of them mark a stage in the evolution of mankind on his fantastic, tremendous journey towards some kind of perfection only dimly seen. This I suspect is the view of history which was taken by earlier societies and among primitive peoples today. It is the view of history that we should take for it is the guidepost for us.

We were talking a few minutes ago of the deeply rooted desire on the part of men not to be isolated—not to be cut off from their past and enclosed in a time capsule with nothing but an appalling vacuum, an emptiness, behind and ahead of them. This need for communication with the past which has produced what we call history, applies to individuals in their professions, as well as to the species as a whole. You have undoubtedly heard it said that writing is a lonely job. I am going to take strong exception to that saying. Writing is not a lonely job at all. Indeed, if you feel lonely when you are writing, you had better examine your work, for you are probably not writing at all but only putting down words. True, when the writer is immersed in his work, he cuts himself off from the world around —from his wife, his children and if possible all the traffic noises. He writes better facing a blank wall. But far from being alone he is surrounded by the creatures in his mind who become alive and appear in words on his type-writer. Yet sometimes he speculates on how other writers worked; men who worked and died hundreds of years before he drew his first breath. He feels a kinship with them, an affection and a sense of comradeship.

A little while ago, reading in an anthology of Irish Literature, I came upon a poem which immediately put me in the presence of another writer. Here are a few of the verses he wrote—about writing—

> I and Pangur Ban my cat,
> Tis a like task we are at:
> Hunting mice is his delight,
> Hunting words I sit all night.
>
> Better far than praise of men
> Tis to sit with book and pen;
> Pangur bears me no ill will,
> He too plies his simple skill.

Oftentimes a mouse will stray
In the hero Pangur's way:
Oftentimes my keen thought set
Takes a meaning in its net.

I was captivated by the man. He was my comrade—my fellow worker. It did not matter to me that he died somewhere in the 800s—an Irish monk, living in a cell thousands of miles from California and one thousand one hundred years ago. His poem gives me strength for my work—the courage the artist must have to continue in the face of his own misgivings. You in your work can also find such comfort and strength from the pages of history. When you stand at the head of a class there stands beside you Bacon lecturing at Oxford in a hall so crowded that students fought to get within earshot of his voice. Beside you too is Socrates and Alcuin the Monk, who helped Charlemagne re-establish learning in Europe at the close of the Dark Ages, and indeed all the great teachers of history—some of whose names are not even known to us. They are there, not dead but living, giving you courage. Even the very stones will speak to you if you will stop a moment and listen to them.

Let me give you an example of what I have in mind. There is in Turkey a dry river bed scoured out in an arid countryside which in winter is cold and windy beyond belief and in summer so hot that one attempts to cool and moisten the air in one's mouth before drawing it into the lungs. The bottom of this river bed is made of those rounded stones which the geologists tell us represent the rubble of the ice age. On one of those stones is carved in Latin the words, translated in English, which say, "The Eighth Legion camped here. Six thousand men." The date is many years before Christ.

That stone tells you many things. It tells you that the legion was below strength, its numbers reduced either by the enemies or the climate or a combination of both. It suggests that there was some fear that the legion might, before getting back to Rome, be obliterated, and for this reason the stone was carved to fix a place where the legion had been. It tells other legions that might come after to have courage, for the eighth legion was there before and up to that point had endured. And it contains, unwritten, a simple unspoken soldier's prayer that the legion whose eagle the men served under should not be forgotton by those who came after. The legion is not forgotten. One has only to stand by the stone to hear it go by—the stones shuffling under the rawhide sandals of the soldiers, the short swords slapping against the leather armor, and some hoarse voice raised in some coarse joke about Rome and what was happening to their wives in their absence.

History, properly viewed, enters a dimension towards which Einstein was reaching at his death—a dimension in which past, present, and future are one; a unified field; unified not by mathematics but by humanity. Some of you have the task of teaching history to young people, and you are required to see that your students are familiar in considerable detail with the history of the United States, come up with dates, list the contemporaries of Jefferson and perhaps produce a paper on John Dickenson of Philadelphia who preceded Neville Chamberlain in thinking that freedom could be achieved by refusing to attribute uncharitable thoughts to one's enemies. All this is necessary to academic achievement and we put a great deal of stress these days on academic achievement. It has its merits. I will not denounce it. But I am saddened by the thought that the process produces thousands of professors of philosophy—and no philosophers. We haven't had a philosopher in this country since Thoreau and we stand in desperate need of one. (I myself am busy writing).

I do not pretend to be putting before you anything which has not occurred to your own minds many times. But with all the required courses which have to be got through and in such detail, history is in danger of becoming just a subject; a set of facts which must be digested and which retreat further and further from milk shakes, hamburgers and a date with that shy little blonde sitting in the corner of the classroom. History tends to become, indeed, its perspective and its life lost, a wearisome subject with no practical application to modern living. A fellow can be driven to mathematics by the lash—by the lash which informs him sharply that he cannot become an engineer or a scientist or an architect unless he is familiar with spherical geometry and the devious ways of logarithms. He will grit his teeth and go to it, for however hard the work, there is a practical purpose to it. There is the reward of a good living and a respected position in society to be gained.

But whatever has history got to do with earning a living? Who cares that Henry the Fifth hanged, before the battle of Agincourt, three lusty bowmen whose services he sorely needed faced with the overwhelming mass of the French, because they had desecrated a church? Of what importance is this little incident compared with the development of the Lazar light which can illuminate from the earth, the surface of the moon? The importance of course is that Henry's hanging of the bowmen was the flickering of another kind of light far more ancient and far more potent—that light which from the dawn of time has shown us that we must not take the things of the spirit even if they are symbolized in vessels of gold, and sell them to buy a jug of wine.

History has nothing whatever to do with making a living. But it has everything in the world to do with living a living—with being fully alive, not locked in the coffin of one's own century but resurrected and transformed and free to roam through all the centuries of man on earth.

The history teacher, and the teacher generally, needs a little help to bring this growing, pulsing spirit into his subject.

May I, with modesty, suggest that some help may be obtained from that curious being, the historical novelist who is rather like the chemical engineer—a man who talks engineering to chemists and chemistry to engineers. The historical novelist talks history to those who are without history, and stories to those who find themselves flattened by tombstones. You will find in your libraries scores of excellent historical novels, freely available to you which will give your students and perhaps yourselves an excitement about history which is often lost when the subject is under close study. They are novels to be sure. But they are not all zounds and rapier work. They are a recreation of the people and the times with which you are concerned and while you will not achieve a degree in history from reading one hundred historical novels—Tolstoy's *War and Peace,* Prescott's *The Man on the Donkey,* Waltari's *The Egyptian*—you will gain or regain a love which will not soon be lost.

When I was a boy studying what is now I find called the Age of Discovery (we learned of it as the Tudor period) my history master suggested that we could learn a lot more about the great navigators if we would go to the library and read Hakluyts "Voyages." His intention was kindly but his psychology was appalling. I never read Hakluyts "Voyages" because I suspected that the book contained the same dull stuff as was contained in my history texts. If I went to a library at all it would be to get a detective novel of Edgar Wallace or Dorothy Sayers. If my teacher had read some of the wonderful prose of Hakluyt to us, if he had got us all interested in the vivid and unbelievable descriptions of what happened to the crews of these great navigators—if he had related only the story of the men who went up the Orinoco river and, leaving their ship for a few hours, returned to find its mainmast draped by a monstrous serpent so that they dared not go back on board—then every boy in my classroom would have been down at the library borrowing Hakluyt, and you wouldn't have found a copy for several months. But he lacked the ability to do so.

What did he lack really? He lacked glasses. He lacked the imagination to see history as it really is—a living part of the present; inseparable from it, vital, fascinating, abounding in color.

If this is your plight then the remedy is simple. Get a pair of glasses. You will find them on the rows of shelves in your public library, where they are curiously labelled "Historical Novels."

Myra Cohn Livingston

# An Afterword: On Sharing Poetry with Children at the Claremont Reading Conference

Juan Ramón Jiménez, the Spanish poet, has told of a time during his boyhood when he cherished, above all, a rubber stamp bearing his name. With this he marked his possessions—clothes, books, papers, hands, every-thing—¿ Quedó algo por sellar en mi casa?¿ Qué no era mío?

Poetry, perhaps, should be like this for each of us; for might we not mark those poems which belong to us, feeling, touching, seeing, hearing their music? May we not be free to choose which poems are ours? Not every poem is for all children. To hold up to them a particular work because it is enlightening or truthful or beautiful seems an artifically imposed stan-dard. The poem may be meaningful to a few, but who can judge what will touch the sensitivities and experiences of another individual?

It seems important, therefore, to take a new look at the poetry we are giving today's child. Rather than approach it in terms of definition, of question, answer, fact (better left to the science laboratory) might we not offer poetry to children on an individual basis, stressing that the individual-ism and sensitivity of each child are qualities to be cherished. Each one of us is different. That which made the poet different, which gave rise to his unique mode of expression, might well be understood in terms of the reader.

If one poet does not sing the tune we, or the children, wish to hear, there are others who will. It is time, I feel that we re-examine the often-heard and done-to-death poems that appear in many anthologies and read-ers, weeding these out and putting in their place poetry that expresses the child of this age; yet retaining what we feel is a universal expression of childhood. To offer poems of romantic love, of old age, of woe, of philosoph-ical implications far beyond the child's understanding or interest, is to lose our children to poetry. To insist that they respond, with questions and answers, to feed back what the poet is saying, at an early age, is to make of poetry another subject for definition and analysis. Poetry is not that.

Searching out fresh poems is not easy. Presenting them is not easy, either, for because poetry often lays bare the emotions, we, as adults, shrink away lest we be thought too emotional. "He will not see me stopping here" wrote Robert Frost in his timeless "Stopping by Woods on a Snowy Evening," (1). How many of us are afraid to be seen as we pause, in the midst of "miles to go" and "promises to keep" to take time out for our emotions. Yet the very nature of poetry, as an art (and apart from pleasant little "rhymes" and greeting-card "verse") demands that the reader, as well as the poet, involve his emotions.

"No meaning—just *feel!*" a teen-ager recently said of the popular music of our time. Is this a reaction against present-day curricula; of definition and analysis until youth itself must rebel and insist upon a balance of individual, emotional involvement?

Reading to a group of Fourth and Sixth Graders means a choice of poetry which covers a range of subjects and sensitivities meaningful to this age group. Not every poem will please every child. Some respond more directly to humor than others. Many have ears attuned only to rhyme. Children have been given the rather false idea that poetry *must* rhyme, and therefore, free or blank verse must be listened to for a bit before it becomes easily associated with poetry.

The poems chosen for this reading ranged from tightly structured forms to freer and more contemporary expression; from the light verse of A. E. Housman or Theodore Roethke to the poems of Langston Hughes, T. S. Eliot, Federico García Lorca, William Butler Yeats, to mention only a few. The effect upon the children of the poems read, varied; in all probability, perhaps only one or two of the forty-old selections chosen had been heard before. One could predict, for example, the hilarious response to X. J. Kennedy's "King Tut" (2).

King Tut
Crossed over the Nile
On steppingstones of crocodile.

*King Tut!*
His mother said,
*Come here this minute!*
*You'll get wet feet.*

And now King Tut
Tight as a nut
Keeps his big fat Mummy
shut.

King Tut,
tut, tut.

But who can gauge the effect of Langston Hughes's "Poem"? (3)

> I loved my friend.
> He went away from me.
> There's nothing more to say.
> This poem ends
> Soft as it began—
> I loved my friend.

Most certainly, each child present was delighted to chant along the sporadic refrain of T. S. Eliot's "Macavity: The Mystery Cat" with a resounding *"Macavity's not there!"* (4) And when three of the children volunteered to do a reading of a three-voiced A. E. Housman poem, the joy was evident for the performers as well as the audience. Yet it would be impossible to judge, even from what seemed to be good response, how "The Cradle Trap" of Louis Simpson, might effect various children (5).

> A bell and a rattle,
> A smell of roses,
> A leather Bible,
> And angry voices . . .
>
> They say, I love you.
> They shout, You must!
> The night is telling
> terrible stories.
>
> But night at the window
> whispers. Never mind.
> Be true, be true
> to your own strange kind.

There is always the child, like one Fourth Grade boy, who showed instant delight at the reading of one poem and came up afterwards to ask for a copy. There is usually a small group of children, scattered among both Fourth and Sixth grades, who find joy in the mere rhythm and music of whatever poems are read. There are always a few who are, on the surface, seemingly unreached, yet who may respond days, weeks, years later—

Sharing poetry with a group of children one has met for the first time works both as an advantage and disadvantage. The reader has no preconceived notions of what might please or displease, and if he risks missing the familiar, he does have the pleasure of introducing new modes of expression with a wide range of reaction. The teacher who knows his children, however, can strive to reach that child who may remain untouched. It is to be hoped that this would be done for each child eventually in a familiar classroom or library situation.

It remains for those of us who believe deeply in poetry to search out poems for the children we know, drawing from more than that body of literature known as "poetry for children." Rather should we think of *all* poetry, choosing that which falls within the child's range of subjective and emotional apprehension. Too often, unfortunately, are clever didactic rhymes mistaken for poetry; too often are poems remembered by adults either from their own childhood, or later, as being "great" thrust at children in the hope of giving them something true and beautiful. Too often is poetry the object of grammar lessons, of lessons in punctuation, spelling, ad infinitum. And far too often does a teacher use poetry as something to mark only special holidays or events. As part of the daily human experience, as an expression of simple joy or wonder it is far too seldom introduced.

"The crime of our civilization," Archibald MacLeish (6) has written, "is that we do not feel." What better way to make a start toward this, than in the sharing and reading of poetry?

"I have learned," said the Philosopher in James Stephens' *The Crock of Gold,* "that the head does not hear anything until the heart has listened, and that what the heart knows to-day the head will understand tomorrow" (7).

### References

1. "Stopping by Woods on a Snowy Evening" *The Complete Poems of Robert Frost* (New York: Henry Holt & Co., 1948).
2. "King Tut," copyright © 1961 by X. J. Kennedy from *Nude Descending a Staircase,* by X. J. Kennedy. Reprinted by permission of Doubleday & Company, Inc.
3. "Poem" *The Dreamkeeper and Other Poems.* Langston Hughes. Knopf, 1932. Reprinted by permission of Alfred E. Knopf, Inc. from *The Dreamkeeper and Other Poems,* by Langston Hughes. Copyright 1932 by Langston Hughes, renewed, 1960.
4. "Macavity: The Mystery Cat" *Old Possum's Book of Practical Cats.* T. S. Eliot. (New York: Harcourt, Brace & Co., 1939).
5. Copyright © 1961 by Louis Simpson. Reprinted from *At the End of the Open Road,* by Louis Simpson, by permission of Wesleyan University Press.
6. *Poetry and Experience.* Archibald MacLeish, (New York: Houghton, Mifflin & Co., 1961).
7. *The Crock of Gold,* James Stephens. (New York: The Macmillan Co., copyright 1912, 1940).